75¢

The Songs and Motets of
Alfonso Ferrabosco, the Younger
(1575-1628)

Studies in Musicology, No. 20

George Buelow, Series Editor
Professor of Musicology
Indiana University

Other Titles in This Series

No. 19 A History of Musical Americanism   Barbara A. Zuck

No. 21 Johann Mattheson's Der Vollkommene Capellmeister:
A Revised Translation with Critical Commentary   Ernest C. Harriss

No. 22 Beethoven's Early Sketches in the 'Fischhof
Miscellany': Berlin Autograph 28   Douglas Porter Johnson

No. 23 Niccolò Jommelli: The Last Years,
1769-1774   Marita P. McClymonds

No. 24 Heinrich August Marschner, 1795-1861:
His Life and Stage Works   A. Dean Palmer

No. 25 Francesco Corbetta and the Baroque Guitar,
with a Transcription of His Works   Richard T. Pinnell

No. 26 The Bass Viol in French Baroque Chamber Music   Julie Anne Sadie

The Songs and Motets of Alfonso Ferrabosco, the Younger (1575-1628)

by
John Duffy

Copyright © 1980, 1979
John Duffy
All rights reserved

Produced and distributed by
UMI Research Press
an imprint of
University Microfilms International
Ann Arbor, Michigan 48106

Library of Congress Cataloging in Publication Data

Duffy, John.
   The songs and motets of Alfonso Ferrabosco,
the Younger (1575-1628)

   (Studies in musicology ; no. 20)
   Bibliography: p.
   Includes index.
   1. Ferrabosco, Alfonso, 1575 (ca.)-1628. Works, vocal.
I. Title. II. Series.
ML410.F2978D8   784'.092'4   80-22513
ISBN 0-8357-1110-2

Contents

Preface		vii
Chapter I	Biographical Introduction	1
	Domenico Maria Ferrabosco	4
	Alfonso Ferrabosco, the Elder	8
	Alfonso Ferrabosco, the Younger	17
Chapter II	Poetry and Music	33
Chapter III	Ferrabosco's Harmonic Practice	47
Chapter IV	The Songs: "Like Hermit Poore" and "So, so, leave off"	51
Chapter V	Other Serious Songs	71
Chapter VI	Tuneful Songs	95
Chapter VII	The Masque Songs	111
Chapter VIII	Masque Songs, 1605-1608: *The Masque of Blackness* and *The Masque of Beauty*	125
Chapter IX	Masque Songs, 1608-1609: A Court Celebration, *The Haddington Masque,* and *The Masque of Queens*	145
Chapter X	Masque Songs, 1611: *Oberon* and *Love Freed from Ignorance and Folly*	161
Chapter XI	Italian Songs	179

Chapter XII	Dialogs	199
Chapter XIII	The Motets	215
	"Ego sum resurrectio," "O nomen Jesu"	221
	"Ego dixi, Domine," "Convertere"	229
	Other Paired Motets with Texts	234
	Other Motets and Anthems	244
Chapter XIV	Lamentations	253
Conclusion		267
Notes		269
Appendix I	Ayres: Concordances	293
Appendix II	Manuscript Songs: Concordances	301
Appendix III	Motets and Anthems: Concordances	303
Appendix IV	Motet Transcriptions	309
	1. Ego sum resurrectio	309
	2. O nomen Jesu	318
	3. Ego dixi, Domine miserere mei	325
	4. Convertere Domine usquequo	332
	5. Ubi duo vel tres	341
	6. Libera me, Domine	350
	7. Domine, Deus meus	359
	8. Noli me proijcere	367
	9. Laboravi in gemitu meo	379
	10. Lamentatio [Lamentations of Jeremiah]	387
	11. Tribulationem et dolorem	413
	12. O Domine	421
	13. Fortitudo mea	428
	14. Sustinuit anima mea	435
	15. Quare dereliquerunt me	444
Appendix V	Table of Variants	451
Appendix VI	Motet Texts and Translations	461
Bibliography		467
Index		473

Preface

Alfonso Ferrabosco, the Younger, is best known as a composer of fancies, dances, and *in nomines* for lyra viol and viols da gamba. It was for these that he was remembered, both in England and on the continent, after his death. His vocal music received little attention until this century save for the unforgiving censure of Burney.

There are several reasons for this neglect. The masque songs, which were such an important contribution to Jonson's early masques for the Jacobean court, must be reconstructed in the mind, placed in their imagined surroundings of dance and allegory, rhetoric and persuasion, before they can assume their proper and convincing validity. The other songs, quite varied in their styles, have been overshadowed by more prominent representatives of English song: Byrd, Dowland, Campion, and the Lawes brothers, not to mention Purcell.

Perhaps a similar reason contributed to the neglect of Ferrabosco's motets in comparison with those of Tallis, Byrd, and Morley, and the anthems of Gibbons. The composer's own reticence may also be a factor, for there simply is not a corpus of works large enough to indicate that Ferrabosco thought of himself as an important vocal composer, at least after 1612, despite the publication of a book of his Ayres in 1609.

Yet, this neglect, only recently countered by studies concerned mostly with the masque songs, is unfortunate, for the vocal music of Ferrabosco provides interesting solutions to problems of form and harmonic organization which enhance our understanding of the changes of style in both solo song and part-music in the early seventeenth century. In this sense, the vocal music complements the instrumental without ever becoming as abstract as the fancies. In addition to the kinds of textual awareness the songs and motets provoke, they present solutions to musical problems which are applicable to instrumental music as well.

I would like to thank those who have helped me, materially and spiritually, in the course of this research. Dr. Murray Lefkowitz has given more than generously of time, advice, criticism and suggestion, and more, even, of support. His personal interest and integrity, as well as his professional guidance, were lights on many a dark night. To Francis Gramenz, Music Librarian at Mugar Library of Boston University, go special thanks for patient help with my many requests of that library.

The index is another admirable example of the work of Linda Solow, music librarian at M.I.T., whose exemplary knowledge, skill, and interest resulted in making this study much more useful.

For materials and assistance, I am indebted to the British Museum, the New York Public Library, and the libraries of Christ Church, Oxford, and St. Michael's College, Tenbury Wells. Finally, to Jeanne go thanks I never will be able to express completely.

I

Biographical Introduction

Of the great families in music history, the Bach family stands preeminent. In the study of English music, the importance of families such as Dowland, Lawes, and Purcell has long been established. Even in the sixteenth and early seventeenth centuries, the musical establishments of the Tudor and pre-Restoration Stuart courts were dominated by members of a few foreign families about which we know very little. Among these the most important were the Bassanos, Laniers, Lupos, Gagliardellos, and the Ferraboscos, and the records of the King's Musick and other court documents show that the influence of several of these families lasted for more than a century. Of these, however, only three individuals were to attain prominence and lasting reputation: Nicholas Lanier (1588-1666), diplomat and art procurer for Charles I as well as an innovator in the recitative style of English song; Alfonso Ferrabosco the Elder (1543-1588), agent for Queen Elizabeth and composer of madrigals; and Alfonso Ferrabosco the Younger (c. 1575-1628), composer of instrumental music and collaborator with Ben Jonson in the early Jacobean masque.

The importance of the Ferrabosco family in music actually begins with the previous generation, the three most important of the Ferrabosco musicians forming a direct line of descent. Domenico Maria Ferrabosco, born in Bologna in 1513, was at one time both a papal singer and employed at San Petronio as *maestro di capella*, travelling between Rome and Bologna with the patronage of the powerful Bentivoglio family. His eldest son, Alfonso, soon entered the swirl of court employment and in 1562, only nineteen years old, entered the service of Queen Elizabeth. A mercurial and versatile fellow, he became very popular among English musicians, although his compositions are rather conservative. What he did in the service of Queen Elizabeth is not quite clear, but he made several trips to the continent as, it appears, her agent, before finally leaving her employ in 1578. A few years later, he joined the court of the Duke of Savoy, abandoning by that act two children who had been kept in England as hostage for his return. In the year before his death he published two books of madrigals in 1587, which were liberally raided during the next decade by the compilers of the English anthologies of Italian madrigals.

Of the children left behind, one, also named Alfonso, the subject of the present study, was raised in music by his warder, Gomer van Awsterwyke, another of the Queen's musicians. At Awsterwyke's death in 1592, the younger Alfonso, then in his teens, entered Queen Elizabeth's service. After the accession of King James, he was appointed instructor to the young Prince Henry and also began a long and important collaboration with Ben Jonson as the composer of many of the songs used in Jonson's early masques. Some of this music appeared in Ferrabosco's *Ayres*, published, like his *Lessons* for one, two, or three Lyra-viols, in 1609. After this efflorescence, however, he published only three other pieces: anthems which appeared in Sir William Leighton's *Teares or Lamentacions of a Sorrowful Soule* (1614).

Ferrabosco's collaboration with Jonson apparently ended after the death of Prince Henry in 1612, and there is no evidence that he actually composed music after that date. His viol-playing was cause for admiration, particularly in posthumous memoir, and his fancies, dances, and *in nomines* for viols, the most important of his compositions, are substantial and contribute to the English development of an early idiomatic instrumental ensemble music. His songs and motets, which are the subject of this study, have not received as much attention. The songs were censured by Burney and, I think, partly misunderstood by Warlock. The motets are interesting in a variety of ways, but most particularly in their marriage of principles of melodic construction with those of harmonic structure. The songs exhibit some of this concern, but their importance really lies in their role in the development of a specifically English declamatory sensibility, a sensibility quite distinct from the Italian *stylo recitativo*.

Three of Alfonso's children were musicians of the court or church, but none made substantial contributions. Thus, with Alfonso's death in 1628, the importance of the Ferrabosco family in music history was effectively ended.

The Ferrabosco family first appears in Bolognese records late in the fifteenth century. That we are able to trace the family's genealogy at all and identify the dozen or so musicians of the family who held professional posts is primarily due to the researches of Giovanni Livi and G.E.P. Arkwright.[1]

Biographical Introduction

Arkwright's work in England developed from his interest in the elder Alfonso Ferrabosco who had served in the court of Queen Elizabeth. Livi, working closer to the earlier biographical sources in Italy, was able to complement Arkwright's studies with a fascinating exposition of the genealogy of the Bolognese Ferraboscos and their close and long relationship with the powerful Bentivoglio family during the sixteenth century. This information also supplemented the incomplete account of the activities of Domenico Maria Ferrabosco, the father of the elder Alfonso and the first of the accomplished musicians in the family, given by Gaetano Gaspari in his history of music in Bologna.

More recent research has unearthed little new biographical evidence concerning the direct line of descent through the three generations which mainly concern us here: from Domenico Maria through the elder Alfonso to the subject of this study, Alfonso Ferrabosco the younger. Only Joseph Kerman's discussion of the elder Alfonso in his monograph, *The Elizabethan Madrigal*, has presented new biographical information.[2]

On September 7, 1460, the records of the parish of S. Maria Maddalena record the baptism of Cecchino, son of Domenico Ferrabosco. This Domenico Ferrabosco is subsequently named in official documents as "famulus" or "familiaris" of Giovanni II and others of the powerful and illustrious house of Bentivoglio which, for nearly seventy years, held the Signoria of Bologna.[3]

This close relationship of the Ferrabosco family with the political and economic leadership of Bologna continued for over a century. The first evidence of special favor shown to the Ferraboscos occurred in 1473 when a house confiscated from a rebel was granted to Domenico by the Commune of Bologna. Presumably, this is the same house which Livi found in the parish of S. Maria Maddalena with the inscription "Ferabosco F.F." appearing around the capital of one of the columns of the portico.[4]

During the same year, apparently as the result of an amorous complication, Alessandro Vaselli was recalled from exile on the condition that he "should marry on the spot, without dowry, a daughter of the same Domenico."[5] Such official concern for the family's well-being was shown even more conclusively in the award of lucrative titular positions, the first of which, the Office of Vicar of Rocca Pitigliana (in the Bolognese Apennines), was conferred upon Domenico in November 1479 and transferred temporarily to his son Cecchino.[6] No wonder, then, that Cecchino's sons, Annibale and Alessandro, should be named in honor of the two sons of Giovanni II who stood as sponsors at their baptism, Annibale and Alessandro Bentivoglio.

Domenico Maria Ferrabosco

The eldest son of Annibale, Domenico Maria Ferrabosco, was, as the accompanying genealogical chart shows, the scion of the branch of the family which would ultimately flower even in England. The first of the many musicians in the family, he was born in Bologna on February 14, 1513, and baptized a week later.[7]

The Ferrabosco Family
[after Giovanni Livi, *The Musical Antiquary* IV (1912/13), pp. 122, 142]

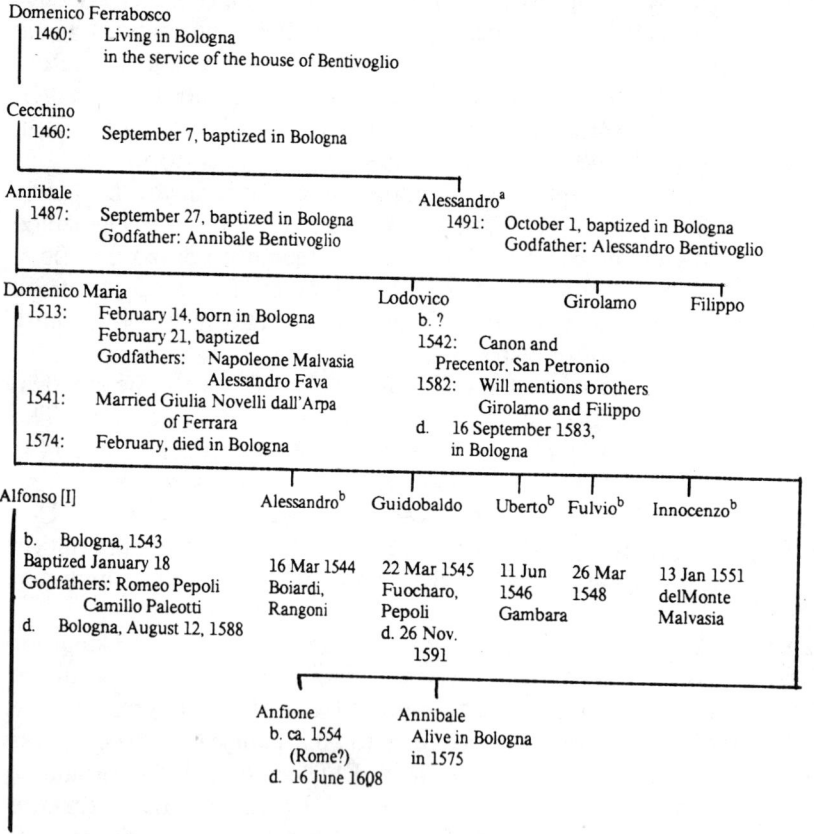

Biographical Introduction 5

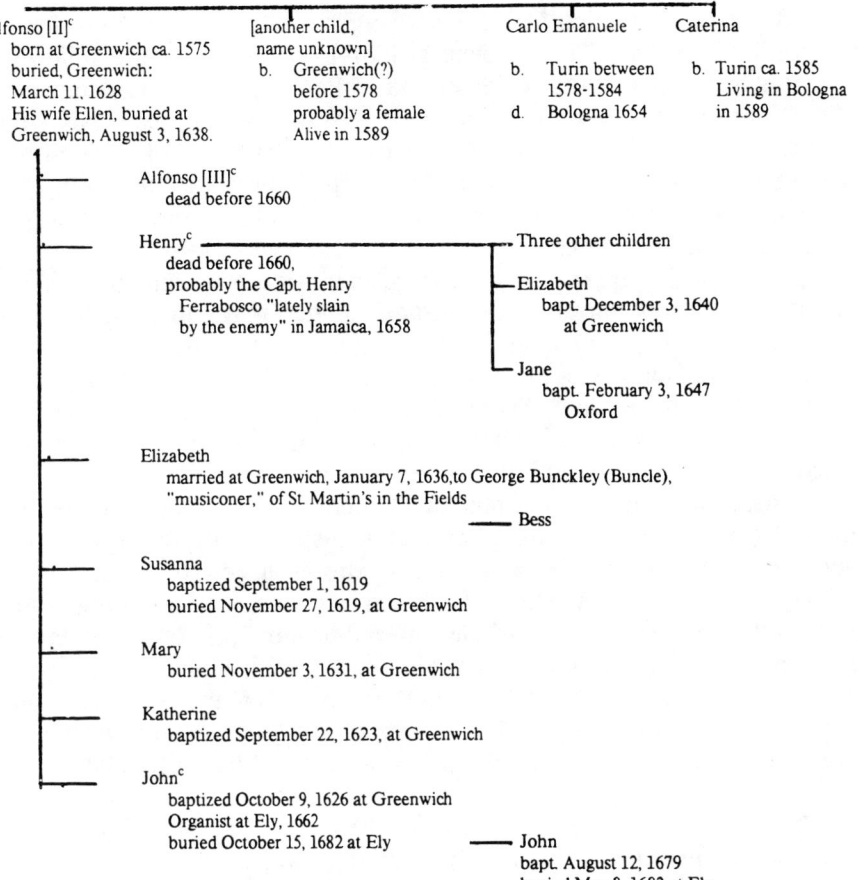

Alfonso [II]^c
  born at Greenwich ca. 1575
  buried, Greenwich:
    March 11, 1628
  His wife Ellen, buried at
    Greenwich, August 3, 1638.

[another child,
  name unknown]
  b. Greenwich(?)
    before 1578
    probably a female
    Alive in 1589

Carlo Emanuele
  b. Turin between
    1578-1584
  d. Bologna 1654

Caterina
  b. Turin ca. 1585
    Living in Bologna
    in 1589

  Alfonso [III]^c
    dead before 1660

  Henry^c
    dead before 1660,
    probably the Capt. Henry
      Ferrabosco "lately slain
      by the enemy" in Jamaica, 1658

      Three other children
      Elizabeth
        bapt. December 3, 1640
        at Greenwich
      Jane
        bapt. February 3, 1647
        Oxford

  Elizabeth
    married at Greenwich, January 7, 1636, to George Bunckley (Buncle),
    "musiconer," of St. Martin's in the Fields
      Bess

  Susanna
    baptized September 1, 1619
    buried November 27, 1619, at Greenwich

  Mary
    buried November 3, 1631, at Greenwich

  Katherine
    baptized September 22, 1623, at Greenwich

  John^c
    baptized October 9, 1626 at Greenwich
    Organist at Ely, 1662
    buried October 15, 1682 at Ely

      John
        bapt. August 12, 1679
        buried May 8, 1682 at Ely

^aOf Alessandro's children, the second, Ercole (baptized January 8, 1520, in Bologna) was a musician. His sons Matteo (baptized in Bologna on July 16, 1550; d. Graz, 1616) and Constantino (b. ca. 1555) also became musicians in various Hapsburgh courts.

By 1540, Domenico Maria was a singer at San Petronio,[8] but it was not until his marriage to a young girl of Ferrara during the following year that we find the first evidence that, like his progenitors, Domenico Maria enjoyed the favor of a number of powerful patrons. His wife, Giulia, was the daughter of Guido Novelli, a member of a family of artisans who was also known as "dall'Arpa," probably indicating his profession as harpist in the Ferrarese court. Giulia's dowry came not from her father, however, but from her Bolognese mistress, Eleonora Campeggi, the legitimate daughter of Cardinal Lorenzo and the wife of Count Alfonso Contrari of Ferrara.[9] One may infer from the circumstances of the marriage and the subsequent, hardly coincidental dedication of Domenico Maria's 1542 book of four-voice madrigals to Guidobaldo della Rovere, Duke of Urbino (son of Eleonora Gonzaga; uncle of Isabella d'Este), that Domenico Maria was familiar with and welcome in the court life of Bologna, Ferrara, and Urbino.[10]

These 45 madrigals, the bulk of Domenico Maria's surviving legacy, are sufficient to establish his place in the history of the early madrigal. But these years of the 1540s also saw the inclusion of several other madrigals in collections with a far larger audience. Most immediately noteworthy are the works included in publications of de Rore: the 5-voice motet "Usquequo, Domine, obliviseris me" was included in de Rore's first book of motets, published by Gardane in 1544, and Ferrabosco's "Piu d'alto pin che in mezzo a un orto sia" appeared in de Rore's second book of five-voice madrigals, also published by Gardane in 1544.

Even earlier, however, Gardane had included three four-voice madrigals of Ferrabosco in his first anthology which appeared in 1542.[11] Among these was "Io mi son giovinetta," one of the most anthologized madrigals of the sixteenth century, appearing in print as late as 1654 and intabulated numerous times; it also served as the basis for two parody masses, one à 4 (published in 1570), the other à 6, by Palestrina.[12]

After his marriage, Domenico Maria made his permanent residence in Bologna, although his work would take him elsewhere. The registers of the Cathedral give evidence of six male children (two more were

---

[b]These sons were not mentioned in Domenico Maria's will of 1573 and presumed to be dead at that time. Innocenzo was a singer at San Petronio. Anfione followed his brother Alfonso through the continent, perhaps even to England. He later held posts at Turin and at San Petronio. The sponsors at the baptisms of these children are among the most influential families in northern Italy: Innocenzo del Monte was Cardinal Crescenzi, Governor of Bologna, and Eriaco Fuocharo was undoubtedly Ulrich Fugger of the German banking family.

[c]In the King's Musick.

apparently born in Rome), the first of which, Alfonso, was born in 1543.[13] The connections with the illustrious and powerful of the time continue to be demonstrated by the participation of various members of the great families of Bologna and elsewhere (Pepoli, Paleotti, Malvasia, Fava, Rangoni, Boiardo) and three cardinals (Gambara, Del Monte, Crescenzi) at the baptism of Domenico's children.[14]

By 1546, Domenico was in Rome at the Vatican basilica, where he was *maestro de capella* and in charge of some of the boys,[15] but the flexibility of that position must have been considerable, for he was soon considered and elected to succeed Michael Cimatoris as *maestro de capella* at San Petronio in Bologna. The election took place on December 1, 1547 and may well have been more concerned with political influence than music, for, besides the family association with the Bentivoglios, Domenico's oldest brother, Lodovico, was a canon and precentor at San Petronio.[16] When Domenico actually assumed the post at Bologna, in January 1548, he also retained his position in Rome.

Despite this evidence of economic favoritism and professional versatility, the Ferrabosco family was in financial difficulty, and Domenico petitioned the Senate of Bologna to exempt him from all City Customs because of the hardships caused by his already large family.[17] That this request came hard on the heels of Ferrabosco's appointment at San Petronio seems no coincidence, and the favorable response of the Senate was but another example of the favor the Ferraboscos enjoyed.

On November 27, 1550, Pope Giulio III appointed Domenico *cantore pontificio*, and this position apparently brought the commuting to an end, for Domenico resigned his post at San Petronio in April 1551.[18] In his new position, however, he suffered the same fate as his colleague, Giovanni Pierluigi da Palestrina. Along with Leonardo Barre, they were expelled from the apostolic choir by the new Pope, Paul IV, because each was married. The final decree was handed down on July 30, 1555.[19] Subsequently, Ferrabosco occupied the position of *maestro di capella* at the church of San Lorenzo e Damaso in Rome until his death.[20]

Despite his employment in Rome, Ferrabosco maintained his ties with Bologna, and no better evidence of the benefits of having influential friends can be given than the appointments granted the Ferrabosco family by the Bolognese Senate. Not long after the birth of Innocenzo Ferrabosco in January 1551, his namesake and sponsor for baptism, the Cardinal Innocenzo del Monte, who was also the Governor of Bologna, sent a decree dated from Rome on August 5, 1552, conferring the post of *Soprastante all'Ufficio delle Bollette per la presentatazione dei forestieri* (supervisor of the Customs Office for the certification of foreigners), upon the young Alfonso, son of Domenico Maria. The position, obviously a sinecure which could be let to a bureaucrat for a small fee, was confirmed unanimously by the Senate of Bologna on October 25 of the same year, and, at the same time, the Senate conferred the position of *Soprastante al Pavaglione* (Silk Market) upon Alfonso's even younger brother, Guidobaldo.[21] Such positions increased the family's income without making demands on the family's time.

About eight months before his death in February 1574, Domenico Maria had his will drawn up by the Bolognese notary Giorgio Agucchi.[22] His death was confirmed by the attempts of his son, in October 1574, to gain leave from his service at the court of Queen Elizabeth of England in order to set the family's affairs in order and preserve his inheritance.

Alfonso Ferrabosco, the Elder

Only four of Domenico Maria's sons lived beyond his death. Of these, the most famous and most important was the eldest, Alfonso, whose standing at several courts, as musician, gentleman, diplomat, and, possibly, agent, was even higher than his father's among the Bentivoglio.

Baptized on January 18, 1543, Alfonso was named in honor of Alfonso Contrari of Ferrara, husband of Eleonora Campeggi who, as mentioned above, had provided the dowry for her lady-in-waiting, Giulia Novelli, Alfonso's mother.[23]

The conferral, in 1552, of a municipal post on the nine-year-old Alfonso by the Senate of Bologna has already been mentioned. For the next seven years there is no evidence of any noteworthy activity by the boy, although it is likely that, through his father, he was introduced to the leading Roman musicians and enjoyed the society of his father's supporters. Thus, it is not so surprising to find Alfonso and two younger brothers in the service of Charles of Guise, Cardinal of Lorraine, in 1559 when they attracted attention for their participation in DuBellay's *Epithalame* presented for the wedding of Marquerite of France and Emanuele Filiberto of Savoy.[24]

By 1562, Alfonso had arrived in England and was in the service of Queen Elizabeth. His stay produced no published music, although there is a tantalizing store of motet and madrigal compositions in addition to those published on the continent and included in the English anthologies of Italian madrigals. The documentary evidence provides only sketchy report of Alfonso's comings and goings. Although he was in England for the major part of the years from 1562 to 1578, his extended trips to the continent and his extraordinarily high salary for a musician indicate that his was not a simple position.[25]

Ferrabosco's appointment at court was for the relatively high sum of £100 *per annum*.²⁶ Paid at the Queen's pleasure, this annuity was the subject of several letters to the court, as Ferrabosco attempted to convince the Queen to grant him a lifetime pension. This was not accomplished until 1568, when the final form of the patent was signed.

There are several possible reasons for the delay. In 1564 Alfonso had returned to Italy. The reason for the trip is unclear, for Ferrabosco traveled in the company of Lord Dudley's Master of the Horse, and the surviving correspondence concerning the trip was addressed to an Italian secretary to the Queen. It can be deduced, however, that Ferrabosco temporarily entered the service of Cardinal Farnese, for the Cardinal would not permit Ferrabosco to return to England. Only by a ruse of pretending to visit his father, Domenico Maria, who by this time had left Rome or was temporarily at home in Bologna, was Ferrabosco able to leave.²⁷ By doing so, however, Ferrabosco left without obtaining the requisite permission from the Inquisition to travel in prohibited countries, of which England was most definitely one, and this hasty departure would cause him later problems.

There apparently was also some reason to suspect Ferrabosco's dedication to the Queen. This seems to be the reason for the first of his surviving letters, dated February 1566, to the Court in which he professed his intent to remain in the Queen's service.²⁸ Then, in 1567, Ferrabosco began a nagging series of letters in which he more strenuously attempted to check up on the progress of his pension. Undoubtedly the Queen had not moved overly quickly in this matter, but Ferrabosco's persistence did not ease the progress. In addition, he was reduced to apologizing for a meeting with the French Ambassador (in public, not privately, so he says), to which the Queen had taken offence, and earnestly pleading his innocence and obedience to the Queen.²⁹

The letters patent for the pension were finally prepared on October 6, 1567, but there was an additional difficulty.³⁰ A week later Ferrabosco wrote a letter of extravagant protest against the assertion that he was the culprit in the murder of a foreigner in the retinue of Sir Philip Sidney. This letter was followed by another, again sent to Court, stating Alfonso's innocence and requesting the confirmation of the Queen's good will.³¹

In this he was finally successful, but only after a considerable delay, for the bond in defense of the patent was not signed by Ferrabosco until March 22, 1569. In return for the lifetime pension, which, of course, would only be paid as long as Ferrabosco remained in the service of the Crown, he swore that, after taking care of his affairs in Bologna, he would not leave the Queen's service "for all the world."³² Four days later the patent was recorded on the Patent Rolls.³³

Thus it was that in 1569 Ferrabosco, as we know from letters to Sir

William Cecil, was on an approved trip to the continent, stopping in Paris and Bologna. At that time his father, Domenico Maria, was suffering from "a long indisposition," and there was discussion of the difficulty of Ferrabosco's position in Italy because he had not, on his previous trip, received permission from the Inquisition to return to England.[34]

It is not known exactly when Ferrabosco returned from this trip, but it is likely that it was another journey which brought him to France in 1572.[35] Certainly, and in what may have been a related activity, Ferrabosco was back in England in June of 1572 when he took part in an entertainment presented before the Queen and the French Ambassador at Whitehall.[36] And it must have been around this time that Ferrabosco married a young woman from Antwerp, "Domina Susanna, filia Domina Balthasaris de Simonibus."[37] Unfortunately, the Latin form of the name leaves the nationality of the family in doubt.

On October 23, 1574, Ferrabosco requested of the Queen permission to attend to the family estate in Bologna following the death of his father, Domenico Maria. In his petition he made reference to his "lunga et honorata servitu" and a bad left leg (which had kept him absent from Court).[38] Despite rather eloquent arguments based on the imminent loss and confiscation of his inheritance by the Inquisition, the request was denied.

It is at this time that we first learn of Ferrabosco's musical skills and how they were regarded by his musician colleagues. In commendatory verses to Tallis and Byrd's *Cantiones, quae ab argumento sacrae vocantur*, published in 1575, one "Ferdinandus Richardsonus" refers to Ferrabosco in the exalted company of Lassus and Gombert.[39]

In eandem Thomae Tallisii, et Guiliemi Birdi Musicam

>Extera quos genuit tellus, cum nominis alma
>Musica praecones cerneret esse sui,
>Illorumque opera per summa cacumina laudum
>Se celebrem vulgo conveniente vehi:
>Orlandum numeros divina voce sonare,
>Edere & immensae posteritatis opus,
>Suavia Gombardum modulamina fundere dulcem,
>Clementem placidos concinuisse modos,
>Temporis Alphonsum nostri Phoenica creare
>Carmina, quae Phoebus vendicet esse sua. . . .

[FOR THE SAME MUSIC OF THOMAS TALLIS AND WILLIAM BYRD

When fostering music perceived that her heralds had been born in foreign lands, and that she, now famous, was reaching the topmost pinnacles of glory by the assent of the multitude through the labor of these men – Orlando, singing with his heavenly voice and composing his works for the ages, Clemens harmonizing his gentle strains, Alfonso, the Phoenix of our time, creating songs that Apollo might well claim as his own. . . . [there follows homage to Tallis and Byrd].]

Similarly, although dating from 1591, are these verses from a poem which concludes John Baldwin's manuscript.[40]

> I will begin with WHITE, SHEPPER, TYE, and TALLIS,
> PARSONS, GYLES, MUNDIE th'oulde one of the queenes pallis,
> MUNDIE yonge, th'oulde mans sonne and like wyse others moe;
> There names would be to longe, therefore I let them goe;
> Yet must I speak of moe even of straingers also;
> And first I must bringe in Alfonso FERABOSCO,
> A strainger borne he was ain Italie as I here;
> Italians saie of him in skill he had no peere.

Like Baldwin's poem, concrete appreciation of Ferrabosco's music, exhibited by the inclusion of his madrigals in the anthologies of Yonge and Morley, did not appear until after Ferrabosco's death. Morley was especially partial to Ferrabosco, commending him "for deep skill,"[41] and recommending his skill in constructing fancies on one point.[42]

Ferrabosco and Byrd had been born in the same year, and no less a witness than Morley reported that the two enjoyed friendly musical competition.

> . . . I would counsel you diligently to peruse those ways which my loving master (never without reverence to be named of the musicians) Mr. Byrd and Mr. Alfonso, in a virtuous contention in love betwixt themselves, made upon the plainsong of *Miserere;* but a contention (as I said) in love, which caused them strive every one to surmount another without malice, envy, or backbiting, but by great labour, study and pains, each making other censor of that which they had done; which contention of theirs (specially without envy) caused them both become excellent in that kind and win such a name and gain such credit as will never perish so long as music endureth.[43]

This subject was brought up again, by Peachum in 1622, perhaps confused by the fact that both Byrd and Ferrabosco had written madrigals with the words "The nightingale so pleasant and say."

> *Alphonso Ferabosco* the father, while he lived, for judgement and depth of skill, (as also his sonne yet living) was inferior unto none; what he did was most elaborate and profound, and pleasing enough in Aire, though Master Thomas Morley censureth him otherwise. That of his, "I saw my Lady weeping," and the Nightingale (upon which Ditty Master *Bird* and he in a friendly aemulation, exercised their invention) cannot be bettered for sweetness of Ayre, or depth of judgement.[44]

Music was not Ferrabosco's sole function, and an incident from the year 1575 gives another representation of Ferrabosco's activities at the Court of Queen Elizabeth. He is almost certainly the Bolognese groom of the Privy Chamber referred to in a letter of February 25 from a mission of three Venetians to the Venetian Senate. The three had been received handsomely at court, and there had been a great deal of mutual compliment with the Italians mentioning that practically everyone at court could speak or understand Italian. The letter goes on to describe the ensuing events.

> We were told that the Queen intended giving us an entertainment to which ladies were to be invited, but possibly from inability to assemble them of quality and in number to her liking, or the requisite number of courtiers, we received instead a message from an Italian, a Bolognese, whose acquaintance we made on arriving in London, and who had become our friend; he is one of the grooms of the Queen's privy chamber, and enjoys extreme favour with her Majesty on account of his being an excellent musician. This individual told us that the Queen, having seen us in our riding gear, which showed that we were in great haste to mount post, was therefore loth to detain us; and then, speaking as of himself, the groom said to us, "Fail not, my Lords, to repeat the Queen's words, and do your best to further her majesty's wishes, as it will greatly benefit your Signory."
>
> On the morrow this same groom returned to London to take leave of us, knowing that we were on the eve of departure, and said he had told the Queen about our intention of making such representations as we understood were desired by her; and that her Majesty answered him saying, "They will not produce any effect, for when the noble Michiel was at the Imperial Court he told my Chamberlain, who was Ambassador there, that he would do the like, yet nothing came of it." The groom then added, "Assuredly, gentlemen, not only should sovereigns themselves be held in account, but also their very words likewise."[45]

At least one of Alfonso's brothers visited or accompanied him to England after his last trip to the continent, for there is a record of an assault at Hampton Court on January 7, 1576 "touching the hurting of Mr. Alfonso his brother."[46] The most likely of the brothers is Anfione, who is described in his father's will of 1573 as being "in partibus Galliae."[47]

Soon thereafter "Alfruso Ferrabolle" is mentioned in regard to a play by Italian players and in a subsequent payment warrant dated March 12, 1576.[48]

During this last stay in England, Ferrabosco and his wife presumably had two children in Greenwich, the town in which their son was to live and affirm as his birthplace. In 1578, however, leaving his children behind in the care of a fellow musician with support from the Queen, Ferrabosco left England and proceeded to France. Herein lies the major cause for speculation concerning Ferrabosco's diplomatic duties, for not only did Ferrabosco remain on the Queen's pay lists until his death, but he was also the subject of a series of letters during the latter half of 1578 which indicate that he was trying to pass himself off as a repentant returnee to the Catholic Church at the same time.[49]

From a letter of Dandino, the Papal Nuncio in France, written to the Cardinal of Como and sent from Paris on June 23, 1578, we learn that an apparently contrite Ferrabosco had rejoined the service of the Cardinal of Lorraine, having been disciplined at the Court of Elizabeth for allegedly assisting the French Ambassador at Mass.[50] His excuse to leave England had been the death of his mother, and his intention was to apply to Cardinal Paleotti, his Godfather, for absolution from his errors.

All this stretches one's credulity, for the Queen had denied exit permission on the more important occasion of the death of Ferrabosco's father.

Dandino was openly sceptical:

> There has arrived here one Alfonso Ferrabosco of Bologna, brought hither by the Cardinal of Lorraine as his musician. Determined against the will of his father to serve the Queen of England, he had been there for many years, requited with honour and pay. But at length, it being alleged that he had assisted at Mass in the house of the Ambassador of France, he was forbidden access to the Queen's chamber and the Court. He has visited me, and told me that, though he is now reinstated in his office and the favour of the Queen, he has resolved to be quit of that servitude, and acknowledge his error, and go home to Italy; and that he has taken occasion of the death of his mother to crave leave of absence for a few months, purposing not to return. And so, he besought my advice, and also letters of recommendation to procure his pardon of his error, and enable him to live at home as a good Catholic and Christian; assuring me in point of belief he had never swerved from the Catholic religion, and that so far as was compatible with secrecy he had not given up the Mass, Confession, and Communion in the house of the Ambassador of France, whose certificate *in scriptis* I have seen. He adds that he desires to apply to Cardinal Paleotti for absolution of his errors, being loath to approach the Pope without his invitation, for fear of imprisonment by the Inquisition, and he begged me to furnish him with a letter to the said Cardinal.
>
> I understand that this Alfonso is a most evil-spirited, evil-minded man, and very knowing, and excellently informed of the affairs of those countries; that the Queen of England makes much use of him as a complotter, in which character he might be employed, so that if one had him in one's power one might learn many things; that it is in order that he may better play his game that he affects to have a grudge against the Queen of England; and that, therefore, he will go to Italy, and, in particular, Rome and Bologna. I know not what of good to believe, as here he has gone to dine with the Ambassador of England on Friday, and has eaten meat, and is constantly busy there; and as I have learned that before setting out for Bologna he desires to know what Cardinal Paleotti's feeling may be towards him, I have warned the Bishop to avoid saying aught in reply that may hinder his going; and my reason for writing to your Most Illustrious Lordship is

that, in case he should come to Rome, the Pope may hear of it. Meanwhile, I have placed persons about him to try if they can penetrate his mind, and I shall apprise you of the result.[51]

Dandino's other letters also imply that all was not as it seemed, and the Cardinal of Como responded, requesting information about persons who were still in the Queen's employ, presumably secretly, in Venice and Rome.[52]

It appears, however, that Ferrabosco in fact had decided to leave the Queen's service, despite his pledge never to do so and the detention of his children in England. A letter, dated February 11, 1580, from Sir Henry Cobham, the English Ambassador to France, to Walsingham, who was in charge of the Queen's intelligence network, implies that the Queen was quite persistent in her efforts to secure Ferrabosco's return, although to no avail.[53]

Later in 1580 Ferrabosco entered into a contract with another citizen of Bologna, an action he could not have taken unless his problems with the Inquisition had been settled.[54] By 1582, Ferrabosco was in Turin, possibly already in the service of the Duke of Savoy, for he wrote from Turin to Queen Elizabeth explaining his long silence and inquiring about his "povero figliolino."[55] Except for a legal matter in which Ferrabosco was only slightly involved, there is no other surviving evidence that he had further contact with the Queen or his children.

From January to June 1585, the Duke Carlo Emanuele of Savoy traveled to Spain to marry the Infanta Donna Caterina of Austria, second daughter of King Philip II. Ferrabosco was a member of this entourage. We know of this from two sources, one of which was a poetical epistle addressed by Pietro Vaz Rego to Giuseppe Torres Martinez Bravo, a musician of the court of the King of Spain, in which "Alfonso Ferabosco, noble Saboyano" is mentioned amid allusions to the most distinguished musicians of the various Chapels Royal of Spain.

> These are, as far as my memory recalls, Your predecessors in that august Royal Chapel: . . . a certain Alfonso Ferrabosco, nobleman from Savoy, at whose fountain Georges de la Hele drank divine sweetness.[56]

Apparently Ferrabosco found time for musical instruction during the trip, taking at least this one pupil. He was, of course, not a nobleman, but a gentleman of the Savoy court.

Ferrabosco received an annual allowance from the Duke of Savoy until, by a decree of March 6, 1586, he was granted a lifetime pension. This decree is particularly important for it not only confirms that Ferrabosco had been in the Duke's service for some time and that he had become a welcome member of the court ("nostro carissimo Messer Alfonso Farrabosco, gentil homo ordinario di nostra bocca"), but it makes reference to a "primogenito" which can only be the young boy, the "povero figliolino," left behind in England.[57] Moreover, a distinction is made between this unnamed "primogenito" and the first of Ferrabosco's two children born in Italy, Carlo Emanuele, described as "suo figliolo legitimo et naturale." This description has been interpreted to mean that the unnamed "primogenito" was an illegitimate child. It seems more likely, however, that such a child would not have received as much attention: Ferrabosco's inquiry by letter in 1582, the Queen's maintenance, and this notice in a decree of the Duke of Savoy. More likely, the mention of the "primogenito" certified the course of the inheritance of the pension. The child was, in fact, lost to Ferrabosco; the Queen would not release him. The question of legitimacy would seem more likely to be a religious problem: the child was born in England, probably to a marriage not yet sanctioned by Catholic sacrament. Thus the child would, technically, not be recognized as legitimate in Catholic lands. The younger Alfonso Ferrabosco never suffered the stigma of illegitimacy in England.

Much of the attraction of the Savoy court for Ferrabosco must have been the recognition he received for his musical talents. In return, Ferrabosco named his two children born in Turin, Carlo Emanuele and Caterina, in honor of his patrons. Presumably the boy was born first, for the girl could not have been born until after the Duke's wedding trip, in 1585, was completed.

Ferrabosco made two other dedications to the Duke and Duchess. The great fire of 1904, which destroyed the Library of Turin, also destroyed a manuscript work, "Dell' historia d'Altimauro, composta per Alfonso Ferrabosco," the two volumes of which were dedicated, respectively, to the Duke and Duchess.[58] Similarly, Ferrabosco published two books of madrigals for five voices in 1587, the first dedicated to the Duke, the second to the Duchess.[59] These books are of not much importance in the history of the Italian madrigal, but they figure importantly in England, for of the thirty-nine madrigals in these two books, fifteen are included by Yonge and Morley in their anthologies of madrigals published with English translations.[60]

These two books of madrigals were published at the instance of the Duke, as the dedications of the works witness.

    (*Primo libro*) ...
        Tra li molti favori, che in diversi tempi V. A. Serenissima se e degnata di farmi, il maggiore, e piu notabile stimo, che m'habbi con suoi commandimenti obligato a porre in luce miei primi madrigali.

> (Secondo libro)...
> il Sereniss. Sig. Duca mio Patrone... commandarmi che io ponessi alcuni miei Madrigali in Stampa:[61]

In the dedication of the second book, Ferrabosco also proclaimed his intention to publish other compositions, in other genres:

> ... mi dara animo di mettere in luce alcune altre mie Compositioni; l'equali tutto che d'altro genere siano....

But death, apparently unexpected, intervened. Ferrabosco died in Bologna on August 12, 1588.[62] He left no will and no provision for his widow and children. His brother, Anfione, was named to his place as musician (only) at the court of Savoy,[63] and, on October 1, 1588, the Duke wrote a new decree, annulling that of 1586 and settling a smaller pension on the widow. There is no allusion to the previously mentioned "primogenito," and Ferrabosco is described as having been "nostro musico e gentilhuomo di bocca."[64]

The inventory of Ferrabosco's estate, preserved at the Archivio Notarile of Bologna among the documents of the notary Vincenzo Orlandini, is dated June 6, 1589. The family was in comfortable financial condition and possessed some property in the Bolognese district. Susanna, Ferrabosco's wife, and the two Italian-born children are mentioned, as are Ferrabosco's two surviving brothers, Guidobaldo and Anfione. These, however, are of secondary interest to the mention of music books located in Turin and Bologna.

> ... Una cassa de libri de diversi autori e diversa sorte de musica in Turino, et in mano de Messer Anfione in Bologna; alcuni libri de musica stampati et altri scritti a penna, opere de M. Alfonso....[65]

Manuscripts of the elder Ferrabosco's works are present in English collections, and these manuscripts contain a great deal of music which was never published. Similar manuscripts have not yet been found in Italian libraries, and it is a tantalizing speculation that some of the English manuscripts may be those mentioned in this inventory. Absent from the listing of heirs in the inventory, as well as from the revised Ducal decree, is any mention of the "primogenito," yet it is that "primogenito" who most successfully carried the Ferrabosco name and musical skill into the next century.

Alfonso Ferrabosco, the Younger

The younger Alfonso, apparently born in Greenwich during the later years (1573-1577) of his father's service in England, was a mystery character in ways quite different from his father. The Greenwich parish registers for baptisms do not begin until 1616, but Anthony Wood, in a note to his discussion of John Wilson, gives Greenwich as the place of the younger Alfonso's birth.

> Dr. Wilson, above mentioned, used to say that, for the honour of his country of Kent, Alphonso Farabosco, born of Italian parents at Greenwich, and John Jenkyns at Maidstone, were admired not only in England but beyond the seas for their excellent compositions.[66]

There is no imputation of illegitimacy in this posthumous description, nor, really, had there been in any of the previous references to the child, as we have seen. The child and, apparently, a sister had been left in the care of Gomer van Awsterwyke, another of the Queen's musicians. Appointed a "musician for the flute" in 1570, Awsterwyke held that position until his death on July 26, 1592.[67] During the later years of the elder Alfonso's life, Awsterwyke had been a proxy, receiving the monies Elizabeth paid Ferrabosco *in absentia* until 1582.

Seven years later, learning of the elder Ferrabosco's death in Italy, Awsterwyke petitioned the Queen for financial support. Because the petition gives so much direct information concerning matters otherwise only speculative, it is presented here in full.

> To the Right Hon. the Lord High Treasurer of England.
>
> Right Honorable: & my very Good Lord: It hath pleased Mr. vice Chamberlain to move her Majesty concerning my suit of the surrender of my patent of £20 per ann. for a lease in reversion according to your Lordships honorable hand, for the good liking of it, I understand that Alfonso Ferabosco is dead, & upon this occasion, I did most humbly beseech her Majesty, to augment the lease aforesaid, in consideration of my keeping of his children, & her Majesty was pleased again, & and said that she would speak unto your Lordship for it. Wherefore I beseech your Lordship to grant me honourable & accustomed favour therein. Right Honorable, the cause of my suit, for the keeping of Alfonso's children is this, I have kept two children of his the space of 11 years, & about 5 years past Alfonso did send commission unto one Lawrentio Dondieno to bring him his children, & also to pay me for their keeping, but then her Majesty commanded me by my Lord Admiral that now is, that I should not let them depart, by reason whereof I am still unpaid for the said children's keeping. And now Alfonso being dead it is apparent that I shall be constrained to keep them still without any recompense, unless her Majesty of her accustomed clemency & goodness, take pity upon her poor servant, that hath performed her command-

ment, most humbly beseeching your honour likewise to consider of it. And I according to my bounden duty shall daily pray unto God for your good L. long & happy life. Your most humble servant

Gomer van Awsterwyke

[Endorsed.] The humble petition of Gomer van Awsterwyke musicōn to the Queens most excellent Majesty. 8 May 1589. The Queens grant to be shewed forth. – W. Burghley.[68]

Apparently as late as 1584, the elder Alfonso still held out hope of bringing his children to Italy, using the services of our acquaintance, the sceptical Papal Nuncio Dandino. Awsterwyke received his lease in reversion, granted for the customary period of twenty-one years, at the annual rate of £21/16s./2d.[69] The patent for the lease states that the award was made "in consideration of service," which must have included, besides his musicianly activities, the upkeep of the children and, in the case of the young Alfonso, musical training as well.

Awsterwyke's petition is the only extant reference to a second child. From the lack of importance given the child in the elder Ferrabosco's letter of 1582 and its absence from the decree of 1586, it is likely that this child was a girl, of whom nothing more is known. The younger Alfonso, however, entered the Queen's service soon after the death of Awsterwyke, for on October 11, 1592, he was awarded an annuity of 40 marks (£26/13s./4d.), "payable to the Treasurer of Her Majesty's Chamber, granted unto Alphonso Ferrabosco, musician for the viols."[70] This was the first professional position for Ferrabosco and serves as confirmation of the posthumous description provided by Anthony Wood.

> From his childhood, he was trained up to musick, & at man's estate he became an excellent composer for instrumental music in the raigne of K. Jam. I. & K. Ch. I. He was most excellent at the Lyra Viol & was one of the first yt set leasons Lyra-way to the viol, in imitation of the old English Lute and Bandora. The most famous man in all ye world for Fantaziaz of 5 or 6 parts.[71]

It was not until the death of Queen Elizabeth, however, that Ferrabosco assumed a measure of musical prominence. Along with the other musicians of the court, he participated in the funeral which marked the end of the Tudor monarchy.[72] Subsequently, he appears as one of the King's Musicians for the violins at Michaelmas, 1604, with an annuity of £50.[73] But Ferrabosco's real entrée into the court life was his association with the young Prince Henry. As early as November 27, 1604, Ferrabosco had been entrusted with £20 to buy two viols with cases and a box of strings for the young Prince.[74] By the following February, a pension of £50 was settled on Ferrabosco for his attendance upon and instruction of the Prince, a pension retroactive to the previous Christmas and confirmed by a patent of March 22 in which Ferrabosco is described as an "Extraordinary Groom of the Privy Chamber."[75]

At this same time, Ferrabosco also became affiliated with Ben Jonson as a writer of music for the masques Jonson and Inigo Jones presented at the Stuart Court. For the first of these, *The Masque of Blackness* (1605), Ferrabosco wrote at least one song, which was later published in his *Ayres* of 1609. His name does not appear in the description of the masque, but his next contribution, songs written for *Hymenaei*, the masque performed at the court marriage of Lord Essex and Lady Frances Howard on twelfth-night, 1605/06, received warm commendation from Jonson:

> And here, that no mans Deservings complain of injustice (though I should have done it timelier, I acknowledge), I doe for honours sake, and the pledge of our Friendship, name Ma. Alphonso Ferabosco, a Man, planted by himselfe, in that divine Spheare; & mastring all the spirits of Musique: To whose iudiciall Care, and as absolute Performance, were committed all those Difficulties both of Song and otherwise. Wherein, what his Merit made to the Soul of our Invention, would aske to be exprest in Tunes, no lesse ravishing then his. Vertuous friend, take well this abrupt testimonie, and thinke whose it is: It cannot be Flatterie, in me, who never did it to Great ones; and lesse then Love and Truth it is not, where it is done out of Knowledge.[76]

Ferrabosco collaborated in at least six more masques with Jonson. Five of these were presented before the death of Prince Henry: *The Masque of Beauty* (January 14, 1608), *Lord Haddington's Masque* (Shrove Tuesday, 1608), the *Masque of Queens* (February 2, 1609), *Lone Freed from Ignorance and Folly* (Christmas, 1611), and, finally, *Oberon*, honoring Prince Henry (1611). In his *Masque of Argurs* (1622) Jonson acknowledges that the music was "composed by that excellent pair of Kinsmen, Master Alfonso Ferrabosco and Master Nicholas Lanier."[77] Whether Ferrabosco's contribution was to the songs or dances is not known, and no songs from the masque have survived.

This association came to a sudden halt after the death of Prince Henry, and the 1616 Folio edition of Jonson's works does not include the handsome tribute to Ferrabosco quoted above. This seems to be more a personal or court matter than an intellectual one, for there is no reason to assume that Ferrabosco was involved with or troubled by Jonson's concern with poetic invention, esthetic validity, or philosophical integrity, i.e., those matters at the heart of Jonson's differences with Inigo Jones.

Thus, the absence of communication may simply be a reflection—not personally directed—of Jonson's feeling that his "invention," the idea of the masque revealed by the text, was the only aspect worth publishing—the only element not limited by particularity or circumstance. More importantly, however, the end of the association may reflect the growing influence of Jones, for as Jones's contribution became more spectacular, his position at court was similarly ascendant, and he gained increasing control of every aspect of the masques. That this was at the heart of the Jonson-Jones argument is established, but it may also have contributed to Ferrabosco's eclipse. Surely, once Prince Henry had died, it was Prince Charles's musician, Coperario, who would receive the most favorable commissions. Jones, who knew well how to flatter his sovereigns, may have been the one to decide that Ferrabosco could no longer be of use to his career.

Ferrabosco's songs for the early masques prior to 1609, excepting *Hymenaei*, appear among the songs published in the *Ayres* of that year and dedicated to his master, Prince Henry. The dedication has an unusual tone, concluding with Ferrabosco's rare and argumentative appraisal of himself and his work. One need only compare this awkward and crabbed dedication with those of the elder Alfonso's madrigal books to understand the penultimate sentence, "I am not made of much speach."

> To the most equall to his birth, and above all Titles, but his owne Vertue: Heroique Prince Henry.
>
> That which was wont to accompany all Sacrifices, is now become a Sacrifice, MVSIQUE: And to a Composition so full of Harmony as yours, what could bee a fitter Offring? The rather, since they are the Offerers first fruits, and that he giues them with pure hands. I could, now, with that solemne industry of many in Epistles, enforce all that hath beene said in praise of the Faculty, and make that commend the worke, but I desire more, the worke should commend the Faculty: And therefore suffer these few Ayres to owe their Grace rather to your Highnesse judgment, then any others testimonie. I am not made of much speach. Onely I know them worthy of my Name: And, therein, I tooke paynes to make them worthy of yours.
>
> > Your Highnesse
> > most humble Servant
> > Alfonso Ferrabosco

Nonetheless, Ferrabosco did include "others testimonie" in the form of commendatory verses by Ben Jonson, N. Tomkins, and some lines by Thomas Campion which address him as "Musicks maister, and the offspring / Of rich Musicks Father / Old Alfonso's Image liuing." That is the only contemporary reference which links the two Alfonsos, as musicians, until after the younger's death. The fanciful nature of the language has led to the inference that there was a physical resemblance between the two men, father and son. It is more likely, in the language of compliment, that the "Image" is one of musical skill rather than of physiognomy.

Shortly thereafter, Ferrabosco published his *Lessons for 1. 2. and 3. viols,* like the *Ayres* "Printed by T. Snodham for John Browne, / . . . to be sould at his shoppe in S. / Dunstones Church-yard / in Fleetstreet. / 1609." These short pieces for the lyra-viol, printed in tablature, are dedicated to Lord Henry, Earl of Southampton. Like the *Ayres,* this publication includes some verses of commendation: a sonnet by Ben Jonson and an Italian sonnet, signed Gual: Quin.

In a prefatory address, "To the World," Ferrabosco states the reasons, common enough in the period, for publishing these pieces: piracy and falsification.

> Lest I fall under the character of the vainglorious man, in some opinions, by thrusting so much of my industry in print, I would all knew how little fame I hope for that way, when besides his, for, and to whom they are, I aimed at no man's suffrage in the making, though I might presume that could not but please others which I was contented had pleased him. But as it is the error and misfortune of young children oftentimes to stray, and losing their dwellings, be taken up by strangers and there loved and owned, so these, by running abroad, having got them false parents – and some that to my face would challenge them – I had been a most unnatural father if I had not corrected such impudence, and by a public declaration of them to be mine (when other means abandoned me) acknowledged kind. This is all the glory I affected, to do an act of nature and justice. For their seal, they had it in the mint or not at all; howsoever, if they want it, I will ease myself the vice of commendation.

The dedication is even more restrained than that of the *Ayres*:

> To the Perfection of Honovr, My Lord Henry, Earle of Southhampton.
> Whilst other men study your Titles (Honourable Lord) I doe your Honours; and finde it a nearer way to give actions, then words: for the talking man commonly goes about, and meetes the iustice at his errours end, not to be beleeu'd. Yet if in modest actions, the circumstances of singularitie, and profession hurt not; it is true, that I made these Compositions solely for your Lordship, and doe here professe it. By which time, I have done all that I had in purpose, and returne to my silence:
> Where you are most honor'd
> by
> Alfonso Ferrabosco

Lord Henry, of course, was also a patron, perhaps more, of Shakespeare, a sympathizer with recusants, and a subject of interest in his own right. The dedication is important, also, as evidence of the patronage, if not employment, Ferrabosco enjoyed outside the court. This is a matter concerning which there is no direct contemporary evidence, only two later notices which appear among the writings of John Aubrey, one of which links Ferrabosco with the Englishman, styled Italian, John Coperario who was a favorite of Charles I and teacher to William Lawes.

> J. Coperario, whose real name I have been told was Cowper, and Alfonso Ferrabosco, lived most in Wiltshire, sc. at Amesbury and Wulfall, with Edward [Seymour] Earle of Hertford, who was the great patron of musicians.[78]
> Alphonso Ferrabosco, the son, was Lord Philip (the first's) [Philip Herbert, 4th Earl of Pembroke] lutenist. He sang rarely well to the theorbo lute. He had a pension in Baynard's Castle [Pembroke's London house].[79]

Thus, it would seem that while Ferrabosco made his permanent residence in Greenwich, the parish in which all the extant family records appear, he had open access to both court and the London residence of one of his patrons, in addition to the estates of the Earl of Hertford in Wiltshire.

The death of Prince Henry in 1612 was cause for an immense expression of grief throughout the country, an outpouring which included musical settings of elegies by Campion, Thomas Tomkins, and others, but particularly Coperario's *Songs of Mourning*. From Ferrabosco, strangely, there was nothing, yet his position at court remained secure and his services as instructor to the Prince were nominally transferred to the younger Prince Charles. After this time there is little, with the exception of the appearance of three anthems in Sir William Leighton's *Teares or Lamentacions of a Sorrowful Soule*, published in 1614, to indicate that Ferrabosco remained active as a composer.[80] The prominence which he had enjoyed at court as Prince Henry's musician was transferred to Coperario, the principal musician of Prince Charles.

In 1623, Ferrabosco was appointed one of the King's Musicians, a position, like the other two he held, he retained after the death of King James in 1625. Also, in the meantime, Ferrabosco had married and began to raise a family in Greenwich. At least two sons, Henry and Alfonso (III), were born before 1616, the date the Greenwich baptismal records begin. Soon after the birth of a third child in August 1619, Ferrabosco entered a partnership which received a patent for dredging the Thames. This should have been a valuable license, for, as the document shows, it was, in effect, a tax on every vessel which used the port of London. Sometime later, Ferrabosco sold this share in the patent "for a great sume of money" to a William Burrell.[81]

> A Graunt for 21 years to Alfonso Ferabosco, Innocent Laneir and Hugh Lydiard for cleansing the River of Thames of flats and shelfes wh^{ch} annoy the same to the prejudice of Navigacon, wth a grant of such fynes and forfeitures as shal be forfeited to his Matie vpon the statutes of 27° and 34° of K. Henry the eight by anie persons for annoying the said River wth power to sell the sand and gravell they shall take out of the Thames to brickmakers or other at usuall prices,

there is an allowance to them of one penny p tonne of strangers goods and merchandises to be imported and exported into or out of the Port of London in ships and other vessles done by order from Mr. Secretary Calvert Subscr. by Mr. Attorney gnrall.
        [Endorsed.]   14 Octobris, 1619[82]

Despite what should have been relative financial comfort provided by the income from this patent and two, then three positions at court, Ferrabosco fell into debt. In January 1626 he announced, in the form of a contract, his intention of paying his creditors and embarking on a trip abroad, presumably to France. In this document, Ferrabosco specified the extent of his debt to Andrea Lanier, also of East Greenw^{ch} and a flutist in the King's Musick, and made provision for the financial support of his wife, Ellen, in his absence. The trip apparently was to take up to three years, but, in fact, it never took place.

    To all Xpian people. . . .Alfonso Ferrabosco of East Greenwich in the County of Kent, gent. sendeth Greeting in our Lord God everlasting. Whereas the said Alfonso is and standeth truly indebted unto Andrea Lanier of East Greenwich aforesaid gent. in the sum of two hundred pounds of curant English money, And the said Andrea alsoe standeth engaged unto divers persons in sev all somes of money for the only proper debt of the said Alfonso, And for that Also the said Alfonso intendeth by Gods permission to travel and make a voyage beyonde the Seas, and is undertain of his returne.. . .In consideracon that the said shall pay or cause to be paid unto Ellen Ferrabosco wife of the said Alfonso Ferrabosco all such Somes of money as shalbe overplus and above the engagement of debts for wch the said Andrea and Alfonso now stand engaged. . . .
    Alfonso Hath therefore given and graunted, assigned and settov and by these p sents doth fully and absolutely give, graunte assigne & settov unto the said Andrea his Executors and Assignes, All the Stipend, Salary, wages & pfitts whatsoev due or to be due to him the said Alfonso from our Sov aigne lord the king's Matie his heirs and Successors ymediately from the date thereof for and during the Terme of three whole yeares from thence next ensuinge. . . .[83]

Perhaps the death of Coperario later in the same year and the subsequent appointment of Ferrabosco to Coperario's position of Composer of Music in ordinary, with its stipend of £40 *per annum*, helped ease the financial crisis. We can certainly infer from this document, however, that the numerous appointments Ferrabosco held were not overly taxing or restrictive, and it is apparent that he expected to be paid even though absent from his duties.[84] On the other hand, we may share with Ferrabosco a certain frustration with bureaucratic procedure. His appointment to Coperario's place took effect on July 7, 1626, yet it was not until November 23, 1626, that the grant was officially recorded.[85]

The other extant records concerning Ferrabosco are warrants for livery or pay records. Of the former, one is of interest, dating from the year 1626. Among the Lord Chamberlain's papers there is a warrant dated June 13, 1626, ordering provision of livery to musicians whose names appear on an accompanying list. Nicholas Lanier, master of the music, is listed first, followed by "Alphonso Ferabosco."[86] Many of the pay records indicate that Ferrabosco remained in Greenwich either sending messengers to pick up his pay or assigning his wages (more and more in the later years) to his creditors, as is the case in the following instance.[87]

> Whereas I am indebted to this bearer Mr George Tite in the Some of Twelve pounds, I desire to deliver unto him my Debent^{es} for payment of my quarters' wages, due to me this present Midsomer 1624.
> Greenwich, March
>
> Yo^{rs} Always
> Alfonso Ferrabosco

The facsimile of another such assignment is presented in the following pages.[88]

Not long thereafter, probably still in debt and undoubtedly aware of the ascendancy of other musicians such as Lanier, Ferrabosco died and was buried on March 11, 1628 in the Greenwich Parish Church, the same church where Tallis had been buried forty-three years previously. His positions were the subject of brief controversy, for his place as Composer in ordinary was first awarded to Thomas Tomkins.[89] This award was rescinded, for all of Ferrabosco's positions were to pass to his sons, Henry and Alfonso, and Tomkins is still listed among the musicians of the Royal Chapel in June of 1628.[90]

In a document dated March 28, 1628, the other three positions were divided among the sons, implying that Tompkins was still considered Composer in Ordinary. The warrant is a piece of windy bureaucratic writing, fortunately concluded with a succinct summary.

> This Conteyneth yor Ma^{ts} Graunt of the severall wages and ffees yeerely in manner and forme following, vizt. vnto Alfonso Ferabosco one of yor Ma^{ts} Musitians 50^{li} p annum lately enjoyed by Alfonso Ferabosco deceased as Instructor to yor Ma^{te}, being Prince of Wales during his naturall life and unto Henry Feraboscó 40^{li} p annum as one of yor Ma^{ts} Musitians and 40^{li} p annum more as Composer of yor Ma^{ts} Musicke during his naturall lyfe from the decease of the said Alfonso Ferabosco their father deceased whoe formerly held and enjoyed the said severall wages & fees for the services aforesaid.[91]

Autograph Note, Front
Photograph courtesy Music Library, Yale University

Mr Cuningham,
I pray deliver to Mr William Tomson
my quarters wages due to me this Michas
1618, and this my noate shalbe yr
sufficient discharge
Grenwch   yr friend
12 August   Alfonso Ferrabosco

October 9, 1618
Received by me William Tomson
gent, of David Cuningeam, according
to the note above written the } to
some of tenn & ould pounds currant } 10 li
money I said receive
of marke of   William Tompson

Autograph Note, Back
Photograph courtesy Music Library, Yale University

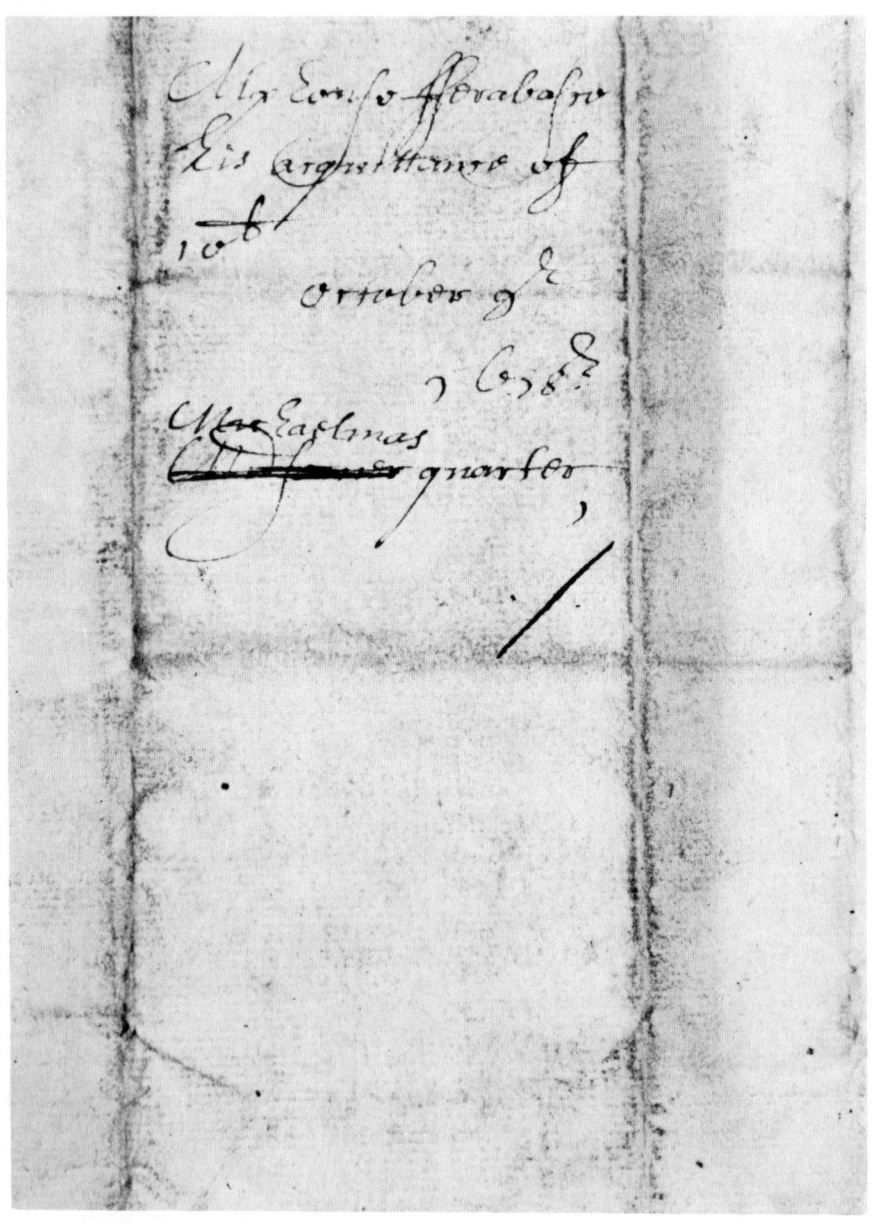

Ferrabosco: autograph note, signed
Music Library, Yale University
Gift, Friends of Music, 1963

Mr. Cuningham,

I pray ' [you] deliver to Mr. William Tomson my quarters wages; due to me this Michaelmas 1618; and this my noate shalbe [shall be] your sufficient dischardge.

Greenwich   your friend
12 August   Alfonso Ferrabosco

[endorsed receipt]

October September 9th, 1618

Received by me William Thomson gent. of David Cunningham,
according to the note written thee--   £
some [sum] of tenne pounds current money of said received -- 10%

The marke of T [mark] William Tompson

[reverse side]

        Alphonso Ferrabosco
        his acquittance of 10 £

                October 9th
                    1618

            Michaelmas
            ---------- quarter

Yet, in a warrant dated the following day, there is no mention of Tomkins, and a note indicates that all four positions were passed to the children.

> Their father enjoyed four places, viz., a musician's place in general, a composer's place, a violl's place, and an instructor's place to the prince in the art of musique. The benefit of all which places did descend unto his sonnes by his Majesty's special grant.[92]

Henry Ferrabosco, evidently named after Prince Henry and presumably born between 1604 and 1612, had joined the King's Musick as a flutist in 1625.[93] He succeeded Innocent Lanier, possibly the same who had been involved in the dredging of the Thames.[94] With his brother, he served in the King's Musick after his father's death until the dissolution of the court establishment. They are last listed in the summary record for 1641 (Alfonso) and lists of musicians in 1645 (Henry), after which time the records are minimal until the Restoration.[95]

In November of 1628, Henry is also mentioned as "one of the musicians for the voices to the king" in a warrant for livery, although he is never so listed in the summaries.[96] He also had charge of a yet younger brother who entered the King's Musick. This boy, John, was the only one of the brothers to survive the Commonwealth, and, after the Restoration, he became organist of Ely Cathedral in 1662. He later received the Bachelor of Music degree from Cambridge (1671), married in 1679, had one child in the following year, and died in 1682.[97]

The last Alfonso Ferrabosco died in 1652 and was buried in the Church of St. Margaret, Westminster.[98] Henry, who was named among the musicians as late as 1645, may have died abroad, for the Report of the Jamaica Committee, dated June 10, 1658, recommends a pension for the children of a Robt. White and Col. Henry Ferribosco, "slain in the service."[99]

The other children of the family were girls. Susanna, named after her grandmother, was born in 1619 and died an infant, in 1621. Two years later Katherine was born, but there is no other record of her. Mary, apparently born before 1616, was buried in 1631. The only surviving daughter who can be traced beyond this date, Elizabeth, was also born before 1616. She married another musician, George Bunckley of St. Martin's in the Fields. Bunckley, or Buncle as other records have him, was a recusant, and, when he and Elizabeth had their first child, Mrs. Ellen Ferrabosco objected to the planned baptism, insisting that the child be "christned according to the rites of the church of England".[100]

Mrs. Ferrabosco, herself, died on August 5, 1638. Pepys mentions a Mrs. Ferrabosco who "sings most admirably" and whom he thought of engaging as a gentlewoman for his wife, later noting that she was in the service of the Duchess of Newcastle.[101] Hawkins mentions a Mostyn Ferrabosco, a lieutenant in the Royal Navy, indicating that the family had not yet died out.[102]

As for the "English" Alfonso, his fame hardly outlived his death. Only in France was he remembered for his great skill in playing and composition. Mersenne quoted one of Ferrabosco's six-voice fancies for viols, "composée par un excellent joueur de viole Anglois de Nation."[103] But the crowning compliment was to come from André Maugars, a French viol player who had been in the service of Queen Henrietta Maria and had come with her to England.[104] Writing from Rome three years after the appearance of the *Harmonie Universelle*, Maugars commented on the Italian players of the viol.

> La Lyre est encore en recommendation parmi eux; mais je n'en ay oüy aucun qui fust à comparer à Farabosco d'Angleterre.[105]
>
> [The Lyre is also in high favor with them, but I have heard no one who could compare with the Englishman, Ferrabosco.]

And, finally, Maugars went so far as to assert that the elder Alfonso Ferrabosco was the one who introduced the viol to England, a pretty piece of speculation to say the least, but it is fascinating to read in this Frenchman's appraisal that the "great" Ferrabosco was the younger, although the father had been more highly praised in England.

> . . . et aussi que le père de ce grande Farabosco, Italien, en a apporté le premier l'usage aux Anglois, qui depuis ont surpassé toutes les nations.
>
> [The father of the great Ferrabosco, an Italian, introduced {the viol} to the English who now excell those of all other countries.]

Perhaps it was that excellence, the excellence of Coperario, Jenkins, William Lawes, and Locke to come, which overshadowed Ferrabosco in his native land both during his life and after his death.

Ferrabosco's activity in the arena of English court music was an accident of circumstances following his father's departure to the continent, and one can only speculate on the relative strengths of nurture and nature which placed him in such a prominent position during the first decade of James I's reign. Apparently Prince Henry was the final key to this success, for after Henry's death in 1612, Ferrabosco seems to have retired from court. His involvement with the masques of Jonson (even, perhaps, his friendship with Jonson—a friendship generously and genuinely expressed by the poet) was probably overruled by Inigo Jones who saw his way to favor more surely guaranteed by using musicians according to their relationship to the powerful at court: Ferrabosco, while Prince Henry was alive; Coperario after Prince Charles became the immediate heir to the throne.

We do know that the bulk of Ferrabosco's music was composed before 1612: the *Ayres* and the songs for the masques, the four-part fancies contained in Tregian's collections, the motets (also copied by Tregian), many of the dances, and the innomines. We don't know for whom Ferrabosco wrote much of this music or the great six-part fancies. Nor do we have anything more than the briefest of posthumous report regarding Ferrabosco's activities at Wulfall and Amesbury, the estates of Edward Seymour, the Earl of Hertford, or at the house of Philip Herbert, the Earl of Pembroke. Other documents concerning Ferrabosco's activities at the houses of his patrons have not been uncovered. It is reasonable, however, to suggest that participation in the music at Seymour's estates may have occupied Ferrabosco after Prince Henry died and his court positions became less promising. These houses, with their independent musical establishment, would be the logical arena for the chamber music both Ferrabosco and Coperario composed in such quantity and quality.

Similarly, we know little of Ferrabosco's earlier activities from the time Queen Elizabeth granted him a pension in 1592 until his first recorded association with Prince Henry in 1604. Here, too, one might suggest that, after Awsterwycke's death, Ferrabosco was accepted at one of these estates which then became his musical home away from court for the rest of his life.

Future research will, one hopes, provide some answers to these questions regarding Ferrabosco's activities before and after his ascendancy at court. Involved are not only the issues of patronage and musical activity, but also those of recusancy, the internal relations of the community of foreigners, and the passage of musical influences and materials between England and the continent. The puzzle is far from complete, leading sometimes to speculations which are more fascinating and fanciful than the evidence can support.

Until we know more, particularly about Ferrabosco's relations with his patrons, we must, however, be guided by the probable assumption that Ferrabosco's work at court is accurately, if not completely, represented by that music which was published in 1609: his songs and compositions for the lyra-viol. The chamber music and motets were probably written in another arena: the four-part fancies and motets before Tregian's imprisonment, the six-part fancies quite possibly composed only after the death of Prince Henry, probably at the estate(s) of a patron (patrons) like Edward Seymour.

Perhaps, too, future research will allow us to know better the man who saw a world of promise denied him, probably because of the political panderings of Inigo Jones, whose rich gifts in music soured in longstanding financial mismanagement and debt, whose accomplishments, once praised by colleagues and friends in poetic compliment and friendly commendation, were dismissed and forgotten in his adoptive country even before his unremarked death—remembered only in posthumous report and foreign memorial.

These questions all remain. We are fortunate to have so much of the music, for without the music we would not care to know the answers.

II

Poetry and Music

> For al theire musicke . . . doth so resemble and expresse naturall affections, the sound & tune is so applied and made agreable to the thynge, that whether it bee a prayer, or els a dytty of gladnes, of patience, of trouble, of mournynge, or of anger: the fassion of the melodye dothe so represent the meaning of the thing, that it doth wonderfullye move, stire, pearce, and enflame the hearers myndes.
>
> Sir Thomas More, *Utopia*
> Robinson's translation, 1551, sig. R5

The appearance of the poetry of Wyatt and Surrey, posthumously published in Tottel's *Miscellany* of 1557, was the first evidence of a break away from the drab, heavy style of contemporary English poetry, the first evidence of those exercises in classical imitation which formed the backbone of humanistic training. Wyatt's Petrarchan sonnets (some direct translations) and Surrey's blank verse translation of Vergil demonstrated that their poetry was a blending of skill *and* learning, an exercise of the mind in which expression was conveyed by the management of rhetoric: meter, rhyme, imagery, argument, convention, and a forceful economy of language.

It remained, however, for the appearance of Spenser's *The Shepheardes Calender* (1579) before the new age of English poetry can be said to have begun. The effect of Spenser's poetry was to convince the reader that form was not the determinant of poetry; elements of form such as rhyme, accent, meter, line length and versification could be both flexible and unobtrusive, serving as vehicles for the thought even while creating the marvelously artificial forms of *Epithalamion*, *The Shepheardes Calender*, or *The Faerie Queene*. The pastoral conventions were here adapted to a variety of subjects while the fitness of style to subject (the decorum) was maintained by variations of diction and poetic scheme.

But it was not only decorum which Spenser and, particularly, Sidney provided. The novelty is recognized in Sidney's *Astrophil and Stella*, a pastoral sonnet sequence written in imitation of Italian models, as the conclusion of the first sonnet:

"Fool," said my Muse to me, "look in thy heart and write." Here the formal perfection of the sonnet was joined with a self-dramatizing spirit, a personality which bespoke a conviction that the divine spark of creativity revealed itself in the heart and speech of the poet.

This, then, was the leading edge of the movement which, in two decades, was to express itself in the extensive, but powerfully compacted metaphors of Shakespeare and the peculiar and individual persuasive force of Donne's diction and syntax.

In most of the poetry of the late mid-century the poets sought "to make the stresses of the language conform to [an] abstract metrical pattern with its strong caesuras."[1] The most common measures, or metric schemes, were the various ballad and hymn meters, usually organized in 4-line strophes, or quatrains. The regularity of this organization is as much musical as it is poetic, for it arises from the consistent division, often for purposes of singing, of the long 12 and 14 syllable lines of this poetry into units of 8 or 6 syllables. For example, fourteeners, lines of 14 syllables, were divided by caesuras into units of 8 and 6 syllables, with a quatrain then consisting of two lines (four units) with the following syllable count: 8.6.8.6.

Hexameters, 12-syllable lines, were similarly divided, with the resulting quatrain having this count: 6.6.6.6. Poulter's measure, consisting of alternating lines of 12 and 14 syllables, produced this syllable count: 6.6.8.6.

When these measures were set to music, there were different results depending on whether the musical meter was duple or triple. In duple meter, the notes were of equal length and word accent was aligned with metrical accent. In triple meter, as well, the long notes were given to accented syllables. That is, the accentual scansion was transformed into a quantitative one, as well.

The caesuras in the middle of the originally longer lines of poetry were often realized by rests in the music, and the 4-measure phrase became the normal length for the musical phrase because it could accommodate both the 6 and 8 syllable divisions of the poetic lines.[2]

Using the symbols / and x (or .) to designate stressed and unstressed syllables, respectively, and − and ∪ to represent the long and short quantitative scansion, the following diagram presents abstract quatrains of each of the three major ballad meters. The manner in which these poetic meters were set to music, in both duple and triple

Poetry and Music   35

meter, is represented to the side. Typically, half-cadences occurred after the second line, full cadences at the end of the fourth line.

                                                                       Music

Poulter's Measure 6.6.8.6.   duple   triple

   1.   x/x/x/   [caesura]   ♩ ♪♪ ♪♪ ○ ▬   ♩ ♪♪ ♪♪ ♪. ▬
   2.   x/x/x/   [line-break]   ♩ ♪♪ ♪♪ ○ ▬   ♩ ♪♪ ♪♪ ♪. ▬
   3.   x/x/x/x/   [caesura]   ♩ ♪♪ ♪♪ ♪♪ ♪   ♩ ♪ ♪♪ ♪♪ ♪♪ ♪
   4.   x/x/x/   [pause]   ♩ ♪♪ ♪♪ ○ ▬   ♩ ♪♪ ♪♪ ♪. ▬
   ∪ – ∪ – ∪ –[∪ –]

Fourteeners 8.6.8.6.

   1.   x/x/x/x/   [caesura]   ♩ ♪♪ ♪♪ ♪♪ ♪   ♩ ♪ ♪♪ ♪♪ ♪♪ ♪
   2.   x/x/x/   [line-break]   ♩ ♪♪ ♪♪ ○ ▬   ♩ ♪♪ ♪♪ ♪. ▬
   3.   x/x/x/x/   [caesura]   ♩ ♪♪ ♪♪ ♪♪ ♪   ♩ ♪♪ ♪♪ ♪♪ ♪
   4.   x/x/x/   [pause]   ♩ ♪♪ ♪♪ ○ ▬   ♩ ♪♪ ♪♪ ♪. ▬
  ∪ – ∪ – ∪ – ∪ –

Hexameters 6.6.6.6.

   1.   x/x/x/   [caesura]   ♩ ♪♪ ♪♪ ○ ▬   ♩ ♪♪ ♪♪ ♪. ▬
   2.   x/x/x/   [line-break]   ♩ ♪♪ ♪♪ ○ ▬   ♩ ♪♪ ♪♪ ♪. ▬
   3.   x/x/x/   [caesura]   ♩ ♪♪ ♪♪ ○ ▬   ♩ ♪♪ ♪♪ ♪. ▬
   4.   x/x/x/   [pause]   ♩ ♪♪ ♪♪ ○ ▬   ♩ ♪♪ ♪♪ ♪. ▬

The stiff regularity of these patterns which tyrannized most of the musical poetry of the period, emphasized by the heaviness of the caesuras and the end-stopping of every other line (increasingly frequently in conjunction with rhyme), can be contrasted to the variety of Italian stress patterns found in the texts in Caccini's *Le Nuove Musiche* (1602). The lines are differentiated by the number of syllables; in each type of verse line the primary accent falls on the penultimate syllable; secondary accents are indicated below by additional accent signs.

        quadernario   1 2 ´3 4

        quinario   1 2 3 ´4 5

        senario   1 ˌ2 3 4 ´5 6

settenario	[ˈ ˈ ˈ ˈ] /	1 2 3 4 5 6̆ 7
ottonario		1 2 3̍ 4 5 6 7́ 8
endecasillabo		1 2 3 4 5 6̍ 7 8 9 1́0 11
		1 2 3 4̍ 5 6 7̍ 8 9 1́0 11
		1 2 3 4̍ 5 6 7 8̍ 9 1́0 11
dodecasillabo		1 2 3 4̍ 5 6̍ 7 8 9̍ 10 1́1 12

In Caccini's madrigals, this flexibility of accent, particularly in lines of 7 and 11 syllables, allowed for more flexibility of musical gesture. The verse for the madrigals was not composed of strophes consisting of lines of uniform length, unlike the poetry for the strophic *arie* which comprised the second part of *Le Nuove Musiche*. Thus, the freer form of the *canzone* poetry of the madrigals was contrasted musically, as well as poetically, with fixed-form and repetitive poetic models.

Discussions of the quantitative attributes of poetry pervaded Europe during the sixteenth century, coming to a head in the latter half of the century. In England, Sidney felt that the ancient quantitative system of prosody was "more fit for Musick, both words and tune observing quantity, and more fit lively to express diverse passions, by the low and lofty sounde of the well-weyed silable."[3] Sidney's and Spenser's discussion of and experiments in quantitative meters, often in conjunction with versification based on Italian pastoral models (e.g., Petrarch and Ariosto and Sannazaro), owe, like Campion's later exposition of musical-poetical analogy, a debt to foreign influence. This influence is most comprehensively represented in the writings of four authors whose ideas become part of the European intellectual climate. Dante, in *De Vulgari Eloquentia*, addresses language as an art of sound and recommends natural speech as being nobler than the artificial kind. Pico della Mirandola, in *Liber de Imaginatione*, espouses the platonic argument that sight is the most important of the senses [this has an importance outside our basic discussion regarding the manner by which poetry expresses itself: its emblematic aspect]. Joachim duBellay, in *La Deffence et l'illustration de la Langue Françoyse* (1549), the manifesto of the Pléiade, claims (as Catherine Ing has observed)

> simultaneously, that the classical languages are and should be models of perfection and richness in metrical expression, and that the vernacular should find appropriate means of ensuring satisfying metrical structure in its own verse which

shall be equivalent to, rather than copied from, the structure given to Greek and Latin poetry by the use of syllabic quantity.[4]

Ronsard, in his *Abrégé de l'art poétique françois* (1565), approaches the problem of grammar and orthography in an attempt to find a solution in the written language for the accurate and subtle representation of the sounds of speech. Baif's quantitative translation of the *Psalter* (1573) and Ramus' *Grammaire* (1562; 2/1572) were also important for their effect on English quantitative translation.

The problems of orthography and pronunciation ("our natural prosodye" as Gabriel Harvey put it in his letters to Spenser in 1580) bedeviled the English as well. In a subtler form, this question was at the root of George Puttenham's impatience, in *The Art of English Poesie* (1589), with syllable counting (meter) which did not produce a satisfying "musicall numerositie," or rhythm.

In this regard, then, it is much easier to view Campion's experiments, set forth in his *Observations in the Art of English Poesie* (London, 1612) as an attempt to achieve that "musicall numerositie." For example, Campion modestly provides that delightful "Rose-Cheekt Lawra" as an example of the second kind of English Sapphic which, following classical models, consists of one line of dimeter (two feet and one odd syllable; the first foot may be either a spondee [- -] or a trochee [- ᴗ], the second a trochee or tribrach), followed by two trochaic lines (with a spondee possible in the first position) and a concluding line comprised of two trochees. The variety here permitted in the quantitative scheme allows the word accents to be coordinated with the long syllables, although such was not Campion's stated intent.

Rose-Cheekt Lawra

Rose-cheekt Lawra, come

Sing thou smoothly with thy beawties

Silent musick, either other

Sweetely gracing

Lovely formes do flowe

From concent, devinely framed;

Heav'n is musick, and thy beawties

Birth is heavenly.

These dúll nōtes we sīng
Dīscordes neēde for hēlps to grāce them;
Ōnly beāwty pūrely lōving
Knōwes no discōrd
But stīll mōves delīght,
Līke cleāre sprīnges renū'd by flōwing,
Ēver perfēct, evēr in them-
selves eternāll.

Campion intended a quantitative reading according to the rules of length which he gives at the end of the *Observations*, but the success of the quantitative reading here is ensured by the fact that the long syllables are reinforced by the natural stress of the language and the syntax.

Such is not the case with the oft-cited "Come let us sound with melody," a lyric which appears in a musical setting in the First Part of Rosseter's *A Booke of Ayres* (1601, no. xxi). The text is set as a strophic song using two note values in the melody: − for a long syllable, ⌣ for a short syllable. Thus, the music specifies the quantitative reading, giving a definitive indication of the scansion, as in musique mesurée. Isolated from aspects of pitch and harmony, that scansion is consistent in each strophe, as follows:

Lines 1, 2, 3 trochee   spondee   dactyl   trochee   spondee
Line 4 dactyl   spondee

The entire poem is given below, with the scansion and musical values indicated for the first strophe. Unlike the reading of "Rose-Cheekt Lawra," this is painfully regular, a result, perhaps, of setting the text to an abstract scheme which must be repeated exactly *because* of the demands of the musical setting.

Come, Let us sound with melody
Come, let us sound with melody, the praises
− ⌣ − − ⌣ ⌣ − ⌣ − −
Of the king's king, th' omnipotent creator,
− ⌣ − − − ⌣ ⌣ − − −
Author of number, that hath all the world in
Harmonie framed.

> Heav'n in His throne perpetually shining,
> His devine power and glorie, thence he thunders,
> One in all, and all still in one abiding
> > Both Father and Son.
>
> O sacred sprite, invisible, eternall
> Ev'rywhere, yet unlimited, that all things
> Canst in one moment penetrate, revive me,
> > O holy Spirit.
>
> Rescue, O Rescue me from earthly darkness,
> Banish hence all these elementall obiects,
> Guide my soul that thirsts to the lively Fountaine
> > of thy devinenes.

This is acceptable, though not convincing, for singing, but conflict of accent, sense and quantity crop up quickly for the reading voice (e.g., "perpetually," "O sacred sprite," even "let us" in the first line, and all but the first of the short lines which have an astonishing variety of accentual patterns), and it is questionable "whether the form of this poem is adequately held together [or described] by Campion's rules alone."[5]

The experimentation with form and rhyme, and with quantity, meter, and rhythm which preceded these efforts of Campion demonstrates two facts: English versification and poetic expression made tremendous strides in the fifty years following the appearance of Tottel's *Miscellany*; and the problems of English measure and prosody are subtle and difficult. Out of the crags of these problems, however, blossomed flowers like these:

> So I vnto my selfe alone will sing;
> The woods shall to me answer and my Eccho ring.
>
> > Spenser, *Epithalamion* (refrain)

and this, from a poem which contains what may be the most beautiful line in all English poetry:

> That time of year thou may'st in me behold
> When yellow leaves, or none, or few, do hang
> Upon those boughs which shake against the cold,
> Bare ruin'd choirs, where late the sweet birds sang
>
> > Shakespeare, Sonnet LXXIII

The conventional Elizabethan persuasive lyric underwent a transformation in the hands of poets like Shakespeare and Donne, becoming a vehicle for personal expression and possessed of an immediacy and urgency to which the conventional (song-) lyric never aspired. Forms such as the sonnet were invested with an intensity unfamiliar to the pastoral landscapes of earlier Arcadias and even to the land of Astrophil and Stella; stanzaic poems were asked to convey arguments which developed thoughts rather than simply to present a succession of pretty parallels of diction, thought, and rhyme. Stress patterns became more prominently those of the speaking voice, and these patterns became an important and necessary part of the experience of the poetry, unlike the patterns of earlier lyric poetry which, by their lack of specificity, contributed only to the sense of the poem's essential generality, artificiality, and distance.

Donne's poetry forces the issue of the crisis, or turning point, of the lyric. Grierson, whose pioneering work on Donne has not lost its basic validity and insight, argues that Donne's is "a poetry not perfect in form, rugged of line and careless in rhyme," yet he continues that it is "a poetry of an extraordinarily arresting and haunting quality, passionate, thoughtful, and with a deep melody of its own."[6] This point, so early recognized in the twentieth-century renascence of interest in the metaphysical poets, is perhaps better presented by Brian Morris, who recognizes the gulf between Donne and the earlier lyric when he concludes that "Donne never conceived his poems in musical terms, and never delivered them as material for a marriage of the arts."[7]

The stiffly limping fourteeners of mid-century, with their drab parade of end-stopped pairs of four- and three-stress lines, paled before the dazzling and supple experimentation of the 1580s. The conscientious efforts of writers to make the English language more literary, a successful venture certainly by the time of Spenser's *The Faerie Queene* (1590-1596) and the publication of Bacon's *Essays* (1597) or Sidney's *Arcadia* (1590-1591), was mirrored by humanistic discussions of literature. Wilson's *Art of Rhetoric* appeared in 1553, but more important was the appearance of Roger Ascham's *Schoolmaster* (1570) which spoke for the Cambridge humanists and advocated (at nearly the same time similar discussions were occuring on the continent) the application of the principles of Latin quantitative verse to English. In 1575 George Gascoigne argued in favor of an accentual prosody, and the debate continued for three decades generating more heat than light.

An awareness of the peculiarities of the English tongue and the assumption that the language was essentially accentual influenced the letters of Spenser and Gabriel Harvey (1580s) without quieting the humanist concern for quantity—a concern the goal of which was not really quantity, *per se*, but a regularization of the language: rules for its formation and use. This goal was thwarted both by inconsistent orthography and by the fact that the language *was* accentual *and* exhibited a tremendous variety of quantities.

Thomas Campion, in his *Observations in the Art of English Poesie* (London, 1602),[8] raised the question again in a particularly important way, for he was an accomplished prosodist, and he applied his prosody to implied or actual musical settings of his metrical experiments. His quantitative prosody, however, was largely irrelevant in English, and his metrical choices were limited to only two (long/short). Even he must have realized that the lyric calm (or the calm lyric) of the pastoral had been too calm, that the immediate voice of Shakespeare and the rhetorical variety of Jonson and Donne demanded a less simpleminded scheme than his, borrowed from the French school of *vers mesurée* and principles of classical Greek and Latin. On another front, however, Campion did not realize the implicit force of his argument. The matching of long and short in English song composition of this period is one of the most interesting problems in the history of song. Although the humanistic arguments about quantity subsided and the lyric lost its position of eminence to the drama, English song writers evolved their own answers to the problems of accent and quantity—answers which are specifically English.

The arguments about poetry of the time had another consistent subject, though one to which less attention was paid: to rhyme or not to rhyme. Campion, in his *Observations*, argued against the use of rhyme, describing it as an easy solution to the problem of ending lines which led to a paucity of poetic expression and device. In response, Samuel Daniel, brother of the composer John Daniel, pointed out (*A Defence of Ryme*, c. 1605) that rhyme is a means of both integration and articulation and that it can be used effectively, for example, in bringing a poem to a close. This argument was anticipated, however, by George Puttenham whose *Arte of English Poesie* was published in 1589 after many years of compilation. Puttenham showed an acute sense of the poetic effort of his time, and he was the first to argue clearly that the basis of length in English poetry was not the foot, but the line: it is the time of the line, not the individual syllable, which is most important to him, and he cites the variable-length lines of Petrarch's *Canzoni* as models for the possibilities of English verse. The proportioning of verse, then, is done at the level of the line, within which the syllables can be well- and variously-weighed. The proportioning of the whole form can be articulated by rhyme. Campion, in fact, also uses the line at his unit of time, implying, as Catherine Ing points out, "that he knows English syllable lengths to be too variable to serve in themselves as measuring-units of time."[9]

In the contemporary progress of the English accompanied art-song, the problems of classification are manifold. In contrast to the ballad, which is textually indifferent and lacks written-out accompaniment, there are the consort song and the lute song with fully written-out accompaniment and increasing textual sensitivity. These were followed by the continuo song, with its separation of bass and voice, improvised accompaniment, and more densely intellectual poeticizing. The distinctions are not altogether clear, for in the period of the lute song, the 25 years following the publication of Dowland's *First Book of Ayres* in 1597, we find lute songs with texted accompaniment parts, lute songs with bass viol parts, and lute songs with written-out, though continuo-like, lute parts.

With this in mind, a distinction must be made which allows us to comprehend the two stylistic extremes of the lute song repertory: the through-composed piece with very specific rhetorical declamation and the (sometimes dance-derived) metrical song with regular phrasing and strophic repetition—in which accent and stress are matched but the goal is neither declamation nor expression, nor even serious persuasion, but entertainment. This latter group most nearly matches the Elizabethan concept of lyric song, while the first is deserving of a distinctive name of its own. Unfortunately, Elizabethan and Jacobean usage included both under the rubric of the "ayre" (a name probably borrowed by Dowland from the French), which is in turn confused by Caccini's use of *aria* to denote his shorter, stanzaic songs in *Le Nuove Musiche*—in contrast to the through-composed solo madrigals which are more representative of the "new music" and which more specifically satisfy Caccini's goal of matching the conceit and form of the text in music.

Like the consort song, both extremes of lute song are accompanied declamation songs. After Byrd, all artful English song was at least somewhat sensitive to matters of declamation. The lute-accompanied declamation songs can be further divided, as above, into those which are essentially strophic and tuneful (lyric) declamation songs and those which, following the lead of the elegiac consort-song laments, more seriously try to reveal the text, and its *pathos*, in the music by expressive affect, declamatory presentation, rhetorical gesture, and a more specific response of the music to the text. Like the consort-laments, these serious songs show a greater integration of the musical material of voice and accompaniment, a wider range of musical gestures which are text-related, and a metrical-rhythmical interplay which is more textually specific and less regular than in the tuneful songs. This causes problems with strophic texts in which successive strophes are not poetic reflections of each other, and, in fact, we can ask of many of these songs whether more than one strophe *can* be sung to the music.[10] The composer as reader, rather than singer, is more evident, and these are the songs from which the English "recitative musick" was to develop, for example in the masque songs which show one way toward the continuo declamation song. These serious songs are the ones which, for a brief period at the beginning of the seventeenth century, married *logos* and *melos*, subjugating neither and often achieving their goal, a sublime expression of *pathos*.

In the consort song, a musical style of great impersonality conveyed the text. It was Byrd's contribution to this style to achieve musical integrity by using pervasive imitation and to treat the words in a way which focused their declamation. Even in the dramatic consort-lament, however, the singing voice does not achieve its own *persona*, but maintains an aspect of undisturbed and exalted contemplation, while the accompaniment portrays the most difficult and intangible moods. The art is focused on the listener's mind, not on the process of interpreting or representing the text. This is the guiding principle: persuasion by decorum — the fitting of style with content — not expression.[11]

The "unliterary" quality of Byrd's settings, as described by Pattison,[12] results from the fact that his is a different convention of text-setting than that which blustered forth from Italy at the turn of the century. It is abstract and generalized in the sense that John Stevens observes: "the suitability of a particular musical style to a particular poem is not a matter of emotional fitness but of convention."[13] Byrd's style was passed on to John Dowland and Orlando Gibbons.

> Byrd's greatest direct successor was Orlando Gibbons, who seemed in his *Madrigals and Mottets* of 1612 to have taken the older master's purely vocal song-style as a point of departure, and who found a form so congenial to his talents in the verse anthem, Byrd's extension of the consort song to composition on a larger scale. But the true inheritor of the native tradition of solo song was John Dowland, whose setting of verse places him closer to Byrd than is generally realized, despite stylistic and textural differences.[14]

Dowland's ayres partake of a variety of English, French, and Italian influences, and among these songs we find the two distinct types mentioned earlier: the shorter, strophic song, often dancelike in character (and origin), and the longer, more serious song, almost polyphonic in some instances. The influences of the French *air de cour* are seen particularly in Dowland's *First Book of Songs or Ayres* (1597), not only in the name[15] and format of his collection which reflected the French part-song performance practice of the *air*, but in the smooth melodic writing, the homophonic four-part ensemble (yet with the sense of accompanied melody), the use of triple-meter and dance-related rhythms[16], short, equal, and balanced phrases with simultaneous cadences in all parts, bipartite structure with predominantly ABB form, absence of imitation, use of strophic poetry, and melodic simplicity with, generally, equal notes set syllabically. Dowland avoided the floridity of the later *air* as much as he did the polyphony of the earlier *chanson*.

Italian influences, publicized and promulgated by Morley, become more prominent in Dowland's later books in which there is more independence among the voices, greater rhythmic variety and complexity of the lower parts, more imitation and different formal structures, more through-composed songs, more "madrigalian" text representation, rhythmical gestures which are textually inspired, and more songs which are presented only as solo songs. Almost all of these latter features, however, are also part of the native song tradition as developed by Byrd, and so it is misleading to attribute these features solely to Italian influence. Although Dowland failed to make his more serious songs popular in England—they were not, after all, vehicles of simple entertainment in his hands—it was in these songs that he succeeded in meeting the problems of a more word-responsive text-setting. Einstein cites Dowland as "the real pioneer in establishing a genuine English 'monody'—one not contaminated by theoretical speculation."[17]

Dowland's early tuneful dance-songs, with their prevailing French influence, found a follower in Thomas Campion who probably remained closest to the French antecedents from which Dowland had derived his earlier ayres. Dowland's more serious songs found some response in Morley and Coperario (both conscientious purveyors of things Italian), but more, and more importantly, in the transition from the lute song to the continuo song, in the serious declamation songs of Alfonso Ferrabosco.

In those serious lute-accompanied declamation songs we see an increasing concern for declamation as we have been accustomed to think of it in light of the principles in Italian recitative: the representation of the text in music. But the English manner was more intellectual and concerned more with meaning than with emotion. It was not until Lanier's attempts, in *Hero and Leander* from the late 1620s, to transport the Italian recitative to England and to impose (unsuccessfully) its practices on English song that there was a large-scale attempt at narrative declamation in music which would mirror the speech-rhythm of the English language.

The declamation of the Jacobean song-writers was nearly as complex, though more conservative and unsupported by theoretical programs, as that of the Italians who tried, *in extremis*, to recreate exaggerated speech-patterns of great intensity in order to achieve dramatic expressiveness. The formal elements of music played a more obviously important role in English song, and the manner in which the Jacobean song-writer expressed the meaning of the text was at all times musically coherent, without an attempt at dramatic realism.

The tools of the English declamatory development were those which allowed a clear reading of the text, which clarified stress and emphasis (both syntactical and prosodic), and which articulated thought. These included: 1) cadence structure and harmonic movement: the hierarchy of stops, ordered by both tonal level and procedure (intervallic or chordal progression), which mirrored the sense of the reading of a poem; 2) attention to stress by the use of duration, varying pitch, and accent; 3) emphasis of stress by rhythmic or melodic gesture and the use of "bar-line" accents coordinated by the activity of these accompaniment and harmony; 4) the use of rests to emphasize or intensify the declamation; 5) the use of repetition (often sequential or with very deliberate musical changes) to emphasize both text and mood; 6) emphatic musical gestures which draw attention to particular words or to the delivery of those words; 7) affective intervals or harmonies which have conventionally acquired expressive connotations and are made specific by the text; 8) word-painting. The use of chromaticism or affective harmonic dissonance was rare in this period of English song—the English madrigal and motet/anthem repertory displays more of these effects, although the larger structure of a song (and its text) was articulated by harmonic area. It was in the combination of these resources, particularly those of pitch, accent, duration, and gesture, that the serious lute-accompanied declamation song was most productive and, in combination with its larger phraseology in "reading" the poetry, most subtle.

The tuneful ayre was content with the formal isomorphism of line and phrase. The poetry was often tediously regular in phraseology and strophic structure (equal phrase lengths; concurrence of caesura and rhyme; regular and repetitive stress patterns, unvaried). As a casual reading of the texts will quickly establish, its wit and sometime sophistication were generally insufficient to sustain its importance. The serious ayre, although its texts are also usually less than compelling by themselves, had, at the extreme, a singularly different goal: its isomorphism was of thought and expression. Thus, the true marriage of words and music is not found in an indiscriminate lumping together of the variegated products of the golden age of English song, but in those songs which succeed in presenting the text authentically, in rhetoric and affect, and in enlarging the experience of the text by means of its musical presentation.

The challenge to the composer was to make his music more specifically responsive to the text without destroying musical coherence. The manner in which English composers met that challenge with the marvelously rich and difficult lyric poetry of the early seventeenth century on the one hand and the Stuart demand for panegyric, in which pretense had to be supported by simple but heroic and ceremonial rhetorical gestures, on the other, shows an increasing sensitivity to the weight and presentation of the text. This concern for declamation approximating natural speech or oratory was never argued through theoretically in England and was most fruitful (with regard to these concerns) only with the abandonment of the written-out accompaniment and the subsequent supremacy of the word which prevailed in the development of the continuo style.[18]

III

Ferrabosco's Harmonic Practice

A brief introduction to Ferrabosco's harmonic practice and, more specifically, to the underlying system of tonal relationships with which he and his contemporaries worked will be helpful to the analysis of the songs and motets discussed later in this study.[1]

Ferrabosco's harmonic practice is both consonant and diatonic. However, it is remarkably flexible while, at the same time, being completely tonal in concept. This tonal system consists of a central, paired (parallel major/minor) tonality[2] and the parallel paired tonalities extending two degrees to either side of the circle of fifths. In addition, the relative minor and major are employed, as are their tonal parallels and the parallel tonal pairs (with important exceptions) one step to either side of them in the circle of keys.

Using C/c as the central tonal pair, this is the tonal arena available:

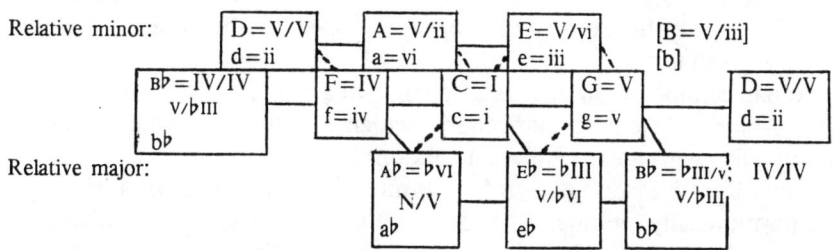

The various fifth and third common-tone relations of these tonal pairs, and individual members of these pairs, are clear and, therefore, so are the 5th (dominant), 3rd (mediant), and 6th (including both submediant and Neapolitan) functional relationships to which they give rise.

That this system "folds" back into itself, closing the arena from further extension (at this time), explains its basic, though inflected, diatonicism. Those elements which might introduce true chromaticism by altering important notes in the tonal scheme (e.g., a♭, e♭, and b♭ minors) are, in fact, excluded, yet every tonal function and all the chromatic inflections which are used by Ferrabosco and his English contemporaries can be explained most convincingly in terms of this system of relationships.

Essentially, the extension of the areas away from the tonic serves to enrich what is, actually, a process of tonicization. The tonal function of the other areas is to embellish the dominant whether by contrast or preparation. The dominant relationship is absolutely primary; the path back to the tonic is always through the dominant. Consequently, any other regions traversed serve to extend the distance, but not the goal of the travel. With Ferrabosco there is neither substantial modulation nor confusion ("bifocality") of tonic. What is important is that the path away from the tonic, which eventually arrives on the dominant, can take many turns. What is ambiguous is not the tonic, but the relationship of a particular area to the tonic at a particular time: e.g., is E♭ heard, in a given instance, as the relative major of C/c or as the Neapolitan of D/d which will then proceed to G. Similarly, A♭, used affectively on the instance of the text, may appear as a "coloration" of the subdominant or as the last stop in a plunge down the circle of fifths, returning to the tonic via the dominant, to which it stands in a Neapolitan relationship.

The chromatic notes used by Ferrabosco are all contained in the basic harmonies of this system, assuming C/c is the tonic: C♯ (VI or V/ii); F♯ (V/V); G♯ (III, or V/vi); E♭, A♭, and B♭ are all within c minor as well as acting as the relative majors of the central tonal pairs. Thus, these chromatic tones are understood as chordal inflections, not as individual note inflections, and they are related to the function of the chord at a given time.

What cannot be shown in a scheme like this is how an individual word *demands* melodic inflection which must be accommodated harmonically without modulation. Examples of this are common in Ferrabosco's more serious ayres and motets. That accommodation *is* made harmonically, emphasizing the fact that Ferrabosco is, essentially, a composer of chordal, rather than contrapuntal music. This also explains the general absence of cross-relations in his compositions (and the frequent awkward handling of them when they appear). Cross-relations are the result of different melodic tendencies (these Ferrabosco does not handle well) or contrasts of parallel modes or areas as represented in this system (e.g. B♭-D; Ferrabosco handles these well).

By recognizing the unity, rather than opposition, of the parallel tonal pairs, the use of E♭, for example, in a piece apparently in C major, is not anomalous and does not have to be described in terms such as "modal borrowing." There are, however, certain limits. There is no use of a♭, e♭, and b♭ minors. Each of these would affect the integrity of the relative major areas (A♭,E♭,B♭) which must maintain the common tone with their relative parallel tonal pair. That is to say, the dominants of F/f, C/c, and G/g must not lose their identity, which would happen with the introduction of c♭, g♭, and d♭. Of course, it must be remembered that within this period, for whatever reasons (e.g., matters of tuning and temperament) keys beyond those containing three sharps or three flats were extremely rare.

This diagrammatic representation also makes clearer why the continued plunge in the subdominant direction acquires a feeling of moving to the minor area. It leads, eventually, to the relative major (understood in the diagram as one of the "foldings" of the system) — typically associated with the minor side of the parallel paired tonic. Similarly, the submediant areas (relative minor) have an affinity to the dominant and the major side of the tonal pair.

Ferrabosco's use of the subdominant/relative major areas is twofold. They are used as balance or contrast to the dominant and for purposes of textual expression. Structurally, however, the subdominant, or relative major, does not approach the tonic directly, but passes first to the dominant. The interest in many of Ferrabosco's motets, in fact, is precisely with the manner he develops this tonal balancing in preparation for and elaboration of the dominant.

Thus, we have a tonal system and a concept of tonicization—a use of tonal balances and dynamics to extend and decorate the dominant without modulation. It is primarily a diatonic concept—as can be seen from the areas which are avoided—based on the resources of the parallel and reciprocally chromatically inflecting tonic pair. Ferrabosco's use of these resources is almost blandly consonant, although harmonically and structurally interesting.

IV

The Songs: "Like Hermit Poore" and "So, so, leave off"

> I have my doubts likewise concerning the *genius*, at least, of the second Ferrabosco, who had the Poets and Dilettanti all on his side; but whose works, that have come under my inspection, seem wholly unworthy of a great professor. . . . [the Ayres] contain as little merit of any kind as I have ever seen in productions to which the name of a master of established reputation is prefixed. These he dedicated, with no great humility, to Prince Henry, the eldest son of James I.[1]

Thus Burney vented his opprobrium on Ferrabosco, as he had also done on Dowland, Lawes, Jenkins, and others. To confirm his opinion, he presented two of the *Ayres*, "Like Hermit Poore" and the three-part "Sing we then heroic grace," so that the reader should "have it in his power to discover such beauties in them as may have escaped my observation."[2]

Despite Burney's engaging style and understated invective, his opinion of Dowland has been found wanting, as, I think will be shown here, is his characterization of Ferrabosco. Burney had, for his perusal, at least the *Ayres* of 1609, Ferrabosco's only published songs. These are 25 solo songs and 3 dialogs, each provided with lute accompaniment and a part for bass viol.[3] To these can be added 9 more songs, another dialog, and 4 striking Italian monodies which appear ascribed to Ferrabosco in various manuscript sources.[4] The tables on the following pages at the conclusion of this volume provide information regarding concordances, attribution, clef, range, form, text, and variant readings of these songs.

The dating of these songs is difficult. The *Ayres* provide their own *terminus ante quem*, and we can specify dates for the songs which appeared in Ben Jonson's masques between 1605 and 1611. But the remainder cannot be dated with any certainty. Several clues exist, however, and the picture which emerges is of a brief, but important flurry of court-related composition. The publication of the *Ayres* and the extent of his work with Jonson serve to remind us that, however briefly, Ferrabosco was regarded quite highly as a songwriter, contributing importantly to that most typical and splendid entertainment of the Stuart court, the masque.

There is no evidence of new songs by Ferrabosco after the celebrated death of his master, Prince Henry, in 1612. Even absent are elegies, such as those by Coperario for the dead Prince, elegies which might have been expected in the orgy of mourning which swept all England. Ferrabosco's sudden eclipse as a song-writer was nearly complete and leads to the conclusion that his career was not only closely related to his service as the Prince's music master, but even, in some important aspects, dependent on that relationship.

Nonetheless, Ferrabosco's songs do not deserve the oblivion which has been their lot, nor the complete censure which they received at Burney's hands, for they provide varied and often imaginative and effective responses to textual problems. Several, such as "Like Hermit Poore" (#1) and "Heav'n, since thou art the only place of rest" (#IV), are beautifully expressive in the manner of the later consort song and Dowland's serious songs. There is charming wit in "Come, my Celia" (#6) and ceremonial pomp and rhetoric in several of the high-flown masque songs. The dialogs point to, but never realize a truly dramatic style, failing mainly because of restraint in rhythmic gesture and harmonic boldness. In the Italian songs we see the monodic, affective recitative style for the first time in the works of an English composer.

Certainly the *Ayres* were met with more approval than Burney mustered, despite Ferrabosco's bluntness and "no great humility" in the dedication. The brusqueness of that dedication, with its insouciant undercurrent of recalcitrant self-sufficiency, is complemented by poems of commendation by Ben Jonson, Thomas Campion, and Nicholas Tomkins. Most of Jonson's praise is directed toward the art of music, expressing the commonplace mythology and legendary attributes of music's origin and powers—which Ferrabosco did not invoke in his dedication. It is an artful and witty use of poetry to commend her sister art, with a graceful turn of focus at the end in the compliment directed at Ferrabosco. Yet, for all this, it sounds as empty praise, though quite proper in the conventions of the period. There is no reason, however, to doubt the sincerity of the praise. Excepting Donne and Campion, Jonson is the only identified English author represented among Ferrabosco's songs, the only one whose texts provide a substantial source for Ferrabosco, and this publication comes during the period of Jonson's and Ferrabosco's close collaboration in the court masque.

The Songs

TO MY EXCELLENT FRIEND
ALFONSO FERRABOSCO

To vrge, my lou'd *Alfonso*, that bold fame
Of building Townes, and making wilde Beasts tame,
Which *Musique* had; or speake her knowne effects,
That she remoueth cares, sadnesse eiects,
Declineth anger, perswades clemency,
Doth sweeten mirth, and heighten pietie,
And is to'a body, often, ill inclinde
No less a soueraigne cure, then to the minde;
To'alledge, that greatest men were not asham'd
Of old, euen by her practise, to be fam'd;
To say, indeed, she were the *Soule* of *Heauen*
That the eight *Spheare*, no lesse then *Planets* seauen
Mou'd by her order; and the ninth, more high,
Including all, were thence call'd Harmony:
I, yet, had vtter'd nothing, on thy part,
When these were but the praises of the *Art*.
But when I'haue saide, The proofes of all these be
Shed in thy *Songs*; Tis True: But short of thee.

Ben: Jonson

Jonson's lovely, ornate lines, with their enjambments and internal rhymes deceiving the reading eye, contrast with the more square and metrically dullish praise of Campion who affects the ornate mode, especially in the concluding alexandrine, and tries to camouflage his heavy trochees by a delicate toying with stanza form. Yet, Campion addresses Ferrabosco directly and speaks of a close relationship between these two contributors to the early masque.

TO THE WORTHY AVTHOR

Mvsicks maister, and the offspring
Of rich *Musicks* Father,
Old *Alfonso's* Image liuing,
These faire flowers you gather
Scatter through the *Brittish* soile;
Giue thy fame free wing,
And gaine the merit of thy toyle:
Wee whose loues affect to praise thee,
Beyond thine owne deserts, can never raise thee.

By *T. Campion*, Doctor
In Physicke

The specificity of this poem lies completely in the almost Shakespearean lines, "the offspring/ Of rich *Musicks* Father,/ Old *Alfonso's* Image liuing." Old Alfonso had departed England 32 years previously, but his legacy remained strong at the century's turn. The revival of interest in his work is demonstrated by the citations in Morley's *Plaine and Easie Introduction* and the inclusion of his works in numerous manuscripts from this period, the most prominent being the Tregian, Myriell, and Filmer collections, and in the English anthologies of Italian madrigals.

Nicholas Tomkins' Latin alcaics conclude the round of praise and include a Latin-Italian pun on Ferrabosco's name which might, blissfully, have remained unnoticed were it not emphasized in the text. This Tomkins, the son of Thomas Tomkins Sr., was the brother of the more famous organist-composer Thomas Tomkins Jr. who later, briefly, was awarded one of Ferrabosco's court positions. The poem, addressed to the "most beloved and excellent in music, Alfonso Ferrabosco," concludes with the following lines:

Ferra-bosco

O Musicae artis quanta potentia,
Non in *ferarum* sola vagum *nemus*,
Sed in virorum plus cateruas
Participes melioris aurae!
Alfonse, dux & rex Lyrici gregis;
Pulsare dignus coelicolum lyram,
Excellis omnes sic canendo
Semper vt ipse sies canendus.

N. Tomkins

[How great is music's power, not only over wild beasts, prowling in the forest (Ferra-bosco = dark wood), but even more over men as they are surrounded by the sweet-sounding airs! Alfonso, leader and king of the lyrical race, master of the heavenly lyre, you excel others so in singing that you yourself will always be sung.]

Such elaborate praise was somewhat at odds with other evidence, for Ferrabosco's songs enjoyed only a restricted circulation in manuscript. From the evidence presented in the tables of concordances, it is readily apparent that only three manuscripts, each of which has been dated before 1630, account for almost all of the appearances of Ferrabosco's songs outside the *Ayres*.

1. Oxford: Christ Church MS 439 is a collection of 74 lute songs set out in 2-stave score, apparently copied from originally published sources. This certainly seems to be the case with the Ferrabosco songs, all of which appear in the 1609 *Ayres*. Ian Spink dates the manuscript in the 1620s.[5] The composers are from the early 1600s with Robert Jones and Ferrabosco prominently represented. There are some semideclamatory songs which appear to be later than Ferrabosco's, but the

real interest of the manuscript lies in the presence of highly embellished versions of the vocal parts of several of the songs, including Ferrabosco's "Why stays the bridegroom" (#11). It is, at present, unknown who compiled the manuscript and on what basis his selection was made or who made use, particularly, of the elaborate ornamented songs.

2. Tenbury Wells: St. Michael's College MSS 1018 and 1019 present rather different problems. Spink dates these c. 1615, only slightly limiting Fellowes' "early 17th cent."[6] Both Spink and John Cutts have concluded that these manuscripts belong together, Spink going so far as to assert that, based on physical evidence, they were "probably a single MS originally."[7] Tenbury 1018 contains *unica* of several songs by the younger Ferrabosco, including several for Jonson's masques of 1611, *Oberon* and *Love Freed from Ignorance and Folly*. Thus we know that the manuscript was still being compiled in or after that year. Almost as interesting is the presence of a number of the elder Ferrabosco's motets, the most prominent compositions in the manuscript before the appearance of the younger Ferrabosco's songs. In addition, there are nearly 30 Italian songs, most of which, in one large group, are attributed to Giulio Romano (Caccini).[8] Four, however, are clearly ascribed to the younger Ferrabosco, and their affinity to the Italian expressive style has no counterpart among his English songs.

The songs in Tenbury 1018 are primarily for voice and bass instrument. Tenbury 1019 consists mainly of a few lute songs with Jones, Dowland, Coperario, Caccini, and Ferrabosco represented by at least one song each. The Ferrabosco setting is of lines from Guarini's *Pastor Fido*, with both English and Italian words—the song was published with the English translation "O eyes, O mortal stars," in the *Ayres* (#25). The prominence of compositions by both Ferraboscos in Tenbury 1018 and the unique appearance of the Guarini text in Tenbury 1019 lead to the conclusion that these manuscripts must have originated from a source close to the Ferrabosco family, if they did not, indeed, belong to the younger Alfonso.

3. The "John Bull MS," Cambridge: Fitzwilliam Museum MS 52.D. 25 contains 22 songs copied slightly later than the instrumental pieces which comprise the main body of the manuscript. Spink dates these additions as being from 1630 or slightly earlier.[9] Composers represented include Ferrabosco, Lanier, Johnson, Wilson, among others, and some of the songs are ornamented in a manner similar to the florid versions found in Tenbury 1018 and Dublin: Trinity College MS f.5.13.

The other manuscript sources for the songs contribute only six more concordances. Except for Bishop Smith's part-books (altus and bassus) in the Carlisle Cathedral Library, these manuscripts are all in the

British Museum: MSS Additional 10337, 11586, 15117, and 24665. Add. 10337 is inscribed "Elizabeth Rogers hir Virginall Booke: Februarye ye 27, 1656" and contains some texted versions of songs and other pieces in two-stave score. Add. 11586 seems to be an overlooked source about which we have very little information. Add. 15117 may have belonged to a member of the theatrical community in London and probably dates from after 1614.[10] "Giles Earle's MS," Add. 24665, is so known because of the inscription "Giles Earle his Booke" which appears on the flyleaf with the date 1615.

Ferrabosco's songs fall into several categories. There are a number of serious songs which are most similar, in manner and construction, to those from the tradition of the English polyphonic consort song and expressive lute song. The masque songs are not uniform in style, but it is in these songs that we find a more impersonal, rhetorically declamatory style which contrasts with the intense intimacy of the serious songs and the casual ease of the tuneful strophic songs. The dialogs attempt conversation in music, and it is interesting in Ferrabosco's pieces to see a movement from the lyrical to the dramatic mode. Quite as interesting as the English songs are the Italian monodies which show, as much as manuscript appearances of Caccini's songs and records of imported music books, that the Italian style of dramatic, affective recitative was known to composers in England, even if they did not succeed in transferring that style to English song.

Despite this categorization, the songs share several important characteristics which will receive more specific examination. The melodic writing is almost always such that, on the larger scale of the entire song, the melodic climax is related to the harmonic structure and textual content. Ferrabosco is generally quite sensitive to the text, both in meaning and accent, and this is reflected not only in the melodic shape and rhythm, but in the harmonic activity within and between phrases. There is little harshness: dissonances are only gently acerbic and harmonic transitions are smoothly accomplished. In addition, these songs have a formal clarity and balance which make them quite accessible; the prevalent structure is bipartite, the most common form ABB.

In *The English Ayre*, Peter Warlock [Philip Heseltine] concluded his discussion of Alfonso Ferrabosco the Younger with this appraisal:

> When Ferrabosco becomes declamatory, after the manner of the so-called "new music" in Italy, he is merely dull and uninspired. At his best he is a melodist and not a monodist. His vocal line is generally smooth, graceful, and shapely, and although his music never rises to any great intensity, he now and again achieves an emotional utterance of real beauty by very simple means.[11]

There are a number of difficulties with this characterization, the most obvious being the description of monody which appears to be based solely on laments and dramatic pieces, foregoing the evidence of smooth, graceful, and shapely melodic lines in songs of no particularly great intensity by Caccini, d'India, and Saracini. If anything, Ferrabosco lacks the extended emotional intensity of the great works of Monteverdi, but it is not unfair to compare some of his English songs with Dowland's better efforts. The masque songs, which are oratorical in their declamation, are not "merely dull and uninspired." Their purpose was different, and rather less personal, than the strikingly affective Italian monody. In their ceremonal guise, Ferrabosco's songs for the masque serve their functions of compliment, persuasion, and education quite well. The style of the Italians, and of Ferrabosco's Italian songs, is only deceptively similar to the style of the masque songs. What Warlock was seeking, the sense of emotional necessity personalized and manifest in the music, was, in any case, not part of the compositional practice in England—as it was in Italy during the last fifteen years of the sixteenth century with the increasing emphasis on and influence of humanistic theories of musical expression. The intensity of Dowland is depersonalized, musical shapeliness and repetition muting the immediacy of even so powerful a song as "In darkness let me dwell."

Similarly, although some of Ferrabosco's songs have moments of great concentration, they do not rise to great intensity for an extended time, but back quickly away from the fires of emotional expression. To be fair, Warlock only knew the published *Ayres*. His appraisal, had he known the later masque songs and the Italian pieces, of necessity would have to be different and more precise.

On their own terms, Ferrabosco's songs are generally quite successful. Those not written for masques, entertainments, or plays are rather easily characterized as serious songs in the consort song-lute song tradition, best exemplified by the well-known serious songs of Dowland, or as more tuneful (though not dance-song) settings of strophic anacreontic verse such as characterize the musical-poetic work of Campion. The character and form of the text are the critical elements: the serious (pathetic) songs far more frequently being through-composed, while the strophic lighter verse is treated in a more casual manner.

The consort song for treble voice and quartet of viols was, basically, a non-representational art, a convention and decorum of form antithetical to the increasing personality and specificity of the contemporary Italian madrigal. Madrigalistic word-painting was largely absent, and the nearly- (sometimes pseudo-) polyphonic accompaniments enveloped the voice rather than setting it off. In the madrigalian sense, the consort song was sublimely indifferent to words, but, in the hands of Byrd, it became a tremendously expressive vehicle for textual sense.

The declamation of text in Byrd's songs might be quite exemplary in terms of accent and rhythmic proportion, but it is never free of the accompaniment in the Italian manner of recitative with continuo. The manner is really one of contemplation rather than expression or exposition, and moments such as "O, let me living die" from Dowland's "In darkness let me dwell" are astonishing for their rarity as much as for their immediacy. Yet even such moments are distanced by the musical shape of the whole, as can be seen in one of the most moving of Ferrabosco's songs.

Pride of place in the *Ayres* was given to "Like Hermit Poore" (#1), the text for which appeared in a variety of literary sources from as early as 1585. It was later attributed to Sir Walter Raleigh, with the fanciful speculation that Queen Elizabeth was the subject. While this may have enhanced the popularity of the poem, the attribution is not substantiated.[12] Burney cited this song in his appraisal of Ferrabosco, as did Warlock who, in contrast to Burney, quoted it for its simple, though very real beauty.

As a lover's lament, this bears comparison to the texts of Dowland's melancholy songs, but it is specifically the restrained and concentrated "Dowland-like" quality of Ferrabosco's setting which is so striking and frustrating. The lute part gives the impression of genuine polyphony and, *pace* Burney, can be reduced to a figured bass only with great loss to the sense of inner movement. Within this web of activity the melody acts to overlap the harmonic and phrase seams with independent cadences. In this sense, Vincent Duckles cites the song as representative of the lute-song *genre*.

> Here is the lute ayre in its definitive form. The solo voice is but one element in the polyphony; its cadences are quite independent of those of the supporting lines. Deceptive cadences prevent the harmonic flow from ever coming to a complete stop before the final close.[13]

Unlike Dowland's more important works in the melancholy vein, however, Ferrabosco's setting remains resigned, uncompelling, never rising to emotional insistence—almost comfortable. But the "comfort" of the song comes from its seamlessness. From the opening knell of "Like Hermit Poore," the musical shape of the song expands in range and in activity until the words "And at my gates, Despair shall linger still" before collapsing back in the final measures. The song never comes to rest until the final cadence which, of necessity, is rather extended; the listener is borne along not only by the words of the singer but by the refusal of the music to stop.

All the more effective in this regard is the setting of those words cited above, "And at my gates Despair shall linger still/ to let in Death...," for not only is the phrase "Despair shall, Despair shall linger still" emphasized by range and sequence and extended by interruption and repetition, but the cadence on B♭ which arrives at the word "still" is only deceptively a stop.

Ex. 1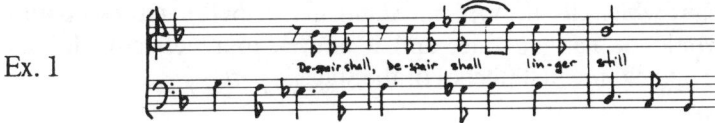

In fact, because the bass continues to lower G, it becomes part of the larger representation of "linger" as the voice similarly extends itself from the b♭ of "still" to the g of "To." B♭ is only a passing relaxation, not the musical goal; nor does the text stop at "still": the rest acts as an affective sigh, at the most merely interrupting the thought.

The overlapping cadences justify, by their forward movement, the apparent awkwardness of the text-setting. For example, the setting of the second and third lines of the poem, "I mean to spend my days of endless doubt,/ To wail such woes as time cannot recure," provides several instances in which the words do not sit well if considered only in their melodic context.

Ex. 2

Yet, a balance of comprehension, melodic weight, and textual accent is achieved by the flexible workings of the accompaniment. The suspensions, delayed resolutions, deceptive harmonic motions, all focus the musical thought as a whole so that the larger arch of the melody is not lost and the text is presented without a sense of misaccentuation. Burney's criticisms would be more appropriate to the bass/voice version he presented, for he was insensitive to the effect of the inner voices and their usefulness in maintaining both a continuous musical thought and a flexibility of accentual weight which depends on a balance of text accent and harmonic stability.

A particularly effective example of this process occurs at the words "of endless doubt." The song had begun with a movement from D to g, as dominant to tonic, a movement confirmed by the progress of the entire song. At his phrase it appears that the tonic will again be confirmed, emphasized by Ferrabosco's mild use of the augmented triad (in which the b♭ is simply a passing-note against the consonant fourth). The deceptive cadence at "doubt" defeats the tonic, and the resolution is on the dominant which, itself, does not stand still. A better representation of "doubt" would be hard to find, and it is even more effective for its emphasis on d and e♭, the first pitches of the singer's part.

Ex. 3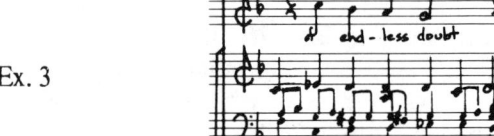

There are other nice touches: the occasional relationship of lute and vocal material, though not nearly as much as in Dowland's songs of this nature, the lingering intensification and sequence on "despair," the ensuing sequence and long-lined final phrase which Warlock found so appealing, the slow emergence of the (obscure) voice from the texture of the lute, and the formal pinning of the piece up on the dominant one-third ("endless doubt") and two-thirds ("find me out") of the way through the song.

The entire piece, in effect, is properly "obscure." The continual avoidance of strong cadences, especially through the use of third-related chords and step-wise motion in the bass, contributes to a sense of transitoriness and "becoming," a sense that when the piece is over it is not because of some melodic or harmonic necessity, but, rather, because the material is exhausted. Only then do we realize that the melodic and harmonic necessities have been fulfilled as well. The melodic arch which so carefully was built over a minor ninth falls down to the tonic just as the harmonic movement of dominant to tonic, presented in prolepsis in the opening phrase, is confirmed at the conclusion. Because the tonal sense of many of the phrases is temporarily thwarted by the continually deceptive or overlapping cadences, our sense of the piece is forced to rely upon the rising curve and intensity of the melodic material. This culminates in the statement of despair which but specifies the condition of the singer unable to free himself from the downward sequences which follow.

This is a private song, best suited for intimate performance. The expression is written into the melodic line and is not overbearing or oratorical, the opening barely emergent and obscure in its own way, yet declamatory in its attention to accent, delivery and meaning. But it must be emphasized that an appreciation of the appropriateness of Ferrabosco's treatment of the words in this song will not be gained by isolating the rhythmic or melodic treatment of individual syllables or by making comparisons with some imagined ideal of speech rhythm. It can be argued that, in the second line, the time given "mean" and "to" would be more pleasing if reversed, but the opening would be quite at home in a continuo song, and the distention of the third line, at the words "time cannot recure," is suspended over a harmonic miasma which confounds the expectations of the ear—just as the text demands—without losing track of the larger sense of the piece. Thus, what we have is not a declamatory song in the sense that Spink discusses the heroic rhetoric of some of the masque songs, nor in the sense of a slavish imitation of speech rhythm. But the declamation of the text is not impeded by the music, nor defeated by it, although the style is intimate instead of dramatically emotional or public and official.

"Like Hermit Poore" was also set by Nicholas Lanier; it is found in John Gamble's Commonplace Book (NYPL:MS Drexel 4257, no. 15); London: British Museum MS Add. 29396 (copied by Edward Lowe between 1661 and 1680); and Playford's *Select Musicall Ayres and Dialogues* of 1652, 1653, and 1659. Its popularity, to which Playford attests by giving it pride of place, is possibly confirmed by the report of Tom Killegrew to Pepys that there had been, during the period before the Commonwealth, no "musique here better than ballads. . . 'Hermit poore' and 'Chevy Chase' was all the musique we had."[14] All of these sources are from the Commonwealth period or later, although their contents may have been copied or collected from earlier sources.

While these sources provide some variants, the essential character of Lanier's setting remains constant.[15] It is a continuo song for solo voice which, like Ferrabosco's setting, does not attempt to overwhelm the text with an affective musical portrayal. The ordered and rather gentle resignation of the text is captured by a similar understatement of musical gesture.

We may assume that Lanier knew Ferrabosco's setting. The opening phrases are rhetorically similar and would appear more so if Ferrabosco's setting were simply for continuo and voice. Lanier's is, however, more vigorously stated, and his setting is characterized by

Ex. 4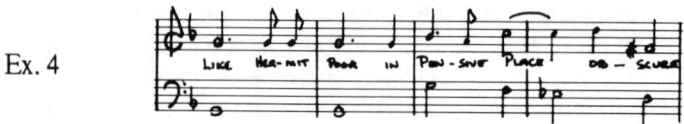

a sectionalism based on strong cadences at the ends of phrases and patterned rhetorical rhythmic figures which begin off the beat at the beginning of phrases: ♪♪♪♩

While Ferrabosco keeps his setting off, but mindful of the tonic in a series of near confirmations elaborated by overlapped and deceptive or passing cadences, Lanier keeps the strophic portion of his setting clearly in the tonic, contrasting that with the refrain beginning "and at my gates" which stays away from the tonic until the final cadence.[16] The simplified tonal focus (which, however, does not intensify the sense of tonal direction) of Lanier's setting can be heard particularly at the conclusion of the first phrase (Ex. 4). In Ferrabosco's setting, the E♭ chord at "obscure" occurs circumstantially, as the result of melodic motion which does not cadence, but in its own obscure way continues on. The E♭ of Lanier's setting, on the other hand, is an inversion which points the movement to and elaborates a D major triad which is clearly related, as dominant, to the tonic G (iv_6-V-i), enhanced by the anticipatory echappée and the irregular leap (in this context) of a descending minor sixth.

The emotional state of the poet-singer, portrayed in the rising melodic line, is affectively intensified by the ornament (particularly the effort to lift to the d"). The continuity of the piece is maintained, despite the phrase-by-phrase setting, by the use of the harmonic expectations which Ferrabosco eschewed. That is, Lanier moves from one phrase to the next harmonically, while Ferrabosco did so much more melodically and without cadences in both voice and accompaniment. Lanier's setting is also more regular and predictable in phrase structure and meter. Because Ferrabosco, in other songs, made use of the same practices of formal regularity, his decision not to use them here indicates a reading of the poem in which the persona of the poet is not so prominent and the text can be presented with the conventional means used in the older consort song.

Ferrabosco set only the first strophe (quatrain) of the poem; all three are given by Lanier, with some particular difficulties of text-setting in the second strophe. The use of the refrain, and the clearer, though more restricted tonal movement avoid the sense of perfunctory close, but the strophic setting with refrain precludes a sense of immediate experience in performance. In Lanier's setting the slow-moving bass, the occasional rhythmic vigor, the modest attempt at affective dissonance are all shams of the Italian style, though it is reasonable to ask if he had that in mind as he did in "Hero and Leander." For this piece, like so many of the early English declamatory and continuo songs, lacks the sense of immanent personality: it is emotionally vague, essentially an acceptable melodic line without the dramatic intensification of affective ornament and dissonance, of the urgent immediacy and specificity of response, not to mention extravagance, of the Italian monodic style.

These two settings contrast manners of reading poetry and setting texts: one is essentially private and restrained, the other more forthright and public, as if the character were speaking, not simply thinking to himself. Yet both are rather smooth melodically and share the same body of harmonic expectations. Ferrabosco, however, provides his melody with an interesting melodic shape and development while Lanier's remains rather lumpish and boring. And, while Ferrabosco confounds the harmonic expectations without denying them, Lanier confirms them all too clearly. When Ferrabosco uses an off-beat pattern, as in the setting of "Despair shall. . . ," it is to intensify the text by rhythmic density, and the rhythmic pattern is accompanied by a rising melodic line and sequence which increases the sense of urgency. Lanier's off-beat formula, however, is used to plump up the rhetorical pose. In more appropriate circumstances, as in Ferrabosco's masque songs, this figure can be used to leap forward in the text, more emphatically presenting it, responding to it and etching it out of the surrounding and supporting accompaniment. In Lanier's song, where it is used to set textual phrases which are arbitrarily placed, the figure becomes trivial.

Ferrabosco's setting is far more successful. Despite its conservatism, it is also the more expressive of the two. Absent from both are the expressive *colorature* and the affective use of dissonance to personalize and intensify which are found in Italian monody.

On the other hand, Ferrabosco could write a song which, though sectional and much more like the continuo style with a slow-moving bass, presents a reading of a poem which provides the composer with more than the usual share of problems. The setting is that of John Donne's poem, "The Expiration" ("So, so, Leave off this last lamenting kiss,"

#7), the first of Donne's poems to appear in print when it was published in the *Ayres*. The poem received another, later and anonymous setting for lute and voice, written in a mature declamatory-continuo style, which is preserved in Oxford: Bodleian MS mus. sch. f. 575.[17] Ferrabosco's is more balanced in its conservative manner of musical construction which accommodates and conveys the sense of the words although it does not attempt to imitate verbal rhythms or create a sense of immediacy.

Donne's poem is in two stanzas and is not readily understood, for it mixes rather high-blown philosophy with more typically courtier sentiments. That the expression is an elaborate *double entendre*, a fanciful play on the Jacobean sexual connotations of "death" and "dying," is not apparent until the second strophe, precisely because the manner of the poem is not at all that of typical courtier poetry. The intensity of the speaker, the imagery, and the long and difficult argument distinguish this poem from the impersonal persuadings of Elizabethan poetry and the just as impersonal posings of the Cavalier poets. It is as polished a poem as the products of either group, but it has an unusual force derived from the vigor and measure of its expression. The scarcity of contemporary settings of Donne's poetry indicates that the composers were aware of the problems Donne's poetry presented, and this poem is far more effective when read than when sung. Its metrical and syntactical life is far from regular or simple, and its verbal music is not the predictable kind so prized by the Campions of the world. Each of these settings of "The Expiration" emphasizes different aspects of the poetic expression and sense; both fail to realize the fact that, for Donne, a strophic poem is not a series of interchangeable structures, but a continuing argument artfully conceived in similar forms. Thus, the use of the same music for the two strophes defeats the necessary sense of development by emphasizing the reciprocal reflections between strophes and, by implication, equalizing their importance. As a result, in this case, both meaning and accent are lost if the second strophe of either setting is sung.

Ferrabosco's setting begins auspiciously, with a vigorous and peremptory gesture, high in the voice and somewhat without measure.

Ex. 5

This is as close as we get to the dramatic voice, however, for the remainder of the song is quite measured and smoothly melodious. Here the accompaniment could be represented by a bass with figures, although it never becomes as static or unmeasured as a later, true continuo bass.

The shape of the song follows the argument of the poem using harmonic movement to articulate parts of the argument, as "Like Hermit Poore" does not. The first section of the poem, the situation presented in the first two lines, is set in a manner which confirms the tonic G and emphasizes the importance of the dominant. The second section, beginning "Turn thou ghost, that way; and let me turn this;" is set in a particularly effective manner, for the command is presented off the tonic, appearing to move toward another tonal area (A/a) at the words "that way." The return to G, via the dominant at "this," is both symbolically and musically important. Moreover, it confirms that the suspected harmonic movement was a textually-based ruse, utilizing the close relationship of third and fifth relations to take a brief excursion (and make an even quicker return) while making use of an additional fifth in harmonic distance in each direction around G. The return to G signals the end of the poet's address to the "other" and the refocusing of his thoughts.

Ex. 6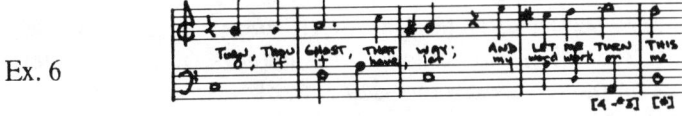

From this example it can be seen that this argument is entirely inappropriate in the second strophe, which does not have the same rhetorical construction nor the same internal organization of lines. As in this line, the entire second strophe is off-balance.

Ferrabosco set the final two lines of the poem as a repeated refrain with an emphasis on the minor mode and some interchange of material between voice and accompaniment, beginning with a prolepsis in the lute.

Ex. 7

Ex. 7
(continued)

As can be seen, however, Donne's argument is now phrased against the structure of the line, doubly so when set with the continental approach which Ferrabosco applies to the division of the 10-syllable line. The meaning is difficult to construe even without the conflict of this setting.[18]

Although this song is constructed differently than "Like Hermit Poore," it shares with the first song a concern for melodic shape and a generally successful approach to "reading" the textual meaning. It is typical of a good number of Ferrabosco's other songs, also, in that it begins spontaneously to convey the intensity of the speaker, but then rapidly moves toward a more musically governed conception. The evenness of melodic motion and the comfortable harmonic movement contribute to a sense of generality, confirmed by the ultimate triviality of the repeat of the refrain. Here the argument is deprived of intensity and credibility: the music serves to emphasize the rhyme (see Ex. 7, above), not the sense. Its repetition—to convince the auditors of the argument which the music confounds or to wind down the long melodic descent?—prettifies the tone of the argument as much as it refutes the original poetic attitude by denying its integrity.

The two settings have been compared in recent articles by Brian Morris and John Hollander.[19] Neither article addresses several problems of the ways in which words and music may be related to provide a satisfactory musical reading of a text. For example, the structure of the songs, both harmonic and melodic, is not considered an important element in the listener's perception, although the way in which the second section of Ferrabosco's setting begins off of, even moving away from, the tonic before returning is vitally important to the understanding of the first strophe of text. The criterion for judgment in both articles is the relationship of the rhythms and gestures of the melody with the accents and syntax of the text. On the surface, this is a reasonable position—if nothing else happens in the song. In the anonymous setting, this is very nearly true, but in Ferrabosco's setting harmonic rhythm, tonal distances, and metric manipulation provide emphasis and understanding as well.

The anonymous setting is much more a continuo song, possibly composed 20 to 30 years after Ferrabosco's, and conceived in a manner which is far freer to respond to the rhythmic instance of the words. Herein lies the problem of Ferrabosco's "musical" setting of the syntactically complicated final lines.

Ex. 8a

Ex. 8b

There is no evidence in the music to suggest that Ferrabosco was intending anything more here than to compose a beautiful ending to the song. In both cases there are gross distortions of accent and meaning, particularly in the second strophe, which result.

As Hollander points out, in contrasting Ferrabosco's setting with the anonymous song, the difficulty is in comprehending the sense of the text.

> For example, the music in a good setting should punctuate the final two lines of the song, with its own rhythms, so as to do something like this:
>
> > Except it be too late to kill me so,
> > (Being double-dead – going and bidding), Go!
>
> Now Ferrabosco's setting realizes neither the speech-rhythm of the phrase "saying, Go!" in the first strophe, nor that of the complex syntax of the second. But at the crudest level of rhythmic fitting of musical downbeat to normal word stress (let alone to phrase stress among monosyllabic groups, or stress maxima in an iambic context) the second strophe will not work.[20]

On the other hand, the anonymous setting admirably realizes the rhythmic requirements of Hollander's *dicta* for the final line of the first strophe, only to distort the second strophe even more:

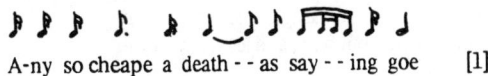

[In the second strophe the anonymous setting] demands two sorts of accentual deformation:

♪ ♪♪ ♪. ♪♪♩♪ ♪ ♫♫♪ ♩ [2]
Being dou -ble dead go- ing - - - and bid - - ding doe

the first, on "going," exacerbated by the long, tied note value on the second syllable, the second, making the phrase "bidding go" syntactically equivalent—through rhythmic identity—to "saying go." But "bidding" is, as we have seen, part of another, complex parenthetical phrase, the very syntactical existence of which dissolves in song. Or, at any rate, in this song.[21]

Actually, both song-writers were faced with a different problem which Hollander does not acknowledge: that of ending the song. The anonymous composer rounded his song by using the music of his first phrase—which complicates the matter by raising questions about the sophistication of his text-setting. Both songs satisfy conventions of their time in trying to deal with a particularly difficult poem. Hollander's observation about Donne is instructive, particularly in dealing with strophic poetry.

> . . . Donne's rhythmic modulation of language is such that even the most musicianly attention to word-stress (and this, indeed, is not always Ferrabosco's strongest point) will frequently not suffice to accentuate correctly the textual syntax.
> . . . the unique problem of English prosody remained a stumbling block in the way of properly "committing short and long," not only in strophic setting but in through-composed ones as well.[22]

Ferrabosco stands near the beginning of the conscientious attempt to "commit short and long" in any more comprehensive sense than simply matching verbal and metrical accents, and his attempt to set Donne's poem, even if only partly successful, is an indication of the willingness of composers to accept the challenges of irregular prosody. Certainly no one will argue about the difficulty of Donne's verbal sense and rhythm. "The Expiration" offers problems of stress patterns and syntax which defy simple solutions, even without the complications of strophic variance of both sense and stress.

A specific example from Ferrabosco's setting may make some of these problems clearer. The third line of the poem, "Turn thou ghost that way, and let me turn this," can be read in two essentially similar ways:

/ \ / / . . / . /
1. "Turn thou (ghost!) that way, and let me turn this."

/ . / / . . / . /
2. "Turn (thou ghost!) that way, and let me turn this."

In each, it is the syntax which demands a pattern of stresses quite different from the rising meter (iambs) of the first two lines, and the roughness, Hollander argues, which appears in many of Donne's lines "comes about as a result of ambiguities in reading the metrical disposition of stresses".[23]

To Hollander, Ferrabosco's setting emphasizes "way" instead of "that," thus missing the point of the line. He recommends the anonymous version.

Ex. 9

The contrastive stress is pointed up in the setting, and at least gross syntactic grouping—aside from any nuances of expression which might grace that grossness—has been satisfied. But, as we might expect, the consequences for the reciprocal line in the second strophe are more disastrous than merely a matter of musical rhythm wrecking word stress. Here, the gasping rest after the poorly treated "if it have, let..." is grotesque and irrelevant.[24]

The anonymous setting does allow for some stretching of note-values which avoids the notated fussiness. This, presumably, is what Hollander means by "nuances of expression." Yet he fails to realize that Ferrabosco makes Donne's point by the combination of pitch accent, melodic interval, and harmonic movement. The meaning of the text is quite clearly conveyed, and the unique way Ferrabosco sets the 10-syllable line at this point indicates that he was aware of the problems.

Ex. 10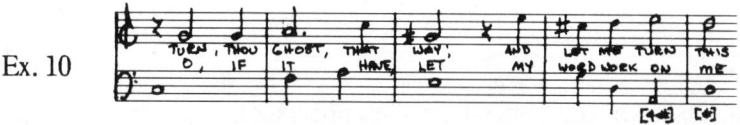

Not only does the harmony move all the way up to an E major chord (in G) for "that way," returning to D (V of G) at "this," but the metrical construction of the phrase forces just the interpretation and reading of the line which Hollander seeks. The triple-time of "Turn thou" is broken by an extension back to duple on "ghost," revealing that the reading is the first one given above. "That" remains an unaccented syllable in scansion, but it is emphasized in three ways: 1) it breaks the hold of "ghost," which, because of the juxtaposition of the triple and duple meters in the melody, both emphasizes the word and catapults it forward to "way"; 2) it has melodic pitch accent which is increased by 3) the diminished fourth, c''-$g\#'$, between "that" and "way." The return to the home tonal area and the use of a higher melodic range effectively distinguish the musical areas of "thou ghost [that way]" and "me [turn this]." Thus, the music allows a combination of sense and scansion which reflects a very deliberate and satisfying "reading" by the composer.

There is no reason to suppose that the anonymous composer knew Ferrabosco's setting. The anonymous song is more fitful, without the melodic fullness of Ferrabosco's musical phrasing. The overall harmonic motion is not as clearly structured and balanced. Performance would, implicitly, be more impassioned and, probably, more negligent of the precisely notated values. The lute sounds its chords not to keep the time, but, as is customary in continuo practice, to serve as a springboard for the singer, a cue for movement which then can be largely free from metric regularity.

Although Ferrabosco makes use of modal inflection in his setting, neither song uses chromaticism in an expressive way. Both, however, ornament the word "lamenting" in the opening phrase. Ferrabosco uses a figure, which can be measured or more directly applied, to heighten the rhetorical urgency of the word without changing the tone of the setting. The more extended figure used in the anonymous setting would, at first glance, appear to be affective, not simply decorative.

Ex. 11a: Ferrabosco   Ex. 11b: Anonymous

But this conclusion is confounded by the appearance of the same figure at the conclusion (at the word "saying"); in fact, the entire first musical phrase is repeated. Thus, while the figure was originally affective and specific, it loses that specificity by being repeated, acquiring the quality of decoration. Similarly, the repetition of the entire first musical phrase at the end of the song serves to extend the mood of the beginning through the progress of the piece and to deny the possibility of hearing the song as the immediate (unmediated) expression of the singer.

V

Other Serious Songs

"Come Home, My Troubled Thoughts" (#2) begins away from the tonic, as did its predecessor in the *Ayres*, "Like Hermit Poore." Here it is a case of word-painting, for the style, though lugubrious, is not that of the consort song. Cadences are clear and coincide with the ends of textual phrases, although those phrases are set flexibly and are not uniform in length. Moreover, the movement from dominant to tonic (g) which characterizes the first section of the song, is balanced by the movement, in the repeated second section, from subdominant to tonic. This sectionalism, in which the harmonic shape provides a balance which is complemented by the structure of the melody, in range more than phrasing, is typical of Ferrabosco. Similarly, there is only one instance of imitation between the bass and voice (in the opening phrase), and the accompaniment could easily be represented by a figured bass.

The movement of the bass is leisurely and steady, and the modest range of the melody is more gracefully than emotionally shaped, bordering on being tuneful without the regularity of the customary lyric or dance song. The attention to words is lyric, not emotional, but there are two instances of affective representations. At the words "False are her wishes" the word accents conflict with the established pattern of the harmonic rhythm, and the composite rhythm of melodic and metric accents catapults into the harsh syncopations of the word "cruel."

Ex. 1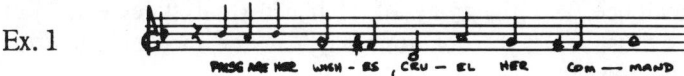

This is a metric play characteristic of the period, in which the melodic declamation of the poem is set off against the harmonic rhythm and the prevailing metrical framework of the song. Such metric play, which enlivens the motet and madrigal literature, creates a more active composite rhythm with rhythmic and metric dissonance, in a sense, which requires resolution and a return to the expected order of metric-rhythmic agreement.

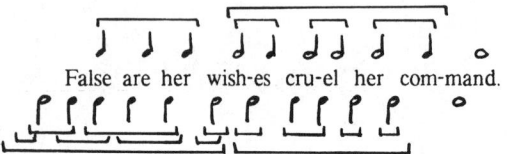

Yet, it is clear that this is also subtle word-painting: the temporary, "false" triple-time "cruel"-ly interrupted by the intransigent return of duple meter, with jarring syncopation in the voice.

Another instance of apparent conflict, also pictorial, occurs at the emotional climax of the piece.

Ex. 2

[must serve you for your pay]

Again there is a temporary mingling of triple and duple, but just as the straining aspiration of the $e^{b''}$ is thwarted from completing the sequence to f', the triple-time collapses back into duple.

Interestingly, the setting of the words "Come away, come away" is either a quotation from the opening of Ferrabosco's song of that title (*Ayres*, #3) from the *Masque of Blackness* or vice versa. It is the only instance of self-quotation in these songs, and the texts are similar enough to indicate a connection, although the one expresses moral intent while the masque song promotes dramatic action, nonetheless moral. The appearance of the songs on facing pages of the *Ayres* is hardly likely to be simple coincidence, and the irony of such a textual statement, "For here vain hopes must serve you for your pay," in the face of a masque song may be quite pointed.

"Unconstant love" (#24), a lover's complaint of more than usual force, though measured and impersonal, looks back to the older consort song in several respects. The bass movement is active and often melodically important, with frequent interchanges with the voice. The tone of the song is superficially restrained, largely as the result of the regular harmonic rhythm and the long arch of the melodic line. Even though the song is in two sections, the first moving from the dominant through the tonic and to the relative major before the second confirms the tonic (c), there is an almost seamless movement through the cadences, new motion beginning before the cadence has time to settle. The inner parts, however, are only perfunctorily melodic, occasionally moving in duet with the bass or filling in an interval or ornamenting a cadential movement.

It is the restraint of the setting which is so reminiscent of the consort song: the neutrality of presentation as seen in the absence of affective dissonance at "most false of all time." The quality of reluctant bitterness and resignation is focused by occasional dissonant melodic intervals (see below) and the structure of the vocal line which, however hard it attempts to attain and maintain the upper g″, falls back to the tonic note. In addition, the melodic motion of the first section is more disjoint and rising, while the motion of the second section is smoother and basically descending. That the second section is repeated only confirms the resignation and neutrality of the expression.

The very opening provides the most interesting melodic movement, with the change from b♭ to b♮ as the figure moves from the prolepsis in the bass to the voice a clear instance of "unconstancy" which gives the sung line a more acerbic tone as well as pointing up the harmony.

Ex. 3

The b♮ - e♭ dissonance is explored in two ways also at the words "Farewell, farewell," where the melodic diminished fourth is a result of harmonic choice (thus kin to Dowland's "Lachrymae" figure) and imitation of the bass, while the b♮ - e♭ in a passing augmented triad (on the second "[fare]-well") is a struck appoggiatura, one of the few affective gestures in the piece. The melodic figure is again repeated in an inner voice of the accompaniment, so that, briefly, we do have a thoroughly integrated musical fabric. Nonetheless, the tone is calm, the insistence expressed by repetition rather than vigor, and unimpassioned in a public way.

Ex. 4

As can be seen in the above example, however, the song is extremely expressive and moving. This is not the case with "Drown not with Tears" (#9), a song of consolation sung by the spirit of one recently removed to heaven and directed to his (or her) partner. The text promises a transcendence of death in that future time when the two will be reunited and "strive with many thousand kisses/ To multiply exchange of blisses."

In this song, also, Ferrabosco clearly delineates the two sections by harmonic areas: the first section (mm. 1-11) emphasizes the dominant and establishes the subordinate role of the subdominant by its place, relative to the dominant, in the second phrase. The progression of the two phrases in this section is the following: G is the tonic. 1) I-IV; 2) I-V-vi(IV)-V-I. On the other hand, Ferrabosco, in the second section, uses the relative major of the tonic, B♭, to portray the vision of the future heaven of bliss in two longer phrases which have the following general progression: 1) ♭III-V; 2) V-I.[1] In both cases, though the means are different, the subdominant and relative major are extensions of and governed by the dominant which guides the movement back to the tonic. This second section is also characterized by extraordinarily long phrases which, unlike the setting of text in the first section, extend over several shorter poetical lines. But it is only in conjunction with the harmonic movement, which does not rest at cadences, that these phrases contrast with those of the opening section: the vocal line has many stopping places, but the harmonic movement impels it forward without allowing the customary broadening at the expected cadence points. In addition, this section, which begins on B♭, stays away from g/G until the final phrase when the song is finally brought to rest, grounded in the most formulaic, simple and understated authentic cadence.

In this manner the song follows the form of the poem, for the last section is one long sentence, shaped by meter and rhyme, while the poetry for the (repeated) first section consists of two strophes comprised of shorter sentences more in the nature of argument than of ecstatic description. The setting of this argument is more discrete, with the cadences confirming the hierarchy of the tonic, dominant and subdominant, particularly at the midpoint. Even the one deceptive cadence of the first section actually impels the movement toward the tonic more emphatically as it slips from vi to IV; unstable even there, it must move on into the final phrase.

Ex. 5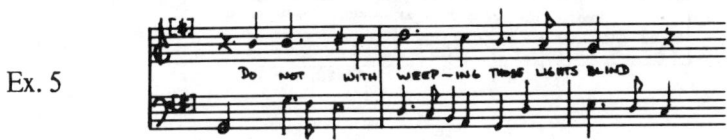

The sense of flexibility comes not just from the freedom of modal inflections, but also from the avoidance of strong downbeats, V-I cadences in root position, and regularity of meter. The metric accents are rarely forceful, and they depend on harmonic confirmation for a sense of arrival. On one occasion this results in an overly extended cadence which would not suffer from the excision of two beats.

Ex. 6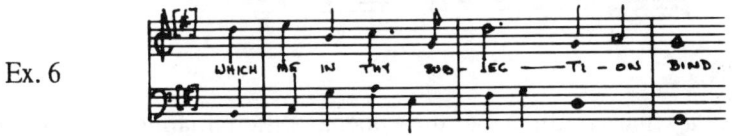

The text can sustain this elongation — particularly in the representative sense of being bound in "subjection" to an imposed musical presentation — although the second strophe is far less apt (see also the second strophe in the following example). The declamation itself, however, is musically dull and ineffective, particularly in light of the many uses of triple-time in the melody of the song, unless organized as follows (in contrast with Fellowes' edition):

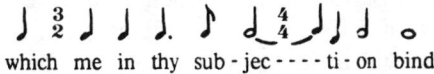

Here the weight of the declamation is more clearly matched to the course of the harmony, with the addition of yet another musical pun in the use of the "binding" tie which (now visually) subjects "subjection" to the root position dominant harmony.

More common, however, is the limpidity with which the second line is set, the graceful movement of the affections specified in the brief triple-time.

Ex. 7

And there is the aptness of the following, in which the textual emphasis is on both the future conditional, "then," and the verb, "will redeem." The setting allows both, as the enthusiasm of the idea is carried forward to expression and the contrast of the trochaic turn of the poetry matched by the move to the relative major.

Ex. 8

This is a fine reading of the poem, differentiating between argument and description, time of waiting and time of fulfillment. The meaning of the poem and the character of the speaker are reflected in the shape of the phrases, the activity of the bass and inner voices (both of which are much less busy in the second section), and the harmonic movement and the tonal areas explored. For all that, it is not a setting of great emotional depth, but one of equanimity, an equanimity particularly evident in the second section of the song because of the avoidance of strong cadences which might stop the musical activity and textual contemplation.

The three manuscript songs which may be characterized as "serious" in tone are of different styles ranging from the devotional to a more profane lament and a little pastoral narrative set in quasi-declamatory fashion.

"Heav'n, since thou art the only place of rest" (#iv) is a particularly satisfying example of Ferrabosco's ability to create an appropriate mood while the singer remains essentially impersonal, a voice without specificity. The text is serious in the moral sense, unencumbered with argument or wit, and the peaceful consolation of the soul is serenely, even dispassionately contemplated. For such a text, this graceful and balanced setting, with its long arches and clarity unperturbed by melodic or harmonic boldness, is suitably unprepossessing.

The opening quatrain is set, line by line, in 5-measure phrases with extensions or adjustments which accommodate both sense and accent. For example, in a poem which is regularly iambic (rising stress), the opening apostrophe to Heaven is given independent stress and thus set apart from the continuation of the poem:

The poet's separation of the *address* is matched by Ferrabosco's emphasis by pitch and duration which, in effect, extends the phrase one measure at the beginning.[2]

Ex. 9

The second and third lines of the poem are linked, in the song, by bass movement, while the third is carried over to the fourth by the singer's common note.[3] Even though the phrase structure is clearly articulated, with emphasis on the predictable areas of tonic (g), dominant and relative major, the bass line is of more than usual interest for it describes, in almost sequence-like manner, patterns which overlap the cadential points until the end of the third line.

Ex. 10

Ex. 10
(continued)

The scope of this line, interrupted only by the representations of the "tempests of all worldly passions"—a pseudo-motion in the bass which portends more harmonic activity than it produces, and the sense of balance, which calls the music back from the relative major to the tonic in the last phrase, contribute to the sense of calm, extended statement, unhurried in declamation and imperturbable in the smoothness of melodic and harmonic motion and rhythm.

Within this calm, it is the subtle effect which counts for much. For example, the emphasis on the word "no" in the second phrase sharpens the point and, in conjunction with the exposed melodic diminished fourth, more closely associates "no" with its object, "peace."

Ex. 11

This is deliberate accentuation for the purpose of rhetorical clarity and effect and shows how flexible the sounding language can be within the general framework of iambic pentameter (rising stress). The iambic reading of the line,

    . / . / . / . / . /
And restless man can find no other peace

is transformed to

    . / . / . / / . . /
And restless man can find no other peace

by the melodic exposure of the lowered third and raised seventh degrees in direct contrast and by the agogic extension of "no" to give it stronger metrical emphasis.

As is typical of Ferrabosco's songs, this one begins with a pronounced gesture and becomes melodically smoother, though without losing sensitivity to poetic sense and construction. In the second section (m. 23 to end), the two lines of text are enjambed, but Ferrabosco ignores the linking, interrupting the progress of the text with a cadence which, though not strongly emphasized, takes enough time to stop the idea from developing. The second and concluding line of the section is set as a variant of the concluding line of the first section, an effective musical rhyme enhanced by a sequential repetition of the first four words of the line. It is also apparent, particularly in the balance of ascent and descent in this last section, that Ferrabosco was concerned with shaping a muscially appealing piece.

The phrases are longer in this section, and the absence of a strong internal cadence to articulate the movement from the relative major to the tonic allows a feeling of extension and integration (contrary to the apparent effect of the text-setting), increased by the interaction of bass and voice and the smoothness of the melody.

That smoothness, particularly in the second section, the gentleness of the text-setting, the regularity of the harmonic rhythm and the easy harmonic motion between tonic and relative major, and the modest arch of the melody (encompassing only a minor seventh), which always falls back in repose, all contribute to the matching of the tone of the song with that of the text. It is the very modesty of the song, with only subtle emphases and gestures, and the motivic integration between sections uniting the two concepts, restless/rest-less ("no. . .peace"), which allow the song to be so moving without having any personal or dramatic quality. In both melodic and cadential activity, the song is conservative, a brother to the serious consort songs of the Elizabethans in tone, if not manner.

On the other hand, "Was I to blame?" (#iii) is a lover's lament, couching a prettily made statement in music both clear and direct. The style of the music is by no means as impersonal as that of Ferrabosco's other more serious songs, and the impetuous frustration of the lover is consistently revealed, as in the vigor of the opening gesture (which, however, quickly melts into the softer melodic shape of memory: "to trust thy lovelike tears").

Ex. 12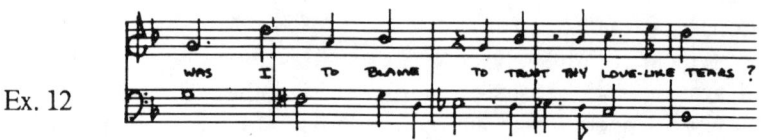

This gesture sacrifices scansion by accenting the first word in the attempt to present a musically impressive gesture which would emphasize "I" by leap and implied syncopation. But it is the gesture's musical content which is most important; it is mirrored by the complementary figure completing the octave g'-d"/d"-g" ("when mine from heads of love..."), with which the second section begins. There, however, the accentuation is not distorted. This is a genuine attempt to represent the emotional intensity of the speaker (see, also, the second line, "When 'tis most just") by asserting the text *against* the metric background. It seems the more out of place because the harmonic movement is so smooth and regular.

The lover's affect is more immediate, his pain more palpable in the exaggerated expression of his smart, and every phrase begins with a gesture of musical hyperbole in which wide skips, high range, or emotionally rushed rhythms emphasize the singer's desperate upset.

The formulaic treatment of the conventional 4-syllable beginning of these lines has become at once more varied and transferred to other 4-syllable groups, even one containing 6 syllables in the case of the extreme "could I suspect that thine" of the second section, where the figures serve to emphasize, even hammer their way toward an accented word.

Ex. 13

At the beginning of the second section (m. 10), the vigor of the opening figure is turned to high-blown petulance, the singer using his despair as an excuse for monumental self-concern. The regularity of the previous section's two 4-measure phrases, delineated by movement from tonic (g) to relative major and back, flows into a more vague 6 measures in which the melodic line plunges bravely into the upper register, unsupported except by imitation in the bass, whence it returns in the lethargic, exhausted extension, "Yet fruitless ran." The despair of these words, the defeat of the singer, are set with full appreciation of their poetic structure as well as their emotional importance: the textual enjambment is observed and the contrast of the singer's reality in comparison with his aspiration is confirmed in the contrasts of range and melodic gesture and harmonic cadence.

Ex. 14

From this point the movement back to the tonic is interrupted as the music takes note of the textual parenthesis of the next-to-last line.

> When mine from heads of love and faith did flow,
> Yet fruitless ran, could I suspect that thine,
> When in my heart each tear did write a line,
> Should have no spring but outward show.

Ex. 15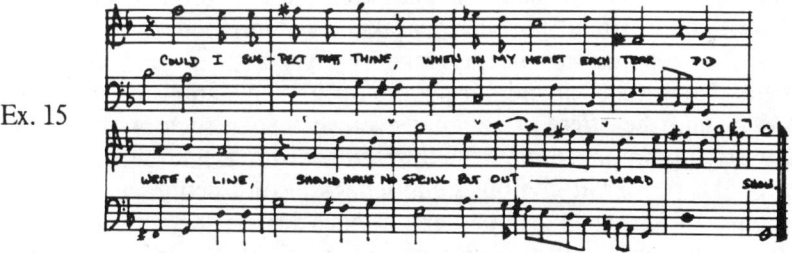

In effect, the suspension of harmonic progress reflects the focus of the lover's energy toward his once-beloved, an unwillingness to let go. For around this parenthesis we have the most flamboyant expression of hurt and outrage. The rhythmic urgency of "could I suspect that thine" barely prepares us for the leaping sarcasm and florid bitterness of the final line with its conflation of meanings ("spring" and fount) and the fanciful imitative overlay of the melody in three and the bass in two. The manner in which the parenthetical expression is woven into the patterns of the bass is extremely subtle, particularly in the connections of the statements of the descending run and the acceleration of imitation as the parenthesis is concluded. The bass begins a full measure before the voice ("Should have no spring"),[4] yet the voice is only a beat behind two measures later ("but outward show"). The entire song, ultimately, is "but outward show." The sense of immediacy which is dramatic, not intimate, is sacrificed to the artificiality of the composer's skill. The vehemence of passionate feeling is carefully balanced and musically shaped; for all the hyperbole, there is no distortion—the presence of the composer intrudes and is felt more strongly than that of the singer.

In this sense the song stands as a paradigm for Ferrabosco's English songs which approach the continuo-declamatory style: because of their musical shapeliness they forfeit the sense of immediacy of event and feeling. Even the minor sixth (d"-f#') at "each tear" is less forceful, the harmonic cross-relation less biting, because of the melody's triple-time phrasing and the pull of both syntax and harmony to the next line and g—as if the f# had been a struck appoggiatura but was here *consonant*. Our response to this is not to the experience itself, but to the expression. This is particularly true when the final section is repeated, as the manuscript directs, for the repetition does not intensify the experience but, rather, places an even greater aesthetic distance between the song and the listener.

It is apparent from this song that the merger of the serious song—which grew out of the elegiac consort-song—with the continuo style and the resources available in that style presents problems of kind. "Was I to blame?" straddles styles, partaking of the mood of the serious song and the resources of the declamatory style and, in part, continuo accompaniment without abandoning some of the conventions of the older style which lend the effect of restraint even to a song such as this. For all that restraint, we are nonetheless presented with a fine and sensitive reading of the poem. It combines subtleties of construction such as the musical parenthesis which sets the textual one, declamatory effects which reveal tone more than accent by means of melodic-rhythmic gesture, and word-painting (the "springing" upward leaps of the last phrase combined with the "outward show" of high range and triple-time) into a musically expressive and comprehensible song.

It is in the portrayal of mood that "Lo! In a vale" (#ii) falls into the category of serious song. Unlike the two previously discussed songs, it is neither moral nor affected. Moreover, it is not a direct presentation of feeling or argument, but a narrative description: an invitation into and recreation of a pastoral scene. At the outset, a distraught shepherdess is "discovered" in the scene, but the song moves quickly from discovery to description (with musically appropriate representations). The vigorous declamation of the first lines is rapidly softened.

Ex. 16

This movement from the declamatory to the pathetic emphasizes the problems of repeating music to new words in this style, for the second strophe simply cannot be sung coherently to the gestures which so startlingly discovered the shepherdess. The problem is no less noticeable after these first measures; awkward breaks in the continuity of thought and misaccentuations abound. In the next phrase it seems that Ferrabosco used the second strophe as his guide—seemingly making various decisions, as he went along, of which strophe he was setting:

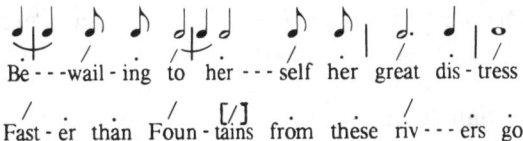

Here the scansion of the second line is matched by the music.

Where the setting is descriptive, however, such as the descent of a seventh at "her downcast head," a related problem emerges. No matter how sympathetic the setting is to the tone of the entire piece, it is pictorially appropriate for only one instance.

Ex. 17

The problem here is also the conflict of scansion and pictorialism, for the "downcast head" leaning on the knee is well described by this descending melodic outline which certainly does not portray "her breast did heave." But, then, "As though her heart-strings strain'd" is better suited than the first strophe to the particular angularity of its setting and the attendant conflicts of stress caused by the syncopations and straining equal durations of "as," "though," and "her," pictorialism notwithstanding.

Ex. 18
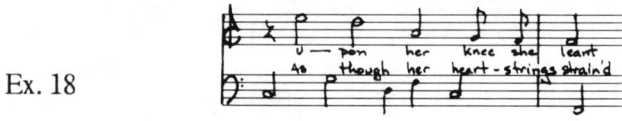

Generally the first strophe of text is the one which fits better, as in the following example.

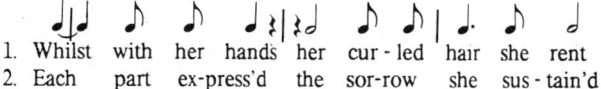

The first setting does not have to endure a separation of verb and object, although both suffer exaggerated stress on the first and fifth (poetically unaccented) syllables.[5]

The melodic writing of the first section of the song is fitful, the harmonic activity dullish. The piece is flatly in B♭, with little variety. The choppiness of the setting is due less to the larger scale of the melodic activity than to the sense of too many stops and starts and the rhythmic rushing of declamation in all-too-familiar patterns. The opening phrase is acceptable, but the similar rhythms of later phrases wear less well.

Ex. 19
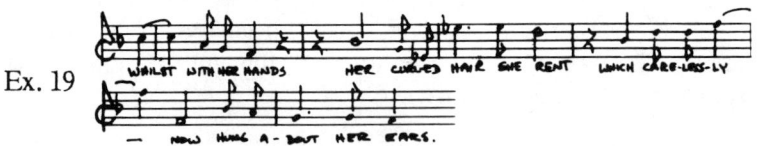

Both the lack of harmonic variety and the particular rhythmic and melodic gestures of the voice are hallmarks of a non-lyrical, almost dramatic style. Yet when the section nears its end and it is time to construct a close, Ferrabosco reverts to the more conventional song style, with imitation between bass and voice (again the bass anticipates the voice in prolepsis) and a well constructed cadence.

Ex. 20

This cadence is the confirmation of a V-I cadence we could have been hearing six measures previously, but did not. Ferrabosco avoided the direct confirmation of the tonic at that point in order to extend the music to match the extended description of the shepherdess's hair.

The shorter, repeated conclusion does not come to rest until the final chord, despite a momentary deceptive movement to the relative minor at the end of the first phrase. In fact, this cadence interrupts the sense of the text at the word "express'd" (which lacks a preceding referent and, thus, remains incomplete) despite the ongoing movement of the bass. Similarly, the grammatical function of the phrase "But by her face and posture," internally interrupted by the leap of the fifth, is clarified only at the end of the song. That fifth, and the ensuing inversion of the first melodic figure (d-e♭-d/g-f♯-g), occurs just after the fourth syllable. Here this is not a natural dividing point, and once more we are made aware of the artifical scansion the music imposes: "But by her fáce."

Ex. 21

"But" is the wrong word, serving no necessary function of contrast or exception; consequently it should not be stressed as if it did. The arbitrariness of the musical setting would be just as clear, however, if the text were changed to "And by her face:" the words have simply been applied to the music.

Nonetheless, in this more tuneful refrain with its active bass

Ferrabosco mitigates these problems. The melodic line of the phrase "But by her face and posture was express'd" is incomplete on the b♭'. It could easily have ended on g', and there made a close on a related harmony. The b♭' is the goal, of course, but here it is deceptive melodically, just as the g minor is deceptive harmonically. The musical idea, just like the textual, is not complete and demands the final phrase for conclusion. The melody achingly moves from the lower g'-f♯' to the upper g" only to fall back (as is characteristic of the entire piece) to the b♭' which completes the more sustained line d"-c"-b♭'. The peripheral movement is the picture of the soul's distress; the conclusive and more sustained line is the narrator's pose of comprehension.

The blandness of the harmonic activity remains a problem, however. The most striking example is at the words "upon her knee she leant" in which the resolution of the syncopation of bass and melody (more appropriate to "as though her heart-strings strain'd"; see above) simply does not satisfy the listener's anticipation. There is no bite to the cadence, despite the implied suspensions.

Ex. 22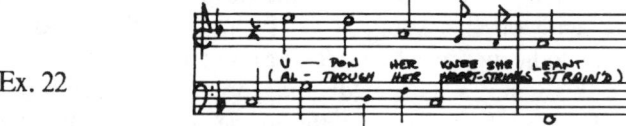

This song is a serious attempt to create a mood in narrative, but its success is partial and reflects only the first stages of mastery of the new style. In a non-dramatic setting, the use of musically rhetorical figures, rhythmic and melodic, is self-defeating, for the energy to maintain those figures and their succession is not justified by the text. Thus it is that, in this song, the most successful aspects are those which relax that vigor and energy into more lyrical moments with smoother melody and more active bass. At those moments the song becomes evocative and expressive, much like the unseen face of the shepherdess. For the most part, the setting is not overly pictorial and remains impersonal. The measured movement of the phrases counters the occasional kinetic melodic figures, and the song moves quite completely from declamatory to lyrical in feeling. Specific expressive devices of chromaticism and dissonance are absent, and it is difficult to gauge exactly how expressive the melodic leaps and rhythms are supposed to be, or whether they are used for emphasis only. Many of the melodic gestures are representational, e.g., the octave leap which might be forceful or burdensome depending on the text ("her curled hair she rent"/"the sorrow she sustain'd") and the dotted rhythms of "The lively image of a soul distress'd" which show an insensitivity to the meaning of the text by confusing "lively" (here meaning "vivid" or "living") with "active."

The piece stumbles when Ferrabosco tries to inject the rhythmic figures of the continuo style (e.g., ♩♪ ♫ ♩) when they are inappropriate or mechanically applied. The use of such off-beat entrances in this song is a frequent miscalculation of style confused with effect and here is just as neutral a manner of text-setting as is the older, more square setting of "But by her face." When the bass is relatively static, the melody is quite active. Here is the key to Ferrabosco's musical difficulties in this song, for he simply does not write a convincing vocal part above such a bass here. Only in the more tuneful sections of the piece, when the bass is active, is there a sense of direction and propriety generated by both bass and melody.

The opening measure of the song promises us something of the flavor and vitality of the Italian style, especially the sense of specific point in the discovery of the "shep-herd-ess," ♪ ♪ ♩ . The promise is never fulfilled, for here we see styles and purposes in flux. Not only do we have problems of decorum in the attempt to set both strophes to the same music—raising the question of whether Ferrabosco was forced to accept self-defeating compromises—but, in addition, there are unique problems which relate to the aptness of text and musical purpose throughout.

There is no other example from Ferrabosco's songs which so laboriously attempts to forge a more responsive style from the old practices by imposition. One has only to look at "Was I to blame?" to see the freedom given by a more continuo-like bass, to "Like Hermit Poore" and "Heav'n, since thou art" for examples of more unified musical conception, or to several of the masque songs for more vigorous and fitting confidence of gesture. For the greatest contrast, there are the Italian songs which succeeded only by almost completely separating the roles of bass and melody, structure and expression.

More in the style of the consort song is the stark "Fly from the world" (#16), the mood and manner of which fulfill the text of the second strophe, "My sighs a strange and stedfast wind shall lend." The steadfastness arises from the unremitting motion of the song: steady, slow, and almost completely stepwise (even the bass is relatively smooth), a wholecloth weaving of thought into a garment of sound, the warp and woof of which is articulated by words. The strangeness of the song, at sight, arises from the older conventional opening off the final tonic and the subsequently smoothly flowing manipulations which keep major and minor sides of the tonic side by side while moving from the opening F major to c/C, using B♭ as a pivot to g. That F major is really V of B♭ is recognized by the fact that, after the cadence at the word "soul," F is not confirmed again but moves to B♭ at the rhyme, "control." C minor is not established by a series of cadences. Instead it is the tonal area in which all the elements of the final section can be conceived as operating, with extra point given by the G major chord at the first appearance of the word "blind."

How much of the tonal-modal flexibility and ambiguity, based on the fluid relationships of third-related areas articulated by stronger fifth relations (F-B♭/g-E♭-G-c/C-F), was intentional, as representation of the vagaries of the passage of the soul to safe harbor, is ultimately a matter of speculation. The final *tierce de picardie* C major is both an effective point of return to the opening (for the second strophe) and point of tentative repose in conclusion. That c minor has been used, importantly, in the setting of the third and fourth lines of the poem ("And where thy thoughts do multiply unrest,/ Tiring with wishes what they straight control") makes the final cadence more convincing.

The great, tiring effort of these moral songs is reflected in the effort expended in heightening the vocal line, only to have it inexorably slip back down. Every additional half-step or step in range is hard won, and the exhaustion is such that the highest point cannot be sustained, nakedly bared above the accompaniment, but collapses upon itself to complete its line.

Ex. 23

Only the sighs and thoughts may fly, for the singer is bound in his lot until death, and there is no relief.

Our perception of weariness and exhaustion is more keen because the text-setting has only sporadic urgency to convey the energy of the poem. As such, the song becomes impersonal, though not without affect. But the steadiness of the harmonic motion and gestures like the following, at the beginning of the song, are not calculated to impart a sense of immediate drama.

Ex. 24

It is the repeat of the word "fly" (m.4) which is not only more representational, but galvanizes the song into action, the eighth-notes of the voice imitated by the bass.

 Ex. 25

Such figural representation is rare in this song. Another instance occurs at the words "multiply unrest" (mm. 13-15), with the long note serving as an extra extension or "multiplier" in the first strophe and as a steady, or "stedfast" note in the second.

In the latter half of the song repetition is used to emphasize words of apostrophe and command, with the two figures combining to outline a perfect fourth which stands in stark contrast to the diminished fourth emphasized elsewhere in the song (see below).

 Ex. 26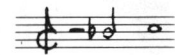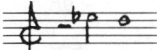

O World   O Thoughts
(O World betrayer of the mind)   (O thoughts that guide us being
                                                              blind)

The generality of the setting is reflected in the fact that the second strophe suffers little from being set to the same music as the first. The exceptions are of two kinds, the first occurring in the opening lines. The opening phrase, though iambic (rising stress), would be read with additional emphasis on the first word:

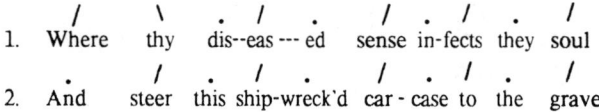

The second line, however, cannot be read the same way in both strophes.

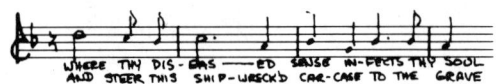

Ex. 27

The second strophe becomes momentarily lost in a snarl of consonants following the verb, while the conjunction, "and," stands alone, preening in its unaccustomed splendor — to no purpose.

Changes of accent in the fourth line demonstrate that the song was composed to the first strophe:

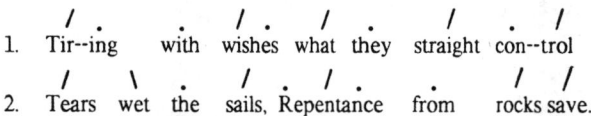

Ex. 28

Both the figure (which is "tiring" by its syncopation and its diminished fourth) and the number of notes belong to the first strophe — so much so that the second is interrupted (this a performer could minimize), and the sense of the important danger to be avoided, the "rocks," is lost. These anomalies are not, in the end, very disturbing because of the strength of the mood of the song.[6]

Other Serious Songs

For a moral song such as this, in which anguish and despair with the mortal lot are sublimated into the calm apprehension of death, the establishment of mood by the conventions of the consort song would be most familiar to contemporaries. The song is reflection, not action; therein lies the strength and aptness of its manner. That it is an antique manner, using intervallic progression and relations more than clearly tonal practices of strong root movement, and subverting our sense of formal clarity by maintaining an ambiguity of tonal focus, only enhances the sense of an inward, meditative contemplation of the release of the soul from the constraint of the flesh.

Even the gestures which could be considered affective are here inexpressive. The figure which sets "Tiring with wishes" is the same which begins the song "Unconstant love" (#24). Here the figure is poignant but pointless, except in the inability to rise above the $e^{b''}$, and the prefiguration in the lute accompaniment is a musical, rather than an expressive device.

Ex. 29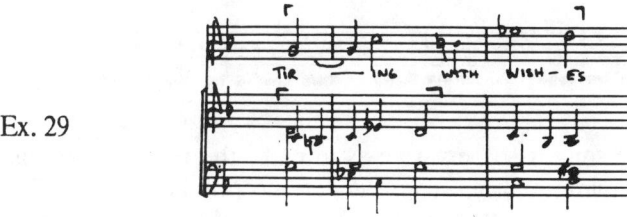

A similar lack of specific expressivity characterizes the melodic diminished fourth at "O thoughts that guide us, being blind."

Ex. 30

The tension of the perfect fourth ("O World. . .O thoughts") and this diminished fourth (especially "being blind," with the reflection of Dowland's "Lachrymae") emphasizes the blindness, the wandering of the song which, itself, does not possess a sure harbor but teeters precariously midway between F and c/C. Only with the performance of both strophes does the "unrest" of the song acquire some "rest." The question is not really which, F or c/C, is the tonic, but what are their relative strengths; the repetition reasserts and confirms the move from F to c/C, but the move is still as tentative, no more confident in its blindness, as the first time.

The breadth of the song comes not only from the manner by which cadences are elided into new phrases, but also from extensions of melodic motion which integrate melody and bass or connect two melodic gestures.

Ex. 31

Similarly, the melody alone presents such an extension at the end of the song, this time ascending. Here word-painting can be argued in both strophes: 1) "guide," 2) "follow," but the effect is of a musical shape being completed, not of a textual idea being represented in the completion of the octave around the rest.

Ex. 32

The tone of the song is so pervasive as to make the fit of the words a matter of secondary importance. There is here no primary concern for the independent life of the text: the abstract musical life of the song is made circumstantially or emotionally specific by the textual meaning. The musical shapes, from the conventional melodic break after the first four syllables to the progress of the melody, even its occasional movement in triple-time, are as much musically determined — to create the shape of the whole melody — as they are shaped to the sense of the word.

Such musicianly care, seen in attention to matters of balance, shape, melodic climax, harmonic flexibility and direction, and regularity of rhythm, without a similar, thoroughgoing attempt to portray the life of the words in a dramatic sense is at the heart of the serious song style. But there are times when Ferrabosco used the serious song manner to impart a *pathos* to more trifling and cavalier texts. This is the case with "Dear, when to thee" (#4), a lover's argument couched in the mode of seriousness, though partaking in a rather obvious way of the *double entendre* of death and sexual intercourse. The feeling of continuity and extension is like that of the serious style, with sham part-writing and cadences in one part overlapped with entrances in the others. The slow, stepwise motion of the melody is not animated for emotional purposes;

rather it seems deliberate in order to make the argument more effective. There is no apparent attempt at making the melodic rhythm responsive to the text, and there are only two instances which can be called affective: the momentary augmented triad, effected by the accented appoggiatura, at "doth my death renew" and the delicious *pathos* of the harmony and the little half-step at "suffer."

Ex. 33

The arbitrary text-setting is occasionally emphasized by an ungainly melodic figure, as at the words "I make" in the opening phrase.

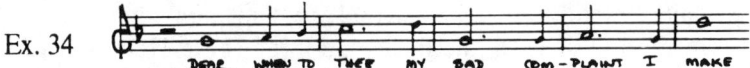

Ex. 34

An example such as this points out how important the smooth melodic style is for such text-setting, for the ear is less likely to be disturbed by indifference in text-setting, in this style, than it is by unconvincing melodic motion and harmonic support.

This opening, emphasizing the first word, is another example of rhetorical effect achieved by the deliberate emphasis on a word in a normally unaccented position. The contrast of first and second strophes in the first six measures is instructive:

```
    /    / .  / .  / .  / .  /
1. Dear, when to thee my sad complaint I make
    /    /  .  /  .  /  .  /  . /
2. But  my  re - ply  is just, that  if  the eye
```

The first word, in each case, is correctly stressed by the music, yet the phraseology of the music fits only the first strophe. The rhetorical ordering of the argument of the second strophe is completely thwarted: there is no break after "just," and the idea is stopped, in mid-flight, after "eye." (See Ex. 34) Similarly, the half-step which characterizes "suffer" (Ex. 33) is out-of-sorts with "delight" in the second go-round. There are even more of these examples which indicate that Ferrabosco composed his setting for the first strophe only, as did most of the lute-song composers; the second was simply underlaid, and it was left to the performer's skill to minimize the problems.

In a way it is only by great compromises of differences that we can talk of all these songs as "serious." The texts range from narrative to sententious, from moral poetry to artful innuendo. What is shared is musicianly concern for shaping the elements of harmony and melody in an aesthetically convincing form, with greater or lesser concern applied to the life of the words and the reading of the text. That Ferrabosco was sensitive to the problems of text-setting, including the unique problems of Donne's poetry, is a matter beyond doubt—even if his solutions were not completely satisfactory or consistent. It is interesting that he paid such matters less attention in a song like "Dear, when to thee" which has little substance, being content to garb the words in puffed-up seriousness, but not taking them seriously enough to attend to them more specifically.

When Ferrabosco pays attention to the rhythm of the words in these songs, however, the result is not uniform. The opening of "Lo! In a vale" is quite attentive to the textual rhythm and the sense of discovery. On the other hand, the declamation of "Like Hermit Poore" is eminently projected—so well, in fact, that Lanier would imitate this opening. It makes little difference that the rhythmic figure is typical in sixteenth-century song, particularly the *chanson*, and that Ferrabosco uses it frequently; it is fitting.

The harmonic resources in these songs are more varied than they are in Ferrabosco's other songs. The extension and continuity of thought is conveyed by flexible use of the resources of major and minor, by third relationships in particular, with more important articulations and cadences being effected by means of fifth relations. Phrases are balanced, though certainly not four-square, and both the melodic and harmonic shapes of these songs follow arches of distance and return. Tonal balances are well-crafted, with several songs starting off the tonic, reaching and confirming the tonic in a manner which emphasizes the textual structure. The subdominant is an important area of contrast and balance to the dominant.

In these songs Ferrabosco resembles Dowland, but without giving his songs the more active inner life of Dowland's greatest works. These songs are basically non-representational and their propriety is one of tone and intellectual appeal more than emotional response, their decorum a mirror of convention rather than a denial of affect.

VI

Tuneful Songs

The more tuneful accompanied declamation ayres, with the exception of "Come my Celia" (#6) which is quite a sophisticated song, are artfully artless. Invariably, they are metrically regular and melodically simple with a direct and unprepossessing presentation of the words which lacks the care, sense of effort, and distance of the more serious song. Although they share several characteristics with the strophic French *air*, they do not partake of the particular rhythmic groupings and triple measure which characterize many of Dowland's French-related dance-derived songs (i.e., the galliards), brothers in spirit with the *chanson dansée*.

The major mode, unencumbered with the baggage of expressiveness, predominates, and the vigorous melodic action which results from the text-setting is shaped into regular phrases shaped by strong and unambiguous cadences. Like the serious songs, the tuneful ayres generally present one note for each syllable. Here, however, the notes are of more uniform length and arranged in shorter, more coherent phrases. In several of these songs, the phrases are even mechanically regular, like some of the refrains of the serious songs. As in those refrains, the result in these songs is a sense of generality in which music and words are only arbitrarily matched, at least regarding rhythm. This is felt even more strongly in the strophic songs in which the music serves primarily to convey a mood which the words of the succeeding strophes make specific.

For example, "Fain I would, but O I dare not" (#5), a song in simple ABB form, is a pretty, teasing complimentg—perhaps a bit naughty—formulated in regular 3-measure phrases of clear harmonic shape (:I-I; I-V:ıı:I-V; IV-V-I:) in G major. The harmonic rhythm is active but predictable, moving at the level of the half-note or, particularly in the second measure of each phrase, the quarter note. The feminine ending of the poetic lines is reflected in the phrase cadences, and, while phrases do not overlap as they might with masculine cadences, they move forward because there is no time lost between the end of one phrase and the beginning of another. Only in the refrain is there an extension of the final phrase, with the harmonic movement concentrated at the beginning of the phrase. Here, too, the two phrases of the refrain are connected by a melodic motion in the bass (a modest prolepsis of the vocal part) which introduces a different harmonic shape to the closing phrase as well.

Ex. 1

Text-setting in these songs is largely only concerned with the alignment of metric and verbal accent, and in this piece Ferrabosco accents the trochaic (falling stress) lines, emphasizing the first syllable by duration and placing it off the beat except at the opening. There is less sense here of the sacrifice of scansion to gesture which often characterizes the structurally important points in Ferrabosco's songs. This is largely due to the trochaic pattern of the poetry which, also, does stress the first syllable.

In two lines, however, the stress of the first foot is reversed, and for these Ferrabosco modifies his practice to accommodate the word accent. The first line sets the pattern:

/ . / . / . / \
Fain I would but O I dare not.

Ex. 2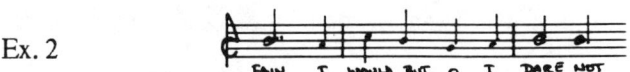

. / / . / . / \ . / /
However, "Thy speech can no higher raise her" and "Thy speech than

. / . / \
thy thoughts are lower" require adjustment.

Ex. 3

In this example, the accents of the first foot have been reversed and the pattern returned to the trochaic form by extending the note on "can" and "than." In the last line (see Ex. 1, above), however, the emphasis on "do" is not derived from considered concern for the text (which should be scanned, "Yét thy thoúghts do nòt hálf knów hèr"), but for the concluding cadence.

The song is witty, not moving. The melodic arch, however, shows concern for the meaning of the text as it stretches to the upper f', unable to progress to the further g", before descending to the lower g'. Thus, too, the frustration of this "speech," which can never ascend to the more sublime height of the "thoughts," is expressed. But it is a deceptive frustration, and the tone of the song gives the impression that those thoughts were not really very sublime anyway.

The difficulty of distinguishing between styles is seen in "I am a lover" (#10), a setting of Bartholomew Yonge's translation of the first strophe of a 6-strophe poem from Montemayor's *Diana*. The translation has its own charm, particularly in the persistent contrast of "ever" and "never," and presents a moving complaint of an unsuccessful lover who now claims oblivion as his only remembrancer. The setting emphasizes the exaggerated *pathos* of the singer by mimicking the serious mode at the very beginning, the first four syllables set to an affective half-step rise and fall.

Ex. 4

But if all this were true, it should be represented despairingly in the minor mode instead of being forthrightly, almost proudly stated in major (G). The mock-seriousness of the lover, revealed in the artifice and tone of his words, is reflected in the regularity of the phrasing and text-setting as well.

The only variance in phrase length, mode, and gesture comes with much huffing and puffing.

Ex. 5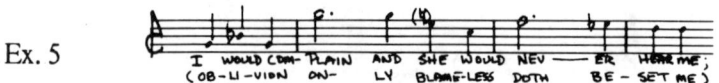

This complaining warrants the large leap of an octave to the extended g", but the repeat, to the words "Oblivion only blameless doth beset me," is rather less deft. "Blameless" is lost in the flourish of the gesture, and its object ("me") remains unclear. The following paradox, "For that [oblivion] remembreth never to forget me," returns to the music of the beginning. The whole song is comfortably rounded; the despair is a sham, a trick known to both audience and performer.

The opening, the description of circumstance, is clear in melodic and harmonic direction, smooth and articulate, even polished. The second section of the song affects not only the mood and gesture of pathetic and impassioned complaint, but incorporates more active inner parts which present a seemingly teeming activity, full of suspensions, deceptive cadences, and voice leadings which temporarily prevent the internal cadences from being as clearly articulated and the chordal progressions from being unambiguous. The ambiguity is also a sham, however, for the regularity of phrasing is maintained, as is the basic harmonic rhythm. There is an occasional feeling of triple time, as there had been more clearly in "Fain I would," but never enough to generate a conflict of metric expectation (see the bass in Ex. 5). It is the temporary emphasis on the minor which permits the ambiguity and *pathos*. An easy return is made to the major, and the lyrical close consigns the complaint to its own oblivion.

The pretense of complaint is as clearly recognized in the teasing text and playful melody of "All you forsaken lovers" (#i). Quite at home in cavalier courtly company, this is a song of utmost clarity and regularity in phrasing, melodic gestures and harmonic rhythm. The text, too, gives the game away, "for love I die," but the song helps the masquerade by using a larger range (an 11th for the singer) and remaining in the minor mode until the very feigning diminished fourth of "unfeigned" completes the dissemblance.

Ex. 6

The charm and musical conception of the setting is such that the awkward fit and roughness of the poetry is unnoticed. Even the untoward stress on "can" is minimized by the motion of the bass pushing forward to the next word.

> All you forsaken lovers come and pity my distress;
> You shall know why.
> All you beloved can pity me no less;
> For love I die.
> Yet hope at least to move pity in her breast. . . .

Ex. 7

The awkwardness ("can") is a matter of prosody as well as of melodic exposure. "Can" is an auxiliary verb, not specific, active, and transitive, and it is rhetorically inappropriately exposed. The parallel of "can pity" and "move pity" emphasizes this distinction.

Ex. 8

The various lengths of the poetic lines are also nicely handled, so that each of the two sections of the song has two phrases which complement each other in harmonic movement. (i-V;v/V-i ‖ i-III;v/V-I).

The song has a curious existence in a pair of manuscript partbooks now in the Carlisle Cathedral Library.[1] While both appearances of the song known to Spink (in the "John Bull MS," MS 52.D Fitzwilliam Library, Cambridge, c. 1620; and the "Elizabeth Rogers Virginal Book," c. 1657, British Museum MS Add. 10337) used the text "All you forsaken lovers," the Carlisle part-books present the music to the words of Ben Jonson's poem "The Houre-glasse."

These part-books, altus and bassus, were compiled around 1637 by Thomas Smith, later to become Bishop of Carlisle, and it is not known how he knew Ferrabosco's song or whether he might have applied Jonson's words to the song himself. Three points, however, argue for a closer relationship of Jonson's poem with Ferrabosco's music: 1) the close friendship and collaboration between Jonson and Ferrabosco; 2) the phrase structure of the song is quite unusual in the uneven lengths of individual sections of larger phrases, and it is thus unlikely that music and text were conceived independently; 3) the imagery of Jonson's poem much more closely matches the movement of the music. [See the transcription of the mildly ornamented version of the song from the Cambridge MS, with the Carlisle text editorially added.] Doughtie observes:

> Thus one might argue that Ferrabosco's music was originally intended for Jonson's poem rather than for "All you forsaken lovers come." Moreover, the Jonson poem fits the music perfectly: the descending five-note scale which does little to enhance the words "pity my distress" and "pity in her breast" in the anonymous text helps illustrate "running in this glass" and "playing like the flye" in Jonson's poem. In Jonson's fourth line, "could you believe that this," a long high note approached by the leap of a fourth gives emphasis to "this," but the anonymous text has a rather awkward "can" at this point . . .[2]

Jonson's poem, first published as no. VIII of *The Under-Wood* in Jonson's *Folio* of 1640, is as follows (here taken from the Carlisle books which predate the *Folio*):

> Doe but consider this small dust
> here running in this glasse
> by attomes move'd:
> could you beleive that this
> the body ever was
> of one that love'd
> and in his Mistress flames playing like the flye,
> burnt to cinders by her eye.
> Yes, and in death as life unbless't,
> to have't express't,
> even ashes of lovers find no rest.

Interestingly, on the page facing the song in both in both part-books of the Carlisle set, the following poem is found. It was written by Girolamo Amaltei and originally appeared in Ramitius Gherus' *Delitiae CC Italorum Poetarum* (1608), I, 73.[3]

> Perspicuus Vitro pulvis qui dividit horas,
> Cum Vagus angustum saepe recurrit iter,
> Olim erat Alcippus; qui Gallae ut Vidit ocellos
> Arsit, & est subito factus ab igne cinis.
> Irrequiete cinis, miseros testabere Amantes
> (More tuo) nulla posse quiete frui.
>   Hier. Amaltheus
>   alias HE.

This, of course, was Jonson's source.

The Carlisle setting differs from the others in minor matters of division of notes; *both* parts have the text, however. There are no written accidentals in the Carlisle books except for the melodic c#" in the next-to-last bar and the bass f# in the second bar. In the melody, the Carlisle set gives g' for bb' in the second measure and an unornamented d" in the next-to-last bar. The bass has additional passing notes in the first, fifth, and seventh bars.

Campion's famous definition of the Ayre, which appeared in Rosseter's *A Booke of Ayres* (1601), implies a simple and closed world not wholly in keeping with the entire Ayre repertory.

> What Epigrams are in Poetrie, the same are Ayres in musicke, then in their chief perfection when they are short and well-seasoned.

Such description is apt for Campion's own output, for he was a much better poet than composer, and his short pieces are seasoned with witty text to spice the sometimes tedious music.

Dowland, too, had appealed to popular taste particularly in the triple-time dance-ayres of his *First Book* (1597) derived from galliards — just as he would succeed, in quite another vein, with the "Lachrymae" pavan / "Flow my tears" relation later.

But "short and well-seasoned" really meant a short tune and a strophic poem set engagingly together: long enough to catch the attention and to present a witty argument (to prepare a "punch-line"), yet short enough not to exhaust the courtier intellect.

Such a song is Ferrabosco's "Shall I seek to ease my grief?" (#17), yet another example of man's delight in love-death, presented by the ubiquitous wounded lover whose subtlety is exceeded, somewhat, by his coyness. The tunefulness of the melody is articulated in short, closed phrases, the harmonic shape of which is as follows:

	A section (mm. 1-9)	Refrain (mm. 10-16)
(g)	i-V/♭III; V-(iv$_6$)V;	
	v-V/v; ♭III-V/♭III-♭III	IV/♭III(V/♭III)-♭III;
		♭III-V-I

Here, then, is part of the "seasoning:" the use of so many of the possibilities (which we have seen in the more serious songs) of the harmonic resources of both modes in an attempt to stress the affect of the text.

In addition, the phrases of the A section are not equal: 1) 5♩, 2) 6 ♩, 3) 4♩, 4) 6♩. The longer phrases each have an additional syllable, and they are balanced. What is subtle is the loss of one ♩ in the third phrase without the ear being aware 1) of an imbalance with the first phrase or 2) a feeling of awkward balance among all phrases.

Ex. 9

The second and fourth phrases are textually and rhetorically matched only in the first strophe. Musically, they provide a closure of phrase harmonically, melodically, and rhythmically with their feminine cadences. The refrain, with similar 6 ♩ phrases to a repeated text, not only emphasizes the sense of closure as it steers back to the tonic (the second phrase of the refrain is, itself, extended to make the return more convincing), but contrasts its descending figures with the rising figures of the A section. Cadences emphasized by root movement of a fifth occur only at the end of sections, confirming the tonal movement of the song. The internal cadences, at the end of the short phrases, are also set off by the rests and repetition of gestures in the vocal part. The vitality of those gestures, with their energetic movement off-the-beat, gives the lie to the professed suffering of this lover. The refrain begins as if pathetic, only to become playful with the bumptious dotted figures both rhythmically and melodically dispelling any possible seriousness.

Ex. 10

"Young and Simple though I am" (#8) is a masterful example of poetry for music by the poet-composer Thomas Campion, and it was set by Campion himself, Ferrabosco, Lanier, and another, anonymous composer in the seventeenth century.[4] The regularity of the poem in matching prosody and diction from strophe to strophe allows the strophic setting to present the words without concern for changes from one strophe to the next.

Unlike our male friend of "Shall I seek" (#17), dying in love, the singer of this song is a woman, a woman rather less simple than first impression would suggest. Campion almost certainly wrote the poem for musical setting, although it is unknown if his own setting preceded Ferrabosco's.

The invariable trochaic pattern of the poetry and the absolute matching of phrases throughout the strophes ease the composer's task, for he could compose a setting which reflected the general tone of the poem, assured that each strophe has similar characteristics.

Only once does this expectation fail: in the final strophe at the words

```
        /  .  /  .  /  .  /
    "Who shall not, I soon can tell;
        .  /  /  .  /  .  /
     Who shall, would I could as well!"
```

where the emphasis is shifted in the second line of the couplet to fall on "shall," in order to balance the contrast of "Who shall not" (which stresses the important word "not") with "Who shall" and to emphasize "shall" to make the statement a question: "Who shall?"

For both Campion and Ferrabosco, the emphasis of these two phrases is not matched by the music, which fits the stress pattern of the previous strophes. In Campion's case the problem is a simple one of time: the meaning is lost in the too quick movement of the word "shall"; for Ferrabosco, the problem also involves harmonic motion and emphasis as "shall" is part of a passing (almost triple-time) movement to V/V.

Ex. 11a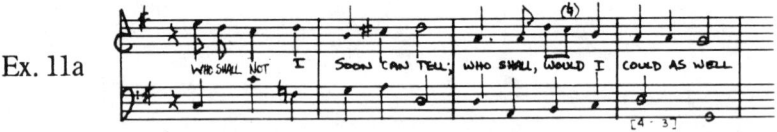

Ex. 11b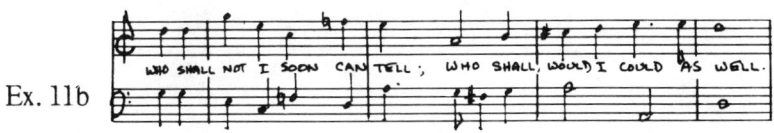

Ex. 11c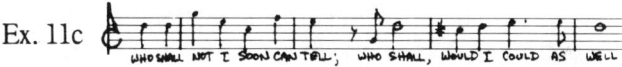

Because this is a strophic song, rewriting (as above, Ex. 11c) would only confuse the other strophes. What was a breathless and coy syncopation, effective for four strophes, is become here rhetorically ineffective and contrary to the meaning of this one line of the poem. The problem lies in the conflict of stress pattern and syntax. The meaning is clear and the statement balanced only if "[Who] shall" is stressed in contrast to the general stress pattern of the poem — easily done if reading, more difficult in the context of a strophic song. That Campion's setting needs one minor adjustment ("Who shall") to accommodate the change is evidence of his (general) indifference to text-setting problems beyond the most basic alignment of verbal stress and metrical accent.

Of the two settings, Campion's is the "simpler" version, cramped compared with Ferrabosco's wider-ranging and metrically more flexible version. Ferrabosco's is more consciously coy, and the harmonic activity contributes to a sense of forward motion which is lacking in Campion's song. Both settings divide the poem so that the final couplet of each strophe is repeated. Campion relies, however, on minimal harmonic variety, and the cadential movement, by phrases, is perfunctory and remains stolidly in the major mode: (G=) I-I; IV-IV; IV-V; V-III: I-V; V-I:. Ferrabosco, on the other hand, introduces more variety in the cadences and explores more harmonic territory, as well as utilizing the minor resources of the tonic: (G=) I-V; I-IV-(V)-I; I-IV-v-V/v; V-V/V-VII:v--ii-V-I; IV-V-I:.

Campion fails, also, to convince that his singer is anything more than charmingly simple. Ferrabosco's singer is wide-eyed, but coy, as the breathlessness of m. 6 demonstrates, when she demurely sings an accented word on the second beat.

Ex. 12

The relaxation of the harmonic rhythm contributes to the effect of lingering on the last line — a line which, in every strophe, prepares for the "observation" in the couplet of the refrain, e.g., "Roses that are overblown,/ Grow less sweet, then fall alone."[5]

In the refrain, as well, Ferrabosco betters Campion, for he inserts a short repetition which contributes, like the syncopation in Ex. 12, to the sense of simple-minded (though knowing) wonder.

Ex. 13

The composer and poet here have combined in a setting which has the sense of the greatest simplicity, yet which gives the lie to the singer's opening line. The delicacy of harmonic movement, including the use of minor resources and the two-fold use of the subdominant — in the A section to prepare the dominant, in the refrain to reverse that tendency and strengthen the cadence to the tonic [IV- -V/V; ii - IV (-V-I): both utilizing third-relations and common-tones], and the contrived grace of the melodic movement are anything but naive.

Campion's setting, with its cramped phrases and conservative harmonic and melodic usage — parallel without variety and energy — is simple, compared with the larger arch and more varied melodic and harmonic shape of Ferrabosco's song. Ferrabosco's is an example, *par excellence*, of the strophic song: the music sets the mood and is made variously specific by the changing text. Moreover, it gives the singer a recognizable character, emphasized in the interplay of strophe and refrain. Poet, composer, and performer conspire to set up the audience for the final line which winkingly deflates all the sincerity of the previous posturing and dispenses with the guise of innocence and the hope of ideal love: "This I know, who e'er he be,/ Love he must (Love he must) or flatter me."

Of all Ferrabosco's songs in the lighter vein, his setting of "Come, my Celia" (#6), a lyric from Jonson's *Volpone* (acted in 1605, published in 1607), is the most subtle and attractive. The poem is a parody translation of Catullus' famous "Vivamus, mea Lesbia, atque amemus," which is perhaps better known in Campion's translation and song, "My sweetest Lesbia, let us live and love."⁶ Campion's translation is more mellifluous and serious, but Jonson's adaptation serves well for the attempt of old Volpone, who is less than graceful and more than blunt, in his ardor to seduce the young Celia. Part of the humor of the song is in the trivialization of the *carpe diem* theme as Volpone makes both the conventional practical arguments (which apply far more to him than to Celia) warning against losing the opportunity for pleasure as time all too quickly passes and the relativistic point that sin is not sin when not observed. Volpone's pretense is matched by the form of the song (aaBRR) which, although each section begins and ends on the tonic, is more extended and varied than the other tuneful anacreontic airs.

It is the sense of dalliance, rather than impetuousity or serious wooing, however, which characterizes the song. The invitation is set, as is the entire poem, with clear and regularly cadencing harmonic progressions. But the invitation is playful, teasingly moving into triple-time or playing off the harmonic motion.

Ex. 14

The impetuosity which appears in the comparative rush of "Time will not be ours forever" and the more extended activity of the melody in the final phrase is deflated in the repeat as charming instance becomes formula.

The relation of specific words to music in this section is arguably awkward and, at the least, indifferent. The dalliance of the triple-time, so charming in proving "the sweets of love," and the melodic line, which by itself is quite affecting and flexible, works against the pulse of the accompaniment as much as with it in the closing phrase. It may be, of course, that Volpone's ardor has gotten the best of him and the music simply represents his excitement. The audience may be inclined to such an interpretation after the unintended self-description of the second strophe, "Spend not, then, [Love's] gifts in vain."

The second section follows the invitation with a question, assuming that the only obstacle to love's success is the curiosity of household gossips (never minding Celia's mute demur). The change of rhetorical stance is reflected in the longer phrases and their emphasis on the subdominant. Modest word-painting abounds, at the words "defer," "delude," and "beguile."

Ex. 15a

Ex. 15b

Ex. 15c

The suspensions at "defer" and the following delayed cadence, the V-IV (F is the tonic) non-cadence which is completed and understood only by the V/IV-IV two measures later, are, then, intentional, not awkward. Similarly, the "delusion" of the next phrase is not simply found in the melodic diminished fourth, but more importantly in the temporary feeling that the song has settled (via B♭) on g — a feeling which is denied by the graceful deceptive move to e♭, avoiding f♯, in the bass and the subsequent, necessary continuation to B♭. Here is a case where the scalar motion of the bass-voice duet is in two complementary portions, the ascending one having to retire into descent as the f♯ is denied and the f♮s do not allow cadences on either g or D.

The third phrase, which concludes the section and returns it to F, uses the instance of the word "beguile" to engage in some syncopations of melody and accompaniment and in the deceptive borrowings of e♭

from the subdominant to prolong the subdominant feeling of the section (by means of the relationship: relative minor of the subdominant = ii of the tonic) before the final phrase concludes with a IV-V-I cadence.

This subtle wooing is too much for Volpone, who finally turns to a different approach to coax the wary Celia.

> Tis no sin Love's fruits to steal,
> But the sweet theft to reveal:
> To be taken, to be seen,
> These have crimes accounted been.

Although Hollander argues that there is a case to be made for grouping together "reveal," "taken," and "seen," thus making the meaning "But 1) to reveal the theft, 2) to be taken, 3) to be seen — *these* are called crimes,"[7] neither the couplet structure of the poetry nor Ferrabosco's setting permits it. Nor does the text itself: "But" here means "except," not "on the contrary." Hollander has simply misread the poem.

The movement from the tonic to dominant is structurally important after the middle section of the song with its emphasis on the subdominant, and the cadence is so strongly presented that the textual idea is stopped, and we expect a new statement.

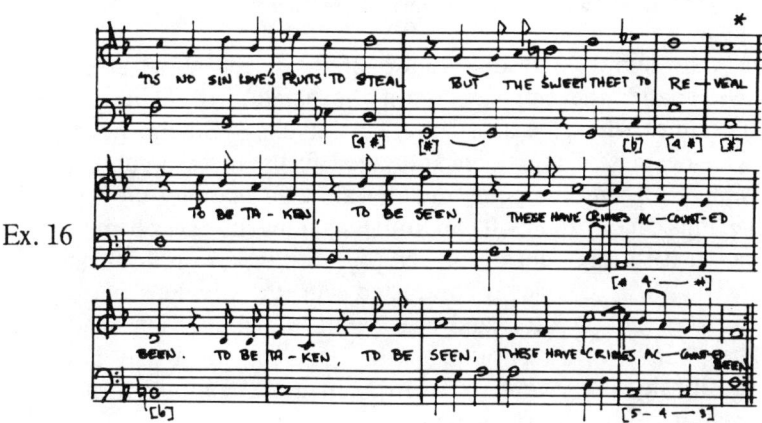

Ex. 16

We get just that in the final couplet (repeated, in Ferrabosco's setting, within the repeat of the entire refrain/final section). The rhythmic activity and melodic shapes, the short phrases, and the repetition of the upbeat pattern all distinguish this couplet from the one preceding, just as this entire strophe of the poem is distinguished from the previous sections of the song by much more direct and forceful melodic activity, simpler harmonic rhythm, and objective tone. This interpretation is corroborated also by the internal repetition of the final couplet following the unusual deceptive cadence on "been" in which the b♮, used earlier to counteract the e♭ borrowed from the subdominant, focuses the motion (as V_6/V) toward the dominant and, thence, to the tonic.

Hollander's comments on the setting of these lines raise another question.

> While the purely melodic effect is lovely and sophisticated—a stylistically forward-looking evaded cadence on the chord of the sixth [first inversion] at "beene," heralding the repetition of the words in a final phrase, *etc.*—it is almost as if the text laid under it were a fairly clever verse translation of that for which the music was composed. The sense of the couplet becomes clear only when we underline the emphatic stress [in reading]:
>
> To be *taken*, to be *seene*,
> *These* have crimes *accounted* been.
>
> "Crimes" needs no added stress, since it refers back to, rather than contrasts with, the "sinne" of the previous couplet. *"These"* (*i.e.*, getting caught, not adultery itself), or, more subtly, *"accounted"* (morality is mere fashion) are the words which take an implicit contrastive stress in speech. According to the setting, the preceding lines of the text would have had to suggest that these were blessings, and "crimes" was then given emphatic development.[8]

If this were simply a reading aloud of the poem, these arguments would be well-made: the emphasis is on the paradox of "These" being "accounted" crimes while the actual theft is "no sin." But in the case of the song, with devices of repetition and tonal focus, these arguments are sophistry, simply missing the point and revealing an inability to deal with the way the music contributes to an understanding of the poem. That the specific text-setting does not emphasize the word "these" is secondary. The *entire* couplet is contrasted with the previous one by its musical structure and gesture, and the point, which Jonson made by placing "These" in a strong position at the beginning of a line, is made here less specifically (*i.e.*, word by word), but more comprehensively in the representation of the governing idea.

The repeat of the refrain softens the connotation of "crimes," and the ultimate recognition is that these "crimes" are not to be taken seriously; they are gentle, playful, and coy. The idea that "morality is mere fashion" is admirably conveyed, and, as in "Young and simple though I am, " the intense seriousness or the immediacy of affect these lines might have had, were they more than part of the game of love, is missing. The setting is one step more artificial than the poem.

VII

The Masque Songs

Masquing entertainments were not uncommon either on the continent or in Tudor England, but the Stuart masque was to make what had been pleasurable into an embodiment of political philosophy. This was the purpose of the masques of Ben Jonson: to inform spectacle and entertainment with meaning.

Unlike the drama, with its separation of players and audience, the masque included the audience and in Jonson's court masques, the exemplars of the genre, depended on the presence of the King. In fact, it was the nature of royalty and courtly society which was the theme variously examined in Jonson's masques.

The form and manner of Jonson's masques are inseparable. The "device" or theme of the masque's narrative content inevitably reaches a point where the masque-world and court-world intersect and where the agency of the King is necessary to resolve a conflict or enable a solution to a fictive problem in the masque. In Jonson's masques, to which Ferrabosco was a major contributor until 1612, the form of the masque action is extremely consistent and emphasizes the central spiritual sovereignty of the King, just as much as the King's central physical position in the Banqueting House at Whitehall.

That Banqueting House was, essentially, a large floor space with tiered seats on three sides. The canopied Royal box was at one end of the floor, roughly two-thirds of the distance from the stage to the back of the Hall, and from this position the King could not only see the dancing and appreciate the perspectives of Inigo Jones's stage designs, but he could intercede in the action which was directed to him.

As stated, Jonson found a variety of ways to make the same points, but, as Stephen Orgel points out, certain characteristics remained constant:

The monarch was at the center, and [the masques] provided roles for members of the court within an idealized fiction. The climactic moment of the masque was nearly always the same: the fiction opened outward to include the whole court, as masquers descended from the pageant car or stage and took partners from the audience. What the noble spectator watched he ultimately became.[1]

Specifically, the way the court partook of the masque, then, was in the dance and in many respects it was the dance, not carpentry or poetry, which was the soul of the masque. For in the transforming and ordered harmony of dance figures the political ordering of the kingdom was reflected. Jonson's "devices" or themes were but emblematic tags which gave specific meaning to the long, choreographed figure or pattern dances of the masquers which were the *real* metaphors, or emblems of order.

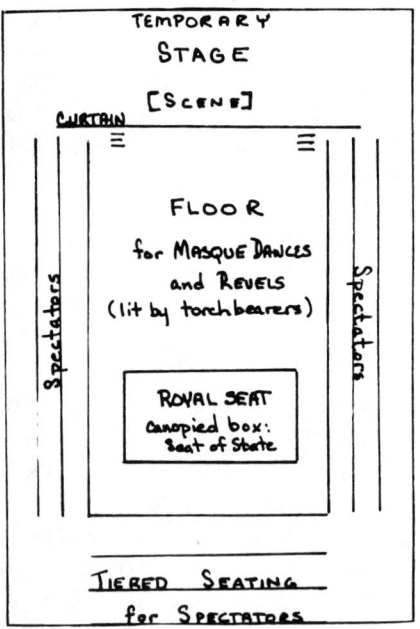

1608 Banqueting House: 120' x 53'
1622 Banqueting House (Inigo Jones): 110' x 55' x 55' (height)

The interpenetration of masque and court made it necessary that the masquers *be* courtiers: their world was a reflection of or analogy to the Stuart court. Misrule could be represented only in the antic manner of professional performers before the masque begins—a conscious contrast of the world without order and the court—the antimasque.

The dances of the masque, proper, were the visual representation of order which could overcome the forces of misrule presented in that preliminary antimasque. The typical narrative "device" of the Jonsonian masque presented the court with a paradoxical situation requiring solution in an ideal society, that is, by the agency of an ideal ruler. That ideal ruler, of course, was James I; the ideal society, Stuart England. The court's participation in this ideal society was symbolized by its participation in the dances of the masque—on one level by the masquer's performance of the patterned masquing dances, but, even more importantly, in the general participation in the revels when the masquers went among the spectators, bringing them onto the floor for dancing.

Jonson's masques are quite consistent in form and serve well as a general model for the court masque. Following the entry and seating of the spectators and an introductory speech, often allegorical, the antimasque would begin. Characterized by lively, folk-like, humorous, even grotesque dancing, the antimasque became increasingly important as light entertainment and (in Jonson's hands) as structural balance to the masque which followed.

The antimasquers were professionals, court-servants, and the end of their antics was signalled by the "discovery" of the masque scene upon the stage. A song generally followed, after which the masquers made their entry dance and descended from the stage to the dancing floor.

There followed a second song and the main masquing dance. This taking place on the floor of the Hall, it could be seen by the spectators, sitting in tiers above the floor, as the moving ("lively") visualization of the allegorical concepts of the masque—the grand conceit, metaphor, and compliment.

At the conclusion of this dance, another song was sung following which the masquers invited members of the court to dance the revels. Unlike the extravagantly choreographed pattern or figure dances of the masquers, the revels consisted of branles, corantos, galliards, measures, and other social dances.[2]

The revels were concluded by a song calling the masquers back to their world (i.e., the masquing stage). During or after a final figure dance the masquers returned to the stage and the conclusion of the masque was often celebrated with a grand choral song.[3]

Thus, the outline for a typical Jonsonian masque is as follows:

```
                           Procession
Prologue
Antimasque
         Professional actors and musicians. Plot in the antimasque is increasingly closely related
         to the theme of the masque.
MASQUE
Discovery of the Scene
                             Song I
    I    Entry dance of the masquers (courtly amateurs) and descent to the floor
                             Song II
    II   Main dance of the masquers
                             Song III
         Revels: social dancing. Masquers invite partners from the audience.
                             Song IV
    III  Return to stage and Final Dance of the Masquers
                           Choral Song
```

The variants of this pattern are of detail, not kind. The importance of the masquers' dances, choreographed in figures and emblems, remains paramount.

The activities of the masque worked on several levels to transform the entertainment into political metaphor and compliment. There was, first of all, a clear relationship between the event being celebrated (or the person being celebrated) and the narrative theme, or "device," of the masque. The ideal society which that "device" invariably implied was realized just before the revels, often, as in the court masques, by the invocation and implicit intervention of the King. Thus the King became more than King, but God as well, for his presence enabled the triumph of order over misrule, right over wrong, happiness over misery. The courtly society of the moment became one with an eternal ideal of order which had a specific political construction. That society which momentarily, through its participation in the revels, partook in a transcendent and timeless social order was certified by the presence of the King—the reflection of that eternal order made specific in the person of James I. In this manner the "more remov'd mysteries" which Jonson spoke of in his description of *Hymenaei* (1606) were given credence in "present occasions."

The songs of the masque are structurally important. They do not partake of the action of the masque directly, standing apart as impersonal comments or directions for action or celebrating the subjects of the masque (and, thereby, celebrating the highest ranking members of the audience) in oratorical fashion. There is no reason to expect in these celebratory songs either the intimate or personal style of a lyric setting or the passionate expressiveness of the monodic manner. These songs, instead, interpret the meaning of the masque, consolidating the response

The Masque Songs

of the audience into a brief gesture of emphasis or triumph which makes specific the interpretation of and reason for the dances. In Ferrabosco's masque songs there is an awareness of the requirements of this type of oratory: to have a clear and simple structure which incorporates such gestures of hyperbole as are fitting to the text.

In his collaboration with Ben Jonson, Ferrabosco provided 13 songs for 6 masques dating from 1605 to 1611. To these, for stylistic and textual reasons, can be added 3 other songs forming one larger work which were published in the *Ayres* and were apparently intended as part of a court celebration in honor of King James I or Prince Henry. From Jonson's own acknowledgments, we know that Ferrabosco sang and perhaps acted as director of the musical preparation for *Hymenaei* (1606) and composed or arranged music for the *Masque of Augurs* (1622).

Ferrabosco: Masque Songs

1605   *The Masque of Blackness*
        Twelfth Night, 6 January
        Old Banqueting House, Whitehall

       "Come away, come away"   *Ayres,* #3

1606   *Hymenaei*
        Marriage of the Earl of Essex and Lady Frances Howard
        5 January
        Old Banqueting House, Whitehall

       [Ferrabosco is commended for his songs by Jonson, but the music is not preserved.]

1608   *The Masque of Beauty*
        [Planned for] Twelfth Night, 10 January
        New Banqueting House, Whitehall

       "So Beauty on the waters stood"   *Ayres,* #21
       "If all these cupids"   *Ayres,* #18
       "It was no policy of court"   *Ayres,* #19
       "Yes, were the loves"   *Ayres,* #20
       "Had those that dwell in error"   *Ayres,* #22

1608   *Haddington Masque*
        Marriage of Viscount Haddington and Lady Elizabeth Radcliffe
        9 February
        Banqueting House, Whitehall

       "Why stays the Bridegroom"   *Ayres,* #11

1609	*The Masque of Queens* [Planned for the Christmas season], 2 February Banqueting House, Whitehall	
	"If all the ages of the earth"	*Ayres,* #23

1609, or Unknown celebration
    previous

	"Sing we the heroic grace"	*Ayres,* #12
	"Sing the riches of his skill"	*Ayres,* #13
	"Sing the nobles of his race"	*Ayres,* #14

1611	*Oberon* Christmas season 1 January Banqueting House, Whitehall	
	"Nay, nay, you must not stay"	*MS Songs,* #vi
	"Gentle Knights"	*MS Songs,* #vii

1611	*Love Freed from Ignorance and Folly* Planned for Christmas season, 3 February Banqueting House, Whitehall	
	"Oh! What a fault"	*MS Songs,* #viii
	"Senses by unjust force banish'd"	*MS Songs,* #ix
	"How near to good is what is fair"	*MS Songs,* #x

1622	*The Masque of Augurs* Twelfth Night, 6 January	

This was the first masque to be performed in the New Banqueting House, designed by Inigo Jones. Fire had destroyed the previous House in 1619.

[Ferrabosco is commended for his music by Jonson, but that music has not survived.]

    The style of these songs is not uniform, nor is their function, although some general characteristics can be cited. The songs have shapeliness, an obvious concern for the construction of the melodic line and the ordering of harmonies (particularly apparent in the cycles with three continuous songs), and a general movement from the more emphatic oratorical gestures and effects to a more melodic winding-down as the song progresses.

Ian Spink cites Ferrabosco's masque songs as being the vanguard of a new style in which "a more declamatory treatment of the voice is immediately noticeable, together with a chordal type of lute accompaniment characterized by a harmonically static bass."⁴

Spink overstates the case by not distinguishing between the kinds of declamation in lute-song and in continuo song (to which he sees the masque song as a necessary preliminary), and it is significant that the traits he finds important and new are found only in the very ceremonial songs of the masque. There the larger-than-life hyperbole of musical expression is necessitated by rhetorical circumstance: the declamation does not imitate natural speech as much as it resembles proclamation and oratory.

Spink's description of the declamatory nature of the voice part and the continuo style of accompaniment in Ferrabosco's "If all the ages of the Earth" (#23, *Masque of Queens*, 1609) defines his idea of the function of the declamatory style.

Ex. 1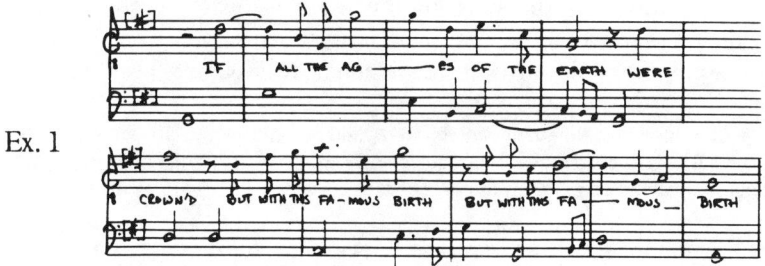

In particular, the opening illustrates the declamatory nature of the voice part and the continuo type of accompaniment. The effect is immediately arresting, and matches the high-flown verse admirably. Its ceremonial character is obvious, and as far removed from the delicious trifling of Rosseter as from the fervour of Danyel. Above all the aim seems to have been to make the words audible in a large hall (a new Banqueting Hall had been opened in Whitehall in 1608), clearly declaimed above an accompaniment sometimes of several lutes. Subtleties of harmonic nuance or polyphonic elaboration were unnecessary.⁵

This latter is an overstatement, for the style of the music is at least as much indebted to its oratorical function as it is to the place of performance. This is true at least in Ferrabosco's case, and his masque songs are stylistically more adventuresome than the contemporary settings of Campion, Coperario, and Lanier and certainly the equal of Johnson. The declamatory features, as Spink would have them, the sharply angled melodic figures and assertive vocal address, quickly become smooth and more regulated. The strict attention to the inflection and delivery of the words, as if in imitation of an exaggerated declaiming or oratorical speech, was usually relaxed as soon as the point had been made, as soon as the audience had been impressed by the significance of what they were hearing. It is rare to find an example in Ferrabosco's songs where his musical sophistication is not felt: in the balance of the structure, in varied, expressive melodic lines the shape of which complements the sense of the text not so much in rhythm as in reach, in coherent harmonic progress, modal flexibility and contrast, in the relation of bass to voice (which generally becomes closer as the song progresses), in the occasional use of syncopation, and in the use of repetitive devices such as sequence and imitation.

It is true that these masque songs owed little to the developments of Italian monody. There is no reason they should. The demands of the court masque were quite different than the concerns for freedom of declamation and personal expressiveness which fostered the Italian monody, and the attractive seductiveness of that style, that is, the ability of that style to move the passions of the listeners, was not suited for a delivery which was meant to impress in an impersonal way.

Thus, again, Spink is partly correct when he claims that

> By and large the lutesong writers were untouched (by the Italian style), and one gets the impression that Italianate composers such as Ferrabosco and Lanier had not so much heard the "new music" as heard *about* it.[6]

Ferrabosco's Italian songs are sufficient evidence to dismiss the second charge, and it was not until Lanier returned from Italy (1627) that he wrote "Hero and Leander."[7] But, just as Italian literature made its greatest mark on England in the period just before the defeat of the Armada, it appears that English music did not have any use for the Italian style, as such, in the reign of King James. The Italian Orfeo could transform the universe through the power of his musical expression, but England waited until Purcell for her Orpheus. It was the King who transformed the world of the masque into a universe of order and right, and music only celebrated this power. In Italy, Orfeo celebrated the power of music; in England, music celebrated the power of the King.[8]

The Italian mode of expression was based on imitation, a conscientious choice guided by the humanistic discussions of the effects of Greek drama and music. The English musicians did not have this theoretical model of what music should be and came much more slowly to a practice in which speech rhythms were more nearly imitated. The declamatory style which Lanier was to attempt in "Hero and Leander," and which would achieve much greater artistic fruition in the songs of William and Henry Lawes, shows a greater concern for the voice to imitate the rhythm and emphatic pitch-movement of spoken declamation.

The Masque Songs

Ferrabosco's manner in the masque songs is not simply a forerunner to Lanier's. Peter Walls emphasizes this, and thereby reminds us of the difficulty and danger of using the term "declamatory" without careful qualification.

> These [masque] songs demonstrate that Ferrabosco's masque song style is not simply an incipient declamatory style, but a medium which could project the dramatic idea that someone is actually proclaiming the joys of the occasion, and at the same time convey a sense of its splendid festivity. It was, in other words, a style carefully suited to the mood of the occasion, the dramatic nature of the entertainment, and the acoustic conditions in which the songs were performed. It is limiting to see it simply as heroic declamation, since that overlooked many of the most characteristic and appealing features of the songs, and since they are so different from the straight declamation that we see in Ferrabosco's Italian solo ayres (or, for that matter, in the English declamation of Lanier). It is important to recognize that the masque songs have a clear musical structure and that this, together with the rhythmic subtleties and harmonic nuances, gave them a sophistication which befitted their courtly context.[9]

Many of the masque songs demand attention to the words for practical, not musical reasons: they must be heard in the theater, and they often draw attention not only to the action and device of the masque but to the royal person in the audience. Consequently, they cannot be obscured in mood or message by excessive accompaniment nor can they be plumped with gratuitous or affective ornament, for the context of performance is inhospitable to such intimacy. Nor did the function of the songs permit such complexity of presentation. The artistic means which supported the political metaphor of the masque included the use of dance to mirror the order of the realm within the universal harmony, the use of stage perspective to focus attention on the sovereign, and the use of royal intervention to permit the solution of dramatic problems.

As mentioned above, songs of the masque could comment on the action, invite, describe, announce, and praise, but they were not vehicles for the singer's feelings. Essentially the range of use was from entertainment to hyperbolic praise, from the tuneful and easy lyric to the exalted and overblown panegyric. It is only in the latter end of this spectrum that the new, oratorical declamatory style evolved. Here is where the oratorical nature of these songs becomes distinctive and characteristic, not anomalous. Many of Ferrabosco's songs partake of exaggerated rhetorical emphasis, often in the use of musical figures which force attention to the manner of text delivery, but not to the customary extent found in his particularly celebratory praise-songs of the masque. Similarly, Ferrabosco's masque songs utilize devices of musical representation as much as, if not more than, his other songs, and both masque and nonmasque songs have coherent musical structure. Thus, a distinction of function must be made, even among the masque songs, for the declamatory oratorical characteristics are far more prominent in the celebratory songs.

Ferrabosco's masque songs provide a view of the development of the new style at its very beginning. Andrew Sabol contrasts Ferrabosco's style with that of another important composer and poet for court entertainment, Thomas Campion, whose metrical style and tuneful ayres received wide circulation.

> Stylistically the masque airs of Ferrabosco are far removed from those of Campion, being more ambitiously conceived and of greater depth. Their vocal lines, seldom as spontaneously tuneful as Campion's, are essentially declamatory and are worthy complements to Jonson's texts, reflecting them as judiciously as Campion's airs do his. Although Ferrabosco's are studied pieces, they frequently produce effects of sheer brilliance in execution. Their sophisticated grandeur was obviously intended to be realized by virtuosos, and they are intended for big voices in big halls.[10]

This description makes the songs themselves sound more esoteric than they are, for what is really missing in our attempts to recreate them in the mind is the panoply of the court masque itself. We can assume the presence of "virtuosos," Ferrabosco included, quite able to realize both the vocal and instrumental parts of the songs. Campion's songs are only pleasant in comparison.

Ferrabosco's masque songs are more emphatically and consistently oratorical than most of his other English songs. Invariably, though, the declamatory element is vitiated; it is only in the Italian songs that rather tuneful declamation is abandoned for impassioned recitative similar to that which Lanier would attempt to compose in the late 1620s. The masque songs are more generally characterized by a tunefulness effected by stepwise or triadic motion and a lack of gestural abruptness. The songs of praise are markedly more emphatic in gesture and far-flung in range, but all the pieces, including those with the strongest opening gestures, become smoother, often closing in a lyric vein with the bass, which often begins with quite static motion and infrequent articulation, gradually and increasingly partaking of the shape and metrical life of the melody and animating the harmonic life of the song. This is particularly true in the three songs beginning "If all these cupids" (#18-20) and "If all the ages of the earth" (#23).

The use of dissonance is rare in these songs, and occasionally the music seems somewhat awkwardly fashioned to the words. That feeling is often alleviated by a gentle application of cadential rubato, not as an affective device, but as a grace which allows the sense of the words to be more comfortably wedded to their accent and weight.

Pinning a definition on these songs (i.e., lute-song, declamatory ayre, continuo song, etc.) is difficult in that they partake of older styles yet tend toward—without fully realizing—styles which were refined and became more popular after Ferrabosco's death. One of the most prominent conservative elements is the use of repetition which, as we have seen in the nonmasque songs, adds to the ornament of the rhetoric but detracts from its immediacy and specificity. This sense of "distancing," combined with the careful melodic shaping and tonal plan of the songs, limits the extent of their dramatic possibility. They also demand a flexibility of performance similar to that required for Dowland's serious songs, particularly in matters of meter and accent. Unlike the freedom of declamation which the use of the basso continuo and improvised accompaniment inspired in the *nuove musiche*, the declamation of these songs never strays far from a metrical frame, though often playing against it in gentle syncopation and varying the weight of the accents of word and pitch by delay or anticipation. Here, too, Sabol's observations are to the point.

> Although all of Ferrabosco's masque airs have duple-meter time signatures, not any of them gives the effect of that meter entirely, so subtly do they fluctuate between duple and triple meter. In almost every air the declamation is heightened with strong accents on unimportant beats. The force of a strong downbeat is frequently vitiated through anticipations or, as in the closing measures of "Why stays the bridegroom," strikingly effective suspensions. At times, as in the concluding phrases of "If all the ages" and throughout the section beginning "How near to Good," in "Gentle Knights, Know Some Measure," the vocal line, with its wide skips is instrumental in character.[11]

It should be specified that there are two distinct ways of emphasizing the words by playing off the metric frame. The first is by setting a figure in triple meter against the prevailing duple; the second is by syncopation (anticipation or suspension). Ferrabosco does both. The latter method is most familiar from the continuo style, although the effect is rarely to vitiate the sense of downbeat, but rather to strengthen it and to emphasize the particular words. In this regard, it is important to recognize that the use of opening entrances after the first beat was to emphasize the voice against the accompaniment. The one exception in which the voice enters on the downbeat, "Nay, nay, you must not stay," presents an extreme rhetorical effect of imperative urgency as the voice and accompaniment begin simultaneously (*ex nihilo*).

The varying relationship of rhythm and meter within a less strongly metrical context than that to which we have become accustomed occurs also between text phrasing and sense. The discrete phrases are often linked together by overlappings of melodic and harmonic shapes or by the simple refusal of harmonic gestures to be fulfilled until the textual sense has been completed. The settings are of mood and meaning, rather than simply the rhythm and shape of the words, and in this regard the settings are conservative, looking backward to the more integrated polyphonic style or to that of the serious songs.

A striking example of Ferrabosco's ability to maintain the continuity of his thought occurs in the conclusion of "Senses by unjust force banish'd" (#ix) from *Love Freed from Ignorance and Folly* (1611). The text has this punctuation and scansion:

/ . / . / . / \
You who late possess'd more treasure

. / . / . / . /
(When eyes fed on what did shine,

. / . / . / . /
And ears drank what was divine),

/ . / . / . / \
Than the earth's broad arms could measure.

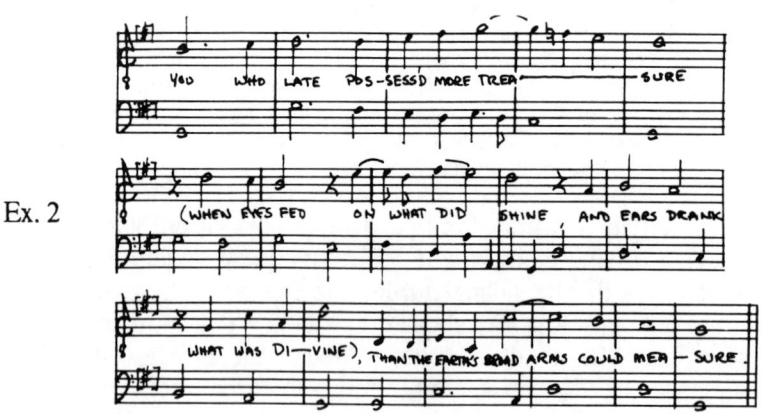

Ex. 2

The parenthetical couplet is distinguished from the outer lines not only by rhyme, but also by the reversal of the first foot and loss of a syllable in each line. Ferrabosco not only delays a "final" cadence until the completion of the entire thought, but he provides a real sense of parenthesis for the inner couplet by musical means. On the harmonic level the first phrase (line) concludes with a played cadence. The next line ends on the dominant, but the movement back to the tonic (6) at the end of the third line is not strongly stated. The fourth line, in effect, picks up where the first left off, concluding with a I-IV-(ii)-V-I progression which, though it includes the subdominant, strongly emphasizes the dominant. The very discrete and distinct bass movement, with slower harmonic rhythm, of the outer phrases—outlining I-IV-I; I-IV-V-I—contrasts with the character of the bass in the inner phrases. There the bass traverses an octave in basically conjunct motion. Structurally the harmonic movement is suspended; there is no real progression.

This harmonic parenthesis is matched by the melodic structure. In the first phrase the voice rises to a climactic g″, concluding on d″. The inner phrases begin and end on he same d″, meandering thereabout without a sense of direction and without exceeding the limits of the octave g″-g′. The anacrusic figure at the beginning of the final phrase, the lower notes which provide the sense of spaciousness in the octave leap, breaks the aimlessness and prepares for the continuation of the descent through the second half of the octave: c″, b′, a′, g′. That the octave descent g″-g′ (larger in terms of structure and time) should incorporate a lower octave leap (c′-c″) shows how well Ferrabosco integrated an awareness of text with the needs of musical structure, for the c′-c″ leap aptly occurs at the mention of the "earth's broad arms." But it is reinforced by the recognition, in the listener's ear, of the longer descent. That the inner phrases could be excised without loss of musical meaning shows that Ferrabosco was presenting a "reading" of the poem. That they cannot be excised without loss of musical effect shows that he, in fact, "could measure" the song, giving it a more than simple representational quality of breadth. Thus, textual function is revealed by the musical structure which provides a most subtle representation of harmonic and temporal spaciousness to inform the final line.

Ferrabosco's masque songs are dispassionate, they celebrate rather than move. That they are well-crafted is particularly demonstrated by those published with lute accompaniment in the *Ayres*. The manuscript sources, for voice and bass instrument, confirm the general tone of ceremonial objectivity, rhetorical ornament, and lack of emotional immediacy. Even the exception proves the rule. The one extant, highly ornamented version of one of Ferrabosco's songs is that of "Why stays the bridegroom" which appears in Christ Church MS 439, pp. 60-61. The embellishments are elaborately ornate decorations, heightening the statement but emphasizing its artificial manner, not despite several instances of word-painting its meaning. (See below, pp. 151-156 for transcriptions and discussion.) There we have a glimpse of the "sheer brilliance" one of these songs could attain, a brilliance which is musically convincing and rhetorically persuasive, not textually responsive.

In these masque songs Ferrabosco did not avoid harmonic nuance or melodic interaction between voice and bass. However, the style was clearly meant to impress the hearers, not to express the text or emotion of the situation. It remained, essentially, a nondramatic style in Ferrabosco's hands, unlike the works of the *seconda prattica* which were intended to promote a dramatic, personal style. The distinction is most clearly seen in the contrast of Ferrabosco's Italian songs with those of the masques.

Many of Lanier's masque songs are formed similarly to Ferrabosco's, i.e., tonal songs beginning with emphatic declamatory gestures which subside into more lyrical passages. Lanier, however, restricts his harmonic excursiveness and, in his dialogues, develops a truer sense of recitative with basso continuo, though without Ferrabosco's sense of shapeliness. But it must be remembered that there is nothing in Lanier's masque songs, or Ferrabosco's, which approaches the recitative of "Hero and Leander."

As mentioned above, Jonson's commendation of Lanier's contribution to *Lovers Made Men* (1617), "in stylo recitativo," appeared only in the 1640 folio volume of Jonson's collected works, not in the 1618 quarto edition of the masque. Without the music for the masque we are at a loss to specify exactly what Jonson meant.

The panegyric or heroic style, which Ferrabosco mastered so well in his brief collaboration with Jonson, is antithetical to the lyric. In the latter, we, as audience, are invited to partake of the intimacy of the situation. In some cases the lyric will be formulaic and generalized, and our delight is in the treatment of the formulas. In others, we are invited (by the music particularly) to participate as if we overheard or identified with the singer without becoming dramatically involved. In the heroic style which informs aspects of the masque, the entire theatre is turned into an arena of praise. There is no intimacy, but there is a grandiloquent stylized expression focused on the ruler who, though present, paradoxically assumed the mantle of gods or legendary heroes. This ennoblement, usually accomplished in a fictive distance of time and place, which by artistic device was made to coalesce with the present at the conclusion of the masque, had to be carried out in the confines of the immediacy of the Banqueting House. Thus, the distance had to be created not only by visual spendour and allegory of device, but by theatrical perspective and the heightened rhetorical style and gestures of the musical oratory.

VIII

Masque Songs, 1605-1608:
The Masque of Blackness and The Masque of Beauty

The songs which Ferrabosco wrote for the masques range in style from the tunefully modest "Come away, come away" (#3) to the obeisant and disjointed "How near to Good" (#x).

Ex. 1a

Ex. 1b

"Come away, come away," from the *Masque of Blacknesse* (1605), is the earliest datable song we know of Ferrabosco, and it is the only song, of the several in the masque, to have survived. In Jonson's text it is simply called "Song," and it appears to call the blackened ladies, whose tale we are following, back to the ocean.

> Their own single dance ended, as they were about to make choice of their men [to dance], one from the sea was heard to call 'em with this charm, sung by a tenor voice.[1]

The very opening of the song is one of its most interesting aspects. Not only is the melody shaped to command attention by the movement over a diminished fourth accompanied by the progression from tonic (g) to dominant, but the declamation of the text is naturally speech-like. That this particular phrase conveys both insistence and resignation is due to the rhythm of the declamation combined with the melodic interval: the first "come away" rushes to the last syllable in dramatic rising intensity, while the second falls back, unable to sustain the intensity and directness, with the doubly slower declamation of expression. It has been remarked earlier that this phrase, text and melody, also appear in "Come home, my troubled thoughts," the song which immediately precedes this one (on the facing page) in the *Ayres*. In that case, as in this song, there is a dramatic justification for the use of the declamatory gesture, for the poet is apostrophizing his own thoughts on human vanity. Peter Walls sees in this dramatic justification the key to Ferrabosco's use of declamatory gestures which articulate the rhythm of the words and, in addition, mirror their inflection and intensity. Wall also speculates that this self-quotation may have significance beyond the aptness of the phrasing.

> Printed side-by-side in the 1609 publication, however, the first song looks very much like an ironic (although possibly unintentional) comment on the vanity of such courtly pursuits as those served by the masque song.[2]

It is in the vocal line that the subtlety of the song lies, for the accompaniment is almost entirely chordal. There are instances of imitation, or relation, between voice and accompaniment, particularly in the use of the filled-in fourth and the device of prolepsis by the bass, already seen in several of the other English songs.

Ex. 2a

Ex. 2b

The relation of accompaniment to voice (in Ex. 2b) is not precisely imitation; at least, it seems that the apparent imitation is not conscientious but results from a quite independent intervallic progression at the words "Sirens of the Lands." This passage emphasizes the expansion of melodic figure: from a third in the opening gesture to the fourth of the second phrase, the fifth of the next phrases, then the return to, essentially, a fourth in the second section. An ascending fourth used in an inner voice of the accompaniment in Ex. 2a is also used in the final line of the vocal part where, expanded to a fifth, it confirms the musical direction of the song (to a cadence on G) as well as emphasizing the figural unity of the musical fabric.

Ex. 3

The song, in fact, presents a reading of the poem in which the cadences and repetitions all serve to clarify the meaning of the text. The first two lines emphasize the tonic. The third, moving to the dominant, states a condition the results of which are presented in the concluding three lines without a rest. These lines are then repeated, but the repetition is more as echo than as oratory. Looking at the last four lines of the text, we can recognize both the structure of the argument and the difficulty it presents to the composer who must acknowledge the enjambments and yet construct coherent phrases.

/ . / . / . /
If you do not stop-pe your ear,

/ . / . / . /
We shall have more cause to fear

/ . / . / . /
Sirens of the land, than they

. / . / . / . /
To doubt the Sirens of the sea.

Ferrabosco molds the cadences of his phrases to the individual lines: G=i-V; / i-i; i-♭III; (♭III-IV)-V-I. What seems to be wanton disregard of the enjambment of the final lines is not; the weak cadence on ♭III does not stop the musical momentum (although the extension of time values in the voice and the falling fifth almost does). In the movement from the second to third lines, the stresses on both "fear" and "Si-(rens)" are reproduced in the voice without a change of harmony to interrupt.

Ex. 4

That the setting of the final line is momentarily out of kilter with the accents of the text, apparently failing to accommodate the change from trochaic to iambic feet in the poetry, is, indeed, a matter of "doubt." Here, as in the first line of this example, the syncopation provides some buoyancy and emphasis.[3]

In the opening phrases, Ferrabosco manages variety and similarity to good effect. Both in time and by extension upwards a step, the second phrase expands the melodic material of the first while, at the same time, including the bass in the material and metric activity of the voice. Instead of simply repeating the declamatory pattern of the first words, "We grow" is given more time, more emphasis. These off-beat figures, e.g., "We" and "if," extending from a weak beat into the strong beat their metrical position would grant them in the poetry, are typical beginning figures for Ferrabosco. They are a sham of syncopation, for the meter is regular, and they operate against that regularity in an anticipatory and anacrusic fashion. Only in the final phrase is their intent and effect that of syncopation, a momentary conflict of accents which is quickly resolved.

Generally, though, the text-setting is not particularly attentive to the qualities of individual words. The success of the setting owes much to the complementarity of the melodic phrases which modestly emphasize the fourths around g. The contrasts of the upper and lower areas are neatly balanced, and the extension to the upper d" is more effective because it follows the lower d' immediately. The one unconvincing melodic gesture occurs at the end of the penultimate line, where the drop of the fifth is an unaccustomed cadential figure and bounces, more than leads, into the next line. But it is in the detail of the lines that Ferrabosco distinguishes himself from a composer like Campion, for although the treatment of the text is basically conservative, the vocal line reflects both declamatory awareness and an understanding of the construction of the poem. There is a modest amount of both visual and pathetic pictorialism: the affective diminished fourth in the first phrase, the sense of melodic triple-time "stop-ped" by the return to duple at "stop-pe," the dubious leaps which span a quick seventh at the words "than they to [doubt]," and the syncopations which follow. The harmonic scheme is simple, but follows the momentum of the text, and the vocal range is an element of the overall structure, as well. So, too, is the shape of the bass line which, in both sections, includes a descent of an octave. Both of these descents are concluded before the end of their respective sections, but while the second section concludes with an authentic cadence, the similarly intended harmonic conclusion of the first section extends into the second—linking and binding the sections together. These features recur in many of Ferrabosco's songs, as does the balance of dominant and relative major areas which contributes to (or is a result of) the modal flexibility of these settings.

The *Masques of Blacknesse* (1605) and *Beautie* (1608) complement each other and were separated in performance by three years' time only because the court required wedding masques for the two intervening Christmas seasons. It is not known if the songs for both masques were composed at the same time, but those from the *Masque of Beautie* share some qualities with the tuneful and clear phrasing of "Come away, come away," which makes their discussion appropriate here.

The songs of the *Masque of Beautie* provide a long discourse on the platonic theory of beauty and love. The first song, for which (like many of the masque songs) we lack a setting, occurs after the discovery of the scene and presents the argument of the masque, its theme or "device," by implication.

> When Love at first did move
> From out of chaos, brightened
> So was the world, and lightened
> As now!
>
> Yield, night, then to light,
> As blackness hath to beauty,
> Which is but the same duty,
> It was for Beauty that the world was made,
> And where she reigns Love's lights admit no shade.[4]

The argument is not rigorously made in this or any of the other songs, but these must rank as some of the most difficult texts to be set in the guise of an "entertainment." The political mythology of order, supported metaphorically by the figure dances and the analogy of James I as invested with the properties of the platonic sun, is the extreme early seventeenth-century example of court panegyric, and the songs begin to match the high-flown intent and expression of the verse.

The first of the songs which has survived, "So Beauty on the Waters stood" (#21), followed the first formal dance and, "sung by a loud Tenor," celebrated the masquers who remained standing on the floor in the figure of a diamond. The elaborate analogy which the masque supports: that the King's power is akin to that of the sun, i.e., Platonic Love, is simply stated in the opening lines which are given a very neatly constructed antecedent-consequent musical setting.

Ex. 5

The symmetry of these phrases, which enclose the tonic (C), is extraordinary: not only are the melodic lines and harmonic progressions complementary, but the vocal rhythms are identical and the bass line varies only to effect the move to dominant or tonic.

The movement of the bass is most interesting in this song, for although it was published as a lute song, there is only one measure of quasi-contrapuntal invigoration of the inner parts. Moreover, that seems to arise in order to accommodate a textual problem by weakening the effect of the deceptive cadence on "taught" in order that the textual idea could continue to completion.

Ex. 6

The bass moves in the same time frame with the voice and partakes in long-range imitations and sequences while still providing a very regular vehicle for harmonic rhythm and tonal focus.

Ex. 7a

Ex. 7b

Except for the moving eighth-notes at the words "And then a motion" and the fall of a fifth to "earth" (which interrupts the larger melodic sequence of the final phrases), there is little occasion for musical pictorialism. An exception is the sense of harmonic and melodic balance of the first two phrases, concluding with the cadence which, aptly, "did with concord all inspire." Peter Walls's assertion that the "rhythmic disposition of the words in this song is undisturbed and as close to natural speech as these ayres ever come" must be qualified.[5] Certainly Ferrabosco's typical exaggeration of the first word-note of a melodic phrase is wholly artificial — a rhetorical device often in opposition to natural speech. Not only is this apparent in the opening phrases, but, even more so, in the awkwardnesses of the long notes used to set "*That elder than him-self are thought.*" These can only be understood in rhetorical context (to emphasize the paradox which must be resolved), for they confound the rhythm and accent of the words.

What we have, then, is description accomplished not only by the text, but by the formality and repetition of the opening lines and the shapeliness of the melody. The smooth passages of the harmonies (and their restricted range) and the rhythmic balance of the song have a lulling quality, as if the argument were decoration and needed no insistence. The textual content of the poem and the manner of the song are related, for the "concord" of the text is surely found in the parellelisms and symmetry of the song, in its balance around the middle phrases, in the matching of ascending and descending motions (in both voice and bass), in the general evenness of delivery and in the quiet, steady harmonies.

The shapeliness of the piece is not only in the smaller phrases. The melodic progress of the song can be heard thus, phrase by phrase.

Even the consistently off-beat entrances of the voice, including the more animated pattern ♪♪♪ of the last line, cannot inform such an arch with urgency.

Following this somewhat obscure text set so comfortably was a second dance, "more subtle and full of change than the former." Jonson's directions, after the fact, give an impression of the effect of these dances.

[They were] so exquisitely performed as the King's majesty, incited first by his own liking to that which all others there present wishes, required them both again, after some time of dancing with the lords. Which time, to give them respite, was intermitted this song, first by a treble voice in this manner:

> If all these Cupids now were blind (#18)
> As is their wanton brother;
> Or play should put it in their minds
> To shoot at one another;
> [: What pretty battle they would make,
> If they their objects should mistake,
> And each one wound (✕) his mother. :]

Which was seconded by another treble, thus

> It was no polity of court, (#19)
> As though the place be charmèd,
> To let, in earnest or in sport,
> So many Loves in armèd.
> [: For say the dames should with their eyes
> Upon the hearts here mean surprise,
> Were not the men (✕ ✕) like harmed? :]

To which a tenor answered

> Yes, were the Loves or false or straying; (#20)
> Or Beauty not their beauty weighing.
> But here no such deceit is mixed;
> There flames are pure, their eyes are fixed;
> They do not war (✕) with different darts,
> But strike a music of like hearts.
> [slightly modified repeat in the song.]

In the *Ayres* these are published as one entity, the three parts distinguished by the changes of mode and clef (singing voice). The first song is a tuneful lyric, which playfully and gently proposes the wounding of Venus by blind cupids (in seeming reference to the cupids on the stage in the masque).

But these stage cupids are not "wanton" cupids interested in simple and trifling pleasures; they have sight, and the tone of the second song becomes more exalted as the second treble speaks of the policy of court. The concluding tenor abandons all pretense of lyric songfulness and indulges in the rhetoric of announcement and flattery rising to an intensity of pitch and decoration unmatched in the previous songs.

In his discussion of the platonic argument which is the foundation of the *Masques of Blacknesse* and *Beautie*, D. J. Gordon explains the meaning of these texts. The sighted cupids have to see,

> . . . because according to the Platonists of the Renaissance, Love is the desire to enjoy beauty, and beauty can only be apprehended by sight. There came, then, to be two Cupids: the "seeing" Cupid who was associated with the higher love, and the blind Cupid who was associated with earthly, sensual love.[6]

Jonson's own annotation confirms this view, contrasting the wanton, blind Cupid, concerned with individual beauties, to these sighted Cupids informed with the idea of Beauty which surpasses in clarity and appeal any individual exemplar.

> I make these different from him, which they fayne, *caecum cupidinem*, or *petulantem*, as I expresse beneath in the third song, these being chaste *Loves*, that attend a more divine beautie, then that of *Loves* commune parent.[7]

The lines of the preceding song, "So beautie on the waters stood / When Love had sever'd earth, from flood!," also require explication, and Gordon cites Ficino.

> The desire to propagate its own perfection is a form of love. Now absolute perfection is in the highest power of God; the divine Intelligence contemplates it, and the divine will desires to diffuse it beyond itself; and it is from this love that wishes to propagate itself that everything is created. Therefore Dionysius says, "Divine Love does not allow the king of the universe to live in himself, without bearing fruit."[8]

Gordon argues that the final lines of that song,

> And then a motion he them taught
> That elder than himself was thought,
> Which thought was, yet, the child of earth,
> For Love is elder than his birth.

are probably a reference to a cardinal concept in Ficino's system, the *circuitus spiritualis*, that "self-reverting current from God, the generating power of which is Love: in Love God created the world and, in Love, every creature aspires to return to Him."[9]

The central idea of the masques, that the King's presence turns Blacknesse into Beautie, becomes a grand apotheosis, more than customary complimentary rhetorical formulae, in which James I is "given the position and function assigned to the sun in the theory of beauty held by the Florentine Platonists."[10]

Such an argument must invade the eyes more than the ears, and, perhaps for that reason, the masque was a suitable vehicle even though the songs strike one as relatively detached from the depth of this textual argument. It seems likely, however, that the three songs beginning "If all these cupids" were intended as a syllogism and were performed as such: the first singer, on one side of the stage presenting the consequences of the apparent "If"; the second, answering from the other side, presenting the policy of the court which stands above such disorder; and the third, stating the reality of the situation ("But here no such deceit is mixed") and thus resolving the implied conflicts of the first two (the apparent and the real) into an ordered vision. Hyperbole of this extreme is appropriate to the masquing stage which consistently portrays illusion in the guise of reality, using analogy and metaphor to create a far more persuasive moment than honest description might. Ironically, "deceit" is the mode of portrayal, artifice the means.

Each of these songs has a basic ABB form (the most customary of Ferrabosco's forms), although this is subjected to some interesting variations in the third song, which is notably more complex than the others. The first song is particularly tuneful, charming in its regularity of phrasing, smooth flexibility of melody, evenness of declamation and harmonic movement, and clarity of musical destination.

That smooth and even presentation of the text is given point in the cute, bouncy beginning of the B section where the playing of the blind cupids is described by means of an angular figure, which is quickly softened, emphasizing the consonant sounds. The textual repetition, added by Ferrabosco, is set to a sequence which is imitated by the bass, as the concluding cadence is brought to the tonic (g/G).

Ex. 8a

Ex. 8b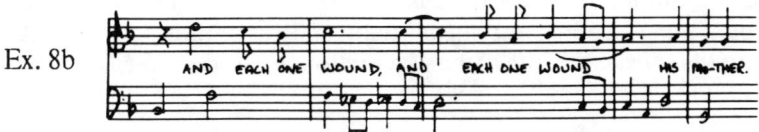

A more convincing instance of word-painting (one is hardly convinced of real "battle" in the example above) appears in the rush of motion at the word "wanton." Not only is the motion melodically wanton, but so, temporarily, are the harmonic rhythm and metric accents. An improvement

Ex. 9

might be made by substituting an E♭ for the g in the bass at "(wan)-ton," to emphasize the implied articulation of the harmonic rhythm and to point the cadence in a manner similar to the conclusion of the first phrase.

"It was no policy of court" changes tone abruptly, although it also begins in the minor. The bass, however, is far less active in the first section, and the melody, with larger leaps and greater variety of phrasing, tends toward a weightier formality. But the opening, strong gestures of the melody, which emphasize rhetorical pose at the expense of scansion, rather quickly loosen into gentler motion. At the same time, the bass becomes more active and, in the lute version, there is melodic participation in several parts introduced after the representational dotted rhythms of the voice and metric play which, in their "sport," recall the "pretty battles" of the first song.

Ex. 10

The artifice of the song is even more clearly presented in the three-line refrain beginning "For say the dames." A consistent melodic figure is shared between voice and accompaniment and contributes, in the final statement, to the musical rhyme of the two sections of the song (cf., Ex. 10).

Ex. 11

The harmonic movement of the phrase "Upon the hearts here mean surprise" is pictorial, and the dotted figure of "Upon" skews the accent and makes the line difficult to understand.

These two songs have dwelt on the witty circumstances of women wantonly captivating the courtiers. The opening seriousness of "court policy" in the second song is soon lost in the playful suppose and the harmlessly teasing repetition of "Were not the men . . . like harmèd?" The formal similarity of both songs, including their use of sequence and of similar figures to end their A and B sections, creates a parallelism which is not disturbed by the differences in the songs (specifically, the greater vigor and higher range of the second song and the contrast of falling and rising figures which end the respective pieces). As we shall see below, the harmonic progress of each song is different, with the second being far more interesting in that respect and in its use of the resources of the minor mode while all the more strongly asserting the major and thus balancing the first song. What is important here, of course, is that, dramatically, these songs are meant to be both parallel and balanced, and that is exactly what Ferrabosco has achieved in the music, even while giving each song its individual tone.

In the final song, the tenor reconciles the two previous songs in the conclusion of the argument, which exalts both the women and the attendant court in the flourish of fanciful rhetoric and melodic and metric decoration beginning at the words "But here no deceit is mixed." Not only does the startling change to the lower voice (indicated in the *Ayres* only by a change of clef) give the opening pronouncement of the song more gravity, but the melodic figures are more emphatic and wide-ranging. The change of gesture and tone at "But here" is revelatory as the emphasis changes from supposition regarding "wanton cupids" to description of the higher form embodied by the women. Melodic angularity and harmonic regularity are seemingly cast aside in metrical conflict between melody and accompaniment, and the cascading, triple-time descents of the voice garnish the hyperbole of praise in a figural *reverence* which temporarily turns the harmony to F major. This F major, of course, is the dominant of the relative major of g minor, but its use is striking here in two ways. First, F has not been used structurally in this manner before in these songs; second, the large scale of the melodic gesture, accompanied by this harmonic turn, focuses our attention on the character of the women — which is now about to be described. Thus the harmonic movement is rhetorical.

Ex. 12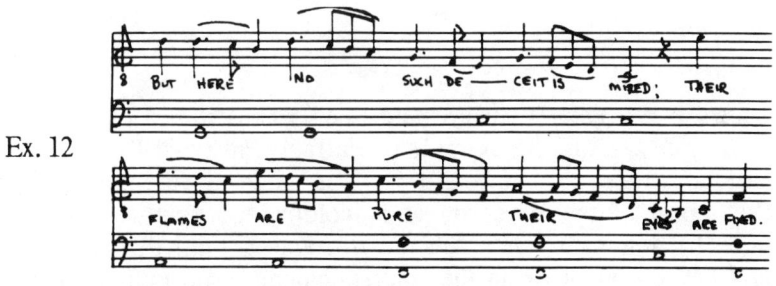

The regularity of the bass and the patterning of the melody is apparent, but of a wholly different nature than that of the previous songs. Their conflict is a "deceit," but quickly resolved, as the text demands.

These sweeping descents are answered by the exalted flights of the final, repeated compliment which informs us obliquely of the fulfillment, in these women of the masque, of the platonic idea of beauty. The syllabic setting, which characterized the first two of the songs, gives way entirely to the impression and expression of grand and sweeping gestures, even the bass enters into the activity of the melody.

Ex. 13a

Ex. 13b

The turn to F major ("their eyes are fixed") is used as a pivot from G major to g minor, a striking example of Ferrabosco's typical use of the resources of both modes. The return to G is made more emphatic by varying the repeat of the B section and avoiding the emphasis of the F/B♭ area. The dominant (D) which did not appear until the repeat of the words "they do not war" in the first statement, is prominent at the beginning of the repeat. The concluding phrase, "But strike a music of like hearts," reaffirms the tonic both in the management of cadences (thus confirming the validity of the deceptive cadence on "darts") and in the completion of the melodic figure in the bass by the movement of an inner part to complete the sequence. The sense of the tonic has never been lost in any of these songs, but its confirmation here is a most apt example of the sense of the poems and representational on a different level than, say, the robust gesture at "war."

In each of these songs musical phrases and textual lines match; the poetry makes no exceptional demands in this regard. Except for the opening of the second and third songs, which are arguably pronouncements, there is no extended sense that the melodic and rhythmic gestures are measured to the words—even, as in these cases,

Masque Songs, 1605-1608

measured against the normal accentuation of the text. More to the point is the difference as the sense of decoration in the first song becomes ceremonial rhetoric in the third; the melodic motion of the first is properly measured while that of the last gives the impression more of rhetorical ornament emphasizing the exaggerated heightening of speech demanded by the compliment, both in the opening phase and in the conclusion cited above. This is not ordinary speech, it is oratory.

Ex. 14

What is most apparently similar between the first and last songs, the melismatic melodic activity (which appears only briefly in the first song) is fundamentally different. In the first, it is applied to the expression for decoration; in the latter it is the expression.

Two other considerations contribute to the sense of weight in this last song. The melodic structure of Ferrabosco's songs, in general, is carefully gauged, and here we have an example of how that structure is enlarged to emphasize the climactic conclusion of the text. The first song has a range of only a ninth, d'-e♭" with the tessitura lying in the fifth above g'. In the second song, the range moves up to the higher g" and the melodic activity almost exclusively stays in the upper octave. The lower fifth of that octave is more prominent in the first section, while the upper fifth, as the voice climbs to the high g", is used in the B section until the final phrase which returns the level of the song to the lower g'. In the third song the range is expanded to a thirteenth, B♭-g', and, although the upper octave is used in the second section, the first encompasses almost the entire field, its d's and e's preparing the way for the f's and g's to follow. That the tenor is singing an octave lower than the previous trebles serves to make this expansion of the singer's range even more effective and forceful.

Similarly, the harmonic activity of these songs assumes increasing range, particularly in the manner by which Ferrabosco makes use of both major and minor chords on each scale degree within the tonality. The associations of G/g are more richly explored and exploited in the successive songs. The progress of the cadences of individual phrases may make this clear.

"If all these Cupids"

A) i-V;I/i-V; ♭III-V/♭III-♭III; iv-V-I
B) /: i-V/V-V; ♭III-V/♭III-iv$_6$-V-I :/

"It was no policy of court"

A) i-IV-I; I-IV-V-I; I-IV; V/♭III-♭III-V$_6$-i-V
B) / : ♭III-V/♭III--i-IV; V/♭III; v/V-I-IV; I-IV-V-I :/

"Yes, were the loves"

A) I-IV-I; v-ii-IV-I-V-I; I-IV-ii-V/♭III-IV-V/♭III
 (IV = V of V/♭III)
B) V/♭III-iv-V-i, V/♭III-i; ♭III$_6$-IV/♭III-V/♭III-♭-III;
 iv-V-I

Looking at the songs is easier than following these symbols, for what is apparent is the flexibility of relative major and tonic and the free use of major and minor harmonies on various scale degrees without losing the sense of the tonic, especially by means of common-tone chords a third apart (which allow movement from D to B♭, for example) or by dominant-tonic movement from a chord in the major mode to one which belongs to the minor mode (C, as IV of G, to F). The contrast of the prevailingly minor tone of the first song with the major of the second is actually incorporated into the third which, after the opening, simply harmonized pronouncements, elaborates the rhetoric of the following lines by modal variety and harmonic extension as well.

Thus, in every respect, the music matches the development and inflated context and style of the texts, from the light to the serious and ceremonial. Occasionally representing a specific word or textual reference by word-painting, the songs more fundamentally represent the texts. Using devices such as melisma and sequence and formal repetition, which are not usually associated with the declamatory panegyric style, the songs present the words clearly, without destroying accent or confounding meaning (if anything, enhancing it), and assume a character, in the last, of oratorical compliment most fitting to the circumstance. With the exception of "If all these cupids," each song from this masque begins with an exaggerated extension of the first note: a strictly musical gesture which draws attention to itself and, consequently, the text by its active opposition to the accentuation of the text. That the final two of these three songs just discussed approach the text, however briefly, in this manner further contrasts their textual concern with the perspicacity and celebration of the court with the first song's description of the fictive, blind cupids, who would exist only outside the arena of the court.

The final song from the *Masque of Beautie*, sung by "the first tenor" between the second and third entries of the masquers, concludes these commendatory acclamations with a moral drawn from yet another obscure philosophical reference.

> Had those that dwell in error foul,
> And hold that women have no soul,
> [: But seen these move, they would have then
> Said women were the souls of men.
> So they do move each heart and eye
> With the world's soul, true harmony.   :][11]

Even Jonson provides two notes to the text, which, from the depth and obscurity of argument, appears rather unpropitious for musical setting, despite its argument that Harmony (in which guise one of the women was portrayed) *is* the world's soul which gives movement to the visible body of the universe.[12]

The figure of Harmony, as Gordon points out, sums up the image of beauty.

> [It] emphasizes how the whole conception of [this] masque is based on that Pythagoro-Platonic tradition which the Renaissance inherited from the Middle Ages, and particularly from Macrobius, and which underlies the philosophy and symbolism of both Pico and Ficino.[13]

It is the specific quality of these women to partake in and to represent the World Soul and, by so doing, to demonstrate their own soul and the "error foul" of those who hold otherwise.

Whether such an argument would be appreciated by its auditors or participants in its entirety is beside the point. It is a marvelous vehicle for compliment, as Jonson's stage directions imply.

> [The dancers] danced galliards and corantos, and with those excellent graces, that the music appointed to celebrate them showed it could be silent no longer, but by the first tenor admired them thus.[14]

Thus, the masque was the most apt vehicle for the argument; the harmony of the music, the ordered harmony of the dance, and the physical harmony, even beauty of the dancers created such sympathetic resonances as to move the singer to respond.

Beginning with the exaggerated length of "Had," another Ferrabosco's typical emphatic opening gestures, the setting of the first two lines of text is an example of rhetorical declamation, even to the emphasis given the word "error" by duration and movement. There is no attempt to imitate natural speech; in some cases the durations serve to emphasize the words (e.g., "had") by their contrast to natural speech duration and stress, making the audience "hang" on the word. In fact, the complementarity and musical self-containment of these lines gives a sense of motionlessness, emphasized by the slow declamation and the even slower and very modest harmonic movement (F=I-V/V-V; I-V-I). The balancing of the harmonic movement in the two phrases is mirrored by the melodic motion: each phrase begins similarly, but the first phrase ascends to the seventh ("foul") where the ascent is frustrated and interrupted. The second phrase turns downward to return to the tonic note.

Ex. 15

The singer is at liberty, with so little activity in the accompaniment, to bend the notated time values considerably, but that flexibility is not really needed here for Ferrabosco has written the rhetoric into the vocal line, even to the point of the subtle agogic accentuation of the word "no" which occurs in a weak position in the poetry and in the melodic line, but is of utmost importance for understanding the *raison d'être* of this song.

The connection between lines two and three is one of idea, not of poetic enjambment, and Ferrabosco does not make that connection overtly: it is the common harmony linking the lines which makes it possible for the performer to continue the thought with only a minimal sense of interruption, the necessary comma to enclose the preceding, explanatory phrase. The vocal gesture at "move," which stirs an imitation in the bass, is a brief example of word-painting (on two levels: 1) the word "move"; 2) the world's/women's soul revealed by the movement it causes), and the announcement "they would have then / Said,:" is masterfully extended over the text line to the V/V, using the diminished fourth to force the conclusion on d'. Here Ferrabosco shows his awareness of and sensitivity to the enjambment and prepares, both rhetorically and musically, for the culminating statements to follow. This is the musical climax — the point of greatest emphasis and distance (V/V). The conclusion confirms the validity of the argument by returning, via V, to the tonic.

Ex. 16

The statement which now reverses the mistaken argument "Women were the souls of men": is set off on the dominant, and the rationale which follows moves from the dominant to the tonic, an apt harmonious and harmonic representation of the text's final couplet.

Thus, the song makes its point in a musical metaphor of the masque's Harmony, following the dances which have provided the visual, spatial metaphor. That all the motion of the song serves this purpose is seen in the brief subdominant excursion which attends the words "With the world's soul." Even this motion is concordant, and the apparent syncopation between voice and bass is yet another example of representation: the response of the voice to the bass reflecting the movement of heart and eye inspired by the women.

Ex. 17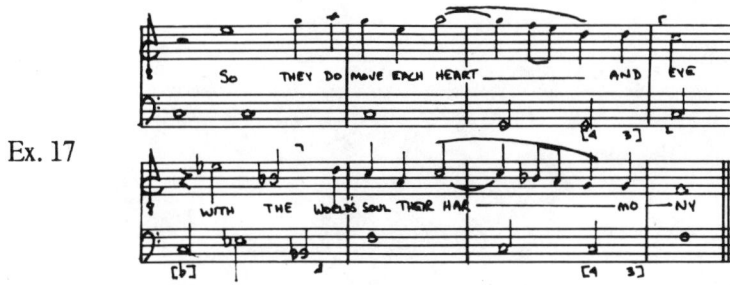

In this last example, it can also be seen that the melody of these lines, with a variation at the beginning of the final line, is derived directly from the melody of the opening lines (Example 13). This rounding of melodic form, more often involving cadential musical rhyme of the two sections of the song, has been the norm for the songs in this masque. So, too, is the carefully shaped arch of the melodic line which is so responsive to the textual rhetoric. This is only in a general sense, for the melodic figure which is so important in the opening and closing phrases admits of no specific "representation" and the individual notes are not as important as the contour. In a line such as "So they do move each heart and eye," the sense of the line is a progression from e-d-c with an extended "lift" or "move" up to g as an extension of e.

That there is little gestural vigor in the song does not diminish its rhetorical polish and extended argument. In a variety of ways the music contributes to the realization of the sense of the text without becoming enmeshed in its particulars. The performer is allowed the leeway of an orator: to shape the intensity of the lines, giving them energy and articulating the syntax which might (particularly at the beginning of the repeated section) otherwise be confounded. In such a manner the performer can achieve the ornate elegance of expression to which the melodiousness and harmonic clarity of the song aspire.

IX

Masque Songs, 1608-1609: A Court Celebration, The Haddington Masque, and The Masque of Queens

The sequence of songs which are numbered 12-14 in the *Ayres* may have been addressed to King James I, by whose coronation the union of Scotland and England, the "Peace that maketh one of two" (q.v., #14), was effected. The British Museum copy of the *Ayres* has an annotation, "A Comp[limen]t to ye Prince," pencilled above the first of these songs, and it is conceivable, by extension of the father's attributes, that they were intended for the young Prince. In any case, we know nothing of the event for which these songs were written, but they have no life outside a court celebration or entertainment. It is possible that they were occasional pieces, specifically composed for the coronation festivities where their homage to King James I would be most appropriate.

The poetry is — perhaps for the best — anonymous; its labored trochaic tread is no compliment to its author. The songs have a ceremonial tone, forthright and not in the least intimate. Together they probably form one long acclamation. Like the similar grouping of songs in the *Masque of Beautie*, they were sung by three singers in succession, two trebles followed by a tenor. Like those songs, these also are ordered carefully with attention to the effect of contrast and synthesis. The two pieces for treble voice are contrasting in mode, although they share the formal pattern aaB. Yet, all three share an opening rhythmic figure which, as we have seen in the song from the *Masque of Beauty*, serves to unify the oratorical presence of these songs. In fact, the figure ♩. ♩ or ♩ ♩. ♩ at the beginning of a textual phrase is a particularly prominent feature of these songs.

The first two songs, similar in form but contrasting in mode, complement each other and create a rhetorical balance. The third song is without repetition, but clearly divided into two sections. It is an invitation to the listeners to join the song of praise and, in its exuberance, it explores a more varied harmonic realm than either of the previous songs had by themselves, combining their harmonic range while reaching a climax of melodic activity and range as well.

In these songs, even more than in those from the *Masque of Beauty*, there is a conscientious sense of oratory. There is even less melodic activity in the inner parts of the accompaniment, and, with particular exceptions, the movement of the bass is less frequent and less interesting melodically. The declamatory effect of the songs comes from the forceful, articulated quality of the melody. This is only slightly related to speech rhythm or to representative melodic gesture, *per se*, arising more from phrase shapes which are derived from concern for oratorical gesture. The phrases, in fact, are like those of a politician: full of pauses but always moving on with emphatic beginnings tailing off into more melodious conclusion. It is the harmony which keeps the movement going and lets the listener know when an idea has been completed.

The stilted formality of expression is a function less of the musical repeat to new words as it is of the regularly occurring and exaggerated cadences and the common, emphatic rhythmic formula which begins each song ♩. ♪ |♩ — exempting them (properly) from an attribute of personal feeling and emotional immediacy. Much more than usual, Ferrabosco simply sets the words without regard to the reading of the poem, allowing the manner of the setting to suffice for more subtle presentation. The entire first quatrain of the first song is treated this way, as four distinct lines which had no other relation than succession, despite the fact that there is a break only between the first two lines. There is no difficulty with this kind of setting: the medium is the message. An integrated part of this medium is the musical concern for formal propriety which presents, in the first two songs, a repeat of the opening phrases of the music to set, also, the third and fourth lines of the poem. Thus, rhetorical pose and musical form take precedence over other textual considerations such as specific word-rhythm and awareness of enjambments in order to present an impersonal, one might even say official, and properly measured, extravagantly formal obeisance.

What offsets the inadequacy of the reading from a poetic standpoint is the effectiveness of the presentation of the words and the harmonic motion from the tonic (C) to the major submediant. The setting is simple and uncluttered, and directs attention to the object of praise—precisely what it should do. The emphasis on the dominant side of the tonic in this song is strong with the major submediant exploiting its common-tone relation to the tonic as well as its role (i.e., A-D-G-C) in the circle of fifths. This is particularly true at the beginning of the second section of the song when the melodic ascent and harmonic extension reach the limit from which they must return.

Ex. 1

The next phrases return the song to the tonic via the circle of fifths, but not without the reminder of modal flexibility at the word "comely" over the subdominant. This last phrase, in particular, is an example of awkward text-setting if taken literally. But there is no need to rush and every reason to stretch the time to avoid rushing the eight-notes and consonantal sounds. The expansion of time is also needed to avoid rushing into the subdominant, which with all the emphasis placed on the dominant side of the tonic, had not appeared previously in the song. It is a charm—"something rich and rare" in the piece—which expands the harmonic range which makes a more convincing cadence.

Ex. 2

Ex. 3

That the rests are used, in effect, as textual caesurae is evident from the treatment of "by nature." They are flexible and allow the singer to respond to the accompaniment—here in a relatively melodious way—without interrupting the piece.

The second song makes considerably greater use of the minor mode in the a sections, and the bass is much more active. But here the problems of style versus sense are more noticeable. The gestures of the melody, hardly more than written-out inflectional ornaments in some cases, do not connect at times. The melodic phrase which succeeds with one text is merely choppy and obtrusive with the second.

Ex. 4

Here, however, is a problem of reading the poem, for the first two lines of the poem introduce four lines of attributes which are followed by a new commendation containing its own problems of interpretation. The repetition of the music for the first two lines of the poem, in setting the third and fourth lines as in the first song, clearly is contrary to the structure of the poetic argument (although not to its rhyme-scheme).

> Sing the riches of his skill,
> Long by studious toil provided;
> Wit that never guideth ill,
> Will that never ill is guided;
> Judgment that can best discern,
> Memory that needs not learn;
> Courage where such thoughts assemble;
> Justly may his haters tremble.

The misfitting of gesture and sense is most obvious in the second section at the end of the second phrase.[1]

Ex. 5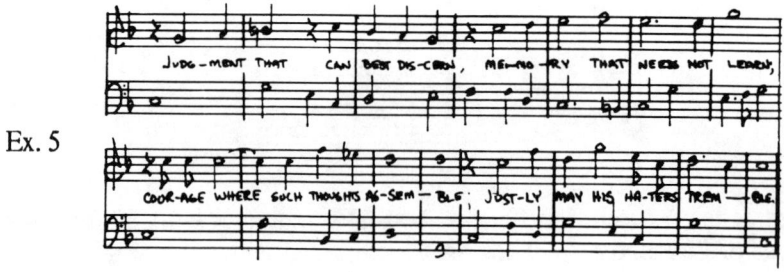

Here (at "Memory that needs not learn") the musical syntax and gesture demand completion, thereby creating the feeling that the text, also, wants completion, i.e., an object for the verb "learn." But, apparently, the poet did not provide one, for the next line begins with "Courage" treated as another attribute, similar to Judgment and Memory, Wit and Will. The reading which the music prepares us for, but does not deliver, is this:

> Wit...
> Wisdom....
> Judgment...
> Memory that needs not learn / Courage.
> Where such thoughts assemble,
> Justly may his haters tremble.

So, Ferrabosco, having set us up for the continuation to the word "Courage," deceives our expectation and presents a cramped and rushed setting (although typically declamatory and subject to more emphasis) of the word which now provides neither the completion (noun-attribute) he implied nor the verb-quality (and the derived, implicit exhortation, "have courage") which the poet intended.[2]

The final line sets up conflicting accents in the midst of the bass-voice imitation, perhaps as word-painting in anticipation of "tremble." The awkwardness of the vocal line is caused by the different demands of the poetry and situation for emphasis and accent. Both "(Just)-ly" and "his" are unaccented in the poetry but given prominent pitch accents in the phrase, "his" being the climax of the melodic line and, by its reference to James I (or Prince Henry), the point to which the song was building. (The reading, "Jústly máy hís háters trémble," is quite justified.) The successive leaps of fourths and the problem of accentuation make this melodic line unique and the most troublesome of the song, but there is no denying the specificity of "his" emphasized by pitch, duration, imitation, and cross-accent.[3]

The final song, like the final song of the cycle in the *Masque of Beauty*, has a larger range melodically (a twelfth, compared to the sixth and octave of the first two songs) and harmonically, although it uses several of the melodic figures and declamatory rhythms present in the earlier pieces. It is in the use of harmony as a structural element, in two ways, that this song is most interesting and illuminating. In the first section of the song, the overall movement is from the tonic (C) to the dominant, but this movement is characterized by an excursion into harmonic areas of the minor tonic (an area explored, though not as far, in the second song) and reached by proceeding plagally down the circle of fifths (revealing a fundamental closeness of the minor and subdominant regions). The second section of the song, which established the return from the dominant to the tonic, uses dominant extensions, the only implication of borrowing from the minor coming at the beginning of the section at the words "Peace that maketh one of two." After that point, the return to the tonic major is complete.

The excursion to the minor realm is also pictorial, beginning at the words "Breaking all the bounds of place," and follows the two short opening phrases which have affirmed the major tonic: 1) I-IV-I; 2) I-vi-iii(I)-V-I.[4] The third-related chords of these two phrases are uninflected, but in the following phrases we find a quick demonstration of Ferrabosco's use, within one tonality, of both major and minor inflections of scale degrees and of harmonies built upon these variable degrees. The words "breaking the bounds of place" are set to a precipitous descent down the plagal side of the key circle: C-F-B♭-E♭-A♭, broken only by the use of A♭ as N/V. This, certainly, is pictorial, but it also demonstrates the aforementioned closeness of the plagal area and minor mode. That the return to the major is made in the next phrase, to the words "Peace that maketh one of two"—an apt pictorialism musically as well as politically.[5]

Ex. 6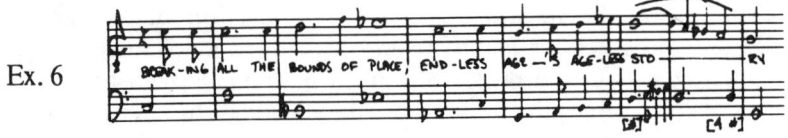

That return to the major uses a third-related harmony, but one which can be comprehended only in the major mode (see also the opening phrases of the first song). Here, then, the submediant in its various guises is used as a balancing agent around the fulcrum of the tonic.

Ex. 7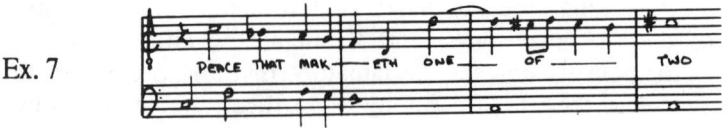

For the most part the melodic content of these songs has been unexceptional except for the careful management of range. The movement has been generally smooth, the delivery moderately stylized until the final flourish. Continuing from the example above, the song concludes with a fanfare of hectoring which whirls the song from a climactic high point at the delayed arrival of the tonic through a sequence of motions which confirm that tonic. The harmonic rhythm changes become quicker and are set off against the vocal sequence; the vocal figure is more angular, moves more precipitously, and is in triple-time. Both relax into the final cadence which uncomplicatedly returns to the previous level of metric activity, grounding the voice in its lowest range, and clarifying the frenzy of harmonic motion with a I-IV-V-I cadence — all of this most suitable for the person in whom we are to find "Justice fixed."[6]

Ex. 8

The final phrase, with the g held over into the F chord ("mercy"), is momentarily awkward, and the entire passage is subject to criticism regarding the fidelity of declamation, but the latter is a concern entirely out-of-place. The passage is a rhetorical ornament which satisfies the musical needs of the piece and the sense and purpose of the text. One would expect that this passage, in performance, would receive an expansive and unhurried performance fitting the intended majestic climax of the expression.

"Why stays the bridegroom" (#11) is a setting of one stanza of the Epithalamion which concluded the *Haddington Masque*, performed, Jonson tells us, "with nuptial songs, at the Lord Viscount Haddington's marriage on Shrove Tuesday at night, [February 9,] 1608."[7] The masque, proper, consisted of this long wedding-song interspersed with dances between the stanzas, four dances in all, "full of elegancy and curious device." Jonson reports on the performance in his description.

> The two latter [dances] were made by Master Thomas Giles, the two first by Master Hierome Herne, who in the persons of the two cyclops beat a time to them with their hammers. The tunes were Master Alfonso Ferrabosco's. The device and act of the scene, Master Inigo Jones his, with addition of the trophies. For the invention of the whole and the verses, *Assertor qui dicat esse meos, Imponet plagiario pudorem.*

The attire of the masquers throughout was most graceful and noble, partaking of the best both ancient and later figure. The colors carnation and silver, enriched both the embroidery and lace. The dressing of their heads, feathers and jewels, and so excellently ordered to the rest of the habit as all would suffer under any description after the show. Their performance of all so magnificent and illustrious that nothing can add to the seal of it. . . .[8]

Although the music for all the songs (stanzas) is attributed to Ferrabosco, only the setting of the fifth stanza, without the choral refrain "Shine, Hesperus, shine forth, thou wishèd star!," has survived. The verse is subtly varied, with numerous enjambments and irregular line lengths.

> Why stays the bridegroom to invade
> Her that would be a matron made?
> Good night, whilst yet we may
> Goodnight to you a virgin say:
> [: Tomorrow, rise the same
> Your mother is, and use a nobler name.
> Speed well in Hymen's war,
> That what you are
> By your perfection we
> And all may see.   :][9]

Like most of Ferrabosco's songs, this has two sections. The first consists of two nearly identical phrases which are harmonically complementary and exploit the area of the mediant (relative major) and the brightness of the tonic major (A) for contrast and effect.

Ex. 9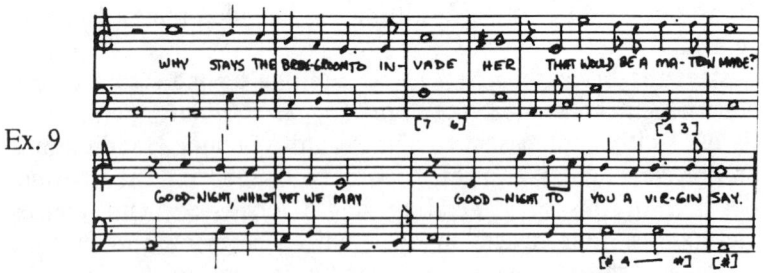

The progression of the first phrase, which veers to the relative major/mediant, is simplified in the second which reasserts the tonic in typical antecedent-consequent fashion. The complementary harmonic relationship of the phrases and their melodic similarities create a feeling of balance, despite the difference in line-lengths. Though this constructive principle is musically oriented, it accommodates the words. For example, the extension of the first phrase's opening to the dominant acknowledges the enjambment of the textual lines as well as incorporating a delay ("stay") of that arrival. It is difficult here, and probably fruitless, to argue that this phrasing is pictorial, for the more important concern, clearly, is the proper reading of the text.

The exception proves the rule in this case, for the octave leap which begins the second section ("Tomorrow rise"), while admirably picturesque and reinforced by the accompaniment, is no surprise, having been heard twice in the first section. The figure has lost much of its capacity for specific allusion by its third appearance, although it emphasizes the upper range of the voice in this song and serves as a spring for the smaller leap to the high g'.

Ex. 10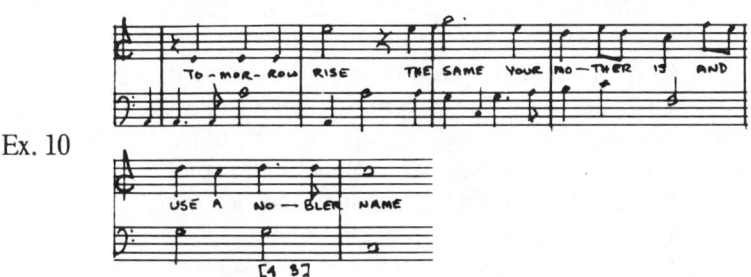

What allows the figure its pictorial validity is the delivery: the phrase emphasizes the word "rise" and does not soften the leap by a descending continuation of the phrase; the entire tessitura has risen in response to the figure.

The conclusion of the song includes another instance of word-painting, although it anticipates the appearance of the word: the introduction of musical perfection (triple-time) to represent the "perfection" of the bride in the accomplishment of her future pregnancy.

Ex. 11

On the whole, the sense of the text is admirably handled, not only in the treatment of the enjambment of lines one and two, and five and six (see Ex. 8), but also in the setting of these final four lines. These lines are not interrupted in the text, nor are they in the music; their sense depends on their continuity, which Ferrabosco preserves. In the poem they are almost a separable prayer for fertility, and this distinction Ferrabosco achieves also, by beginning the solemn declamation of the address on the submediant (F): "Speed well in Hymen's war."[10] The melodic ascents of the second section contrast with the descents of the first until the final couplet turns back down to rest. But the return is more complete and subtle, for, at the word "perfections" the bass clearly recapitulates the melody from the beginning of the song. One beat later that melody is restarted in the voice and passed to an inner voice of the accompaniment. This rounding of form attends the return of the voice to its middle range, as used in the first section, and the completion of the long, arching descent of the second section after its initial rising gesture.

The expansiveness of this song, both in range (an eleventh) and in phrasing, combined with its formal clarity and sensitivity to the poetic text, make it one of Ferrabosco's most satisfying pieces. Another contributing factor is the suave management of balance around the tonic, in which the third related areas from the minor mode are used to articulate the phrasing, while the dominant-tonic relationship defines the larger formal divisions.

This song appears anonymously in Christ Church MS 439, pp. 60-61, in a version for voice and basso continuo. It is one of several highly ornamented songs in the manuscript, and, as can be seen from the accompanying transcription, the ornamentation is no more affective than the original unadorned setting. It adds decorative flourish, a gestural effusiveness fitting to both text and circumstances. The figures contribute nothing to the words, but increase tremendously the rhetorical effect of the song and the stylization of its performance. Not simply decorative and not purposefully expressive, the ornaments serve their rhetorical function by being a little of both.

We cannot tell if this is Ferrabosco's ornamentation or whether this was a singer's "working" copy. There is no conclusive evidence that this setting, or one similar, was actually performed during the presentation of the masque, although it certainly would be appropriate, its rhetorically ornate filigree fitting the complimentary style.

The added notes are either inflectional and considered part of the note to which they lead, as at the beginning, or decorative, occurring primarily at cadences. Although these latter take extra time, there is no difficulty coordinating the cadential actions of accompaniment and voice.

While there must be some delay for the figures to be performed, the cadence tone is anticipated in the decoration and the antepenultimate note is reached with such security that the arrival of the cadence is uambiguous. None of these ornaments are dissonant or affectively expressive. The effect is still to transform the modestly garbed and somewhat monochrome version we know from the *Ayres* into a splendidly stylish and brilliant reflection of the pose of the masque itself.[11] Particular problems with this transcription from the manuscript certainly remain. Specific examples, aside from the bass c at the beginning, have to do with whether the ornaments are performed on the beat and when the sixth and seventh degrees should be raised at the conclusion of the song (f/f#; g/g#).

The *Masque of Queens* was "Celebrated from the House of Fame, by the queen of Great Britain with her ladies. At Whitehall, February 2, 1609."[12] It culminates in speeches by Heroic Virtue and Fame, both presented as they are depicted in Ripa's *Iconologia*, honoring Queen Anne. These speeches are followed by the descent of the masquers and three songs, only the second of which survives with music. Jonson's description of the proceedings after the discovery of the scene and the first song emphasizes the importance of the dance.

Here they lighted from their chariots and danced forth their first dance: then a second, immediately following it; both right curious and full of subtile and escellent changes . . . the first was to the coronets, the second to the violins. After which they took out the men and danced the measures, entertaining the time almost to the space of an hour with singular variety; when, to give them rest, from the music which attended the chariots, by that most excellent tenor voice and exact singer her majesty's servant Master John Allin, this ditty was sung.

SONG
When all the ages of the earth
Were crowned but in this famous birth,
And that, when they would boast their store
Of worthy queens, they knew no more,
How happier is that age, can give
A queen in whom all they do live![13]

There followed another dance, graphically disposed into letters honoring Prince Charles, designed by Thomas Giles. Then came some galliards and corantos, with the whole concluded by a final dance after which the dancers

took their chariots again, and triumphing about the stage, had their return to the House of Fame celebrated with this last song, whose notes, as of the former, were the work and honor of my excellent friend Alfonso Ferrabosco.[14]

Unfortunately, there is no trace of either the first or the last of these songs with their references to Fame and Virtue and to "Th'Assyrian pomp, the Persian pride,/Greeks' glory, and the Romans'." The song which remains, "If all the ages of the earth" (#23), sung to give the dancers rest, is grandiloquent, though short.

It was the ceremonial opening of this song which Spink cited to illustrate the "declamatory nature of the voice part and the continuo type of accompaniment."[15] This opening gesture is the most vigorous and striking of all the published *Ayres*, matched only by some of the songs in manuscript. It is a gesture which completely sacrifices the scansion of the first words for rhetorical effect.

Ex. 12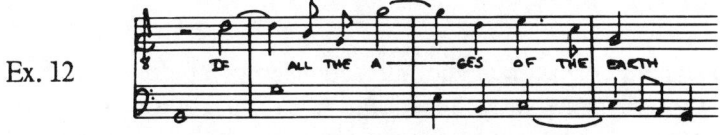

The energetic sense of celebratory fanfare and complimentary excess continues throughout the song, in an extraordinarily high tessitura. In many ways, however, it is not typical of Ferrabosco's output. The triadic figures are motivic and do not shape a melodic line. Propelled by the continuo, particularly in the first section, they provide successive surges of energy to support the hyperbole of the textural sentiment and the sustained rhetorical and musical height of the song. After the relaxation of pitch at the end of the first section and the relatively more sustained melodic structure at the beginning of the second, it is the return of overtly rhetorical gestures which provides the impetus to compel the conclusion: the imperious and impetuous sequence ("of worthy queens") and the marvelously adroit compliment which recalls the triadic figures of the first section ("Were crowned, but with this famous birth") and now crowns the entire piece: "A queen in whom they all do live". This textual summing up, reflected in the sustained height of the melodic line, is exactly the kind of political philosophy which the masque sustained: the body politic represented in the figure of the monarch.

The bass participates actively in this sense of motion. Its melodic interaction with the singer begins as early as the sixth measure (Ex. 13a), reaching a climax in the middle of the second section where the bass sequence at "Of worthy queens" is abruptly condensed: a successful and genuinely rhetorical gesture which carries the music forward (Ex. 13b).

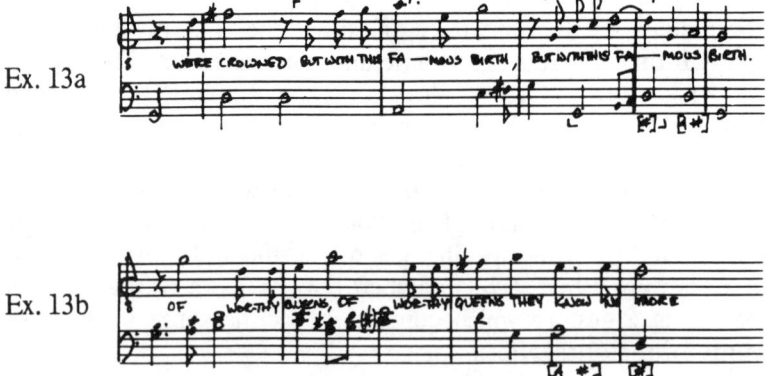

Ex. 13a

Ex. 13b

That these instances of bass-melodic interaction occur at the only times the text is repeated makes those repetitions even more emphatic. One need only compare the only other example of melodic interaction between voice and bass to contrast the rhetorical efficacy of these examples with the casual nature of that one which occurs at the beginning of the second section: see Ex. 14, "And when that they."

In the oratory of this piece, the text-setting is illustrative of the problem of defining "good declamation." In fact, text-setting does not appear to be Ferrabosco's concern here. He uses musical gestures suitable to the tone of the text, but not necessarily to the textual shape and weight of the words if taken by themselves — even interrupting the progress of the text in several instances. Devices of repetition and sequence, rhythm of delivery, melodic-rhythmic gesture, interruption, harmonic movement and melodic range all support a presentation of the text true, not to the weight and accent of the words, but to the nature of their purpose: to celebrate.[16]

In this manner the distinction between the later English recitative and this celebratory declamation can be seen, and it is the paradoxical accomplishment of this song that Ferrabosco manages to maintain, even enhance, the rhetorical tone of the beginning in the very place where the song becomes more melodic and where the textual sense is most frequently interrupted musically or disrupted by textual repetition.

Ex. 14

The clarity of harmonic expectations, and their fulfillment, and the interaction of bass and melody maintain the sense of forward motion which the melody lacks by itself. The aural spectacle of the song, though not virtuosic, is convincing. The music is apt, but not specific—like a fanfare, it exists not in itself but only for what it announces. As such, though not as song, it serves very well.

Virtuosity would focus attention on the performer, and such complimentary graces as we found in the MS version of "Why stays the bridegroom" would not find a home here with the absence of strong phrase cadences. The rhetorical impersonality of the song is emphasized by the repeat of the second section. The marriage of musical resource and rhetorical effect, at the expense of more specific concern for the unique qualities of individual words, is seen in two additional examples where the rhetoric of the music enlarges that of the text. First there is the resemblance of figures used at the conclusion of each section—the stereotyped odd-beat figures of the slightly later continuo style used here with harmonic point, particularly as they are combined in the expansion to the major seventh stretching to the ninth before the inevitable return to the octave.

Ex. 15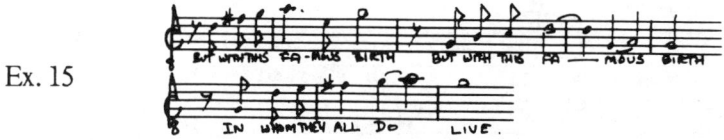

Also interesting is the turn to the minor mode at the words "How happier is that age" (see Ex. 14). Occurring at the very climax of the compliment and at the return of the tonic, this can only be accounted a rhetorical device of solemnity, a specific contrast to the "mere" brilliance of the worthy queens who live no more. It is a deft touch, and makes the concluding G major chord even more effective.

X

Masque Songs, 1611: Oberon and Love Freed From Ignorance and Folly

Ferrabosco's contributions to the 1611 masques *Oberon* and *Love Freed from Ignorance and Folly*—his last settings of Jonson's texts—are preserved solely in Tenbury MS 1018. Only two of the songs from *Oberon* have survived. "Nay, nay you must not stay" (#vi) follows the first dance of the masquers and is an exhortation to the fictive fairies of Oberon to continue dancing. The second song, "Gentle knights" (#vii), bids the dancers conclude their revels before the morn. Both songs partake then not of the hyperbole and compliment which characterized "If all the ages," but actually participate in the process of the dances and are directed not only to Oberon-Prince Henry, but to the entire group of masquers.

The setting of "Nay, nay" is forthright: regular in its phrasing and relatively smooth in its melody. The first six lines of the poem are irregular in length and meter and are divided into two groups of three lines by their sense.

>Nay, nay
>You must not stay,
>Nor be weary yet;
>. . . . .
>This is not time to cast away
>Or for fairies to forget
>The virtue of their feet.

In the first section of this bipartite song, Ferrabosco follows the sense of these larger groupings rather than setting the lines separately, thus creating longer melodic lines and fewer divisions. This is accomplished by not allowing the line-cadences to settle convincingly until the movement to the dominant (D) at the end of the section is emphasized by the use of V of V. The phrases, of about two measures each, link into each other, with the best example of this being the manner in which Ferrabosco observes the enjambment of the last two lines: both melodic line and textual sense are incomplete at the word "forget," although the cadence to the tonic is secure.

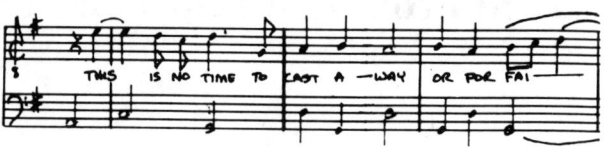

Ex. 1

Despite the near regularity of the line cadences (counting the first two lines of text as one), the impression of this passage is of asymmetry, not only because the second "half" is longer than the first, but because the second half moves on where it might be expected to stop. The dominant-tonic seesaw and the structure of the harmonic rhythm in the third and fourth phrases emphasize the harmonic expectations which usually are satisfied in such phrases structures. But both text and the shape of the melodic line do not allow pause on "(for)-get" (compare the effect of melodic c'-a-g "to for-get"). The text needs continuation, the melody needs reversal, and the extension into the next textual line is also a harmonic extension to V, bringing all the elements into balance—but not on the tonic.

The final quatrain of the poem is much more squarely written, four stresses to the line, and that regularity is reflected in the similarly measured phrases of Ferrabosco's setting. The music is also descriptive: the bumptious, angular quality of the music for "knotty legs," the smoother melody and metrically elusive cross-rhythms more fitting fairies' feet. Thus the invitation to resume the dance contrasts the earthbound and charmed motions implied by the text.

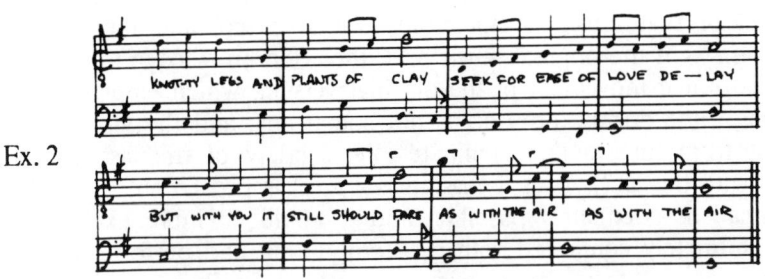

Ex. 2

The bass motion of the first example is more active and disjunct at the beginning, an immediate contrast to the preceding measures, as is the absolute evenness of the phrasing and the repetitiousness of the harmony (I-V; I-V). The melodic progress of the second excerpt is smooth, although the upper g' is a touch which, at first glance, would contradict the sense of lyrical melodiousness by which it portrays the airy lightness of the fairies' dance. Consider the position of the note in other respects, though. It is the weak beat of a triple-time pattern (if it is to make textual sense) and thus avoids the accent of the down beat and of its own pitch, setting up a cross-rhythm which floats to the final cadence over the evenly moving I_6-IV-V-I of the bass. Linking two text lines, it leads not to the g which follows, but to the c' ("air") which then continues the descent from d' to g which had been prepared twice before (m. 5; m. 16, ff., see Ex. 2), but not completed. The figure also appears in an imitation n the bass at m.5. The bass figure in the latter phrase (mm. 17-18) had been presented in part or in variant twice before, at mm. 3-4 and 13-15 where the arrival at the tonic was in the wrong position of the harmonic rhythm and the progression continued to the dominant. It also appeared in the melody at mm. 9-12 (see Ch. IX, Ex. 6) where what could have easily been a cadence on the tonic was turned toward the dominant.

The manuscript presents one problem of intention in the final measures: one measure is crossed out and the underlay has been altered.

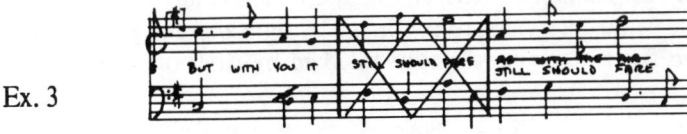

Ex. 3

Spink[1] attributes the alteration to a later hand, but one must wonder how the copyist of that music, if not close to Ferrabosco, and the "later" annotator first got the original music and, then, the knowledge to correct it. The harmonic movement of the original version, which emphasizes f for the only time during the song, is not convincing, and the loss of the movement from line to line eliminates the subtlety of the last phrase ("fare/As with the air"). Thus, omission is a great improvement, although the "original" is adequately passable, and it would be more likely that someone intimately connected with the composition and performance of the piece was, in fact, the copyist and reviser — perhaps Ferrabosco himself.[2]

Ferrabosco, or the copyist, also made a change to Jonson's text for the last line. In the printed masque the line reads, "As with the air of which you are." It is moot whether or not the text of the song is a slip of the pen; the point of Jonson's text is made by the airy triple-time patterns in the music.

This is one of two of Ferrabosco's masque songs to begin on the downbeat. The usual practice of setting the voice off against the continuo or lute chord would have been possible here, but this opening more satisfactorily fulfills its rhetorical function: the strong and vigorous protest against the cessation of the dance. It is the only gesture in the piece which actually emphasizes the words. For the rest, the concern with words is general and figurative or representational. The vigor of the opening subsides into smoother melody just as the asymmetry of the early phrases (both text and music) gives way to the regularity of phrasing and harmonic rhythm in the second section.

The other surviving song from *Oberon*, "Gentle Knights" (#vii), invites the dancers to conclude the revels (which had been in progress) before the arrival of Phosphorus, the day star. Particularly at the beginning the slow movement of the bass and the larger intervals of the melodic line suggest the declamatory-continuo style. But, as happened in "Nay, nay," that impression is soon revised when it becomes clear that the smooth sweep of the melody (over the span of a thirteenth) and the even tread of the harmonic rhythm are benedictory and spacious, rather than heroic or impassioned. The vocal part lacks any urgency of expression. The wide intervals are set in a rhythmically relaxed fashion and the melodic figures are increasingly filled in by division as the song proceeds.

J.P. Cutts, who identified these songs in manuscript with the masque of *Oberon*, remarked that they were "pleines d'effets charmants et exquises à chanter."[3] The appeal of "Gentle knights" owes much to its harmonic simplicity and clarity and to the balancing of its melodic activity. The song is a gentle aubade, a winding down of activity, and its style is ornate, though uncluttered, as is proper to the circumstance of the fictive spectacle. Unlike the commendatory masque songs, it does not bear the weight of focused communal expression and, thus, does not partake of the effort and puffery necessary to sustain hyperbole.

The overall form of the song is ABB' with the B section being slightly longer, more wide-ranging, and more interesting in its use of the relative major (the tonic is g/G). The first section consists of two pairs of lines each of which is set to an ascending figure followed by a (relatively) smoother descent. The harmonies progress as follows: I---V; ♭III-V/♭III, V-I(i). The same complementary pairing of melodic gestures continues in the setting of the two pairs of lines of the second section, where the harmonic movement is much more varied and off the tonic: i-V/V-(v), ♭III-V/♭III-♭III; ♭III-V/V-V, ♭III-V-I.

But it is the melismatic motion in this song which is its characteristic and unique feature. In contrast to the florid coloratura of the MS version of "Why stays the bridegroom", this embellishment is modest divison, giving the song a sense of effortless passage. Wide intervals, such as those traversed directly at the opening of each section, are heard in a more relaxed frame after the long melismas of the second section are performed. Like the wider melodic leaps of the opening measures, the scalar motions of the song are consonant and tonally unconfusing. Both emphasize chord tones and do not, in themselves, contribute to a sense of forced motion.[4]

In the second section, the textual lines are set to progressively longer (and wider ranging) melodic material (except for the first appearance of the last line): a musical "tarrying" or reluctance to conclude which is portrayed by both the progressively longer lines and the varied repeat of the entire section.

Ex. 4

Ex. 4
(continued)

From this example the pictorial aptness of the eighth-note motion is apparent—the descent on the word "motion", complemented and "varied" by the ascent at "Fairies." The variation and repetition of the setting of the final line at the conclusion—the two-fold descent starting first on the f', then overlapping that to begin on the still higher g' in an even longer curve—aptly portrays the word "tarry" as well as it ultimately grounds the "airy motions" which have soared so high. And it is no accident that the exploitation of the relative major in this section begins at that phrase: "And their motions so they vary."

It is misleading, however, to consider the changes in the repeat of the final line simply "tarrying" in the sense of word painting. This is an elaborate closure which befits such decorous entertainment, an expansive gesture making the close all the more convincing by enlarging the setting of the line and allowing a more certain arrival and confirmation on the tonic through the sequential repetition which, in its downward sweep, encompasses all but the lowest step of the range of the song and brings the motion to its final rest.[5]

In Tenbury 1018, between the two songs from *Oberon*, there are three more songs attributed to Ferrabosco. The first and third are settings of texts which appear in *Love Freed from Ignorance and Folly* (1611). The second, though not appearing in the printed masque, is fitting to it in subject and mood, and may have been composed for the masque but either omitted in performance or removed from the text of the masque when Jonson prepared it for publication.

The first song, "Oh! What a fault" (#viii), is sung by a priest following the first dance of the masquers. In the masque it is a rhetorical question answered by a chorus and, as can be seen from the text quoted below, takes part in making the point of the masque.

Although the manner is different, this function is similar to the songs of the *Masque of Beautie* with which this work shares its theme—it is the sighted love which is freed from ignorance and folly.

A bipartite song for treble voice, "Oh! What a fault" begins energetically only to subside into seductive melodic smoothness and harmonic regularity, the mirror of the "beauty" of the text. That text is short and divides after the third line:

A	O what a fault, nay, what a sin In Fate or Fortune had it been So much beauty to have lost!
B	Could the world with all her cost Have redeemed it?

Ferrabosco's setting is, as might by now be expected, a full-fledged reading of the poem, attentive to the text in both sense and shaping. The division of the poem is followed, with the first conclusive cadence on the tonic (g/G) coming at the end of the third line. The movement of the harmony does not really rest until that time, reflecting the continuity of the poet's thought through the three lines. The cadence to B♭ at m.7 is not allowed to conclude; the voice enters too soon again and the bass-voice imitation in mm. 7-8 reveals the B♭ to be linked to the ensuing e♭ in both parts.

Ex. 5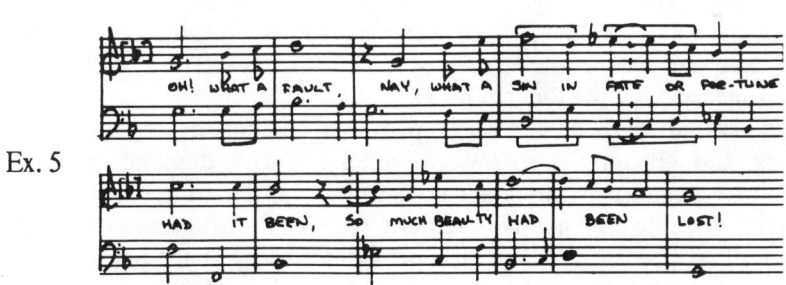

The opening of this song, like that of "Nay, nay," counterfeits a declamatory style with rhetorically emphatic and vigorous gestures which reverse the iambs of the poem for effect, accenting the expressive, intensifying words "Oh" and "Nay" by metric position, duration, and their springboard effect which catapults them toward their even more emphasized objects, "fault" and "sin."[6]

```
          /  . /   .   / . /
      ·
      Oh, what a fault; nay, what a sin
```

becomes

```
      /   . . /  /  . . /
      Oh! what a fault! Nay, what a sin! . . .
```

But the bass movement soothes the effect of the melodic reach toward the seventh and the setting becomes smoother and more sustained. The seventh descends to its starting place, and the rhythmic vigor of these first measures is transformed into playful limpidity as the brief triple time of the following measures carries the motion forward with the sense of the textual enjambment. Not only does the rhythmic activity serve to link the two lines ("sin / In fate"), but the failure to establish the dominant at the end of the first line — the ascent to f and the avoidance of f♯ — makes it a (re)turning point, not a stopping point.

In the second line the harmonic motion is smoothly extended to b♭ (the relative major) without ever really resting there — not because of a lack of harmonic preparation but because the singer's line does not allow the harmony sufficient time to settle. Rather, it picks up ("So"), forcing the bass to move on (in prolepsis of the melody) until the textual statement and the melodic descent from f' to g' can be completed and the tonic reasserted. The third line marks a change from iambic to trochaic stress pattern in the poetry which would normally have left a dead spot between the lines, if the accents had been followed slavishly. But the voice emphasizes the change by advancing the setting of "So," at the same time carrying the thought forward.

The second part of the song provides another example of the interesting, though simple, contrast of ascending and descending lines, and of how Ferrabosco's important contribution to the understanding of the poem, specifically in management of tonal structure and the extension of a prevailing harmony, provides passing harmonies while essentially going nowhere, in the setting of a repeated text.

Ex. 6

As in the first section, the melodic movement of the second section forms an arch of ascent and descent. The harmonies are simpler and uncomplicated by intimations of movement away from the tonic. But it is the way in which the vocal line descends through the octave which is structurally important.

In this section the repetition of textual lines is more deliberate than in most of Ferrabosco's songs where the repetition is usually of a smaller phrase or of an entire section of the song. In the measures of the first phrase of this section, the bass had been simply tonal support for the voice, moving from the tonic to dominant, a movement complemented in the final phrase, the repetition of the words "have redeem'd it," which returns to the tonic without melodic activity in the bass.

At the repeat of the words "Could the world with all her cost," however, the bass begins a stepwise descent which is reflected by the voice. This descent, ending on the tonic, also supports the first statement of the question's conclusion, "have redeem'd it?," which ends off balance and needs melodic conclusion. The poem itself ends mid-line with this question—its meter needs completion just as its question needs an answer. Ferrabosco has set the question, but in two ways, one of which envelops the other. The internal question is set to end as if incomplete, and a look at the music will show that neither the harmonic arrival on the tonic nor the vocal line are convincing as completion. The entire octave descent of the bass is an insert, in effect, surrounded by another setting of the question which leaves off and picks up at the same level and provides a conclusion to the song which confirms the tonic and completes the melodic descent of the voice.

By doing this, the question exists on two levels. The inner one, with the lack of fullness and a strongly articulate bass line, is poignant in its sense of loss and incompletion: thus becoming the answer, by representation, to its non-question—it *is* the representation of the "loss" proposed by the text. The outer question, however, transforms the entire activity to the level of a rhetorical question, removing the song from dramatic time into an esthetic distance and perspective in which the song itself becomes another representational answer to the question of the poem in the context of the redeeming powers of the court—where loss can be redeemed. It is absolutely convincing musically, and entirely at home in the artificial and secure world of the Jacobean masque.[7]

The primary reason for considering the next song, "Senses by unjust force banish'd" (#ix), as intended for the same masque is that the three songs appear run-on in the Tenbury 1018 with only changes of clef and signature to interrupt them. Another collaborative argument can be made that the text is related in meaning and reference to the previous one, the "beauty" of the earlier being the "object of your pleasure" in this.

A
: Senses by unjust force banish'd
From the object of your pleasure;
Now of you is all end vanish'd.

B
: You who late possess'd more treasure
(When eyes fed on what did shine
And ears drank what was divine)
Than the earth's broad arms could measure.

In addition, the division of the poem after the third line and the parenthetical couplet in the final quatrain are dealt with in a manner similar to the formal procedures we saw used in "Oh! What a fault."

The first section of this song does not come to a conclusive cadence until the completion of the first three lines of text, and the manner of maintaining the motion of the piece between the second and third lines is almost identical with that of the previous song: the voice continues without allowing the (relatively weakly achieved) cadence to settle.

Ex. 7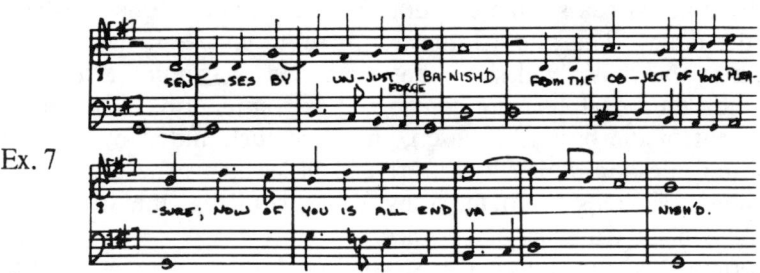

Though the harmonic motion is simpler (and entirely on the dominant side) in this section, the weighting of the cadences is similar to the earlier song with a direct movement to the dominant followed by a feigning movement back to the tonic which must be confirmed, at the end of the section, by a more assertive authentic cadence and the return of the melody to the tonic note. The textual enjambment of the first two lines is handled in a different manner, however, as the sustaining of the harmony does not interrupt the thought and the sequence, with its expansion of interval, creates a sense of enlargement and continuity. Once again, the third line enters "early" and the concluding figures of the first section in both songs are almost identical, save for mode.

Similarly, the logic of the text is accommodated in the second section where the parenthesis is, in effect, set within an independently complete musical thought, elaborating on it, but not changing it.

You who late possess'd more treasure:
(When eyes fed on what did shine
And ears drank what was divine),
Than the earth's broad arms could measure.

Ex. 8

The twofold movement of the bass through the descending octave (mm. 14-18; 19-25) and the clear and slower harmonic movement in the outer phrases (I-IV-I [. . .] I-IV-V-I) articulate the structure of this section on one level. But so, too, does the melodic structure, with these outer phrases contributing first an exploration of the upper fourth of the song (d'-g'-d') which is then complemented and grounded by an augmentation of the descending figure from d'-g which also concluded the first section. On the other hand, and contrasting with the shaping of these phrases, the inner phrases meander, only to end, melodically and harmonically, in the same place they began and without the sense of having purposefully gone anywhere else. Thus the setting of the two outer lines subsumes the parenthesis as surely as the marvelously pictorial gesture of the octave leap in the last line "measures" the scope of the song.

The use of contrary motion between bass and voice is more consistent in the song than in any other by Ferrabosco, focusing the harmonic tendencies and giving impetus to harmonic progressions. Where there are instances of imitation or prolepsis, it is more difficult to tell if they are intentional or simply fortuitous, as in the following example:

Ex. 9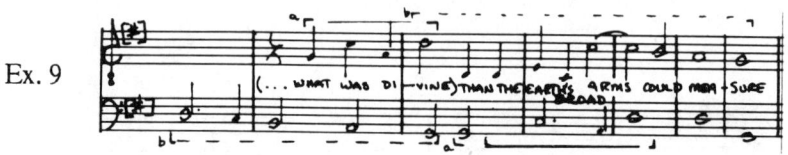

    While the sense of the text governs the overall dynamics of the song's energies, the musical gestures are only occasionally related to specific qualities of the words, excepting their accent. The cadences are carefully balanced to aid the listener's understanding of the poem, and the devices of tonal expectation allow a flexible, yet thoroughly comprehensible setting of the textual material. The sophistication of this particular setting (and it shares this quality with the preceding song) lies not just in the grace of its motion and the scope of its rhetorical suavity but in its handling of specific, larger textual problems. It is not the speaking voice we hear in this song, but the *idea* of the poem itself, and an intellectual understanding of the poem leads directly to the aesthetic expression of it in music.

    The song which concludes the Revels, "How near to good is what is Fair" (#x), poses several problems. Its extreme range covers two octaves in the voice (G-g'), and there are several instances which call for a gentle recomposing or emending of the manuscript version. Even more of a problem than the range is the way it is traversed: the entire first section consists almost solely of three figures, in succession. Two of these are disjunct and outline chord tones, the kind of figures occasionally found at the very beginning of these songs. Here, however, these figures are repeatedly stated, mindless of the difficulty they pose to anything more than an implacably arbitrary presentation of the text. The form of the whole is as follows:

A	a	i-V/♭III-♭III
	a'	i-iv-V-i
B	a"	i-^{V}/V/♭III
	b	v-V/V
	c	ii-IV; vi-V-I

The reasons for the primacy of the formal division proposed above, despite the figural similarities of the a, a', and a" phrases are based on harmonic form and complementarity and on the melodic shape of the B section which traverses, in essence, the octave g' to g in the three phrases.

The first section consists of two parts, as shown in the example below, with the figures labeled a, a' and a".

Ex. 10

The third excerpt, the first part of the second section, shows a slight variation in the figures and an incomprehensibly ineffective passage ("and prove / What way we may") as it tries to take advantage of motion to the relative major similar to that which had taken place in the first section. Unlike the two parts of the first section which had exploited both the dominant and relative major associations of the tonic, this part tries to do both, losing the connecting thread in the middle in a deceptive and confused movement toward the relative major which is never confirmed, stumbling over itself to its own dominant. That the music then resolves itself (mm. 21-23) into the same form we saw at the end of the first section (mm. 11-13) is a matter for some rejoicing, for at least now the song has regained focus, despite the vocal gymnastics required.

The song might be better served thus:

Ex. 11

In fact, the song almost allows for this, sliding from the V of V in m. 18 to ♭III (in what should be a deceptive cadence) which, disappointingly turns out only to be a i_6. The insistent presence of the g in mm. 19-20 thwarts the movement toward B♭, and this is why the emergence of F is not convincing — we don't know where we are until the next part of the second section begins.

If it were Ferrabosco's intent to experiment with motivic construction in this song, he did so at some loss to sensitivity of text-setting. The angular gestures soon become ploddingly boring and must be smoothed over by a very limpid singing style if our senses are to be taken by these musical "lines" and their "outward air." The difficulties are most apparent at the beginning of the second section (following m. 14). Jonson's text, in the Folio edition of 1616 reads differently from the text of the song, and is, perhaps, a bit more clear.

> We wish to see it still, and prove
> What ways we may deserve.
> [*Ayres*: We wish it still to see, ...]

This is an arguably ambivalent variant which may indicate a revision for publication, but the question of whether the adverb belongs with "wish" or with "see" is not as clear from the song as it is in Jonson's text. In fact, the music suggests, by emphasis of interval and duration, an even less plausible meaning: a command to halt in order, then, "to see and prove."

Ex. 12

This is taking the difficulties to their extreme, but the adherence to these melodic figures not only creates problems such as the one above, but their unrelieved repetition, with their sea-like down-and-up and wary rhythmic uniformity, is both tedious and mechanical. The irony is that these gestures are associated with the more firmly etched melodic assertiveness of the emerging declamatory style and continuo song, but here there is no sensitivity to the words themselves, or their import. There are only those "lines and outward air," not the informing substance.

On the other hand, the setting of the last lines of the text deals admirably with problems of rhetorical tone, melodic shape, harmonic point, and the use of sequence. The false emphases and stops of the first section and the granitic inflexibility of those musical gestures are absent. In their place is a long melodic descent from f' (carried from the g' in m. 14) to g supported by two very different harmonic sequences and a governing harmonic progression which emphasizes the dominant area and directs us surely to the tonic.

Ex. 13

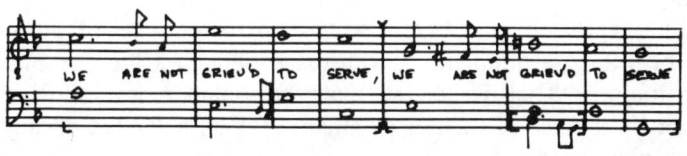

In the first sequence the just preceding movement to the dominant of the relative major (arrived at *from* its dominant) is countered, both in area and direction, by the movement from the minor dominant (d, also the relative minor of F) *to* its dominant. That overall movement is embellished within, and the larger movement of voice and bass,

$$f' - e'$$
$$d - a$$
$$(v - V/v)$$

is prefigured in the setting of the first two words. The third part of the sequence is extended to recapitulate the first, though now with an awareness of movement down the circle of fifths.

176   *Songs and Motets of Alfonso Ferrabosco, the Younger*

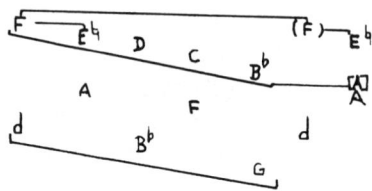

It is the simple and subtle touch of emphasizing the tonic harmony (g minor) by extending its length, then passing over the d minor (which should have been major in the sequence) lightly on a weak beat of the harmonic rhythm, which reminds the ear of the level which must be reaffirmed before the song is complete. The variability of the sequence is also its charm, melodically as well as harmonically, with the extension of i on the word "more" accommodating the sweep past the expected dominant both musically and pictorially. The melodic descent and ascent of the seventh (f ' -g: another prolepsis of the entire melodic activity of these concluding phrases) which pivot at that point are so smoothly coordinated that one is not as much aware of the interval as of the scope of activity.

The song, itself, had been boosted up to the level of the dominant briefly, beginning around m. 21 with the cadence on the dominant of the relative major. That is to say that the balance was shifting to the dominant by the use of further dominants for an extended enough period nearly to give the dominant its own validity. The sequence just discussed confirms that movements by implicitly preparing to end on the dominant. When the sequence pattern is broken, however, the relationship of tonic to dominant is reestablished, and the movement to the V/V becomes an overextension, which prepares the return to the tonic itself.

That overextension is balanced in the two-fold sequence (to the repeated words, "We are not griev'd to serve") both by the reduction of V/V to ii and by emphasis on the subdominant. The sense, in the preceding sequence, of upward harmonic motion by fifth is here followed by a complementary descending fifth while the melody completes its descent by step to the tonic.

Ex. 14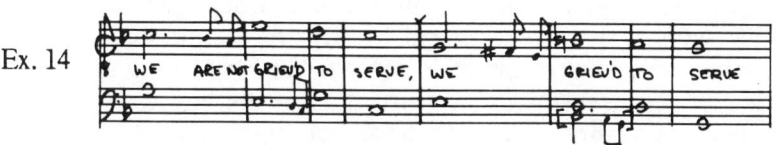

The first four measures end on the subdominant which previously in the song had functioned as the V/V of the relative major. Here, however, it serves as the preparation of the V-I cadence to follow. The strong bass movement by descending fifth in the latter two measures of each statement of the sequence, contrasts with the common-tone progressions in the first two measures of each part and the link between the two statements.

$$\begin{array}{c:c} \text{ii-IV}_6 & \overbrace{\text{V/IV-IV}} \\ \overbrace{\text{vii-I}_6} & \text{V - I} \end{array}$$

They also contrast with the rising fifths of the preceding sequence, as does the serene evenness, the regular harmonic rhythm of the progressions.

In the manuscript the sequence is not followed strictly in the second statement, as the suggested emendation in the above example points out. The harmonic progression remains the same, but the bass line, in the manuscript version, lacks vigor just where it most needs it—before the final cadence.[8] The conclusion of the descent of the octave in the voice transforms the mode from minor to major, in contrast with the prolepsis of this descent given in the first sequence (see mm. 24-28 and the outline of the passage on p. 176).

In these final measures Ferrabosco forces our attention to the pronoun "we." Excepting the first word of the entire poem (as was customary for him), he had not placed weakly accented words in a strong metric position, and, in an iambic text such as this one, the first word of a line should normally be unaccented. But the English language is marvelously, if frustratingly variable, and, as we have seen in "Oh! What a fault!" and "If all the ages of the earth," these patterns are flexible when sense, syntax or rhetoric demands. "We are not griev'd to serve" has no rhetorical point and little, even trivial metrical interest. By reversing the first stress pattern and reading the line as Jonson intended the emphasis of meaning, "We are not griev'd to serve," both subject and verb are highlighted. After the series of emphasized verbs: "We court, we praise, we more than love," this focus is appropriate and does not impede the text. Rather, after a song characterized by weak-beat entrances and odd-note groupings, this metric emphasis sets the final measures apart as a culmination of the poem's sense, confirmation of the musical statement, and mirror of the forthright tone of masquing compliment.

The first section of the song, however, seems to be willfully misconceived, possibly even a conscious experiment. Its melodic gestures, mechanical feeling, bass writing, harmonic lack of definition (mm. 18-20), and absence of a sense of the relation of text to musical phrasing contradict Ferrabosco's usual ability to combine melodic shapeliness, harmonic clarity and direction, and textual sense. These are precisely the attributes found in the latter half of the second section wherein a long melodic descent to the tonic is married to harmonic sequences which direct and enhance our expectation of arrival while the text is set in a way which modestly emphasizes its rhetorical quality.

XI

Italian Songs

There are five songs to Italian texts which are ascribed to Ferrabosco in the Tenbury MSS 1018-1019. The world of these songs is much more impassioned and full of more urgent expression than we find anywhere else in Ferrabosco's vocal compositions, for here is found the affective manner of the monodists. The high-blown oratory of the masque songs is superficially similar to this style, but where that manner was official and commendatory, these Italian songs attempt to be expressive. They give, at least in their opening measures, a much more direct sense of the experience of the song's *persona*—as if there were no intermediary between experience and expression.

The gestures of these songs are more responsive to the emotional impetus of the text and the emotional state of the singer, even though they are less colored by dissonance and *colorature* than their genuinely Italian contemporaries. Like other of Ferrabosco's songs which begin in a declamatory rather than lyric manner, they evince a concern for structure and overall form. This prevents the harmonic activity from becoming incoherent or dissociated from a sense of phrase. Generally, also, it results in a two-section song, the second section of which is more smoothly melodic than the rhetorically declamatory opening and which returns the harmonic activity securely to the tonic. Thus, the problem of closure in this quasi-recitative style—i.e., how to be responsive to the speech qualities of the text without losing a sense of shape when the textual material is exhausted—is satisfied and solved by musical means which organize the energies of the song in a musically coherent fashion.

Nonetheless, in England these songs are astonishing for their time. It is a likely assumption that they were composed at about the same time as the masque songs of 1611 which also appear in Tenbury 1018, although there is no real proof that they were not written later. These songs lack the attention to detail in declamation and expression which makes a song like Caccini's "Amarilli mia bella" so exemplary. Nor do they exhibit the fluid and sometime extravagant embellishment which contributes so much to the expressive presentation of the text in the Italian monody or the dissonance of Monteverdi's harmonic mastery. Leaving aside the possibility of improvised *affetti* or *fioriture*, as found in the Christ Church MS 439 version of "Why stays the bridegroom?," Ferrabosco's songs nonetheless demonstrate that the English knew the Italian style.

One of the songs does double duty, for it appeared in the *Ayres* with the English text, "O eyes, O mortal stars" (#25). In Tenbury MS 1019, however, it is found with two texts in a setting for a voice and lute: the English text, known from the *Ayres*, with an Italian text beneath. The Italian text is a madrigal by Giovanni Battista Guarini, "Occhi, stelle mortali," which appeared in his *Rime* (Venice, 1598) as Madrigal XII. The English text is a translation of the Italian original.

The English setting has not provoked much interest. Ulrich Olshausen even observed of the manuscript appearance, "Als Alternativtext ist eine italienische Übersetzung des Originals unterlegt."[1] Ian Spink and Edward Doughtie have corrected that misconception, and it is now surprising, in retrospect, that the specific problems of the song did not earlier suggest the primacy of the Italian text.[2]

The primacy is more than just one of translation, for the musical evidence indicates that the song was first composed to the Italian text, the translation applied later. If this were simply an English song published in 1609, as was thought until recently, two general musical problems concerning gesture and accent might strike the hearer. Of the first, two examples will suffice. The opening invocation is an impassioned rhetorical formula of address (and lament) known to contemporary Italian song. It belongs more to the continuo style of semi-dramatic song than to any of the varieties of English song of the time. It is a gesture far more assertive and passionate than is customary with Ferrabosco, excepting some of the masque songs, and certainly unfamiliar in the styles of composers like Dowland, Campion, and even Johnson.

Ex. 1

In addition, no other song by Ferrabosco uses a forceful gesture over and over with such awkward texting as occurs at the words "If closed you annoy me,/ Being open you'd destroy me."

Ex. 2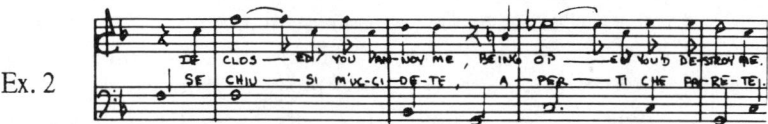

Even ignoring the ill fit of the gestures and text in English compared with the Italian, the text-setting itself gives pause, not only in the above example, but more obviously (i.e., where an over-ruling musical pattern cannot be the culprit) in the setting of the third line, "Thát in slúmb'ring wáge wárs." Unlike the iambic trimeter which surrounds it, this line twice reverses the stress. The setting does not take this into account, and the accents are askew.

Ex. 3

There is the possibility, one might argue, that Ferrabosco put the melody into triple-time at this point to accommodate the problem of the English textual accents. If so, the accompaniment effectively "wars" against the success of that intent. The seven-syllable Italian line, with its primary stress on the penultimate syllable and a secondary stress on the second syllable, matches the accents of the melody:

"Che'n sóg-no an-co mo-stráte."

Similarly, the problems of gesture are best understood in light of the Italian text. The vigorous, cutting figures used to set the concluding lines of text (Ex. 2) make much more pictorial sense with the Italian words, "Se chiusi m'uccidete, aperti che farete" (more specifically and accurately translated: "If, when closed, you sever me [kill me by cutting],/What would you do if open?"). The limp inappropriateness of "annoy me" to convey the sense of "m'uccidete" and to inform the force of the musical figure makes the point. The English text lacks the Italian text's gestural correspondence with the musical gestures.

Unlike some of the other Italian songs which more consistently aspire to dramatic recitative, this song is regular in phrasing and harmonic motion. The characteristically emphatic off-beat entrances of the dramatic style are not used, except in the opening phrase, and the voice and bass, for the most part, move in the same time frame.

The harmonies are simple, with a balance of subdominant and dominant activity which is ordered so that the subdominant, though it balances the dominant, is clearly subordinate. In the first section this is quite clear: F=I-IV-I; V-V/V-VIII-IV-I; I-V-I. The second section, beginning at m. 9, consists of two parts, the latter of which is written-out variation of the first. Here the melodic activity is based on the figure cited above, and the harmonic activity is more interesting. In the second statement, the voice soars to the upper g″ in a slight variation of the figure. Although we lose the piquant diminished fourth, the extension of the figure is more pathetic and expressive, and it gives an entire octave descent in a fulsome sweep before the arrival on f′.

Ex. 4

It is also in that second phrase that the harmony is most expressive, using the inflection of the dominant minor (m. 20), although the basic progress of the harmony remains the same: I-IV; V/V-V; V-I; IV-V-I.

In light of the numerous Italian poems which were translated and imitated by Elizabethan and Jacobean writers, not to mention the presence of large families of Italian musicians at court, it is not surprising to find a setting of a translation of an Italian poem in a Jacobean book of ayres. What is unique is that it appears that this song was originally composed to the Italian text and the composer, himself, was responsible for the publication of the English setting. We can be grateful to the compiler of Tenbury 1019 for making it possible to understand "O eyes, O mortal stars."

Four Italian songs for voice and continuo appear in Tenbury 1018 attributed to "Alfonso Farabosco." In addition, the manuscript contains other songs by Ferrabosco which were used in the masques of *Oberon* (1611) and *Love Freed from Ignorance and Folly* (1611). Preceding these are motets of the elder Alfonso, and a large group of songs by Giulio Romano (Caccini) follows. Three of Ferrabosco's songs have texts from Guarini's *Pastor Fido* (written between 1581 and 1590, published by G. B. Ciotti in Venice, 1602). The fourth text is anonymous.

These songs are much more rhetorical, seeking effect by contrasts of range, affective gestures, harmonic changes, and rapid variability of melodic activity and bass motion. Yet, Ferrabosco is never able to abandon a basically musical approach to these texts, and these songs partake of an appropriate pastoral lyricism, even though many of the gestures are more immediate and direct than in any of his other songs.

For example, "Udite lagrimosi spir'ti d'Averno" (#xi) begins with a free address to the spirits of hell, a declamatory recitative similar in style, if not means, to the powerful choral recitative Monteverdi had presented in his fourth book of madrigals (1603) in pieces such as "Si ch'io vorrei morire" and "Sfogava con le stelle." The singing part, over a practically motionless bass, is intense and disjunct, and the leap of an octave, at the repetition of the command, "Udite," is particularly effective in commanding attention. Nevertheless, the setting of the first three lines demonstrates a musical shape which ensures comprehensibility, despite apparent wrenches of harmony.

Ex. 5

The opening phrase is answered by one a major third higher (the common-tone, b♮, is the pivot) which substitutes an apparent I-V-I progression on B, for the more solemn I-IV-I on G. The concluding phrase, however, moves quickly to a confirmation of the original tonic, linking the phrases together by revealing that B was the dominant of the relative minor, e. This, then, is reincorporated into G (mm. 13-17) and concluded with an authentic cadence on G.

This is a mirror of the specific text, "Mirate crudo affetto in sembiante pietoso," for the powerful passions which engender the song (or, at least, seem to at this point) — and this harmonic movement — are artfully clothed in aesthetically pleasing fashion, even to the point of using the melodic diminished fourth in a well-shaped phrase to mitigate the horrors of the "crudo affetto." The melodic "affetti" — the use of the descending minor sixth, part of the monodists' stock-in-trade, at the words "crudo affetto" and, later, "crudel" and the surging octaves of the first two phrases, in addition to the diminished fourth — combine with the rhetorical declamation of "Udite" to create a much more exaggerated sense of expressiveness than, for example, was present in "O eyes, O mortal stars," even though both texts eventually are revealed as anacreontic rather than tragic.

Beginning at m. 18, the second of the song's three sections is even more adventuresome harmonically. The first section has used relations of a fifth within areas a third apart to emphasize the mediant and submediant (as V/vi and vi) about G. Here, however, the common-tone linking passes through the ♭VI to ♭II (V/♭II - ♭II) giving a neapolitan-phrygian feeling (here unbalanced on the mediant/ relative major side) to the depth of "L'inferno" and the pain of "morte." The entire section, in fact, has been lowered onto the minor subdominant, creating a balance of the first two sections: the first with its emphasis on G, surrounded by B and e and confirmed by the use of the dominant; the second on c, surrounded by E♭ and A♭.

Ex. 6³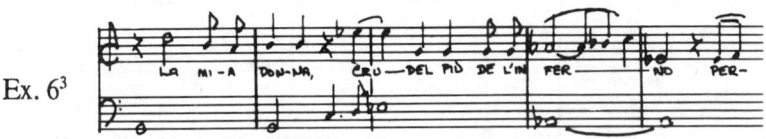

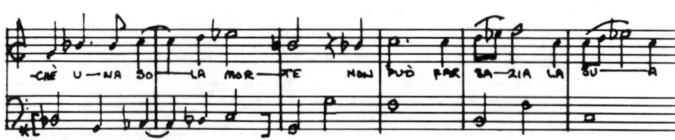

Ex. 6
(continued)

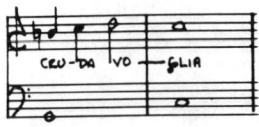

Even here, however, the melodic line is smoother throughout, not just in the closing figures of phrases as in the first section. The harmonic excursion is not allowed to meander and is, in fact, rather short.

The final section (mm. 31-45) is a two-fold confirmation of the tonic (G) in which the melodic writing is more animated, much more metric in quality, and closely related, by imitation, with the bass. The harmonic activity, so rich and flexible in the preceding section, is simple. Although there is one instance of word-painting, the descending seventh at "perpetua morte" which recalls the opening section, the metric regularity and the quick, patterned movement of the melody reveal the essential playfulness of the text.

The two parts of this section form an interesting linked structure: the first part (mm. 31-38) is nearly identical with the second. The differences (and the details) are quite important, for the first part moves from IV to V ("[mor]-te"), with the arrival on I at "mi commanda ch'io viva" somewhat distinct from the formal parallel—an interjection which concludes the first part musically but begins the second part textually. That second part, now beginning on I ("Perche la mia vita," m. 39), recapitulates the earlier progression with the dominant given stronger emphasis. The movement from IV to I included V/V-V to overcome the strength of the subdominant influence in the first part. In the second, IV is clearly subordinated to the dominant, and the tonal hierarchy of the entire piece is heard when the validity of the tonic is established by the concluding IV-(I)-V-I cadence which reflects the harmonic motion of the whole song.

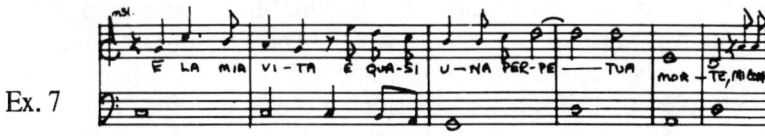

Ex. 7

Ex. 7
(continued)

This final section is also interesting in its manner of phrasing and text-setting. The opening of the piece promises great and awesome horrors of dramatic import; the final section is sprightly and playful, reflecting the textual turn from exaggerated horrors to their somewhat stylized cause: a surfeit of love. Occasionally using the conventions and manner of affective expression (e.g., the descending seventh, previously mentioned, at "perpetua morte," though in a very comfortable and consonant harmonic context, which recalls the similar leaps of the opening section), this second section presents simple, regularly occurring harmonic movement with an absence of chromaticism, generally smooth, though active melodic lines, neutral and patterned text-setting (somewhat indebted to the text for the repetitions of "mille"),[4] imitations between bass and vocal lines, and sequences which delight rather than terrify.

The feeling of this last section is almost wholly tuneful and lyrical, not dramatic or impetuous, or serious. Thus, the game of the text, with its overblown apostrophe to "wretched spirits" promising to reveal a yet more lamentable and fearful circumstance, is revealed as an amorous tease by the music used to convey it.

"Eterni Numi" (#xii) also begins with wide-ranging rhetorical gestures of a mixed declamatory-arioso style: the intense and immediate melodic angularity pursued for its own sake. The first phrase, with its extended and only secondarily pictorial emphasis on "e-[terni]," is another example of Ferrabosco sacrificing scansion for rhetorical effect—the anacrusic surge propelled into the lofty range of "numi." This song is also in two sections which differ in mode and melodic phrasing, relationship between bass and voice, and textual content: the first section, by oratorical description, contrasts the lofty ease of the gods who bestow grace with the difficulties of men's thoughts to rise to those inaccessible heights (to achieve grace).

Ex. 8

The ceremonial address of the first section, in an exalted range, proceeds over a slow-moving bass which only in its last phrase becomes melodically linked to the vocal part, and measured of necessity, thus emphasizing the move to the dominant. The harmonic movement is simple: I-I;I-V;V-I;I-IV-(v)-V/V-V. The address to the gods is ceremonial, but not emotional, and there is no expressive use of dissonance. The high range of the singer is both pictorial and rhetorical: the emphasis is on the vocal declamation which proceeds with lofty emotional neutrality though great rhetorical intensity, even to the extent of textual repetition. The vocal entrances are given some metric flexibility, until the final phrases, by being presented over static harmonies. Thus, they basically begin off-the-beat. This allows clearer articulation of the words and gives them a sense of greater importance, a sense of "edginess" contrasting with the harmonic foundation, which permits the performer(s) considerable leeway in an ostensibly metric scheme. The performers can use the "downbeat" as impetus, a springboard, and the notation is only suggestive as measure, except where coordination *is* necessary, as it is in the second section of this song.

Thus an expressive or emphatic rubato, a negligence of exact measure, is possible, even necessary here as part of the intentional contrast between the relatively free, declamatory first part of the song and the second, more measured section. Even more negligence is permitted here than in the more contrapuntally and metrically conceived lute-song where the performer could stretch the musical fabric only slightly for effect, either to accommodate the words or to give a musical gesture impact or fullness, especially at cadences. The sounding of the continuo articulates the harmony (with which, in this case, not against which the singer works) and also provides the "springboard" energy for the singer whose declamation is a succession of new beginnings, new leaps of vocal gesture in response to the continuo. At the end of the first section we hear the counterpoint of these various articulations in an even more interesting manner as measure becomes more definite, and the voice and continuo anticipate each other, in turn and at closer intervals of time, impetuously pushing each other forward. The harmonic movement is also quicker and more varied, with the triple-time (mm. 14-15) accentuating the arrival of V/V and the brief use of harmonies from the relative major anticipating the beginning of the second section.

The more lyrical second section of the song is characterized by a much closer metric and melodic relationship between melody and bass (e.g., the bass prolepsis in mm. 21-22), greater melodic shapeliness of the bass, and an affective shift to the parallel minor (g), making use of the relative major as a contrast. The most interesting aspect of this section is the manner by which Ferrabosco returns from the brief excursion on the relative major exemplified by the movement in mm. 21-22 and repeated more conclusively in m. 25. In the first instance, the diminished fourth in the bass (b♭-f♯) is not simply a prolepsis of the melodic figure a measure later, but signals the move I-III$_6$ (in B♭) which is quite quickly understood as [B♭] I-III$_6$ = [g] V$_6^1$-i. When the figure occurs the second time, in m. 25, it is prefaced by i, and the conclusion on i is more strongly confirmd by the addition of V/V and by metrical position: i-♭III-V/V-V$_6$-I.

Ex. 9

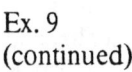
Ex. 9
(continued)

This reestablishment and confirmation of the tonic is both careful and ingenious, involving a scalar descent in the bass which is repeated and expanded to emphasize those elements which contribute to focusing the harmonic movement: the medial cadence on the dominant (m. 27) and the substitution of a iv-i-V-I progression at the end of the song for the weaker V^4_3-i (mm. 23-24) which had concluded the previous textual phrase.

The contrapuntal and structural interest of this second part may be part of a word play ("fallaci e torti"). If so, it is surprisingly mild harmonically, and the distance between B♭ and g/G rather directly covered. The primary interest is in the contrast of the general, descending line of the bass and the specific ascent of the vocal line, "al cielo." The circuitous nature of the passage to these inaccessible heights of the gods (arriving at the same pitches of "alti inaccessibili") is emphasized by both textual and musical repetition.

Thus, despite the oratorical beginning of the song, the melody here is more pictorial than dramatic or rhetorical, its effect residing in the representation of height by extreme range (admittedly a rhetorical effect, as well), especially in this more measured and tunefully shaped section. The bipartite structure of the song is revealed in the contrast of the vigorous, though shapely overall, recitative-like introduction with the more conjunct, measured, less assertive, tuneful conclusion. The harmonic motion of each section, however, is simple and complementary in the balance of nearly equally long phrases:

	First Section	Second Section
1st phrase	I-I	i-V/♭III-♭III
2nd phrase	I-V	♭III-V-i
3rd phrase	V-I	(i)-♭III--V/V-V
4th phrase	I-IV-V/V-V:	i-♭VI-V; iv-i-V-I
Or, in major structural sense:		
	I-V	i-♭III-i-V-I

Thesse schemata denude the progressions of their specific elaborations and manner, but they show how clearly Ferrabosco created his tonal working-space.

"O crudel'Amarilli" (#xiii) is more impassioned and sustained than Ferrabosco's other settings of Guarini texts and more resembles the contemporary monodies of Caccini and d'India: never too startling or disjointed, its rhetorical immediacy and emotional urgency is enhanced by modest, stinging dissonances and by a more flexible delivery which is more responsive to the emotional movement of the words.

Unlike the case with the previously discussed Italian songs, here Ferrabosco seems genuinely comfortable with an arioso style somewhat between recitative and metric song. The continuo is much less a melodic voice, remaining relatively static and following the singer without straying so far from participation in and articulation of a metrical frame that the sense of composition is lost. The voice works around the frame of the bass with familiar rhetorical gestures such as the upbeat (odd-note) off-beat entrances which intensify the delivery of the text, cadential elongations, occasional dissonances of anticipation which serve expressive purposes (quite resembling Monteverdi's similar use of such figures), and quickly ranging melodic gestures which mirror the agitation of the singer.

Even when stylized, the vocal part is emotionally expressive in this song, not at all distanced and ceremonially proper. The very opening measures, the addresses to Amaryllis, assume a more intimate direction and sense of immediate and urgent feeling compared with the openings of the other Italian songs. The vocal gesture bears a family resemblance to the pathetic, idiomatic "Ohime" settings of contemporary Italian monody and opera, the descending minor sixth embellished by harmonic dissonance (as in this case) or stunning harmonic change. This example is somewhat gentler in its harmonic effect than the sevenths of Marenzio, Monteverdi, or d'India, but its piquancy is greater, the bitterness and tenderness of expression yoked together less forcefully but no less certainly.

Ex. 10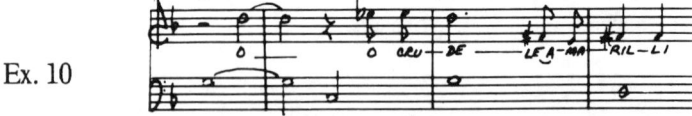

The Guarini texts which Ferrabosco set are not, properly speaking, dramatic. "O crudel'Amarilli" is the only one in which protagonists are named, and it is, in effect, a comment from an outside vantage, from a narrator, if you will, or a *persona* functioning in the manner of the ancient dramatic chorus or speaking for the audience. In that sense the text lacks dramatic personality, although not dramatic validity. The other Guarini texts are not narrative at all; they do not participate in our

Italian Songs

understanding of a dramatic situation (even in the conventions of pastoral drama). They range outside the bounds of time or place and, even, particular characters: the love-death trifles are specific to anyone, hence no one, and the address to the gods is sufficiently Olympian in tone to make us realize that, while we might share the sentiment, we cannot share the expression.

But the "narrator" places the situation is a different guise. He can describe the circumstance and, by his manner of description, invite us to participate in it, while he, himself, retains the aspect of observer and commentator. In the case of "Lo! In a vale" (#ii), the narrator was content to describe a circumstance. Here, however, the narrator-chorus responds to the actions of a character and, in situations of this type, much of the narrator's success depends on the sense of the present importance of what he is saying. That is, it depends on how he says it. This, then, is the composer's challenge: to inform the text with musical urgency without destroying it with emotional excess. Of this type, Monteverdi's *Il combattimento di Tancredi e Clorinda* is the paradigm, arraying the forces of music for representation, expression, description, and narration in such a way that the drama takes place in the music: its sounds, its rhythms, its pace, its shape, its tensions.

Ferrabosco's is but a small contribution when measured against Monteverdi's. But "O crudel'Amarilli" succeeds in some of the same ways as does the music of his Italian contemporaries. The song is kept moving by the reciprocal influences of singer and continuo: the downbeat of the continuo provides, as we have seen, a spring for the singer; the upbeat figures of the singer direct their energy into the continuo's downbeat. Thus, the freedom from metric regularity is bound up in the unremitting responsiveness of the singer and continuo which continually energize, if not regularize, the musical time. These features are characteristic of Ferrabosco, not limited to this song alone, and in these Ferrabosco was unique among his fellow Englishmen in the first decade of the century.

Ex. 11

Again, the song is bipartite in construction with the first part being more impassioned and less measured as the bass articulates and propels the voice forward rather than participating in its movement or expression. The second section, beginning at m. 35, is more regularly metrical with greater participation of the bass at the metric level and in the melodic material of the vocal part. The regularity of meter, the management of harmonic rhythm, and the use of sequence and repetition in this section play a great part in both the confirmation of musical goals and the effective creation of a sense of closure. The sharpening of formal determinants, such as the metricization of harmonic progressions and their repetition, also allows the listener both aesthetic pleasure and distance. Time and again with Ferrabosco we find that we are never far from the pleasure of a well-shaped song. Especially with regard to the progress of the harmony, this contributes to the sense of almost wistful gentleness which is present even in the opening measures of this song. There is no astounding conflict of sense and expectation, no clash of perception and understanding as the ear finds, for example, in some of Gesualdo's madrigals and in Monteverdi's *L'Orfeo* at the arrival of the fateful messenger.

The repeat of material in "O crudel'Amarilli" is as interesting as that in "Eterni numi," although it is quite different. The sequences and repetitions of motive-like figures in the second section are modified and expanded in quite tonal fashion.

Ex. 12

The harmonic movement of these examples is complementary, with the second part a confirmation, by expansion and elaboration, of the first.

1. G=I - V/V; V-(I - V)-I
2. I-IV-V/V-V; V-(I-IV-V)-I

The use of subdominant to emphasize the final cadential progression is characteristic of Ferrabosco, as we have seen also in the other Italian songs.

The sense of reflection between these two parts of the second section is not limited to harmonic matters. The use of contrasting directions in setting "E'l vomitasti fuore" to figures which expand to an octave and the expansion of the upward leap of a fifth to an octave in the settings of "per non l'aver nel core" are two other, melodic examples. The leap of an octave also provides an instance of musical rhyme, for the concluding line of the first section of the song, which just begins to partake of the metric quality of the second section, anticipates the shape of the final line.

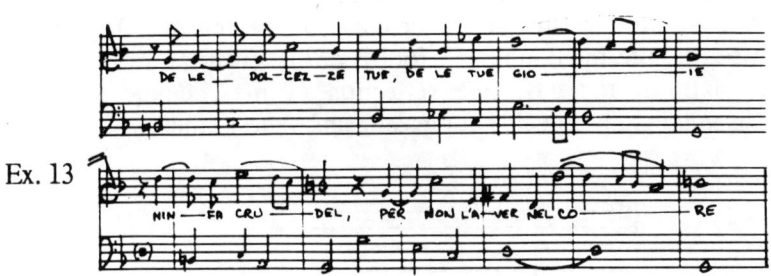

Ex. 13

And there is the subtle expansion of the cramped figure used to set the words "ninfa crudel," an expansion which delivers us to the tonic, instead of merely preparing us for it.

The astringent affect of the first statement, "O crudel'Amarilli," is mitigated by the petulance of the qualifying sequences and repetitions of "ninfa crudel." The interplay of continuo and voice in the first section effected a refusal to stop: a constant surging, forward-moving agitation which refused convincingly to settle on the tonic until the word "gioie" and canceled expectations of relaxation by using both major and minor harmonic inflections. The second section, in its formalism, reminds us that this is artifice, not life; song, not drama.

The use of dissonance in this song is instructive, for Ferrabosco never cultivated an affective dissonant style, and he generally uses dissonances only in suspension or in passing, primarily at cadences. Here, however, we have two similar instances of dissonances of anticipation on a weak beat, approached by leap, from a minor sixth and a diminished fourth, respectively.

Ex. 14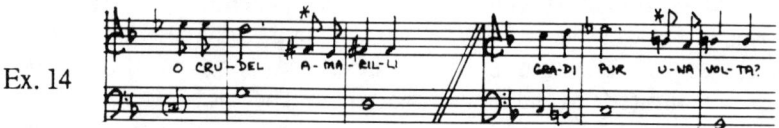

In the first instance we can argue both expression and word-painting ("crudel'"). In the second, we hear the first, but with a sardonic overtone befitting Amaryllis' "insidiosa bocca." Each moves quickly to its harmonious reconciliation with the bass, leaving only a fleeting impression. Ferrabosco's style is not that of profound expressive affect, and these instances of dissonance charm more than jar.

Another example of this effect occurs in the setting of "Or l'odiato nome" which, despite the diminished fourth of the singer and the leap of the minor sixth in the bass (the reflection of the melodic sixth of "crudel'"), is not dissonant at all, but pleasing and almost tuneful.

Thus, the pastoral distance is maintained, and the essential difference between the solo song as a contained art-work and the opera arioso and recitative as a dramatic presentation exemplified.[5]

The last of the Italian songs presents a variety of problems. The author of the text is unknown, the text has no known concordances, and it is difficult to read in the manuscript, confusing not only in its legibility but also in its sense.

> Lacrimar sempre il sommo diletto;
> Il rider doglio, l'assenzio e tosco.
> La notte affanno, il ciel seren'e fosco
> E duro campo di battaglia il letto.
> O bellezze! voi siete belle e vaghe per costei,
> E siete sole perche siete in lei.
>
> [To weep forever; of delights my all!
> Laughter is pain, poison and bitt'rest gall.
> Clear were the heavens; now clouded is their light,

Italian Songs

> And bed a battlefield i' th' breathless night.
> Beauties! Th'art fair and lovely still (I know)
> Because th'art in her: thus she makes thee so.][6]

It is hard to place the circumstance and object of this burdened, marinistic soliloquy, the patterned contrasts of which war against each other in oxymoron just as the lovers war on the field of love. Yet, it is not action which is presented, but reflection—although a reflection which could be used by a composer for re-presentation.

Of all Ferrabosco's songs, this begins most closely to assume the *recitativo-arioso* style: seemingly without measure and able, in both melodic and rhythmic gesture, to respond to the immediate instance of the text, while using repetition to increase the *pathos* of expression. Yet, even in the first section of the song which, typically, is metrically more free than the setting of the concluding couplet, the declamation and expression never stray so far from metric regularity not to be able to lapse into the ever-immanent metric frame. What we find is a very "composed" setting which uses text repetition (and, most likely, improvised ornamentation—there is none written into the setting) to give the effect of intensity in delivery.

The assertion of the meter serves to emphasize the text in an expressive way.

Ex. 16

The coordination of bass and voice at the words "l'assenzio e tosco" not only focuses the listener's attention but is absolutely necessary for both the imitation and the effect of the $a\flat$—which is not simply a melodic inflection but an expressive bending of the harmony. While the rest of the phrase can be delivered in a rather free manner, this must be "in time."

Also in strict time are the "representative" battle figures used at the words "di battaglia" (see below) which, crossing the accompaniment with the voice, are properly combative. They are somewhat out of place with the mood of the song, particularly as we have become accustomed to Ferrabosco's ability to convey mood throughout a song without episodic interruption. But it is this very episodic quality of contrast and representation of a suggestive text which the Italian composers emulated. Here, it indicates a more dramatic leaning, an experiment on Ferrabosco's part, toward a more representational style (i.e., *stylo rapprasentativo*, not simply word-painting).

The repetitions of text in the first, less regular or songlike section are musically interesting, for almost every textual half-line is repeated immediately to the same musical figure, but at another pitch level, in a manner which emphasizes the harmonic clarity (and objectivity) of the lament.

Ex. 17a: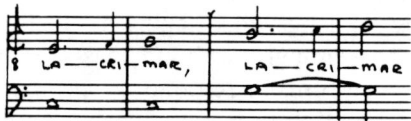

sempre il mio sommo diletto

Ex. 17b:

Il rider doglio, l'assenzio e tosco
    (not repeated)

Ex. 17c:

The subdominant here is not only a minor harmonic inflection, but it anticipates (and, therefore, in retrospect affects) the subdominant plunge in the next phrase, i.e., the word-painting at "La notte affanno."

La notte affanno

Ex. 17d: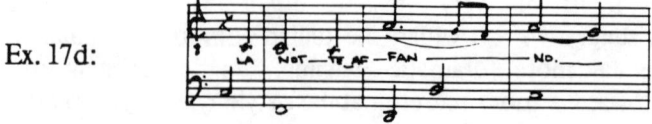

Il ciel seren' e fosco

Ex. 17e: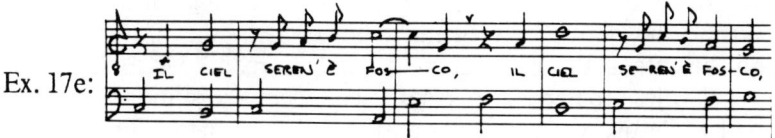

E duro campo

Ex. 17f:

di battaglia(il letto)

Ex. 17g:

Interestingly, it is in the setting of lines which are not repeated that we find the most affective harmony and an emphasis on the subdominant. This emphasis is immediately countered by the dominant presence in the last line, just as the heavy, lingering setting of "La notte affanno" is countered by the vigor of "Il ciel." The word-painting is not obtrusive, until the unusual emphasis given representation at "di battaglia," and is, as seen above, carefully shaped and balanced when it occurs. Even the figure at "Il ciel" is not extreme and is complemented, in turn, by the downward turn of "seren' e fosco."

As we have come to expect in the concluding sections of these songs, we find here a more metrical feeling and greater use of musical process, such as sequence, to articulate more clearly the structure of the section. Bass and voice move more closely together, particularly in the closing phrase which elaborates the final cadence, IV-I-V-I.

Ex. 18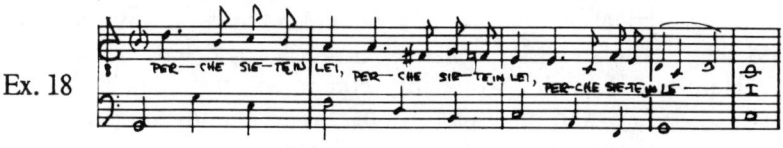

The sequences focus the tonal energies, which had not really been unclear before, although the movement of the preceding phrases of this section were to the dominant (generally, however, by the movement I-V which only heightens the expectation of the return of the tonic). The tuneful regularities (balanced phrases, sequences, repetitions) of this section tend to defuse the emotional and more immediate expressiveness of the first section, establishing aesthetic distance between the listener and the thing described. In the masque songs, a similar change of musical style is used rhetorically to increase the compliment by suave emphasis.

On paper this is a tedious song, chopped up phrase-by-phrase into short, repeated snippets of text held together by harmonic logic. The absence of chromaticism, except for the phrygian sense of the minor inflections in the middle of the first section (m. 10), and unprepared dissonance bears witness to the relatively unadorned style which, we have seen, is characteristic of Ferrabosco's English songs as well. That the song fails to sustain either emotional intensity or lyric bloom is not, thus, unexceptional. But a performance of this song, in particular, might be quite different than its appearance would imply. The possibility of ornamentation and expressive improvisation must be considered, at least until the words "di battaglia." The declamation of the words can be almost entirely free of regular meter, except where cited in Ex. 15 above, and the realization of the continuo, even in a modest style as suggested by Spink, is extremely important in creating the sense of "thinking aloud" and declaiming in music.

These songs, in which music and words are joined, but in which music is still the prevailing partner, are clear evidence that Ferrabosco was aware of the contemporary developments in Italian music. He had no reason to be as directly concerned with the humanistic arguments about the function and manner of music which resulted in the early, experimental Italian *recitativo*. If the date of these songs is correctly gauged to from around 1611, the date of the last masque songs, then it is not surprising that these songs do not demonstrate mastery of the continuo song and dramatic recitative styles. Ferrabosco was more eclectic. He was sensitive to words, but he was not involved with theorizing about affect or quantity. Even in these songs he is never far from the almost lyrical early monodic style which could, at any moment, burst into song. The English "recitative musick" would have to wait for Lanier's "Hero and Leander" (probably composed after Lanier's return from Italy in 1627), and the mastery of the continuo song was not achieved until the time of William and Henry Lawes.

XII

Dialogs

We might expect to find a dramatic style in Ferrabosco's dialogs, for it was in this genre that some of the earliest approaches to recitative are found, particularly in the slightly later works of Johnson, Lanier, Ramsey, and Hilton. By the time of William and Henry Lawes, the dialog enjoyed a greater popularity in England than its evident model, the *dialoghi* of the earlier Italian monodists, did on the continent. Those *dialoghi* were stylistically incorporated into the chamber duet/cantata and the conversational recitative style of later mid-century opera.

The characteristics of the English dialog consist of the alternation of voices in the first section over a continuo-like bass, often progressing from the simple repetition of musical material by each voice, to overlapping, even imitative entries, and a concluding concerted duet in more measured and note-against-note style. These dialogs took place between pastoral lovers, mythological characters, biblical personages, even moral or instructional attributes—sometimes between characters from various of these categories. Except for the biblical and moral dialogs, the subject of discussion was usually love: true love, lost love, false love, faithful love, etc.

Here, however, there was a different necessity which governed the style. Unlike the expressive monologue of the late madrigal, e.g., Monteverdi's *sestina* from Book VI: "Lagrime d'amante al sepolcro dell'amata" (1614), and the narrative representation which was developed from one stunning moment in *L'Orfeo* to its full powers in *Il Combattimento di Tancredi e Clorinda*, the dialog needed to present both contrast and unity. Thus the declamation of speech was important—to isolate, characterize, and rationalize the participants—but so was the measured coordination of song in which both characters could simultaneously agree.

The form which accomplished this, then, allowed the (dramatic) juxtaposition of the characters in the more declamatory mode and concluded with a unifying/unified duet. As the century progressed, the symmetry of alternation in the first section became less important than the dramatic contrast of the characters and the individuation of their expression. While this is seen very clearly in the dialogs of Henry Lawes, the beginnings of the more dramatic dialog style are seen in Ferrabosco's dialogs.

Of Ferrabosco's four dialogs, three appear only in the *Ayres*, while the fourth is found in the "John Bull" MS where it is marked "i pte," although no sequel follows.

Faire Cruel Nymph	*Ayres*, #26
A Dialogue between a Shepheard and a Nimph	
What shall I wish	*Ayres*, #27
A Dialogue	
Tell Me, O love	*Ayres*, #28
A Dialogue betweene a Shepheard and a Nimph	
Say, Shepherd Boy!	Cambridge:
A Dialogue i pte	Fitzwilliam Museum, MS 52.D.25, ff. 100^v-101
	(*Manuscript Songs*, #v)

None of the texts has been identified, and there is no evidence of particular performances or events for which any of these might have been composed.

"What shall I wish" (#27) is a moral dialog, its text tediously austere except for the trappings of rhyme. Completely impersonal, it lacks any sense of the dramatic which informs the poetic and later musical representations of soul-body dialogs. The other three songs are settings of pastoral dialogs in which a love-smitten shepherd is eventually comforted by an entirely sympathetic, though often coy and teasing nymph.

Particularly in the last of the *Ayres*, "Tell me, O Love," (#28) and the manuscript dialog, "Say, Shepherd Boy!" (#v), we are at the brink of an affective style which, while it does not approach recitative, attempts a musical characterization of the participants. Spink rightly points out that

> [Ferrabosco's] style is insufficiently flexible to serve as a vehicle for naturalistic musical conversation, but the continuo tendencies in the accompaniment are clear, and this was a necessary preliminary before the vocal parts could loosen up and develop declamatory suppleness.[1]

Spink's use of "declamatory suppleness" in conjunction with "naturalistic musical conversation" at least lets the reader know what kind of declamation he is discussing, for in many of the works examined in these pages several aspects of declamation have been admirably handled without approaching a "naturalistic" expression. We are caught in changing traditions, for English song had typically been neutral or unconcerned with regard to many aspects of text-setting. The emergence of a new style which placed much more emphasis on verbal qualities, especially those peculiar to the English language, went through several stages before it was comfortably presented in the works of Lawes and composers thereafter.

Dramatic monolog or soliloquy, focusing attention on the *persona* of the speaker, had been the raw material for the affective monody. The dramatic narrative, on the other hand, was ideally borne by the representative style. Both shared resources of harmonic affect, florid ornament, and a naturalistic, if intensified, recitative style which could be varied at the whim of verbal or dramatic circumstance. The more introspective and non-dramatic interior monolog or meditation was characteristically more conservative.

In effect, the pastoral dialog was non-dramatic entertainment, though shamming as drama. It belonged to a world in which strong feelings, pain, and death were alien. It was the insistent emphasis on strong feelings in the Arcadian world of the Italian madrigal which ultimately destroyed the genre, transforming it from impersonal entertainment into personalized drama. The bucolic world of Ferrabosco's dialogs knows no such disturbance. Following a brief exposition of love-pain and sympathy, shepherd and nymph sing together a concluding chorus of harmonious joy and union. No one is fooled; the dialog was all a game, a delicious trifle, played with artfully phrased and chosen words, affected pain, and mock seriousness.

The dialogs are comfortably framed in a variety of ways: the poetry is regular and rhymed, and this is reflected in the music; the participants appear sufficient unto themselves, there is no intrusion from outside (one has only to recall how the essentially idyllic and pastoral landscape of *Die schöne Müllerin* was lost with the intrusion of the hunter); the chorus provides agreement, conclusion, and musical distance (a sense of "happily ever after"). There is no sense of universal response. There cannot be, for there is no projection of personality.

In this non-dramatic milieu, a dramatic style would be insupportable; it would overwhelm the content. At his best in these dialogs, Ferrabosco provides modest musical characterizations which merge in an invariably tuneful chorus where a sense of urgency is avoided in both harmony and melodic gesture. Voices alternate, rather than interrupt, or sing together; there is no dramatic confrontation.

There are no characters, no moral conflict in "What shall I wish" (#27). Rather than dialog, it has the feeling of reflection between two equal voices which share point of view and, hence, melodic gestures. If anything the song is too simple and unsophisticated. The melodic range is a ninth, but that is misleading, for almost the entire piece, vocally, stays within the fifth above c' (the tonic).

The opening section of the song presents the typical alternation of voices, with chordal accompaniment, creating a small melodic arch from the tonic to the fifth and back. The text setting is arbitrary, with no evident concern for any rhetorical possibility. The text is presented smoothly in discrete snippets which rely on the overlapping of the singers' entrances to maintain continuity.

The second section, repeated in the *Ayres* (this repeat is overlooked by Fellowes), moralizes in a concerted duet with welcome melismatic activity twining up and down the same fifth at the words "Flattery brings pleasure." The conclusion, to the severally repeated text "Happy are they that never knew deceit," employs a neat marriage of imitation and voice exchange after a cadence on the dominant.

The first section is in the minor mode, as is the beginning of the second, and both are flavored by the use of the relative major. The interesting aspect about this typical procedure here is that the subdominant of the relative major, A♭ (which is also related to the tonic by two common tones) is the vehicle for the transition. This allows greater ambiguity, not only with the tonic, but with the dominant (G) itself to which the a♭ melodically points (as N of V).

Ex. 1

The use of the relative major and the dominant as internal stopping points alternates by smaller units, with the first part of each section utilizing the implications of the relative major, while the second establishes the primacy of the dominant-tonic relationship.

The final, imitative section affirms the major mode as the locus of all that is true ("happy are they that never knew deceit"), which, stretching things a bit, could argue that the slippery relations between ♭VI, i/I, ♭III, and v/V have been the miasma of deceit from which the singers now happily are freed. The contrast is neatly made, however, with the antecedent-consequent phrases combining to fill out a descent of a major scale in contrast to the earlier, repeated (though varied in specific manner) ascending and descending fillings-out of the lower fifth in the minor mode.

Ex. 2

The range of the song, its simplicity and unsuitability for consideration as either great art or secular entertainment, and its didactic tone with a lesson emphasized in major mode might suggest that this is a very early song—which even if true, cannot be proved—or, as it stands in the *Ayres*, a song for two, probably young and beginning singers—proper food for young minds and young musicians.

"Faire cruel Nymph" (#26) is a genuine dialog, its two characters differentiated in range and, at the beginning, aspect. The anguished shepherd's lament strains upward a minor sixth, answered by the nymph's pert descent of a seventh to the tonic, G. The shepherd's pain is none too real, however, for his moan turns to the relative major and is smoothly reversed by the nymph's reply ending on the tonic major. And touches like this petulant dotted figure characterize the playful nymph much better than words could do.

Ex. 3

The opening section of this dialog is in two parts. The first of these is a prolepsis of the whole, for the second repeats the melodic procedure, in different detail, before the final duetting begins.[2] On a larger level, it presents a confirming movement (very nearly a modulation) to the relative major which returns to the tonic only by sleight-of-hand (passing movement to the third-related dominant) in an artificially extended cadence.

Ex. 4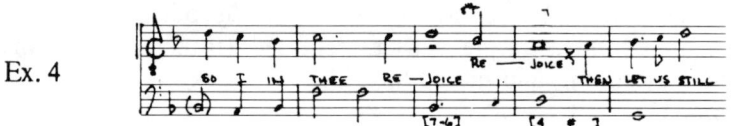

When singing alone, the shepherd's melodic motion is continually falling back, unable to sustain melodic height, while the nymph's, rhythmically more assertive, seems bold in comparison.

Ex. 5

The fancies of the shepherd's mind are portrayed in the metric malleability of his line, as, pretending to be languishing in despair, he flatters the nymph into compliance; his words are allowed to linger expressively in descent. The effect is made not by accenting the vocal line against the accompaniment, as if these were syncopations, but simply by following the word accents and allowing a temporary, fanciful, delirious metric ambiguity.

The melodic shape of the song is carefully gauged to this game of love, for the shepherd who, by himself, can reach no higher than e♭, (though he certainly aspires to the nymph's f) suddenly, in duet, takes the lead, completing the octave to g' ("As thou in me"). The two then share their range equally, albeit an octave apart, as they celebrate their climax in a relaxed, twin descent to the lower, fundamental octave.

More interesting, in the measures which begin the duetting, is the manner Ferrabosco draws the two characters together by rushing their responses, overlapping them at different intervals of time, interlocking the melodic lines, and animating the delivery of the text. This loving tug-of-war has two stages, and in the second the shepherd, as mentioned above, dramatically o'erleaps the nymph causing her breathlessly to "rejoice."

Ex. 6

Unlike the earlier statements made individually by the characters, throughout this example cadences are thwarted by suspensions and melodic motion in the bass until the return of g minor. At that point, the duetting becomes regularized and the cadences synchronized, the harmonic movement more stable and restricted. Both voices share a melodic arch of a seventh, and the final cadence concentrates the attention on g by both harmonic and melodic progression and by contrary motion between voices and bass for several measures.

Compared with the stodgy text-setting of "What shall I wish?," that of "Faire cruel nymph" has more rhythmic animation and variety, as well as greater melodic scope and harmonic interest (which is shared by the accompaniment). Also, there are no egregious violations of normal textual accent. The closest examples are the exaggerations of "As thou in me" which, fittingly, borders on the ecstatic.

Ex. 7

The first instance is simply awkward misaccentuation; the second is willful and affective emphasis.

Another amorous situation is more interestingly handled in "Tell me, O love" (#28). In this a love-smitten shepherd seeks confirmation that he is indeed loved by his nymph. This, in itself, is not unusual, nor is the standard *double entendre* in which death and the act of love are joined. Much more noticeably than either of the previous dialogs, which made no essential musical characterization of the participants, this one identifies the shepherd and nymph by contrasting musical styles which merge as the distance between the characters diminishes. Specifically, the shepherd is presented in the guise of traditional lament, while the nymph, much more animated — and perhaps honestly disturbed — responds in a vein closer to continuo song. The shepherd, though his expression is moderate and measured, acquires the chromatic inflections of a more passionate style and finally the two sing in a manner not as ornate and sustained, but not unlike the duetting style of Monteverdi. That duetting arises from both textual and musical impetus, regularizing the asymmetry of styles and phrasing and resolving the differences between the characters.

Beginning in the manner of the serious lute-song, replete with a pseudo-contrapuntal imitative introduction, the shepherd breaks in before the accompaniment cadences. The web of superficial part-writing, overlapping entrances and cadences, and the conventionally neutral text-setting (in which the musical gestures, such as the opening leap of a fifth, and the text have no apparent relation except for the constantly thwarted aspirations of the melody which is unable to keep from falling back on itself) hearken back to the laments of the consort-song repertory.

Ex. 8

Ex. 8
(continued)

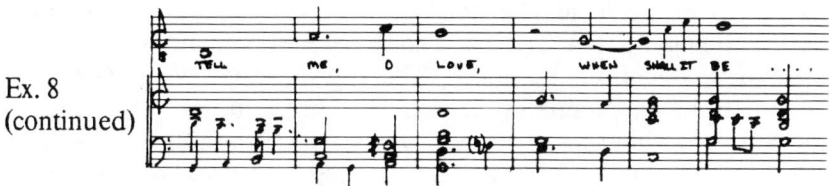

The fluid overlapping and the expansive leisure of the vocal line create an impression of impersonality and inwardness which changes during the song as Ferrabosco moves away from this starkly antitextual style.

The nymph, on the other hand, is all in the here and now. She responds to the shepherd's laborious (and patently fictive) agony with an immediate, if teasing, concern expressed at the outset in an agitated near-recitative (over a continuo-style bass) which rather quickly abandons its seriousness to rhetorical pose, metric games, and, finally, punning and melodiousness.

Ex. 9

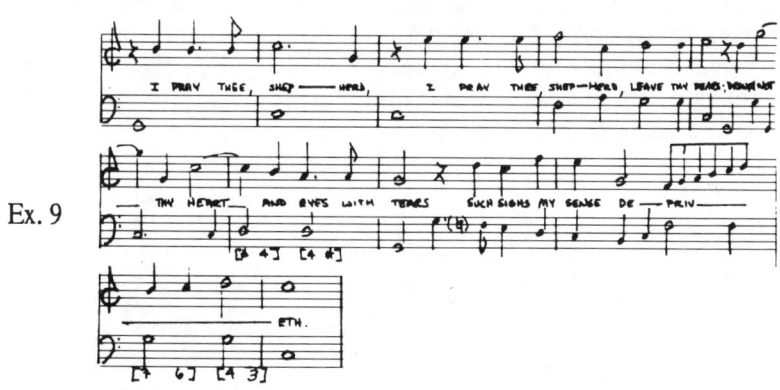

The exaggerated pronouncement, "Drown not thy heart. . . .," might be imperious in another circumstance, but here, by rhetorical license, it is merely a counterfeit of celebratory declamation. The sense of accent and harmonic focus is temporarily lost at the punning setting of "my sense depriveth."

The structure of this dialog is more complicated than that of its predecessor in the *Ayres*. The balance of the alternating or duetting voices is predicated on the text, but, after the first, extended statements of each character, their responses come more quickly and the harmonic palette becomes more interesting. The opening lament of the shepherd is presented on the dominant, to which the nymph responds on the tonic.

The second set of entrances, about half as long, finds the shepherd drawn reluctantly to the tonic after a brief exploration of the circle of fifths begun by sliding from a C major chord to E major (V of vi). The steadfast nymph confirms the tonic. The real duetting recapitulates this movement to the upper side of the circle of fifths until the return to the tonic, "And sing this song with me," which is signified by overlapping imitation between the parts. (The measures just preceding, during which the move was made back from the implications of a, the relative minor, presented the voices in successive imitation: see Ex. 10c.)

At particularly moving passages, such as the various, dolorous appearances of the word "Alas," the affect is enhanced by harmonic chromaticism, and it is this which spurs the activity on the farther reaches of the dominant side of the tonic. The chromaticism is always consonant, entered through a common-tone or fifth-related harmony. That it is always a major, not minor construction and without prominent melodic affectation indicates that this expression is not one of pathetic seriousness (for which Ferrabosco typically used the subdominant and/or minor regions). The direction of the melodic line confirms this. In the first example cited below, the shepherd affects disappointment in the falling intervals, his *dolor* prettily expressed in the sweet dissonance of the cross-relation. In the second, dawning joy is heard in the ascent which is found also, more extended and aware, in the third.

Ex. 10a

Ex. 10b

Ex. 10c

This last example provides the textual clue to this little game of love, for now our shepherd, by this time fully recovered, and our nymph, no longer fretful, duet away in carefree, tuneful style.

But the contrasts of the consort style, the pathetic mode, the continuo song, even the plumped-up declamatory episode, with the final duetting is a game in itself. Here are all the styles, *in nuce*, except the intensely expressive declamation of, say, Dowland's uniquely moving outburst in "In darkness let me dwell."

To be sure, these are not all masterfully presented. They are, more properly speaking, counterfeited, imitated, or implied. We infer more from their contrasts and balances than we would if they were presented separately.

Ultimately, though, each of the "styles" devolves quickly into the melodious, harmonically predictable and metrically regular character of lyric song.

Despite the tendency toward a continuo style necessary for the voices to achieve declamatory flexibility and the kind of expressiveness that permits, the lyrical mode lies close to the surface. Even the sham consort style of the opening, which did not partake of the more severe modal flavor of the older laments, rather quickly becomes chordal as the bass becomes less melodic and more fundamental.

Both changes of tempo and flexibility of presentation are called for here, as the styles change, and the aspect of this song which is most convincing is not its approach to our concept of recitative, but its juxtaposition of these various styles for the sake of musical characterization.

Ferrabosco never did develop a consistently dramatic recitative responsive to both the circumstance and the finer detail of the speech rhythms of the words. Like the poetry he chose to set, the formal regularities of the dialog settings restrain the rush of words and the immediacy of response. Yet, in his one unpublished dialog, Ferrabosco did reach the brink of true recitative.

The implicit, coy drama of "Say, Shepherd Boy!" (#v) is suitable for staging or inclusion within a larger theatre entertainment. It is all sham as we have a none-too-shy nymph (unseen, hiding, or, more brazenly, holding her hands over the shepherd's eyes) who accosts a sorely grieving shepherd about his condition. His love-pains confessed, she reveals herself, and the two join in an imitative, exuberant chorus wherein they somewhat remarkably aspire to fill their hearts "with chaste and holy fire."

To be sure, this is but another of the variants of cavalier pastoral encounter, neatly shaped and ephemeral. More important to the student of English song is the freedom of the vocal dialog compared with the more lyrical pastoral pieces in the *Ayres*. It is a freedom, however, based on the principle that "less is more," for the flexibility of the dialog is permitted by a restriction of harmonic movement and a reduction in the melodic activity of the bass.

Thus, a true continuo style is approached. Over a slow-moving bass the voices are free to move, rather negligent of the notated time-values, responding to the impetus of that bass more immediately than the rest would allow as well as stretching the interior of the lines for affective expression. The vocal lines also use a greater variety of time-values, which give a sense of elasticity and greater naturalness and direction.

The beginning is a good example of these points, as the nymph insouciantly calls the shepherd, emphasizing her brashness by lingering on the words "Say" and "Why?", and then delicately teases his pain with a diminished fourth.[3]

Ex. 12

The flexibility of the setting is particularly conspicuous compared with the regularity of the iambic text. As he has in other instances we have discussed, Ferrabosco emphasizes the first word of these phrases, reversing the accent for rhetorical purposes three times in succession. In each of these cases, the word normally accented in the text is given slight emphasis by prominence of pitch (tonic accent) which keeps the word from being lost. But it is the eighth-notes rushing toward the next textual accent which really enliven the declamation and, in the case of the $e^{b''}$ on "so," intensify the feeling. One need only compare the above examples with a smoothed-out version to hear how much of the life of the words and situation is incorporated in Ferrabosco's setting.

Ex. 13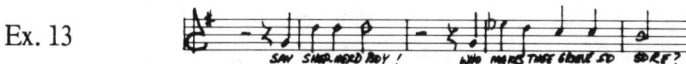

The more varied use of longer and shorter time-values in the setting of the text, the frequent off-beat entrances, and the use of smaller note-values after long notes (particularly those tied over an imaginary bar-line or metric accent or striking of the bass) contribute to the sense of a freer, more speech-like rhythm. But the metric frame is always immanent, ready to reassert itself and organize the expression in a temporally comprehensible manner, thus also regularizing the harmonic progressions into greater focus. The shepherd's lament is never far from tuneful song, and it provides an example of movement from relatively free expressions to measured song, from the declamatory "Ah! Glad am I" to the lyrical bloom and pictorially ecstatic emphasis at "phoenix."

Ex. 14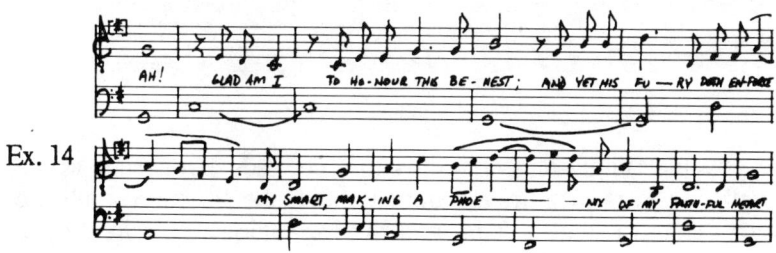

The nymph never abandons her rather imperious manner, although it softens in the last measures. There is no command in Ferrabosco's English songs more forthrightly stated and appropriately exuberant than hers to the shepherd.[4]

Ex. 15

"And take me swain" is unfortunately set in a way which only confuses the syntax. The ascending melodic line demands a g" for completion, yet the word "swain" should be set apart as a noun, not an adverb. Here is the case for a Hollander-like argument that what we expect to hear is something on the order of "and take me now" instead of (with clarifying punctuation) "and take me, swain, whose heart thou long last had."

That g", however, is the climax of the dialog and the culmination of a very discreet ascent by the nymph. The ecstatic moment of revealing takes us almost from duple to triple time, at least in the vocal writing. The bass and voice act at cross-purposes, with their triple-times coming at different points, and this metric play is possible only because the metric frame is relatively secure. Such is not unique with Ferrabosco, but this dialog is an excellent example of how the near-recitative and melodic styles can merge in and out of one another and how dependent that relationship is on the character of the bass.

The only inexplicable difficulty is at the words "Love is the sweet of life."

Ex. 16

If it were possible simply to ascribe this to a copyist's error, such as we must do with the extra measure mentioned above, the situation would be much easier. Here the metric frame and the harmonic rhythm have gone mutually amuck, the implied movement toward D thwarted, and bass and voice hobbling together as if in a sack race. It is unique in Ferrabosco's songs, and, without additional concordances, it must stand.[5]

We return to the tuneful measured style in the chorus, which, in the uninhibited exuberance of the runs on "Sing" and the imitations which follow, resembles that of "Tell me, O love." The greater regularity of the chorus lacks neither vigor nor variety, though it is required for the ensemble and to provide a means of closure. It ends so quickly, even when repeated, that we are induced to think of the entire song as a trifle, entertaining and artificial, pleasant for the moment but, ultimately, unremarkable. That is unfortunate, for this is a piece worth attention. Even in the chorus, Ferrabosco focuses attention on the words by musical and metrical means. The setting of "Sing we of love," while aptly representative of singing, plunges headlong into the word "love," impelled by the abrupt change of the harmonic rhythm.

Ex. 17

These amorous dialogs have relatively assiduously plied the major mode and, in particular, the dominant side of the tonic. At the conclusion of this chorus, however, the use of the borrowed f of "chaste" transforms the sound, though it might not convince the sceptical auditor that the description is deserved.

Ex. 18

It is in this dialog that we see most clearly the prototype of the dramatic style: a harmonically interesting continuo bass which moves freely from almost unmeasured to measured participation with the voice, vocal parts which are asymmetrically presented and interact as well as connect and which have an immediate vigor of rhythmic and melodic gesture and an ability to coordinate in ensemble in addition to maintaining their individuality of expression. The responsiveness of the vocal setting to the words is both rhythmic and gestural as well as occasionally pictorial. The style is not, in these dialogs, an emotional style, either in vocal ornament or in harmonic dissonance and contrast. For such, we must look to Ferrabosco's Italian songs. But it is an apt style, ripe with possibility, rarely losing its harmonic or melodic shapeliness and direction, and, in this modest context, very satisfying.

XIII

The Motets

Unlike his songs, which are in many respects quite progressive and reflect contemporary modes of song composition, Ferrabosco's motets are conservative. We do not know when or for whom they were written. They almost certainly, like the four-voice fancies, were written before 1609, the year young Francis Tregian was removed to Fleet Prison where, before his death in 1619, he compiled his great manuscript collections. One of these, the Sambrooke Book (now NYPL MS Drexel 4302), is our only source for all the motets. In addition, another source, Thomas Myriell's *Tristitiae Remedium* (British Museum MSS Add. 29372-7), was completed in 1616.

The real problem is the absence of Tregian's original source or sources. The variants and the numbering of motets in the Bodleian set (MSS Music School c. 45-50) and in the more important of the British Museum sources (MSS Add. 29366-8) are similar enough to argue that the Bodleian set might have been used as the source for the latter. But neither would have been adequate for Tregian, and the ordering of the motets in Tregian's manuscript is different. Moreover, the Bodleian set was copied with certain incompletions (described in the Table of Concordances) and with a mistaken clef at the beginning of the quintus part of "Ego dixi domine," which would indicate that these part-books were not used for performance, otherwise the necessary corrections would have been made.

Therefore, of a total of 13 motets and a set of *Lamentations*, only 8 motets and the *Lamentations* have fully or partially texted concordances outside the Tregian collection. Another motet appears without text or attribution in the Bodleian set. Because the Tregian collection provides at most the text of the bass and cantus and sometimes only the incipit of these, the absence of fully texted sources for the *unica* makes it difficult even to surmise what the texts might have been (cf. especially "O

Domine"). Since it is unlikely that the Tregian collection served as a source for any of the other manuscripts, or vice versa, we must postulate at least one other set of "ghost" partbooks which have yet to be identified or are lost. The one inexplicable anomaly among these concordances is the appearance of the *Lamentations* as a 5-part piece in Tregian's score, while only the cantus and bass are provided in the Bodleian set (which had provided the only fully texted concordances of 8 of the motets). No reason for this can be demonstrated, although one could assume that performance by 2 voices, or voice and instrument, would have been acceptable.

If these motets were completed by 1612, the year of Prince Henry's death and the abrupt end of Ferrabosco's active artistic ascendancy in collaboration with Ben Jonson, it is no wonder that they do not partake of the emerging verse-anthem style explored by East and Gibbons. These are still representative of the principles of the psalm-motet: non-liturgical texts presented in a series of imitative sections. The texts represent the generally more personal attitude which had developed toward the choice of words for a motet from the time of Byrd's early works. Though most are Biblical, their arrangement is manipulated in an individual way, and several of the texts are apparently original (e.g., "O nomen Jesu").

The musical settings emphasize this concern for the specific text and, rather than church usage, imply domestic or private devotion: perhaps in the house of a patron (with the patron the arranger of the texts?), the house of the Ambassador of France, or even the Queen's private chamber. The individual motets vary considerably in their manner, but the characteristic mode of construction is multisectional and through–composed. The characteristic compositional technique consists of a succession of points of imitation, sometimes two used simultaneously, each of which conveys a textual phrase. After the exposition of the material in all the voices the phrase gathers into a cadence which, unless there is a clear ending of a textual idea, is not completed before the imitative procedure introducing the next textual material enters, overlapping and redirecting the cadence concluding the previous text.

It is arguable that composers such as Byrd, Palestrina, and Lassus, to mention the most prominent, were word-oriented and even oversensitively aware of the text. Such an observation is witness to the sense of sublime enlargement of the text which takes place in the works of these composers through the subtlety of architecture, the detail of accentuation (often varying in various voices), and the restrained drama of timbral contrast and harmonic movement and inflection. This sense is muted and mediated, different from that which informs Monteverdi's choral recitative or inspires the growing sense of dramatic *persona* in the continuo madrigal or verse anthem.

The matching of musical figure to textual phrase, however, is a sticking point for which we have not yet developed the art of comparative and critical evaluation. Composers who are successful are so in variety, as is attested by the multitude of successful settings of the mass ordinary—or by the parodies of works "reworked," the refractive passage of ideas resonated through decades, and centuries. The unsuccessful works, however, are not the ones overshadowed by their towering brothers, but those which, in this sense, succeed only perfunctorily in conveying the text.

In this regard, Ferrabosco is successful, but on a small scale. His works participate in the freedom of imitative counterpoint and the variety of melodic material, as well as the use of homophony and textural change for expressive purposes, which Byrd (and Tallis in the latter regard) introduced to the English scene from the 1570s on. And his works display a large-scale concern for harmonic construction which emphasizes tonal relations. This is true not only of the motets in two *pars*, which must be considered together because they are complete musically only at the end of the second motet whether or not the textual units could be separated, but even more so of the *Lamentations*, in which the large, three-part structure first contrasts, then balances the dominant and subdominant sides of the tonic.

Textual units within the motets are set to different musical figures, as is to be expected, but each of these units is set in a manner which emphasizes a movement creating a tonal harmonic structure. It is the clarity of these structures, their tonal order, which keeps them from sounding "antique." For here even more than in the songs, the use of the resources of parallel tonal pairs (e.g., G/g) results not in confusion of mode, but in enrichment of the tonic.

The clarity of construction, however, points to a problem which results in the impression of insubstantiality of expression. Although there are a multitude of examples which militantly stand forth against such a statement, such as the moving opening of "O nomen Jesu," the problem really seems to be one of talent. All the elements of the compositions are in basic order, yet the overall sense is sometimes mechanical. Except for rhythmic shape, the points of imitation are as often guided by musical needs as they are by textual specificity, mostly consisting of triads or perfect intervals whose shape is filled in passing. This alone would not distinguish Ferrabosco from his betters; what does is the absence of a sense of necessity in the expression of the music: the absence of the coruscating rhythmic dissonance pointing a climactic moment of the text, of the dramatic variety of timbre and procedure which pervades Palestrina's later works, of a more interesting use dissonance and harmonic juxtaposition, or of a sense of fullness at the end of a work. To be sure, even a brief look at these motets will reveal much to recommend Ferrabosco. But to hear a motet of Byrd and one of Ferrabosco is to enter into the text at different levels. A motet of Byrd serves the text wholly; the dynamic tension of the expression and the ebb and flow of energy fill and move the piece. Ferrabosco lacks that sustained and sustaining energy in his motets, just as he does in most of his songs. In both, shapeliness substitutes for intensity and immediacy. But is is only by knowing works such as these that the genius of Byrd or Gibbons or even Weekles can be assessed.

The use of homophony, or, more specifically, homorhythmic declamation, is infrequent in the motets and *Lamentations*, reserved for moments of particular effect. In two of the most striking examples, the opening of "O nomen Jesu" and the concluding "Jerusalem, Jerusalem" of the *Lamentations*, this chordal declamation is presented with contrasts of the lower and higher four voices. But such contrasts of timbre and overt use of homorhythm are rare, although Ferrabosco will more frequently begin a section with the voices (from two to five) presenting the text at almost the same time, or with four beginning followed by the fifth, but quickly trailing off into a more relaxed quasi-contrapuntal or imitative procedure. While the cantus and bass are the most important parts and are distinguished from their fellows by their relative sedateness and greater clarity of textual presentation, there is no consistent sense of one voice stepping out of the ensemble and contrasting with it. "O nomen Jesu" povides a notable exception in which the leading voice (or voices) is exposed against the background of the ensemble. But this remains a sense of response, such as is known from the serious consort-song, in which the words make specific the shared musical experience of the participants. There is no sense of personalization as found in the later madrigal, no dramatic persona.

The bass is both a melodic voice and harmonic foundation, and the character of its lines varies considerably in the performance of these two roles. What is most characteristic, however, is the appearance of forthright leaps of a fourth or fifth at the beginnings of sections or at structurally important cadences. At less important cadences the movement of the bass is frequently conjunct, and the cadence is achieved by intervallic, rather than chordal, progression. Where the structure needs articulation, and at the end of the motets, however, the bass moves directly by leap. In this way, the hierarchy of the motet structure, the importance of the various harmonic movements, is emphasized. This structure is reflected by the successive new phases of imitation, only rarely by textural variety (except that which arises as the new points emerge from the preceding cadence) or by full, internal stop.

The voice parts lie within one ledger line of whatever clef is used, and the one exception to this actually proves the functional relation of clef to range. In the conclusion of "Omnes amici" in the *Lamentations* the bassus (normally with bass clef) is asked to sing up to e♭'. But at this point, which places the bass a full third higher than he had previously sung, the tenor clef is used, and the extra ledger lines are avoided. Vocal ranges generally extend an eleventh or twelfth. The lower extremes of the four upper voices are used, but not greatly, so the tessitura vary from the upper ninth for the cantus to the lower ninth for the bass. The *Lamentations*, using ATTBarB clefs, is certainly for men's voices. The motets with two treble clefs, (like similarly scored madrigals of the time in both England and Italy whence the practice originated) exploit an uncomfortably high part of a woman's or boy's range today, and lead one to wonder if there was a different pitch standard. The clefs used in this case, TrTrMsABar ("Ubi duo"; "Libera Me"), correspond to Morley's "high key," and the clefs of the *Lamentations* are those he describes for compositions for men.[1] Morley makes no mention of transposition, but a problem arises when he goes on to say

> It is true that the high and low keys come both to one pitch (or rather compass) [Morley had just used "compass" to describe the vocal range relative to the staff] but you must understand that those songs which are made for the high key be made for more life, the other in the low key for more gravity and staidness, so that if you sing them in contrary keys they will lose their grace and will be wrested, as it were, out of their nature.[2]

Morley appears to be caught in a contradiction here concerning the reason for using high or low clefs and his assertion that both "come to one pitch (or rather compass)."

However, he continues:

> For take an instrument as a lute, opharion, pandora, or such like being in the natural pitch, and set it a note or two lower, it will go much heavier and duller and far from the spirit which it had before.[3]

And then, to make clear that he is *not* recommending transposition, he observes:

> Even so if songs of the high key be sung in the low pitch and they of the low key sung in the high pitch, though it will not be so offensive as the other, yet it will not breed so much contentment in the hearer as otherwise it would do.[4]

Even if it be not always true that "songs made for the high key be made for more life, [those] in the low key for more gravity and staidness," there is no indication of transposition based on clef-combinations. It is more likely that the "high key" pieces were genuinely higher in pitch than "low key" compositions. It is also demonstrable that the clef combinations allowed the simplest key signatures; therefore, the pitch standard was probably flexible unless fixed-pitch instruments were used in accompaniment. The compromise employed by Peter Platt in his edition of Richard Dering's *Cantica Sacra, 1618*[5] was to transpose pieces in "high key" (i.e., having two sopranos) down a minor third. This is understandable from a singer's position, but it does prejudice the relation of such a piece with "low key" compositions which are presented untransposed.

Matters of clarity of notation and instrumental performance undoubtedly affected the overwhelming predominance of clef-combinations with signatures of, at most, one flat or sharp. A flexible pitch standard might allow for modern-day transposition, but not for an arbitrary theory (here, at least) of *chiavi trasportati*. The transcriptions of Ferrabosco's motets, which appear as an appendix to this study, are untransposed — there being no compelling reason for transposition.

Ferrabosco's response to the texts has two aspects. On a large scale he is well aware of the relationship of phrases to each other, and his musical structures carefully reflect those textual elements which are subordinate or lead to another phrase and those which are contradictory or vocative. The various stages of the textual progress are also reflected in the tonal structure of the motets. On the level of individual words, there is occasional highlighting of an important word, both by gestural prominence and, where pictorially appropriate, melodic vigor and shape. Often particular words will be given a rhythmic "motto"

| ♩. ♪ (♩)

(e.g., "do - mi - ne")

which is always used for that word in a motet, whether appearing in a single voice or, at the other extreme, simultaneously in all voices. What Ferrabosco does not achieve, as Palestrina does even in a mass setting like the *Missa Aeterna Christi munera*, is the impression of an accumulating density of declamation which serves the words, sometimes effected by contrasting groups of voices. With Ferrabosco, the effect remains diffuse, the words seeming to serve as attributes of the music instead of the other way around. The moments of musical pictorialism and affective expression show an aspect of Ferrabosco's awareness of words, but it is an awareness without mastery.

"Ego sum resurrectio" and "O nomen Jesu"

Although not so designated in the manuscript sources, there are several indications that "Ego sum resurrectio" and "O nomen Jesu" form a motet in two *pars*, just as do the next three pairs of motets in the major sources and one additional set in the Tregian score. The words of Jesus, from the Gospel of John, are answered by the worshipping believer who responds to the message of Christ. More convincing even than this textual interpretation is the manner by which the music supports the argument. "Ego sum" works out its material in the minor mode and ends incomplete, one might argue, on the dominant. Just as the "I" of "Ego sum" needs the company of worshippers for completion, the dominant, which concludes that piece, needs the tonic ending of the next motet. The ecstatic affirmation of the validity of Christ makes whole that which was not finished: the opening measures of "O nomen Jesu" bring the work back to the tonic major, thus asserting the power of that name, and the opening homophony and contrasts of texture reflect the universality of the response.

I.	1. Ego sum resurrectio et vita		$g=i$	iv_6-V-i	(g)
	2. qui credit in me,		m. 21		
	etiam si mortuus fuerit, vivet			V/iv-iv	
	et omnes qui vivit et credit in me				
	non morietur			V/IV-IV	(C)
	3. in eternum		m.50	iv-V	(D)
II.	1. O nomen Jesu			$G=I$	
	nomen dulce			V-I	
	nomen delectabile			I-V	
	nomen confortans			V/ii-ii-I-IV	(C)
	2. Quid est enim Jesus		m.22		
	nisi salvator			IV-ii	
	Ergo Jesu			ii-IV/IV-IV	
	Propter nomen sanctum tuum			V-I-IV	(C)
	3. Esto michi Jesus		m.40	V-i-V	
	Et salva me			I - I / IV	(G)

Both motets are in three major sections in which the balance of subdominant and dominant is of particular interest, as is the flexible movement between tonic minor/major and relative major. Each motet also concludes with a short coda with a pedal in the upper voice, in which the pedal tone (D in the first case, G in the second) is the note of finality against which a subdominant pull is exerted—in effect, a plagal cadence considered as a I$^{(\flat)}{}^6_4$ suspension to balance the authentic cadence which led into the coda.

The close relation of text to music on this larger scale is characteristic of the motets in two *pars*. The internal balances of dominant and subdominant, and of tonic and relatively major areas, and the flexible intermingling of all of these by third-related movement utilizing voice-leading rather than direct chordal movement are also characteristic, as is the use of a plagal coda. These two motets are unusual in that they try to represent two different *personae* by different musical styles: the musical, imitative procedure of the first is contrasted to the more homorhythmic declamation (and greater subdominant emphasis) of the second. The *Lamentations* similarly attempt to distinguish between description and admonition, as well as between the text, the Hebrew letters, and the introductory announcement. Most of these motet texts do not call for such distinctions.

The inner voices of "Ego sum" provide a polyphonic web, while the cantus stands somewhat apart in range and gestural immediacy, its progress rather less busy than that of the inner parts. Moreover, the cantus answers the tonic entrances of the other parts by entering on the dominant (mm. 7-8), outlining a major triad for the first time in the piece. This is a moment of great affect: the individuation of the cantus as the "Ego" of the text, the speaking voice, is quite effective.

With the integration of all the parts by imitation this piece straddles the ground between the serious consort song (as developed by Byrd) and church motet. Because the lower voices do not continually isolate themselves against the cantus, however, the debt is clearly more to the church motet in which all voices are related, their musical integrity independent of the text.

In general, the musical figures have little textual specificity, the rhythmic point of "etiam" and "mortuus" and the lively eighth-notes of "vivet" and "vivit" being exceptions. These latter fall in the category of word-painting, as does the long-held note at the end of the cantus ("in eternum") and the descents at "si mortuus" and "non morietur" where depth and death are allied. What is more interesting is the use of the "vivit" figure at the end of "O nomen Jesu" to represent the nature of salvation ("et salva me") promised to the true believer, certainly a textually justified association and structurally striking since both occur in the codas concluding their respective motets.

One wonders how subtle Ferrabosco was in the setting of this first motet, for he does not employ dramatic effects to their full extent where they might be opportune. The setting of "et omnes" (m. 34) shows how close he comes, and yet how far he remains, from a dramatic portrayal of the text. All the voices are almost brought together here. In the larger sense of the text, however, a dramatic textural change would be inappropriate, disruptive of the idea of the text and the manner of presentation previously developed. Ferrabosco saves that dramatic turn for the response, "O nomen Jesu."

Except for the beginning of melodic figures, the vocal lines are generally smooth.[6] Both rule and exception can be found in the opening measures. The bass, which often and understandably has a less melodic contour than the other voices, is here smooth and elegantly shaped, while it is the tenor who, in m. 5, must make a double leap upward of a minor seventh and quit that by leap also.

Ex. 1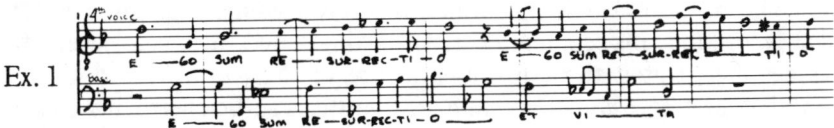

Such a double leap is unusual not only in its outer limits but also in the fact that the smaller ascent is made first, contrary to the practice of Palestrina. The disjunct character of this line is emphasized by the text-setting, while that of the following line, also sung by the tenor, is exposed as the lowest part where it emphasizes how important intervallic progressions remain in this style.

Ex. 2

The presence of cross-relations reflects mostly the flexibility of modal inflection which permeates Ferrabosco's motets. There are inconsistencies in the sources and times when one might wish to hear passages differently, but Ferrabosco does not often use cross-relations in the manner of Byrd and Tallis—for the biting acerbity they contribute to cadences. In an example such as is found in the fourth voice at mm. 28-29, the application of the b♮ seems wholly arbitrary; it would have been more understandable a beat earlier. This is, however, the point where a precipitous movement down the circle of fifths begins, and this startling suddenness, triggered by the b♮ and seconded by the e♮ in the cantus on the next beat, may well have been intentional.

The circumstances are different in m. 32, where the b's, both flat and natural, can be explained melodically, and in m. 33, where the b♮ in the cantus nicely points the cadence. In cases like this, the emphasis on the e♭-b♮ relationship serves paradigmatically to represent the flexibility of movement afforded by the modal inflections in the parallel tonal pair G/g, standing in contrast, as it does almost immediately, to e♭-b♭ or e♮-b♭ (and, much less frequently, e♮-b♮).

The cadence at m. 34 concludes a textual idea and is presented with both preparation and a drop of a fifth in the bass. Cadences of less structural importance are not so strongly presented, as the next one, in m. 40, demonstrates. Its shaping is intervallic, although it would not be recognized in today's harmonic terms as functionally different from that in m. 34, and its effect is much more quickly passing. In this manner, Ferrabosco (and his contemporaries) distinguished between levels of cadences and related them to the structure of the work. This does not mean that bass movement by fifth or fourth is sufficient to indicate a cadence, for that begs the basic elements of cadential preparation: aspects of repetition and reduction of harmonic rhythm among them. But it points out that the resources of voice leading are used by Ferrabosco in all parts, and they contribute to the hierarchy of cadential effects, just as they do for Byrd and Morley.

Contributing to the awareness of structural importance of the cadences are other practices, such as suspensions or continued polyphonic working out which will not allow the cadence to settle. In an unusual manner, too, Ferrabosco will often present only an open fifth, even at major, structural cadences (see m. 21, m. 33). These cadences give the effect of only a half-ending and demand further action to fill the void of root and fifth. In each of the examples in this motet, the quality of the chord is established quickly by the ensuing counterpoint. Because this counterpoint is moving away from the cadence, however, and not confirming it, the cadence remains insufficient and incomplete to our ears, providing another kind of contrast with the complete triads in other cadences and the final chord. Unlike the music of a century before, when such three-voice cadences were the result of a deliberate cleaning out of the texture to focus on the modally essential tonic and fifth, the appearance of the archaic open fifth is shocking in its emptiness, for these cadences proceed to the open fifth not only by melodic clearing away (intervallically) but also by harmonic chord progression enhanced by voice-leading and suspensions which can fill out the sound. Thus, "Ego sum resurrectio," in its internal cadences, exploits a range of intervallic and chordal practices to establish a structural sense in which motion is clarified but not stopped.

Although these cadences serve to coordinate and define the activities of the successive sections of imitation, the harmonic activity of the entire motet and the final cadence, in particular, exhibits a flexible sense of harmonic propriety. On the one hand, the important centers of harmonic weight, which include the dominant, subdominant (major and minor), and relative major, do not compromise the recognition of the tonic. This is confirmed by the feeling that the motet "Ego sum" ends "up" on the dominant and that the motet "O nomen Jesu" is necessary for its musical completion. The sections of this motet form a larger-scale movement of i-iv/IV-V, a movement recapitulated by implication in the very last measures and the final coda under the dominant pedal.

The opening section, which begins and ends on g, establishes a relationship between D and g in which D is subordinate to and leading toward g (as we expect of dominant-tonic relationships), arriving there only after several tantalizing attempts. The next textual phrase moves away from the D-g arena in the subdominant direction and cadences (V-i) on c. But this cadence is not as secure, nor is it established as strongly as the first. Moreover, it is followed by contradicting harmonic movement. Ultimately we are led further down the subdominant course toward F as IV of C (m. 54: n.b., not as V of the relative major, B♭) only to return, as we must to balance the first section, to an apparent forthcoming cadence on g.

That cadence is delayed, however, until the ending of "O Nomen Jesu." G is never properly prepared, nor does it arrive at the right place in the harmonic rhythm. Instead, the ending slides up onto D (recognized as a dominant because of the g-D juxtaposition), balancing there momentarily, for it is a fact of hearing this piece that the sense of g is the stronger. That the coda, like all the many other codas in these motets and *Lamentations*, is plagal with a pedal tone maintaining the note of resolution (so the coda can be considered a $^6_4$ double suspension), is further demonstration of Ferrabosco's use of the subdominant relationship for structural balance while he uses dominant relationships to heighten cadential finality, i.e., to articulate the structure.

Even the approaches to the codas in these motets exemplify this point. The coda in "Ego sum," which only thwarts our sense of arrival on g, is approached iv-V — that is, the approach implies a movement to i which, in a sense, then occurs only to be recalled.[7] At the end of "O nomen Jesu," however, the longer coda, with its tonic pedal and subdominant influence, is approached from the dominant, V-i. The subdominant "grounds" the arrival, so there will be no further movement, by balancing the preceding dominant and, more importantly, the dominant influences in both works.

The balance of subdominant and dominant areas in these two motets are remarkably similar. Both begin by emphasizing the dominant side and then move toward the subdominant, with the tonic major acting as a dominant itself. This movement is moderated by the influence of the relative major which turns back to the dominant, whether the reestablishment of the tonic follows. Not all the motets work in exactly this manner, but the prominence of the subdominant area is even stronger than that of the relative major (to which it is related). The flexibility of relations between these areas reflects the modal freedom of this tonal thinking.

"O nomen Jesu" affirms the tonic of "Ego sum", thus acting not only as a response to but a completion of the message and music of the first piece. In mood and member, however, it contrasts with "Ego sum," for "O nomen Jesu" is, with the exception of some shorter parts of the *Lamentations*, the most effective of Ferrabosco's motets in its use of homophony and textural contrast. It is the expressive use of two levels of textural contrast at the beginning which sets the example. There, and throughout the motet, the cantus presents the essential text and musical figures while the other voices respond directly or weave their figures in the background, supporting the prominent and exposed threat of that upper voice. In addition, homorhythmic groupings of voices occur at the beginning of several phrases, giving the text greater clarity and concentration (mm. 1, 20, 22, 27, 39). Contrasts of voice-groupings are also used, most notably at the very beginning and at m. 31 ("ergo Jesu"), where the upper voices are joined by the lower voices with the effect of tremendous enlargement of the statement.

As is customary in the motet literature of the time, the rhythmic variety of Ferrabosco's motets is restrained, ranging (in the 2:1 reduction of the transcriptions) from sixteenth-note small ornamental figures normally two notes long and the eighth-notes which are mostly passing or structurally unimportant notes to the half-notes of the harmonic rhythm and the whole notes of cadences. The basic motion is in quarter and half notes, with the shorter notes being used decoratively or, as the piece progresses, to give the work animation. The tendency of the vocal lines is to begin in longer values, then break into increased activity, with the result that the melodic activity becomes smoother as it increases, while the harmonic rhythm stays at the level of the half-note or, in cadences, the whole or dotted whole. It is the harmonic rhythm which governs the sense of "bar-line," although Tregian's score, unlike the part-books, rigorously aligns the parts in 2/2 measures. For the most part this is satisfactory; it does not prevent the kind of individual flexibility and metrical freedom the cantus displays in mm. 6-9 and 46-51 where, as in some of the songs, the melody is clearly organized in triple time.

Ex. 3

As in "Ego sum" the subdominant is structurally important in "O nomen Jesu" and is developed by the use of its own subdominant as well. But, rather than the use of the subdominant minor in conjunction with its relative major, we find here the appearance of the subdominant major only — and the fulcrum of the return to G is the transformation of a, the relative minor of C, into A, the dominant of D (mm. 40-50). That this is done more by intervallic treatment of voice-leading and dissonance can be seen in the counterpoint of cantus, bass, and second voice in mm. 43-44.

A minor is only the means, not the end: it is used here and earlier (mm. 29-31) to delay the resolution on C. As a third-related extension of C, it can enhance the means of "staying on C." At the same time, however, the addition of c♯ denies C and turns back quickly toward G. The return to G is colored by the tantalizing intrusion of b♭ following the dominant (m. 47). This combination would normally be the occasion for the peculiar English fondness for the augmented triad, in this case d-f♯-b♭, and the working out of its several suspensions before this momentary deceptive excursion into minor is "restored" to major in the coda (m. 51) at the words "et salva me." Instead, however, Ferrabosco avoids the dissonances and is content to flavor this passage only with prepared suspensions.

The move to minor allows the final arrival on G a freshness which otherwise would have been impossible, but such grace of modal effect is not the only attractive feature of the piece. The part-writing is very smooth, except for some opening figures in a point of imitation, and the bass is treated as both a melodic and harmonic part, as its first phrase and continuation show:

Ex. 4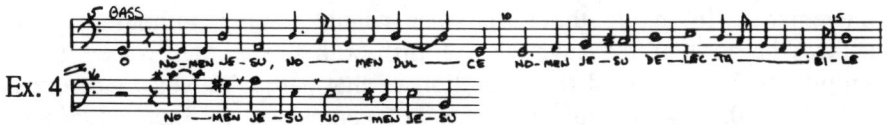

The one difficulty in singing this part from a part-book, the c# in m. 16, is anticipated by a c# in the cantus and participates in a predictable harmonic progression.

The ecstatic energy of the meditation on the name of Jesus effects a change of mood from humility to exultation seen most clearly in the transformation of the figure of the second voice in mm. 8-9 into that of the cantus at m. 16, followed by two of the other voices.

Ex. 5

In the first instance, the figure, lying comfortably within the relationships of dominant and tonic, contributes to the easy sense of the passage which concludes on the dominant at the word "delectabile." In the second case, however, this figure takes the lead in moving away from the dominant, with the energy increasing as the figure is passed from cantus to bass to the second voice. Thus the repetitions of "nomen Jesu" become ecstatic, only to be startingly transformed and softened by the disarming agency of a minor, into a sublimely deceptive cadence on C at "confortans." But it is this tremendous, sublimated dominant-tending energy which sustains the expectation of G through the end of the motet, and the opening section of this motet presents Ferrabosco's skill at its highest.

This is also one of the easiest of the motets to sing. Its range is modest, and the awkwardness of text-setting minimal. The shapeliness of the melodic writing does not contradict the metric felicity and textural organization discussed above, and the voice-leading, which shapes many of the cadences by intervallic logic, is smooth. Contributing to that shapeliness is a better than usual fit of words to music, particularly in the use of longer notes for accented syllables and the occasional animating use of dotted figures to propel the text forward (e.g., "nisi salvator," mm. 27-28; see also the next motet, "Ego dixi").

The smoothness of the part-writing extends beyond the individual lines, for Ferrabosco sometimes will use one line to resolve a movement begun in another, particularly when there is the danger of parallel voice-movement. In m. 26 the third voice cannot resolve without parallel octaves because of the augmented fourth with the second voice. It is simply left hanging, and the resolution of that particular voice part does not affect the sound, only the sense of completion of that voice-line. While this is not pure contrapuntal practice—in fact it breaks down the contrapuntal integrity of individual voice-parts—it occurs in a passage which is governed entirely by the intervallic laws of dissonance and consonance. A similar situation occurs in the cantus at m. 11, where the resolution is delayed by one beat of rest. This treatment of the vocal parts is possible with five voices, perhaps even necessitated by the problems of parallelism which five voices can engender, problems shared by Ferrabosco and his contemporaries.

There could hardly be a better example among these motets of the "drive to the cadence" which culminates in the return of the original tonic area (deceptively delayed by its own minor mode) and the invigoration of the melodic writing by melismatic passages in all voices and particularly, in the final measures, the lower voices billowing up underneath the cantus pedal. It was not by mistake that Arkwright chose this motet to publish in his important article, "Notes on the Ferrabosco Family," where he went on to say that,

> While his motets are written with a less rigid adherence to the rules of the purest modal counterpoint (as is to be expected at the period when he wrote), he is in some ways the more attractive composer [than his father, highly regarded by Peacham and Morley], and when set beside Philips or Dering (who are the writers with whom he may be most fairly compared) he will be found to hold his own.[8]

"Ego dixi, Domine" and "Convertere"

"Ego dixi domine" and "Convertere Domine usque quo" also constitute a motet in two *pars*, unified by tonal organization and textual content. The same textual contrasts or tonal progress found in the previous motet-pair are not found here. It is the tonal structure of the motets which is most interesting—articulated according to the text into three large sections in
each motet.

III.	1. Ego dixi Domine	C=I		
	Miserere mei		I	(C)
	2. Sana animam meam	m.22	I(vi)-V/vi-vi	(a)
	3. Quia peccavi tibi	m.37	vi(V/ii)-IV/ii-	
			V/ii-V/v	(D)
IV.	1. Convertere Domine usque quo		ii-V/V	(D)
	2. Et deprecabilis esto	m.18	I-V/V-V	(G)
	3. Super servos tuos	m.39	V-I; I -I	(C)
			IV	

The cadences of these sections delineate important aspects of the overall progression, without implying modulation (there is none). These cadences are *only* "marking" places and do not give a sense of their relative tonal weight. Particularly important in this regard is the cadence on (not in) a, which has little relative weight in itself but serves as a pivot from C (a=vi) to D (A=V).

C - a/A - D; d/D - G - C.

Both motets conclude with the by now familiar plagal coda and pedal. The harmonic movement of these sections can be seen as a move down the circle of fifths from the relative minor which creates a harmonic sequence, A-D; G-C. But the progress is not as direct as that. The establishment of the tonic, and, even more, its reestablishment, is accomplished by the elimination of divergent tendencies. Unlike the restrictive procedure of harmonic progression in dance patterns, this is a "tonicization" in which the tonic is identified by the strength of its associated attributes. Thus, the tonic is confirmed as fundamental without regard to mode, and all the resources of the tonic, including modal relations, contribute to the sense of tonality and tonal perspective. We are clearly dealing with pieces which revolve around pitch levels, not modal patterns.

The intermediate section of each motet serves as an ambiguous intermediary, cadencing on a note which carries tonal implications for both the opening and closing areas. The movement to a in "Ego dixi," for example, involves a great deal of confusion with C before the nature of the progression is confirmed, yet the confusion by thirds is one of the balancing tricks so important to the establishment of the tonal hierarchy: we later learn the significance of a/A when it proceeds to take us to D.

This ambivalence is seen within a section as well, for instance in conjunction with the movement from d minor to D major (itself a word painting) in the opening section of "Convertere." That D is V of G, not the ultimate tonic, is confirmed by the progress of the intermediate section which, in fact, moves to G (as V of C, ultimately) rather than to its dominant, A.

The final section of each motet focuses on its tonal goal by restriction of association, not by force of statement. And, because the movement of the first motet away from the tonic is, in a sense, a preparation for the tonic return in the second, there are several levels of association and dissociation at play. Instead of the meandering kind of progression and understated confirmation of cadential destination found in the middle sections, the harmonic movement in the final sections becomes limited primarily to dominant and subdominant relations.

The fascination of these last sections is actually in the balancing of dominant and subdominant around the final tonic and the way in which the balancing, itself, contributes to the sense of propriety and completion in the final cadence. The coda of "Convertere," for example, appears to threaten the sense of tonic completion by the use of b♭, as if the goal were yet one more step further down the circle of fifths. But its balancing function is neatly accomplished and the settling on the tonic convincingly effected because of the tonic pedal in the cantus which suspends the sense of motion, creating a feeling of balance and restful closure.

Thus, the tonic is confirmed by balance and elimination; tendencies away from the tonic are balanced (subdominant/dominant), transformed (the common-tone movement to the relative minor pivoting and returning down the circle of fifths), or not supported (influences of g minor in the middle section of "Convertere"). That is to say, dominant and subdominant are balanced, relationships of thirds are clarified (partly by avoiding the ambiguities presented in earlier deceptive progressions), and modal inflections are ordered rather than interchanged. The result is a fully emergent tonal structure emphasizing dominant relationships while employing means which are far more ambivalent.

Several aspects of motivic treatment are of more than passing interest in these motets, particularly the use of dual, though not paired, motives in "Ego dixi" for the phrases "sana animam meam" and "quia peccavi tibi." In each case, one of the figures is more active, and that figure is also musically dominant, with the motion of the figure and, in the case of "quia peccavi tibi," the vigor of the musical gesture characterizing the entire section of the piece.

Ex. 6a

Ex. 6b

The middle sections of the motets are most active melodically; the settings of the words "sana animam meam" and, in particular, "et deprecabilis (esto)" make small fantasias of almost wordless music to themselves.

232 Songs and Motets of Alfonso Ferrabosco, the Younger

This brings us to the problem of vocality, for the upper voice lies unusually high, generally maintaining a fifth above the second voice. Nor is there particular grace in the matching of word and musical gesture. In fact, both of the examples of active figures cited above are no more than marriages of convenience, arbitrary associations of word and tone sometimes defying even the customary observations of accent. Usually Ferrabosco is not this casual, but the opening figure of "Ego dixi" is additional evidence. It is not until the words "domine" and "miserere" that there is a sense of particular concern for the text in the lower parts while the cantus follows the accentuation but, like the second voice, in triple-time.

The variety of ways in which the text is presented does include the use of homorhythmic address by various groups of voices after m. 7, but Ferrabosco simply does not seize the opportunity to make a strong statement with the text. Instead, he conveys the sense of address, i.e., "Domine, miserere mei," without affecting the manner of address. The modesty of the supplicant, perhaps, is here revealed, but it would seem to be unintentional. Ferrabosco chooses to pay attention to textual suggestion in these motets with the affective intervals of "miserere" and "convertere," using the same minor thirds and sixths endemic during this period in settings of these words. Otherwise, these motets give the impression of having the text applied to them.

The working out of musical ideas, to which the text is added, is exemplified by passages such as the following from "Ego dixi" (Ex. 7), and from "Convertere domine" (Ex. 8).

Ex. 7

Ex. 8

That a bass line should give such an impression is not unusual considering the dual role it performs, but an even clearer example of a specifically harmonic use of the bass is found at the beginning of the same motet.

Ex. 9

Here, in its simplest form, is the girding of the motet set out in equal half notes, oblivious to text, except for the borrowing of the rhythmic and melodic cliche which shapes "convertere." Yet in contrast to the abruptness of this bass line stands the long line of the cantus, gradually welling upward before its graceful and easy descent—a process which, although larger intervals are used, is essentially stepwise.

The importance of the harmonic rhythm, and the patterns of expectation which it sets up, is particularly in evidence at the coda of "Convertere" in which the subdominant pull is not strong enough to topple the tonic, yet effective as a balance to the dominant preparation for the coda. The coda begins with the arrival of the cantus at its tonic pedal. What is unusual about this arrival is that it follows, in effect, an extended 3/2 measure on the dominant. The harmonic rhythm is momentarily expanded, making the arrival at the coda more decisive and establishing the fact that the tonic is heard on the downbeat of the harmonic rythm while the subdominant is heard only on the upbeat. Thus, notwithstanding the presence of b♭, the subdominant always goes to the tonic rather than the reverse. A similar effect is achieved within the shorter coda of "Ego dixi" (mm. 50-51), where the sense of closure and arrival was not intended to be so definite.

The peculiar "English cadence," in which a suspension and its resolution sound simultaneously, is used by Ferrabosco, though not with the pungent effect of Tallis.[9] In fact, the effect of the suspensions is preempted, since Ferrabosco does not complicate matters with cross-relations, as Tallis does in this sublime example from *Lamentations II*, the ending of the letter "Daleth."

Ex. 10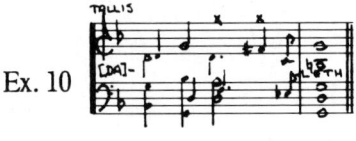

Ferrabosco's style, indeed, seems to be militantly consonant, the avoidance of such possibilities intentional.

The structure of these motets is reinforced in many ways: the textual phrases conclude with cadences on important levels of the tonal design, the texture differs from section to section in terms of the melodic shape and activity (although not usually in terms of voicing) while the progress of each section culminates in a fullness of vocal texture; harmonic relations are confirmed at the structural level, resolving ambiguities which occur in passing at a more superficial level. In almost every way, the musical aspects of these motets are satisfyingly, if not excitingly, treated. The texting is not objectionable, but it is certainly of secondary importance in determining the musical decisions of the pieces. Questions of vocality arise, particularly at the words "quia peccavi tibi," but it can also be said that such vocal writing was not uncommon, nor was it objectionable to contemporary standards of text-setting as presented by Zarlino and, later, by Morley. That these motets show an awareness of individual words is demonstrated by the affective inflection of "miserere" and the rhythmic point of "domine" and "animam." The guiding concerns, however, are musical: the musical gestures are justified by their autonomous efficacy, not by their service to the clarity of presentation or interpretation of the text. That is the function of the work as a whole.

Other Paired Motets With Texts

The next two pairs of motets also have C as their tonal center, but their movement ranges farther up the circle of fifths, with particular use made of the relation of C to its relative minor, which then, by change to major, acts as a secondary dominant pointing the way of return down the circle of fifths. [See the following structural summary.] Not only is the move to A/a made more emphatic by the application of its dominant, but the ambivalent functions of A/a are stressed to a greater extent, for these pairs of motets are more flexible in their internal sections. In fact, the third-related sleights-of-hand, which are more numerous and more varied in these pieces, do not allow the clearer sense of sectionalism which the first four motets presented.

V.	1.	Ubi duo vel tres congregati fuerunt	C=I	I-V	(G)
	2.	In medio eorum sum in nomine meo	m.29	V/ii-ii	(d)
	3.	Dixi, Domine	m. 55	V/V-V-I; IV-ii-V/ii	(A)

The Motets   235

VI.	1. Libera me, Domine		V/ii-V/V
	de morte eterne		V/V-V/ii (A)
	2. In die illa tremenda	m. 21	ii-V/IV-IV
	Quando caeli movendi sunt		vi-V/ii
	et terra		V/V-V-I (C)
	3. Dum veneris judicare seculum	m. 41	I---V-I
	Per ignem		$\underline{\text{I}}$ - I (C)
			IV
VII.	1. Domine, Deus meus	C=I	I (C)
	2. Ne queso intres in iudicium	m. 13	
	cum puero tuo		
	delicta iuventutis meae		
	et ignorantiae meae		-V (G)
	3. Ne memineris unquam	m. 35	(iii,V,I)
	neve in finem iratus		I
	mea mala reserves		V/vi-vi-ii
			V/ii-ii-V/ii (A)
			(orVI-iv/VI-VI)
VIII.	1. Noli me proijcere a facie tua		(A)
	in tempore senectutis		VI-vi (a)
	et cum defecerit virtus mea		V-I (C)
	ne derelinquas me	m. 21	
	usque ad senectum in senium		i (c)
	2. Ne declinas a servo tuo	m 36	(i)-V
	Sed in pace		♭III-V/♭III
	Recipe animam meam		V-i (c)
	3. Et misericordias tuas	m. (57)58	V-I
	In eternum cantabo:		V
	Domine, Deus Meus		IV-V-$\underline{\text{I}}$-I (C)
		m. 69	IV

The arch of these motet-pairs does not emphasize their differences. "Ubi duo" has a very interesting middle section which extends the third-relationship of C-a to F-d without detracting from the dual role of d/D plays as ii of C or V of G.[10] That dual role is particularly ambiguous because the two major cadences in this section (m. 41; m. 52) end in an open fifth and octave respectively. The structural separation of d and D is reversed in "Libera me" where we are first returned to D, then must return to the secondary dominant and come back to d (with its relative major, F) before the reestablishment of C major, which can encompass all these changes.

Although the movement away from C is just as far-reaching in the next motet-pair, the grounding on C is much more secure: "Domine, Deus meus" arrives at the dominant only in m. 35 – more than halfway through the piece. Here, too, it is the relationship of G to e/E which allows the piece to proceed to A, rather than the previously used connection of C-a. The return from A to C is more direct in "noli me," but not convincing. For this reason, C is confirmed a number of times, the first of which uses these third relations still with strong emphasis on the minor dominant-related members of the relative tonal pairs C/a and G/e, ending with C in a stronger position, though not convincingly established. What follows exploits, finally, both the tonic-dominant relationship and the parallel tonal pair C/c, presenting a strong feeling of c minor to which the open fifth cadences contribute. This is contradicted only in the final third of the piece by the movement to and long confirmation of the major tonic in which the opening section of "Domine, Deus meus" is repeated. Both of the concluding motets have plagal codas with upper voice pedals, and both pairs show a concern for the text which is directly manifest in the structure of the motets.

Fully the first half of "Ubi duo" is devoted to the first textual phrase, and perhaps this is the reason this section, unlike its counterparts in the previous motets, moves away from the tonic to the dominant, rather than staying squarely on the tonic. The second section, which concludes the Biblical quotation (but with the rearrangement of "in nomine meo" to follow "in medio eorum sum") is not set to balance the first but to move further away from the sense of C—in preparation for the response of the speaker whose intrusion and vocative address to the Lord is announced and begun in this concluding section. It is here that the tendencies toward d minor are consolidated—A has no independent validity as a tonal center, so the conclusion of this motet points to the beginning of the next, both musically and textually. The dominant function of A is confirmed in the opening section of "Libera me" which moves first to D major, turning then to d. The return to C at the end of the second section—and its confirmation in the concluding measures—is a reminder that this is a prayer for release, born of faith as much as of fear.

The general absence of homophonic pairings of voices in these motets heightens the effect of their occasional appearances as at "in nomine meo" and the final "Deus, Deus meus." This is also particularly telling at a textually significant moment such as occurs at the words "congregati sunt" (in "Ubi duo") where the textual "two" or "three" are literally gathered together.

Ex. 11

Such word-painting is more than just a pleasant moment during which the little variations of text-setting provide opportunities for the singers to explore the possibilities of duration and accent of the same words without breaking away from the basic choral homorhythm. The gathering together is structurally important: a concentration of energy moving onto the dominant, the articulation of that harmonic movement, and the confirmation of its importance.

The conclusion of the piece is built with similar care. Beginning in m. 41, the voices are first paired and then completely intertwined with close imitations leading to the first statement of the words "dixi, Domine." The arrival on D, with the open octaves defined now as major, is emphasized by the homorhythmic grouping of voices; the surge of excitement and activity which conveyed "in ncmine meo" is concentrated and transformed into the preparation for the second motet: "Dixi, 'Domine, /Libera me. .'" only by this concentration of energy and dramatic sense of continuation is the lifting of the cadence to A possible; there is no sense of completion or ending here.

"Libera me" has neither the same drive to a cadence nor a like quantity of homorhythmic passages. In mm. 21-24, however, there is one of the finest passages in Ferrabosco's motets.

Ex. 12

On the surface, this is not unlike the setting of "in nomine meo" in the previous motet. Here, however, the textual response is more marked. After the long notes and chromatic figures of "de morte eterne," Ferrabosco momentarily presents a triple time which surges forward, presaging the imminent movement of the heavens. The isolation of the upper voices contributes to a dance-like feeling, but this triple-time is not a dance, it is an expansion. The harmonic rhythm becomes briefly triple, with hemiola, before returning at the end of m. 24 to its regular half-note pulse. Thus the "tremendous day" is portrayed by subtle enlargement of experience through contrast of range, rhythm, movement, and of time itself.

Not accidentally, the progress of this section brings the motet back to C (at m. 41), grounding the violent figure used to represent the movement of the heavens in the earth.

Ex. 13

Although the essential shape of this musical figure remains within the Ferrabosco canon of triadic outlines and primary intervals (filled-in or not), it attains unusual vigor, its angularity assuring the prominence and articulation of the syllables "cae-li" as much as it reflects the agitation of the heavens on that fateful day.

Both of these motets use double motives, especially "Ubi duo" in which they are found in the first three sections. But again, characteristically for Ferrabosco, they are not used as paired motives, but as complements. For example, the figures used to set "Ubi duo" at the outset are used in combinations which vary from the nearly palindromic to those which fill out an octave:

Ex. 14

These are the clearest examples, but the other double motives of "Ubi duo" are also short and melodically simple, featuring filled-in fourths or fifths which are sometimes ornamented or expanded (though not in the consistent fashion of Byrd), without losing the essential prominence of the perfect interval. The opening section of "Libera me" also exhibits these qualities. Where single motives are used for the point of imitation, they tend to be more developed, longer in breadth and larger in span, than the double figures. Even so, the basic outline of a perfect interval or a triad is the most important concern in the structure of all these figures.

The melodic importance of the sixth in these motets give them a sense of greater arch. In "Ubi duo" the sixth is found in ascent and returns to the fifth or fourth above the starting note, acting as an upper neighbor and upper limit to the melodic thrust.

Ex. 15a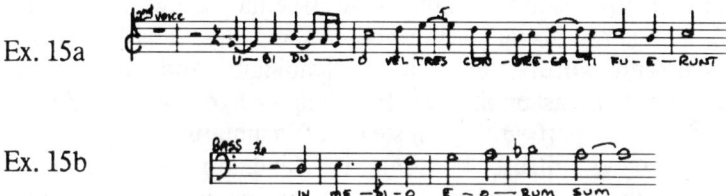

Ex. 15b

The ascending sixth is also found in "Libera me," particularly in the cantus, mm. 8-12, and at the opening of the third voice, where it is stretched to a seventh. It is the inversion of the sixth, however, which is most telling at the words "de morte (eterne)."

Ex. 16

This gesture, which counts also as word-painting, momentarily and remarkably interrupts the smoothness of melodic construction, precipitously redirecting the meandering, generally rising melodic progress. There is no evidence that Ferrabosco used these sixths in a self-conscious fashion to integrate the thematic material of these motets, but that is exactly what has happened.

The archaism of cadences without thirds has been mentioned above. One such cadence occurs at the change of mode from minor to major (on D) in "Ubi duo," where the cadence arrives on bare octaves.

Ex. 17

D minor has held sway for the previous 17 measures, and this transformation is akin to those in the antiphonal music of Gabrieli and Schütz (where, however, the change occurs directly at the cadence). This cadence is a vacuum into which the trio of inner voices rushes, defining the quality of the mode as it fills the triad. Such examples, though usually with open fifths instead of bare octaves (see the cadence in m. 41, just previous), are not unusual in Ferrabosco's motets. His intent is, apparently, clear and worthy: to maintain ambiguity and still create contrast, yet the effect is disappointing. In examples like this, the reason is easy to find. The part-writing, instead of maintaining vigor and independence, becomes diffuse in similarity (and, in this example, parallelism). Thus the tension of expectation is lost, as is the fullness of sound, even if only for a beat, and the energy of the piece has to be reestablished.

Problems of another kind are present in the cadence to F in "Ubi duo":

Ex. 18

This little hint of a Viennese waltz is presented, remarkably, in all three sources. The most obvious solution to this shared anomaly would be to remove the sharp and, perhaps, rewrite the middle part.

Another instance of manuscript consistency which may still be in error concerns the usage of b♭/b♮ in mm. 48-51 of "Ubi duo."

Ex. 19

The real difficulty is in m. 50 where the two forms occur only a beat apart. If the effect were really the delighting of the ear, there would be no quibble, for the passage does pass by quickly enough to be easily overlooked. The result, however, is a confusion and inconsistency for which there is no textual explanation nor recognizable purpose. Each of

The Motets

the notes can be "explained" by reference to an earlier form of the melodic figure which serves as the basis of imitation or to the use of b♮ in the upper voices, while b♭ is used in the lower. The b♭ is strengthened by the preceding b♭ in the bass (m. 49), while the b♮ can revel in the wisdom of hindsight when the turn to D major is apparent and the third voice, itself, uses b♮ (m. 51; this having been the voice with the conflicting b♭). Ferrabosco does not take advantage of cross-relations in an affective sense, but he does make modal distinctions, and that is what is wanted here: a maintenance of the minor until m. 51, and, consequently, a consistency has been editorialized into the transcription. The use of b♭ (or f♮/f♯) in this sense of describing structural units is also found in the middle of "Libera me" and is important in establishing areas of contrast and balance.

There is no liturgical or traditional reason for these texts to be set together, and their ingenious linking here remains a mystery. The words of Christ and the responsory text (also used as the offertory in the service for the dead) are related only in that the promise of Christ is the liberation from death. This absence of liturgical authority is yet more evidence that these motets were written for private devotion and performance.

The next pair of motets also display a textual quilt which has no liturgical connection but which balances a concern for youthful indiscretion in the first motet with a prayer for sustenance and mercy in old age. The unification of vision is demonstrably intentional in this case, for the music of the opening invocation is used at the close of the second motet: the only musical borrowing or recapitulation in all these motets.

The conservatism of Ferrabosco's motet style can be seen in the beginning of "Domine, Deus meus." Although such an address might well have been set homophonically for rhetorical effect, this effect is saved for the conclusion of "Noli me." Instead, the musical figures used in imitation are starkly presented in their independent integrity. They also contribute to the absence of rhetorical effect, because the opening figure is answered at the lower fifth and thereby creates a sense of vacillation between tonic and subdominant. Moreover, the long, winding lines which extend after the head motive, do not reach a climax or develop intensity.

Only in "Noli me," at a textual point of utter humility, is the independence and diffusion of the isolated voices singing "do not reject me from Thy service" ("ne declinas a servo tuo") concentrated in the essence of the prayer, "but in peace receive my soul" ("sed in pace recipe animam meam") "and I shall sing Thy mercies for all eternity,

Lord, my God." This moment is stunning (m. 48ff.) as all the voices speak as one, thwarting the confirmation of the tonic by moving to the relative major. It is a moment out of time as much as it is out of harmony. In the first regard, it is a coalescence of tendencies which are inherent in the manner of composition: the imitative, polyphonic weaving tends to converge at cadences; this declamatory invocation is the ultimate convergence, its essence momentarily suspending the movement of the voices. It is, thus, out of time, and the following return to imitation takes place *sub specie eterne:* it is a transformation of the timely supplication for grace (mortal) into the eternal, and therefore also immediate and ever-momentary, song of joy.

This transformation is effected on an E♭ chord (m. 48) which also sets this most humble and intent request apart from the surrounding music. The preparation for this E♭ comes from the e♭s in the two previous measures, the only implication of c minor in this pair of motets to that point. This excursion is quickly over, however, and the c which was expected at m. 48 appears in m. 51, with the return to C effected at the next textual phrase (m. 59). The textural and harmonic aspects of this passage are the more effective because of the arresting use of rests, particularly the one preceding the first statement in m. 48: the cessation not only of polyphonic activity, but of the sound as well, setting off the following statement.

The tone of seriousness which governs these motets is nowhere more in evidence than in the restrained setting of "cantabo" ("Noli me," mm. 65-69). Ferrabosco does not take this opportunity for musical effusion to indulge in wide-ranging lines and melodic delights, but, rather, is content with plain syllabic presentation leading to the return of the text "Domine, Deus meus." It is this return which confirms the quiet intensity and solemnity of these motets, as the text and music which began "Domine, Deus meus" is made the conclusion of "Noli me." This is a stunning effect, the directness of the quotation camouflaged by the invocation, "Domine," presented in all voices (prefigured by the setting of "in eternum [cantabo]" in m. 63ff. which bonds the musical material of conclusion and coda).

Thus what had begun as an earthly prayer for grace is transformed into an eternal song of praise. More convincing evidence of the unity of conception of these two pieces could hardly be adduced, but even more important is the service that the music renders the text, reflecting its structure, but at the same time elevating it from the level of meaning to that of experience.

Until the passage "ne declinas" (in "Noli me"), these motets are set completely on the dominant/relative minor side of the tonic. The more complicated structure of "Noli me" reflects the varied delaying tactics used to avoid a sense of final arrival on the tonic, but what is more unusual is the use of secondary dominants reaching all the way up to V of iii and the relatively long time the motets stay "up" in the area of the relative minor or V of ii. The contrast with the appearance of the minor mode and the relative major, beginning with the pictorial descent at "ne declinas" — with its subdominant movement and change of mode — is therefore all the more effective and affective. This is further evidence of Ferrabosco's awareness of tonal resources and his structural use of them in service of the text.

The dynamic of tonal balancing which we have remarked in earlier pages are again exemplified in the cadential preparation of "Domine, Deus meus." Ferrabosco does not let us entirely forget C major after m. 21, for he feigns a return in m. 52, a return which is unconvincingly presented and moves on toward a. From m. 56 on, it appears that the piece will close on D, as V of the G which would appear at the beginning of the next motet. Actually, we are left hanging on V of D: just before the final chord there is an expansion of the harmonic rhythm so that the arrival on A is made on a downbeat (compare m. 56 and m. 58). This expansion and cadence revolve about an inner pedal, and it is this pedal which leads the way to the next motet, "Noli me," which begins at the same pitch. "Noli me" never does "arrive" on D; the A becomes so top-heavy that, in effect, it falls of its own weight all the way to C (m. 21; confirmed in m. 36). The process is not entirely direct, for A is relieved of its dominant characteristics by m. 9, after which time it ceases to be a directing force and becomes a substitute for C.

There are more steps in the structure of "Noli me" than in the previous motets. The obvious reason for this is the longer text with so many separable phrases. However, it is the levels of tonal certainty which are interesting in this structure. The return to C is made by m. 21, after which there is the ambiguity of a/C until m. 36, when C is once again reached in an authentic cadence. This, in turn, is followed by a movement to the dominant during which it becomes apparent that the minor tonic is the destination. This is reached, albeit by implication in an open cadence, in m. 55, whence the return to the major is effected by m. 63. From that point, the tonic and its quality are not in doubt, the plagal coda being unusually short because the structural coda really began at the return of the words "Domine, Deus meus" in m. 69. The concluding measures contain some of the more interesting examples of Ferrabosco's rhythmic counterpoint, particularly in m. 82 (where the repeat of mm. 1-12 of the first motet is concluded by the short coda) with the bass singing in triple time, albeit briefly.

Other Motets and Anthems

Of Ferrabosco's five remaining motets, only one, "Laboravi in gemitu meo," appears outside the Sambroke Book, and even that concordance (in mss. Add. 29366-8) is untexted and not placed with the other motets by Ferrabosco which appear in that source. The final motets in two *pars*, "Tribulationem et dolorem" and "O Domine," present only incipits in the bass and are otherwise without text, although the motets "Sustinuit anima mea" and "Fortitudo mea" do have texted bass parts.

Despite the inexplicable restriction of these motets to one source, there is no general distinction between these and the previously discussed pieces. "Laboravi" is more modestly decked out than the others, its part-writing becoming less animate as the motet progresses, and the tonal movement is restricted to the exploitation of the minor/relative major relation of a to C. The shared tonal area of F used as a subdominant balance to G (around C) and submediant balance to C (around a).

IX.   1. Laboravi in gemitu meo   a = i   i-III   (C)
      2. Lavabo per singulas noctes   m. 18   (C)
      3. Stratum meum lacrimis meis   m. 31   (A)
         Rigabo $\frac{I-I}{iv}$

The first third of the piece moves from a, via F, to C, and the emphasis placed on C in the second section of the motet would lead one to think that it was the true tonic (a convincing "bifocalism" which works too well). The final section, does not convincingly move back to a/A, this being the one case where the tonal balances are not resolved. The impression given is that we are on the dominant of D/d, an impression encouraged by the appearance of d in m.42. If this were the first of a pair of motets such as we have just seen, we could anticipate the possibilities of the second motet. Here, however, there is not sufficient dominant strength to enforce the integrity of the presence of A, and, top-heavy, it falls to d.

That pull to d had been strong from the beginning of the motet, where it was shunted along toward G, thence to C, and is the occasion of one of the more interesting of Ferrabosco's deceptions. This occurs in m. 10-12 in a passing cadence which, because of the presence of an augmented triad, would normally have been handled in a different manner. Instead of developing the suspensions of the upper two notes relative to each other and the lowest note, Ferrabosco here spices what are essentially parallel major triads by treating the lower two notes as suspensions against the upper. As this passage suggests, the establishment of a is not strong in the beginning, and it should be argued that, more than any of the others, this motet seems in transit without having established a real starting place and certainly without an arrival at a clearly recognized destination at the end.

In contrast with this, the paired motets, "Tribulationem" and "O Domine" form a complementary movement from G to its dominant and back, with particular emphasis on the subdominant area and the tonic minor in "O Domine."

XI.	1. Tribulationem et dolorem inveni		G=I
	2.	m. 14	-V; -♭III
	3.	m. 36	IV-I-V(v in ms.)
XII.	1. O Domine...		v/V ---IV
	2.	m. 23	V-i/I-IV-V-I

Rather plodding quarter-note movement, which can be seen at the end of "Laboravi," is also found at the beginning of "Tribulationem" — a motion which quickly leads to a sense of chordal, rather than melodic, movement and which obscures, even in this simple context, the rhythmic mixtures of triple and duple time.

It is the opening of "Tribulationem" which is the most interesting, for the imitative exposition of the textual phrase is brought to a complete close. What follows is without text in the manuscript, although the third and fourth voices duplicate the opening voices of the motet. Unlike the beginning of the motet, however, this rebeginning is accompanied by another figure which soon dominates the musical content (m. 14ff.). The great unhurried breadth of the beginning, which is so conservative as to be meditative rather than expressive, creates an arch of ascent and descent, a self-contained kernel of the motet set off from the continuation by a fermata and double-bar. The continuation incorporates the material of the opening with new, decorative figures which give the piece animation — and which are derived from the complementary descending figure of the opening (m. 8ff).

The bass part in both of these motets is often dull and perfunctory, only occasionally partaking in the motivic and imitative life of the music. More often its melodic activity is superseded by its harmonic functions as arbiter of rhythm and foundation of chord. The harmonic activity of the motets, as a whole, is not very extended, a movement in the direction of the relative major (B♭) beginning in m.30 of "Tribulationem" being the most effective of balances to the dominant and more strongly stated than the subdominant in m.44.

The final cadence of "Tribulationem" uncharacteristically avoids the raised third, a mistake in the manuscript most probably, despite the argument which could be made for a contrast with the opening of "O Domine" on the dominant. This opening is similar in declamation and the contrast of voicings to "O nomen Jesu" and "Hierusalem," but this motet, like its partner, is modest in melodic activity as the choral invocation spins out into the exposition of rather uninteresting figures. Beginning in m. 23, however, is a figure which is used for the remaining half of the piece, a figure which includes a diminished fourth usually elaborating a second:

Ex. 20a

Ex. 20b

The strong feeling of g minor, to which this figure contributes, is abruptly revised to major in mm. 40-41, although the result is a hodge-podge of cross-relations which are more irritating than acerbic or effective. The concluding measures present a rare authentic cadence unadumbrated with any plagal coda or pedal notes. The absence of the coda and pedal notes, used in the motets discussed earlier, is consistent in these and the last two motets. In conjunction with the generally less active melodic content and the more restricted harmonic movement, and the unique appearance of these motets in Tregian's score, it is reasonable to surmise that these pieces may have been written at another time, probably earlier, than the motets with wider circulation and more interesting musical substance.

Nevertheless, the part writing in the unpaired motets "Fortitudo mea" and "Sustinuit anima mea" is more interesting. In these, with more of the text available, it is easier to discover where the text has informed the musical setting and choice of musical figures. The forthright opening figure of "Fortitudo," which bears a family resemblance to the example cited above and is a witness to Ferrabosco's consistent use of primary intervals in the structure of his motives, is an example.

Ex. 21

"Fortitudo" is in a minor, but it avoids frequent use of the dominant. Its overall harmonic progress is from a to C, followed by a small excursion borrowing from d minor before a movement onto D is effected (mm. 31-35 ff.). The final section of the motet uses the dominant to return to a/A, and the final measures of the piece recapitulate the III-IV-V movement of the entire work, concluding with I. [See also the prolepsis of this movement in mm. 13-14.] Although the dominant is not emphasized, the progression, at both levels, is clearly directed toward a. In this regard and in the appeal of the close imitations (e.g., m. 30 ff.) and textural changes, this motet is very satisfying.

XIII.	1. Fortitudo mea et laus mea	a=i		(F/C/a)
	Domine		V-i	(a)
	2. Et factus est mihi in salutem	m. 14	III	(C)
	Vox exultationis et salutis	m. 24	-IV	(D)
	3. In tabernaculis justorum.	m. 35	V/V-V-I	

"Sustinuit" is also more interesting in variety and arena of its activity. The serious tone of the text is reflected not only in the opening gesture, which bears a resemblance to the figures we have seen on works like "miserere" which require an effective gesture, but also in the timbre of the relatively lower voices. In addition, after the opening section of the piece establishes d minor and then moves to the dominant, the tone of the motet changes and the harmonic motion leads to the relative major.

XIV.	1. Sustinuit anima mea	d=i		
	in verbo eius			
	Speravit anima mea			
	in Domine		-V	(A)
	2. A custodia matutina	m. 26	V/♭III	
	usque ad noctem		[subdominant area of] ♭III	(F)
	3. Speret Israel in Domino	m. 49	♭III-V/♭III [N/V]	
			V----I	

At the words "usque ad noctem," however, the harmonic movement becomes word-painting as the voices are led down the subdominant side of F and back and the lowest voice closes on F, its lowest note which had not been so strongly stated before. This section is so complete, that the ensuing, contrasting conclusion of the motet comes as quite a surprise. The serious mood of Israel's night is broken by a joyous transformation appropriate to the words "speret Israel in Domino."

What had been profound now dances: the temporary drift (in transcription) to 3/8, the dotted rhythms, the faster harmonic rhythm, and constant suspensions all move one metric level faster than before. The vigor here is more rhythmic than melodic, in contrast to the figures used in "Ego dixi" ("quia peccavi tibi") and "Libera me" ("quando caeli movendi"). The move back to d minor is made quickly, confirmed, but then revoked in mm. 55-57 where it appears that the piece will conclude on F. The final turn to D, the light of faith which illumines the darkest night, is without parallel in these motets. The part movement suddenly stabilizes and returns to the former level of activity, as the I-V (in F, or so it seems—i.e., the relative major) is transformed by chromatic alteration and common tone connection and suspension into V-I in D. This is an example of the rare beauty of which Ferrabosco was capable. Typically, it passes by quickly; there is no sense of extension. Despite this, the closure is complete and satisfying. The ear is delighted, even though the means are modest, and the architecture of the piece is fulfilled.

Another Latin piece by Ferrabosco survives, the four-voice motet "Quare dereliquerunt me." In most respects it is similar to the five-part pieces with the exception of a consistent fullness of texture and the lower range (AABarBar) of "Quare dereliquerunt me."

The appearance of "Quare dereliquerunt me" in two sources next to (B.M. Egerton 3665) or close to (B.M. Add. 29372-5) the elder Alfonso's four-part motet "Fuerunt mihi" raises questions of attribution, despite the clarity of attribution in those manuscripts. On stylistic grounds, however, there are three aspects of the composition which point clearly to the younger Ferrabosco.

The first is the use of the subdominant area in conjunction with the tonic minor (c) in the opening half of the pieces, mm. 1-34. Only in the second half of the motet does the piece move up to the tonic by emphasizing the dominant influence. Here the dominant is balanced (relative to the tonic) by the subdominant minor so that the tonic is strongly felt to be minor throughout the piece. Because the subdominant is so strong an influence there is ground for a suspicion that the motet ends on the dominant, not on the tonic—a crucial problem for the latter-day listener who is used to thinking of tonic definition in terms of the dominant. It is the motivic shape which provides one of the major clues in this problem. The affective leap of a minor sixth, a figure which is first used in m. 45 and generally involves g-e♭ or c-a♭, returning toward the dominant (d) or tonic (g).

The other clue lies in the harmonic rhythm, for the strong position of the harmonic rhythm, after m. 45, is denied the subdominant except in passing (m. 55), or in the preparation of a harmony which, in turn, is part of the movement to the tonic (mm. 48-49), or as an extending element of closure (m. 59). This last instance occurs in a coda (m. 57-end) with a pedal in the second voice. If the coda were rewritten to make obvious the metric accents of the three moving parts, the closing extension of the harmonic rhythm would be more obvious as the combination of 6/4 and 3/2 measures of the bass shows.

Ex. 22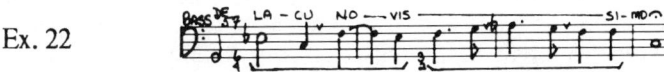

This plagal coda and the preceding twelve measures of the piece complement the opening both in general motivic shape and in the sense (now) of f→C/c, compared with the earlier C→F. The coda, itself, is a Ferrabosco convention, however tentatively it resolves the C-F balance.

So, too, are the clear harmonic articulations of form at the end of individual textual phrases (m.20; m.34; m.45) and the modest, though effective use of word-painting at "inundaverunt" (m.20). But it is the sudden reining of the melodic activity at m. 34, the move from question to address and from the imitative and flowing setting of "inundaverunt" to the decisive, homorhythmic address of "Dixi, Domine," which is a hallmark of Ferrabosco's style: the brief declamatory outburst sets the address apart from both the narrative aspects of the circumstance described and the ensuing counterpoint which, by the use of affective intervals (min. 2 and min. 6) specifies the quality of this desperate cry.

All of these features we find in the five-part pieces, and the only substantive distinction lies in this setting for two pairs of equal voices.

The four-voice anthem included in Leighton's *Teares and Lamentacions of a Sorrowful Soule* (1614), "In thee, O Lord, I put my trust," is set for four high voices, all written in treble clef. The range is comfortable today only for professional singers, and it seems most reasonable to assume that this short piece was written at its notated range to avoid, as much as possible, accidentals and the use of other clefs: the plainness of text-setting also suggests the possibility that, whatever the reason for its inclusion in the collection, this is a piece for young, student singers. The text setting of the second voice, interrupted, for no necessary reason, in the fourth measure, the wide range of these high parts, and the modest imitative activity are unusual for Ferrabosco and raise questions of when and why the piece was written.

The similarly short five-voice anthem, "O Lord, come pity my distress," is set for a more customary grouping of voices (SATTB) and employs two figures of imitation at the outset: one for the inner voices, one for the cantus and bass. These outer voices are deliberate, forming a self-sufficient duo. The distinction of character between outer and inner voices is lost, however, during the second phrase ("see how I sigh and moan") in which most voices use the earlier figure of the inner voices while the fourth voice pronounces the text to the figure of the outer voices. The final phrase (m. 9 ff.) is more interesting for the way harmonic movement of the bass and the intervallic logic of the part-writing combine to make a satisfying conclusion (cf. especially mm. 11-12).

The effect of the anthem is emphasized not as much by the shape of the motives (although one could argue that the phrygian character of the opening cantus and bassus phrases were important in this regard) as by the two occurrences of augmented triads. The first of these, amidst a description of sighs, groans, and tears, appears in passing, setting in motion an evasive resolution which is a prolepsis of the concluding cadence of the anthem. There the augmented triad is more forcibly and more conventionally, if less interestingly, resolved as an ornament to a $V^{b{6\atop4}}$ double suspension.

This little anthem, about the length of one of the sections of the Latin motets, is unexceptional in its harmonic range. Nonetheless, it is wonderfully scaled and serves well as an example of Ferrabosco's control of melodic curve, harmonic rhythm, tonal focus, and the combination of intervallic process and tonal harmony.

The text setting of the second voice in mm. 3-6, however, is particularly awkward and arbitrary.

Ex. 23

The opening figure and the rhythmic point of "pity" (♩ ♪: both lose their specificity in m. 6 when they appear to new words) are oddly coupled with the ensuing music which is relatively disjoint and diffuse. The octave leap (m.6) occurs only to wed the fourth (m.6) and third (m.7) voices, emphasizing the isolation of the cantus which, like the voice-part of a serious lute-song or (because of the integration of the five parts) consort song, soars beyond the lower voices of the accompaniment.

"In death, no man remembreth Thee" is only slightly longer than these anthems, but its structure is more varied by a movement to the dominant (m.9) which emphasizes the contrast of statement and question in the text. In a sense the entire anthem is word-painting: the question "how is he to celebrate Thy glorious name?" is answered not so much by the imitative activity ("celebrate," m.13; at the return to the tonic) as by the anthem itself: the manner of celebration is suggested by the musical activity, the form of celebration by the anthem itself.

The conventional imitative passage of the opening measures is brought to a standstill on the dominant, followed by a dramatic rest which precedes the low setting of "in darksome grave." This abrupt turn to declamatory homophony demonstrates how clearly chordal Ferrabosco's writing becomes when the words are aligned. The imitative passages of this piece, after the first few measures, are simply animated homophony. The process, in reverse, is seen by the transformation of the declamation into animated celebration (mm. 10-13): the harmonic rhythm remains steady, only the words are no longer aligned and the voices are more active and varied in combination; the concentration is released, the celebration erupts even from the grave.

The focus of the tonal thinking is clear: the modal variety of the second section, contrasting the inflections of minor with those of major in the opening, only strengthens the sense of g/G. That the modest architecture of the anthem is delineated by both harmonic and procedural means emphasizes Ferrabosco's concern with form. In this anthem the harmonic practices used are essentially chordal—Ferrabosco's typical preference for any kind of structurally important articulation.

XIV

Lamentations

The polyphonic settings of the *Lamentations of Jeremiah the Prophet* form a genre of their own. The original Hebrew text was written by unknown author(s) in the period between the destruction of Jerusalem in 587 B.C. and its restoration, and it is read each year on the ninth day of Ab to memorialize that destruction. In the Christian church these texts were incorporated into the matin services of Holy Week beginning on Maundy Thursday, where they introduced and set the tone for the celebration of the most serious period of the Christian year.

The form of the Hebrew poetry is important. Of the 5 chapters of *Lamentations*, only the last is not an acrostic poem. The first, second, and fourth chapters each have 22 3-line stanzas beginning with the consecutive letters of the Hebrew alphabet. The third chapter has 66 stanzas arranged into 22 groups of 3, proceeding similarly through the alphabet. The final chapter also contains 22 stanzas, but does not have an apparent external organization. Catholic usage did not abandon the oratorical effect and symbolism of the Hebrew acrostic, and St. Jerome's *Vulgate* retained the Hebrew letters at the head of each verse. In the chants for the Office of Matins these letters were little more than signposts, but in the polyphonic settings they provided opportunity of great moment, an opportunity for wordless music, for meditation, for illumination, for announcement.

The first of the known polyphonic settings of the Lamentations is Dufay's commemoration of the Fall of Constantinople (1543), the *Lamentacio sancte maris ecclesiae Constantinoble* found in Codex 2794 of the Biblioteca Riccardiana in Florence (anon.) and Codex 871 of the Abbey of Montecassino.[1] *Lamentations* by Ockeghem and Busnois, though listed in accounts at Cambrai, are lost or no longer extant. With the publication by Petrucci of 2 volumes of *Lamentations* in 1506, the dam was opened, and the sixteenth century saw a tremendous number of these settings, most of which, of course, set only part of the text. Tinctoris, Genet, Agricola, de la Rue, Sermisy, and later, Victoria, Lassus, Handl(Gallus), and Palestrina, who wrote at least 13 complete sets of *Lamentations*, are only the leaders and most interesting of the continental composers who contributed to this outpouring.

The English response was more modest in number, with only 10 settings by 7 composers. The 2 (a5) by Tallis are rightly well known, for they remain exemplars of the art. Less well known are the 4 others which also appear in *Tudor Church Music*, 2 by Robert White (a5; a6), and 1 each by Osbert Parsley (a5) and William Byrd (a5). 2 settings by the elder Alfonso Ferrabosco (a5; a6) and one each by John Mundy (a5) and the younger Ferrabosco (a5) are known only from manuscript.

Part of the reason for this small number of settings certainly stems from Henry VIII's break with Rome and the subsequent establishment of the Anglican liturgy in which the *Lamentations* were of little significance and the Tenebrae services eliminated.[2] Thus it would appear that these Latin settings in England were intended for private use, for they are decidedly serious works intended for special occasions, or possibly, as a comment on the state of the Catholic rite in England following Queen Elizabeth's excommunication in 1570 and England's subsequent official fall from grace (Pius V: *Regnans in Excelsis*).

Like the psalm-motet, the *Lamentations* offered the composer a rich arena of textual choice—a choice which, in England, was independent of liturgical propriety. As with favorite motet texts, composers could represent, in an individual style, a shared experience: the English composers of Latin *Lamentations* were all recusants or of Catholic background. Thus, they paid homage to their predecessors while staking their claim to a specific expression within the general, shared expression represented by the succession of settings. There can be little doubt that the English composers viewed the *Lamentations* as a special genre in which unalloyed seriousness was reflected in the craft of composition and the sonorous timbres of the lower voices (excepting White's settings) selected for the voice-parts.

The most well-known of these settings by English composers are the two by Thomas Tallis which succeed in moving the art from expression to meditation. The younger Ferrabosco's setting, like Tallis's, uses the verses from the beginning of *Lamentations* which depict the solitary Jerusalem, bereft of friends and weeping her fate, while the prophet keeningly invokes her to return to her God. One of the most compelling aspects of Tallis's setting is his manipulation of textures by which voices respond to each other, or against which a single voice is etched. Tallis occasionally has the singers sing as one, homorhythmically, with telling dramatic effect as the swirl of melodic activity is cast away and the text is revealed in nugatory concentration. But much of this succeeds in Tallis's setting because there is a flow from section to section. The motion stops only for rhetorical purposes, to articulate the lamentation; otherwise, the effects of expression are accomplished almost entirely by texture and movement and by discreet and poignant use of dissonance and cross-relation. The elaborate and constantly amazing refractions of the Hebrew letters, standing as musical analogues of the great illuminated capitals in medieval and Renaissance manuscripts, lead on to the verses, although standing apart in style, as if conveying the energy of the finger of God pointing to what follows. The sectional cadences are overlapped with the result that the thrust of the prophet is not lost or trivialized, like a politician's speech, by constant stopping.

Not as compelling as Tallis's, Ferrabosco's *Lamentations* lack a similar breadth of vision, concentration of purpose, iridescence of sound, and expressive control of the material. Each of the sections—there are eleven in all—comes to a close which, even though only momentary, deprives the setting of the grand sweep which befits the visual imagery, the emotional integrity, and the prophetic charisma. Nonetheless, the sonority is weighty and impressive, and this piece, like so many others lost in the shadows of greater exemplars, deserves performance.

Ferrabosco's *Lamentations* appear in sources which are outside the usual group of English manuscripts containing *Lamentation* settings. The only other *Lamentation* in the Tregian score is the setting a6 by the elder Ferrabosco, and there is no other *Lamentation* in the Bodleian Music School set. Ferrabosco was the youngest of the composers by a full generation and quite probably had not written his setting until after the other manuscripts had been compiled (e.g., the most important of them, Christ Church mss. 979-983, compiled c. 1600 by John Baldwin).

Several problems exist because our only complete copy of the setting appears in the Sambrook book, without full text, while the Bodleian Music School set gives the complete text but only the outer parts. The texting of the inner parts is a problem familiar to any researcher of the motet and mass repertory, but it is mitigated here by the short sections and textural clues in the music itself. We can be reasonably sure that the Tregian score was not used for performance, unless by instruments, although its sources might have been, and we are faced with the implication in the Bodleian set that performance could be "stripped down" to simply cantus and bass. This is not unreasonable, for the cantus is the prominent voice and somewhat stands apart while the others, excepting the bass, are less distinctive and overlap considerably.

There are a variety of factors which contribute to the demarcation of sections of these *Lamentations*. Some of these emphasize the separation of the individual units while others, by variety and balance, contribute to a sense of a larger and more inclusive whole. The most obvious elements of separation are the formal cadences at the end of each section. These themselves are varied, however, with several (e.g., those at the end of "Quo modo" and "Non est") clearly preparing for the next exposition of text.

That these sections are not merely additive in an arbitrary fashion, one simply following another, is also shown by the difference of treatment of these cadences. "Aleph" emphasizes the dominant and presents an authentic cadence to the major tonic, G. "Beth," however, arrives at the same tonic but only with a twist, for it has been in g minor and utilized the minor subdominant as preparation to the final tonic. The contrast of parallel modes and of dominant and subdominant in these two pillars of larger formal division emphasizes the importance of the harmonic arena in determining a sense of formal balance and contrast.

The variety of individual sections is manifest in changes of texture, both in voicing and presentation. The range is tremendously flexible in this style, and Ferrabosco takes advantage of much of it, from the homorhythmic declamation of "Princeps provinciarum" to the fantasia-like instrumental brilliance of "Ghimel." There are occasional contrasts of vocal timbres, such as the repeated statements of "Hierusalem, Hierusalem" in which the lower four voices are answered by the upper four a fifth higher, or of vocal groupings, as in the paired entries of "Aleph."

The aspect of timbre cannot be too far separated from the practice of imitation, for imitative procedures are the glue of most of these sections. In the three Hebrew letters, especially, the imitation of a musical figure by the voices, either paired or individually in succession, is most rigorously presented. That is, entrances are made at regular intervals until all participating voices have presented the material. After that point, as in the other sections, the procedure becomes more flexible with often only a tag of the motive being presented or musical filler provided with no melodic relation to the original gesture. All voices participate in this activity, but not to the same extent all the time. In several movements the bass and cantus are most closely involved (see "Incipit" and "Quo modo") while the other parts participate much less, if at all. All the voices participate in "Migravit," although rather freely, and the homophonic, homorhythmic opening of "Hierusalem" opens out into a plaintive, imitative texture which continues into the codetta at m. 15. It is harder to characterize the setting of "Omnes amici" which begins with a homorhythmic statement by four voices answered by the fifth and then focuses on the forceful word "spreverunt" by the use of a distinctive melodic figure wich is highlighted as it is passed among the voices.

Thus, imitation is neither pervasive or consistent in these pieces, but is used for variety and for extension of musical ideas as well as for rhetorical effect, whether it be the focusing on "spreverunt" or the stretto-like accumulation of energy which leads to a cadence. Imitation, as a structural device, is used less in these works than in the motets, and it is used with less regularity (i.e., of entrance and voicing). As in the motets, the imitation is not strict: the motives which are filled-in perfect intervals are adhered to fairly closely, but the strong gestures with leaps ("spreverunt," "Ghimel") serve only as models for approximation. A short, identifiable figure which shares some characteristic of the head-motive, such as direction and interval or rhythm, is all that is required. Imitation allows a different approach to the density of musical activity than does homorhythmic treatment of the text, and Ferrabosco utilizes the spectrum between the two to good effect, providing variety, structural clarity, and a sense of inner motion which is consolidated at the cadences. The larger form of the *Lamentations*, however, is dependent on the harmonic areas explored. This larger form follows, predictably, the text with the three letters standing as the pillars of thesis, antithesis, and synthesis. From the diagram which follows it can be seen that the "Incipit" is also a musical introduction, a passing from the dominant to the tonic of the *Lamentations* proper. The subsequent three sections, articulated by the Hebrew letters, emphasize the dominant and subdominant/minor area and then balance the two. The entire work is tonal in outlook and essentially harmonic in procedure, with the melodic activity and the sense of intervallic progression less extended and varied than in the individual motets. As in the motets, the immanent ambiguity of mode (G/g) is emphasized by the use of resources of each mode, particularly the use of B♭ and E♭ and c borrowed from the minor, while C, a, and D and E are related to the major. F/f is doubly ambiguous, for F is borrowed from the minor but also used in conjunction with C, while f extends the range of the minor extensions. What this amounts to is a pool of resources related by common tones and dominants, and that is the way Ferrabosco uses it: there are no juxtapositions of unrelated harmonies for effect, no startling harmonic diversions. The last large section of the work, beginnning with "Ghimel" demonstrates this flexibility as it moves to the subdominant minor (ending of "Ghimel") to the subdominant major (ending of "Migravit"), and then emphasizes the major/minor ambiguity in "Hierusalem."

Lamentations of Jeremiah

I.	1.	Incipit lamentio Jeremiae prophetae	g/G=i	V-I	(G)
	2.	Aleph	I(i)	V-I	(G)
	3.	Quo modo sedet sola civitas plena popula			
		Facta est quasi vidua			
		Domina gentium		i-V	(D)
	4.	Princeps provinciarum		V(V/V)-V	
		Facta est sub tributo		♭III-♭VI-IV-V-I	(G)
II.	5.	Beth		i-iv-I	(G)
	6.	Plorans ploravit in nocte		I-i	v-i
		Et lacrimae eius in maxillis eius		V-I	(G)
	7.	Non est qui consoletur eam			I
		Ex omnibus charis eius		i-♭III-V/V-V	(D)
	8.	Omnes amici eius spreverunt eam,			V-I-iv-V
		Et facti sunt illi inimici.		V-I; I/IV-I	(G)
III.	9.	Ghimel		I-IV	(C)
	10.	Migravit Juda propter afflictionem	temp.[C=I]	vi-V/ii-V/V	(C)
		et multitudinem servitutis;		ii-V/IV-IV	(C)
		Habitavit inter gentes,		V-I, IV-I	(C)
		Nec invenit requiem.		IV-I	(C)
	11.	Hierusalem, Hierusalem,	[G=I]	IV-I; I-V	(C)
		Convertere ad Dominum tuum.		V-I; I/IV-I	(G)

This architecture works on the ear unnoticed as the attention is focused more directly by the use of homorhythmic sections and affective repetition (e.g., the opening cries of "Hierusalem") and the thematic highlighting of certain words by imitation. The smaller, sectional ebb and flow of activity, which generally begins with uniform or regular exposition and a basically syllabic text-setting before relaxing into a looser, more effusive musical play, is directed to the cadences which gather up the parts and regulate their activity within a small arena. The outer parts confine the action, both in vocal range and in musical scope, for they brake the less sedate activity of the inner parts, keeping it in line with the harmonic rhythm of the bass and melodic-textual impetus of the cantus. But it is the overall formal conception of the *Lamentations* which makes them as satisfying as they are, allowing the listener to hear beyond the individual verse. Less ornate than Byrd's, less rich than Tallis's, this setting is nonetheless humbly worthy of such company.

The brightness and predictability of Ferrabosco's *Lamentations* lies largely in the use of tonal resources which confirm or enhance the expectation of arrival on the tonic, particularly by means of secondary dominants and a distinctly harmonic bass. The opening measures are an example as the establishment of G/g as the tonal center of the entire work is begun on the dominant. It is immediately quite clear that D is not the tonic, but the dominant, and when that dominant function is thwarted, as it is briefly in the harmonic meandering which follows the deceptive resolution at measure 5, the result is felt as a delaying of the real goal.

Ex. 1

Several factors are at work here: 1) D is recognized immediately as the dominant of g, because the relationship cannot be reversed convincingly (i.e., g is not felt as subdominant to D, particularly with the strength of the intervallic movement of the upper four voices in mm. 3 and 4); 2) the e in the bass at m. 5 is clearly deceptive, pushing the cadence off to the subdominant; that is the only time in the piece, until "migravit," that e is used, and it is not entirely convincing here where it also affects the quality of movement to the open fifth on C a measure later.

As has been mentioned above, Ferrabosco varies his vocal forces, more in style than in number, without abandoning the basic five-voiced texture for more than a few measures at a time. The settings of the Hebrew letters are the clearest example of the variety of ways the voices can combine and intermingle in relatively free musical play. On the other hand, the sonorous "Princeps provinciarum" depends for effect on its essential homorhythm even more than on its harmonic structure which focuses on the tonic (G) from the dominant and relative major sides in successive phrases. This is an example of the startling, dramatic clarity which declamatory homophony provides in the larger context of 5-voice polyphony. Only in the even more chromatically inflected and expressive "Jerusalem, convertere" is such an effect recreated, there for the first time combined with a real sense of a leading voice which bears the text, while the others, like the accompaniement of a concert song, create a musical mediation out of the same material.

Yet this final section is one of the easiest to text, and the voicings are so deliberate that there is no question of the parts being nonvocal. The metaphor of "turning" is achieved by the "return" to G in the final cadence, but that arrival was never in doubt. The common-tone chromatic twistings of the opening measures, repeated then at the upper fifth, never confound a sure sense of reference, partly because the bass does not participate and also because there is no complication of register exchange of the kind which makes the opening of Gesualdo's "Moro lasso" so much more difficult to sing. Only one note is chromatically inflected at a time, and the progression is based on the circle of fifths.

For the most part the melodic lines are smoothly filled in with leaps answered by a return of direction. This rule of smoothness is openly flouted at the beginning of "Ghimel" by a melodic figure which has its antecedent in the very beginning of the work. The incorporation of a harmonic ornament (implied suspension) into the beginning of the point makes the opening of the "Ghimel" quite angular melodically and rhythmically. The diminished fifths which are required in mm. 5 and 6 are not, in themselves, demanding of the singers, but the second voice (m.6) not only sings the diminished fifth but careens thereby into the midst of an augmented triad with no textual impetus.

Ex. 2

[original appearance of the figure, from "Incipit"]

What permits this all to make aural sense in performance is the reality of the texture in contrast to the appearance of the voice parts. The c♯ of the second voice is derived from the d of the third; the harmonic ornament which comprises both the augmented triad and the suspension (which never quite touches base with a neat a-c♯-e) can maintain its unresolved piquancy precisely because the firm sense of d is present and confirmed in the first half of the next measure, before sliding down to B♭.

There are times, however, when the handling of the major/minor ambiguity and smaller touches relating to modal contrast is not as effective as one might wish. In the first section, as the "Incipit" leads to "Aleph," the connection is smooth: G to G, with only the change of texture and procedure to set off the dramatic evocation of the awesome letter. The modal contrast does come, however, with the e♭ at the end of the first measure and the b♭'s in the second measure. But it has no structural effect, being localized and merely coloristic. Ideally, it would also be preferable to have f♯ sounding (in the fourth voice) before the reapparance of b♮ preceding the final cadence, lest the early appearance of the b♮ preempt the effect of the cadence even more than is already done by having the b♮ appear only in the final chord where it serves as a shimmering inflection of g minor. Similarly, the f♯ in the bass at m. 3 seems only half-good. The first one, explained away as a cross-relation in context and a leading tone to g in purpose, confuses matters, while the second, the resolution of a suspension and leading back to g, is quite acceptable. The confusion comes about because the cross-relations are not born of melodic intent, but are arbitrarily applied, presumably so that the bass voice will outline a major third in its opening motive. Such consistency is not a necessary attribute of the piece or of this passage and defeats the movement to the minor begun just a measure earlier and continued until the cadential preparation. In each of these three instances the dramatic effect of this letter is diluted, and it is the lack of care with details like these that most essentially sets Ferrabosco apart from his contemporaries, Byrd and Gibbons.

The combination of textural concern and free imitation is demonstrated in "Quo modo sedet sola civitas." The musical-textural fabric is here much denser and given a variety of colors both by voicing and by the changing amount of imitative activity. The activity of the inner voices is infrequently imitative, except for word rhythms and the general responsiveness of the second voice to the first; the outer voices have a life of their own. Nevertheless, the activity of the inner voices never overwhelms the clarity of the upper voice which, buoyed by, but soaring beyond, the confines of those lower voices, rises to a climax of contemplative reflection of this city, once great among nations.

That contemplation is stunningly and forcibly focused on the present state of the desolate city by the following section, the contrasting declamation of her plight, "Plorans ploravit," which wrests the contemplation from D back to G, expressively using a path from the relative major. But one might ask how it is possible so to invoke the minor mode with there being only one chord of minor quality in these phrases—and why did Ferrabosco avoid the sublime effect of loss which a conclusion on g minor would have afforded? To the second question there can be no satisfactory answer.

To the first, however, the answer is at least two-fold and is based on the principles outlined in the introductory discussion of Ferrabosco's harmonic practice. In the first place, the progression of chords, related by third (common-tone) and fifth (dominant) relationships, is governed by nonmelodic bass movement which is unconfusingly related to the g/G tonality. The use of chordal inflections from both members of the parallel tonal pair prepare and ornament the dominant. The g/G tonality had been previously exposed sufficiently to be comfortable to the ear and to serve as orientation for the harmonic combination of the relatively simple vocal parts. The crossing of voices obscures the importance of the manner by which intervallic harmony, melodically inspired, contributes to what we hear as chordal progression, particularly in mm. 3 and 7-8. The effect of this statement of the condition of Jerusalem, this trombone chorale of lament, concludes the first verse of the *Lamentations*.

Like a mighty flame in the darkness, the letter "Beth" is etched against the lament, contrasting its resolute minor mode (turning to major only at the final chord), presented in wave after wave of imitative activity and undiluted sobriety, with the major sonorities which had just preceded. It is a model of constructive effect, with the upper voice first riding over the imitative weavings of the others as it presents in longer notes the motto with which it had also begun "Aleph." Then, when it takes up the imitation, it soars well beyond the lower choir's range as the harmony moves to the depths of the minor subdominant, from which the return to the tonic is made without the intermediary of the dominant. This is an important distinction, for with the exception of the brief and deceptively resolved dominant in m.5 this is a more severe movement than we had heard before, one which has the flavor not just a g minor but almost of g, then c dorian.

The affective climax of the work is "Plorans ploravit" with dissonances constantly tugging at resolution, the weeping augmented triads of the first two measures stretching the expressive capacity of the harmonic fabric, the chromaticism of the first and second voices wailing slightly out of synchrony before they are joined by the next two voices picking up their lament. In fact, the opening of this movement could be reduced to a rather uninteresting progression. As it stands, however, the bitter gnashing of the harmonies, apparently thrashing around in quest of resolution, obscures the clarity of their progression through the concatenation of augmented intervals, suspensions, and the use of sinuous chromatic inflection and neighbor tones.

The rising minor sixth which is used expressively to represent "lacrimae," appears with modifications as a motive. It appears first in the bass and is answered by the cantus. After these statements, only the rhythmic shape and melodic contour is retained. Even the expressive half-step descent following an ascent of a minor interval is briefly abandoned in mm. 13-14, to be reclaimed in the following statements. What is important, of course, is that the rising sixth, or its substitutes,

What is important, of course, is that the rising sixth, or its substitutes, cannot overcome the gravity of its expressiveness and is unable in resounding to break the bonds of its melodic logic. The universal resonance of this figure through the five parts and in varied forms confirms the infinite grief and present weeping of the city, as much as does the inability of the lament in the same measures, 13-14, to move away from g minor to the relative major, B♭.

"Non est qui consoletur" and "Omnes amici" stand together both textually (as circumstance and reason) and musically. The emotional outpouring of weeping of "Plorans ploravit," with its imitative reverberations, is focused into description and near homorhythm in two phrases of great breadth and vocal range. The sense of breadth is due in part to the full texture but also owes as much to the melodic descent of the bass in the first phrase and the slower movement of the voices, necessary to accomodate the chromatic inflections and cross-relations. The logic of the movement in the first phrase, even to m. 8 when the cantus reaches its pedal-like final note, is intervallic rather than chordal, although the result is no less convincing harmonically. But in this piece, which moves from G/g to rest on the dominant as preparation for "Omnes amici," the lack of a strong authentic cadence at the end of the first phrase allows the movement away from the tonic to be less forceful.

The change of mode between the two phrases is discreetly handled and is quite effective, partly because the use of b♮ has been consistent in the first phrase and partly because the change serves as a precursor of the similar transition in the next movement. As we have come to expect, the modal contrast is affective and, in conjunction with the extremes of range of the bass and cantus, heightens the effect of the solitary upper voice, extended and exposed at "eam."

The transformation from D to d in "Omnes amici" at the words "et facti sunt illi inimici" is one of the stunning effect: the turn of friends into enemies reflected pictorially by the transformation as well as expressed emotionally by the suspensions which form augmented triads in the midst of the passage (m.14, but see also m.5). After the relatively declamatory and homophonic opening, this movement opens up into a more expansive and imitative piece, the expression conveyed by musical gesture (e.g., the figure used for "spreverunt") and by imitation and the manipulation of texture and melodic interval rather than by force of declamation. Both the bass and the cantus are plain in comparison with the other voices.

These two movements form an arch from tonic to dominant and back and share an expressive change of mode at their midpoints, while being of different style in their declamation and imitative procedure.

Their pairing is given even greater structural identity by the coda at the end of "Omnes amici." Here, as we see in several of the motets, the tonic is reached, with dominant preparation, at m. 19 when the cantus reaches its last note. That note is then held at an upper tonic pedal with the minor subdominant (I^6_4) balancing the previous dominant. This also creates a conflict of e♭ and b♮ (briefly exposed in m. 5), the effect of which is to prolong the possibility of movement to c and to color, by emphasis of the exposed diminished fourth, the setting of "inimici."

The management of harmonic rhythm is also particularly effective here, with the movement of c to G occurring every measure on the first and second half-notes (as transcribed). In order for the resolution to occur on G, it must be reached on the first beat of the measure, that is, c must be extended through an entire measure. That is what happens after the bass establishes a double pedal in m. 21.

Curiously, in this coda, the bass is given the tenor clef in ms. and suddenly sings as high as e♭, while the fourth voice becomes the lowest sounding. The bass imitates the figure of the cantus (from m.16) but with the important change of perfect to diminished fourth (b♭-f:e♭-b♮) which not only creates a cross-relation at a distance and fails to complete the octave, but points the motion toward c. Both aspects, the cross-relation and the harmonic point, are also present in the most conclusive statement of the diminished fourth, by the fourth voice in m. 21, when it becomes clear that c is structurally inferior to the pedal g. The use of the subdominant area is a welcome stroke and expands the arena of these *Lamentations*, but the importance of this move will be clearer in the next section.

The imitative flourishes of "Ghimel" trail off into free play after a distinctive beginning, until the cantus breaks away from the activity and moves more deliberately to the cadence (m. 11ff.) on C. In fact, the nature of the opening figure is a harbinger of this move, for the descending leap of a minor sixth (g-b♮) is heard as moving to c. It is heard even more clearly due to the form it takes: that of a dominant suspension in which, after the suspension is resolved, the dominant must move to the tonic (or, as in m.4 to a deceptive resolution). Only at the sonorous m. 12 does this expectation of chordal progression confront the intervallic procedures of individual melodic lines as the bass does not complete its figure but proceeds to f which pulls us quite clearly out of the realm of g minor and clarifies our arrival on c/C. That arrival is brought home by the dominant suspension (the familiar figure is augmented, in the second voice) in the next-to-last measure. This movement to c/C is important, for by its strength here it makes possible the excursion involving a minor at the opening of "Migravit" and with a conscious attempt at harmonic contrast of the dominant and subdominant poles about the tonic.

The abrupt angularity of the opening figure has been mentioned before as recalling the figure at the word "lamentatio" in the introduction.[3] Here, also, that angularity is presented in an arena of harmonic clarity, although the leap into an augmented triad (m.6, second voice) might argue against such an assertion. In fact, however, that leap is not so startling when the other voices are included: the g-c♯ by itself is difficult, but the c♯ is heard as emerging from the d in the third voice. Thus the effect is cushioned and only mildly astringent.

The movement to the subdominant area (c/C) is achieved by going beyond and moving as far as the subdominant of the subdominant, with the tonic now acting as a dominant to balance about c/C. The crux of this flexibility is the B♭ in mm. 7-8, where once again the bifocal relationship between tonic and relative major is exploited and the subdominant implications of that relationship explored: g-B♭, F/f, c, G, C. That is, the relative major returns to the tonic, or in this case the subdominant, by progressing up the circle of fifths.

"Migravit" provides an even more extended example of the use of the subdominant, this time in the sense of an area which always returns us immediately to its upper fifth. The opening, rising, arch-like fourth is the mirror image of such motion. The a minor with which the pieces begin (relative minor to the previously heard C), is undermined by the lack of a confirming g♯, and the emphasis is really on F and d, the areas to which the a minor keeps slipping, with the brief movement to F in m. 13 a confirmation of what the ear expects although reached by intervallic progression in the outer voices rather than by strong bass movement.

From this point, it is clear that the a minor of the beginning was a subtle trick, a nexus of deception which could guide us toward D, which we know as the dominant of g/G, or, as here, F, which can either direct us to g via B♭ or act, as it does, as the subdominant of C. From m.14 on, the piece confirms C as its goal, and in this confirmation the bass takes on a more assertive contour emphasizing the harmonic fundament. G is used, though never in the proper metric position for a preparatory dominant in a cadence (i.e., the move to C never occurs on a downbeat after G). It is involved, in passing, to balance the sense of F, so that the ear does not expect to conclude on F. That balancing and the repetition of movement from F to C (mm. 17-18; final cadence) enable the movement to C, intimated and begun in "Ghimel," to effect a local resolution, a temporary balance.

That balance succumbs to another force in the final section of the *Lamentations*, "Jerusalem, convertere ad Dominum tuum." The weight

Lamentations, "Jerusalem, convertere ad Dominum tuum." The weight of the entire piece is brought to bear here, and the return to G is a confirmation of the inexorable granitic and uncompromising character of the prophet's admonition, a statement in the eternal present tense. The sense of "turning" is effected both by the return to G and by the more active use of the dominant (D) to effect that move. Largely unused in the previous two movements, the dominant is reached very quickly in the sequential opening statements of "Jerusalem" which lift the piece from C to G. The timing, too, has changed, with G being a destination reached on the downbeat. At the midpoint of the movement there is a structural division (m. 8) where the sublime B♭ is refracted into a more immediate g minor which is subsequently confirmed several times by both harmonic progression and the melodic leap to the descending third, the reaching for the Lord, "ad Dominum."

In mm. 12-15, the balances are heard more clearly: a sequence of V-I's deceptively brought round to the dominant by interrupting the sequence on the relative major. Here, also, there is a coda with the cantus and third voice providing a tonic pedal. The cadence to the tonic is ostensibly thwarted at m. 15 and pointed toward the subdominant by a biting suspension. But when that suspension is resolved, the timing and quality of the ensuing suspensions all point to G: m. 15 is, in effect, a 3/2 measure, with the c in the bass on the weak third beat; moreover, the suspensions do not have range to extend the movement back to c—there would have to be an f as the suspension over the bass c or another e♭ to work against the d (in the fourth voice) at that point to allow the suspensions to continue. Besides, the suspended d, over the bass c, has lost some of its effect by having the note of resolution sounding as the bass. The result is convincing only as it is pulled up to G, and the effect of the coda is once more to provide a balance to the strength of the dominant without contradicting the confirmation of G as the tonic of the entire work. Our ears recognize G from the rest of the work, and now this cadence completes the procedures and balances of the preceding movements.

Conclusion

The briefly luminous career of Alfonso Ferrabosco presents more questions than answers. But in his works we see a composer who, Janus-like, looked to both the past and the future. It is the native tradition of English song which is the strongest influence in his songs, and the style of the continental (and English) Latin motet still resounds in Ferrabosco's conservatively written motets.

Nevertheless, in the ceremonial masque songs Ferrabosco exploited a manner of declamation infrequently found in earlier English song: a forceful, oratorical style which, while it did not attempt to reproduce speech rhythms, succeeded in fashioning song into rhetoric, in matching the oratorical style with musical gesture. And in the Italian songs which approach the monodic style of his continental contemporaries, Ferrabosco far exceeded the practices of English song in the service of expression. Yet in all these songs, there is not one instance when musical considerations are forgotten. Phrases may be asymmetrical, but overall structures are balanced and tonal clarity is always maintained.

This is true also of the motets which, while they ape the style of the contrapuntists, are tonal in concept and design. In fact, the most interesting aspect of the motets is their tonal construction which reveals, even more clearly than the songs, the tonal system which, however implicitly, informs English composition of this period. Moreover, it reveals that Ferrabosco is an essentially chordal (harmonic) composer. As in the fancies, there is a lot of melodic motion without much harmonic movement. In addition, the imitation Ferrabosco presents in the motets is an imitation of gesture rather than content—free imitation which avoids the constraints of rigorous counterpoint.

Ultimately, however, it is as a "reader" of his texts that Ferrabosco is most interesting, for in songs and motets which are "well-made" musically he often provides solutions to the understanding of texts. He accomplishes this by musical means: setting off one phrase from another, suspending harmonic action until a parenthesis is completed, not allowing phrases to cadence completely until a thought is completed, emphasizing levels of argument by harmonic area, confirming the arrival and validity of a concluding statement by the return to the tonic, etc. His harmonic structures, in both songs and motets, reflect not simply the apparent structure of the text, but, even more, the inner fiber—the marshalling of argument, the contrast of position, the characterization of mood and manner, and the importance of various textual elements.

That Ferrabosco should be compared with Campion and Dowland is inevitable. Both were more facile than Ferrabosco, but only Dowland surpassed Ferrabosco as a master of almost every phase of composition and expression. Campion, on the other hand, with his predictable regularity and limited harmonic palette, is not as interesting a composer as Ferrabosco. The whole generation of song-writers from the first third of the seventeenth century in England suffered almost total eclipse, and we are only now beginning to understand how varied the arena of English song was between Dowland and the Lawes brothers. Ferrabosco played an important, though brief, role in that passage.

Chapter I

1. Arkwright's first articles dealt with the elder Alfonso Ferrabosco, whose madrigals were included in the English anthologies of Italian madrigals and whose skill was later praised by Morley and Peachum: "Un compositore italiano alla corte de Elisabetta," *Rivista Musicale Italiana,* IV (1897), pp. 1-16; "'Master Alfonso' and Queen Elizabeth," *ZIMG,* VIII (1907), pp. 271-77. A short article, "Alfonso Ferrabosco the Younger," appeared in the periodical *The Musician* in 1897 and was reprinted in *Studies in Music,* edited by Robert Grey (1901), pp. 199-214. These were followed by a larger article, supplementing Arkwright's previous work, "Notes on the Ferrabosco Family," *The Musical Antiquary,* III (1911/12), pp. 220-28, and IV (1912/13), pp. 42-54. This latter article bore fruit in the form of a response by Giovanni Livi in which a great deal of information about the Italian Ferraboscos was presented for the first time: "The Ferrabosco Family," *The Musical Antiquary,* IV (1912/13), pp. 121-41. Livi refers the reader also to Gaetano Gaspari, "Memorie risquardanti la Storia dell' arte musicale in Bologna al XVI Secolo," in *Atti e Memorie della R. Deputazione di Storia Patria per le Provincie di Romagna,* Ser. II, Vol. i, pp. 13-21 (*anno* 1875), which provides more information about Domenico Maria Ferrabosco, the first of the Ferrabosco musicians.

2. Joseph Kerman, *The Elizabethan Madrigal* (American Musicological Society, New York, 1962). The pertinent information was also presented in Kerman's article, "Master Alfonso and the English Madrigal," *The Musical Quarterly,* 38 (1952), pp. 222-44.

3. Livi, *op. cit.,* p. 124.

4. *Ibid.,* note 1. "Ferabosco F.F." is an abbreviation for "Ferabosco fece fare"("Ferabosco caused to be made.") Livi explains the presence of the inscription by suggesting that the house was first of simple design, with a wooden portico. During the rule of the Bentivoglios, when the city was almost entirely rebuilt, the house was remodeled and embellished with a new brick and stone portico which bears the inscription cited. Interestingly, the family name underwent many variants in spelling. The form found here, with one "r," prevailed until a century later when, in the generation of the elder Alfonso, the spelling with two "r's" became more accepted. In the text of this study, the spelling has been made consistent with the later practice.

5. *Ibid.*

6. *Ibid.*

7. *Ibid.,* p. 125. The chart follows information presented by Livi. The records of the court of the Bentivoglios were lost during political difficulties in 1507, so we are at some disadvantage in speculating about the exact nature of the participation of the Ferraboscos in that court. Livi quotes Domenico Maria's baptismal deed: "1513 die xxj februarii – Domenego Maria fiolo de Anibale de Cechino Feraboscho, nacque a di 14 de febraro lunedi de sira a ore meza de note, e fu bategeato a di 21 del soprascrifo (*sic*) mexe. Tenelo M. Napulione de la Malvaxia e Lisandro de la Fave." (*Ibid.,* note 1.)

8. Robert Eitner, *Quellen-Lexicon* (Leipzig, 1900: reprint, Graz, 1959), Volume III, p. 416. Eitner does not give a source for this information and much of his article on the Ferrabosco family is confused, but, in the light of Domenico Maria's subsequent career, this position is certainly plausible.

9. Livi, *op. cit.*, p. 126. The dowry contract was drawn up on January 31, 1541, by the Bolognese notary, Camillo Morandi.

10. *Ibid.* Livi points out that there was a close relationship between the princely houses of Bologna and Ferrara resulting from the marriage, in 1487, of Annibale Bentivoglio and Lucrezia d'Este, daughter of Ercole I, Duke of Ferrara. The book of madrigals was published by Gardano in Venice: *D'il Ferabosco il Primo Libro de Madrigali/ a Quatro Voce* novamente posto in Lvce / con Gratia et Privilegio / Venetijs apvd Antonivm Gardane / MDXXXXII. The dedication begins, "Al' Illvstrissimo et Eccellentissimo Signor / Gvidobaldo Dvca d'Vrbino / il Ferabosco."

11. The original collection, published by Gardane in Venice in 1542, was titled, *Il Primo Libro d'i Madrigali de Diversi / Eccellentissimi Autori a Misura de Breve / . . . a quatro voci.*

12. A modern edition of "Io mi son giovinetta" is handily available in Alfred Einstein, *The Italian Madrigal*, translated by Alexander H. Krappe, Roger H. Sessions, and Oliver Strunk (Princeton: Princeton University Press, 1949), Vol. III, p. 56. In its various appearances this madrigal was also attributed to Giaches de Wert, Lasso, Alfonso Ferrabosco, and the enigmatic cleric, Fr. a Bosco.

13. Livi, *op. cit.*, p. 125, note 4, remarks on the difficulty of tracing the female children, if there were any, from the particular records he was using. As can be seen from the genealogical chart, however, it would have been very difficult for Giulia to have borne any more children until 1549 at the earliest.

14. *Ibid.*, p. 126.

15. Gaspari, *op. cit.*, p. 152, note 2. Domenico is similarly described in the records of his consideration for the position of *maestro di capella* at San Petronio in 1547. Gaspari cites those records in full (*ibid.*, pp. 150-51).

16. *Ibid.*, p. 153. Domenico had expressed a desire to attain the post as early as February 1546. Gaspari cites the registration of correspondence between Domenico and Vincenzo Magnani, a singer, in which Ferrabosco makes this wish known (*ibid.*, p. 152).

17. Livi, *op. cit.*, p. 126, note 1. The decree included the whole family and was passed by a vote of 27 in favor, 9 opposing.

18. Gaspari, *op. cit.*, pp. 152-53 and p. 152, note 2.

19. *Ibid.*, pp. 153-54. The record of exclusion indicates that the severance was handled in a manner which did not financially penalize the musicians:

"30 Julij 1555. Eodem die fuerunt exclusi de capella Leonardus Bare, Dominicus Ferrabosco, et Jo. Luis. Palestrina: quia sic voluit Papa, et dedit motum proprium illis, ut de cetero non serviant in capella, quia sunt uxorati, et in loco ricompensae Papa jussit illis dare scuta sex (in ogni mese) pro colibet. Omnia ista sunt facta in praesentia omnium."

[30 July 1555. On this day Leonardus Bare, Dominicus Ferrabosco and Jo. Luis. Palestrina were dismissed from the choir as the Pope ordered, giving the reason that they should not serve in the choir for they were married. By way of recompense, the Pope gave them six (6) *scuta* per month as agreed. All this was done with all parties present.]

Gaspari cites this from Giuseppi Baini, *Memorie storico-critiche della vita e delle opere di Giovanni da Palestrina, compilate da Giuseppe Baini* (1828), Vol. I, p. 56.

20. *Ibid.*, p. 154, note 2. Gaspari cites Matteo Fornari's unpublished manuscript, *Narrazione istorica della cappella pontificia di Matteo Fornari*, for this information. Fornari also asserts that Domenico was a disciple of Josquin. This is highly unlikely in the direct sense of "student," for Josquin probably never met Domenico. In another sense, however, the statement is plausible, for Domenico may well have admired the master's works; he certainly had the opportunity to study them at Ferrara, if not Bologna.

21. Livi, *op. cit.*, pp. 127-28.

22. *Ibid.*, p. 125. The will provides information by its silence concerning the sons who were no longer living and by the mention that Anfione was then "in partibus Galliae."

23. *Ibid.*, p. 127. The record of baptism, preserved in the registers of the Cathedral of Bologna, is given by Livi:
"1543, die xviij januarii.
Alfunsus, filius Dominici Marie Feraboschi, baptizatus ut supra. Compatres Magnificus Dominus Romeus Pepolus et Comina Portia Savignana et Dominus Camillus Palaotus, bononiensis patritius."

24. Kerman, *The Elizabethan Madrigal*, p. 76. The actual reference can be found in Pierre de Ronsard, *Oeuvres complètes*, ed. Laumonier, Vol. IX, pp. 53-54, where Alfonso is described as sweetly singing to the lyre.

25. The best sources for this information remain the articles of Livi and Arkwright, supplemented by the records collected and published by Arkwright in *The Musical Antiquary* and Henry Cart de Lafontaine in *The King's Musick*. This information, of course, is available in various state documents, though at much less convenience. Kerman's discussion of Alfonso's madrigals in *The Elizabethan Madrigal* remains the only one of any substance. J.V. Cockshoot, the author of the Ferrabosco articles for the forthcoming, sixth edition of *Grove's* has studied and scored the motets in his unpublished Oxford dissertation (1964), "The Sacred Music of Alfonso Ferrabosco, father (1543-1588), with Critical Commentary."

26. The documents attesting to this payment are printed in the introduction to Peter Cunningham's *Accounts of the Revels at Court* (1842), p. xxvii. They are reprinted in Arkwright's article, "'Master Alfonso' and Queen Elizabeth," *ZIMG*, VIII (1907), p. 272, whence they are quoted here:

"Payde to John Bapta Castiglion grome of the preuy Chamber upon the Q. Ma^{ts} warraunt dated at Westm^r the xxviijth of March A^o iiij^o bee by him deliured over in way of the Queenes Ma^{ts} reward to Alphonso Ferrabosco Italion Musicon the some of xx^{li}.

Payde to Alphonso Ferrabosco Italyon upon the Q. Ma^{ts} Warraunt dorm dated at Greenwich the xvjth of June A^o iiij^o for his Annuytie of C marks per ann. payable q'rly during pleasure dew for halfe a yere ending at Mychas A^o iiij^o xxiij^{li} vj^s viij^d."

27. Arkwright, "Notes on the Ferrabosco Family," *The Musical Antiquary*, III (1911/12), pp. 223-24; IV (1912/13), pp. 42-43.

28. Arkwright, "Un compositore Italiano alla corte di Elisabetta," *Rivista Musicale Italiana*, IV (1897), p. 9.

29. Arkwright has printed these letters in the articles appearing in *ZIMG* and *RMI*.

30. These letters patent are printed in Thomas Rymer's *Foedera* (3rd ed., London: George Holmes, 1743, reprinted New York: Gregg Press, 1967), VI, part IV, p. 134. Rymer cites the Auditor's Patent Book E.403/2452, f. 152^v.

31. Arkwright, "Un compositore Italiano," *RMI*, IV (1897), pp. 12-14.

32. *Ibid.*, pp. 14-15.

33. *Ibid.*, p. 16, and Arkwright, "'Master Alfonso' and Queen Elizabeth," *ZIMG*, VIII (1907), p. 273.

34. Arkwright, "'Master Alfonso,'" *ZIMG* VIII (1907), pp. 273-75.

35. Livi, *op. cit.*, p. 129, cites a contract dated May 31, 1572 which describes Ferrabosco as then "in partibus Galliae morantem." No information is given as to the nature or provenance of the contract, or its source.

36. Arkwright, "Notes," *MA*, IV (1912/13), p. 45, cited Feuillerat's *Documents relating to the Office of the Revels*, pp. 159-60.

37. Livi, *op. cit.*, p. 129. Livi claims that she is so described in many legal documents, but he does not given sources.

38. Arkwright, "Un compositore Italiano," *RMI*, IV (1897), pp. 8-9. There has been confusion about this letter because of careless dating on Ferrabosco's part: he had dated the letter 1564. As Livi points out (Livi, *op. cit.*, pp. 128-29), the circumstances of the father's death and the reference to long service demand the 1574 dating.

39. Morrison Comegys Boyd, *Elizabethan Music and Musical Criticism* (2nd ed., rev., Philadelphia: University of Pennsylvania Press, 1962), p. 113. Ferdinando Richardson was a pseudonym of Sir Ferdinando Heybourne (c. 1558-1618), an amateur composer who had been a pupil of Tallis. The poem follows other tributes in the publication. The translation is by Boyd (pp. 288-91).

40. The manuscript is now in the British Museum (Royal Music Library MS 24. D. 2.) and contains motets and miscellaneous pieces. Boyd, *op. cit.*, pp. 310-12 gives the poem in full. Ferrabosco heads the list of foreigners who include Marenzio, deMonte, Orlando, Crequillon, deRore, and Willaert.

41. Thomas Morley, *A Plain and Easy Introduction to Practical Music* (London: Peter Short, 1597, ed. Alec Harman, 2nd ed., New York: Norton, 1973), p. 294.

42. *Ibid.*, p. 271.

43. *Ibid.*, p. 202. This description occurs in a discussion of canons, and the above mentioned canons are registered as having been published by East in 1603 under the title *Medulla Musicke.* No copy is extant.

44. Henry Peachum (the Younger), *The Compleat Gentleman*, 1622, cited in Boyd, *op. cit.*, p. 214. The titles, of course, are translations of Ferrabosco's original Italian texts. The use of Morley's phraseology is interesting, but Peachum misunderstood Morley's "censure" which concerned one instance of consecutive fifths in "Sich 'io mi cred 'ho mai," from Ferrabosco's second book, which Morley justified on the grounds "of jollity." (Morley, *op. cit.*, p. 148.)

45. *Calendar of State Papers, Venetian,* 1575, no. 617.

46. Arkwright, "'Master Alfonso,'" *ZIMG,* VIII (1907), p. 275.

47. Livi, *op. cit.*, p. 138, note 2.

48. Arkwright, in "Notes and Queries," *MA,* IV (1912/13), p. 260. This may be a performance of the comedy in preparation mentioned in a letter from the painter Ubaldini to the Queen, cited by Arkwright, "Notes," *MA,* III (1911/12), p. 224; IV (1912/13), p. 44.

49. In a communication to the *Review of English Studies,* VII (1932), pp. 201-02, B.M. Ward summarized the information concerning Ferrabosco available from the records contained in the Teller's Views of Payments. These records began at Michaelmas, 1569. Ferrabosco's pay is listed at £100 until 1576, when it is reduced to £50. The records for the year beginning Michaelmas 1570 are illegible; those for 1582-83 are missing, as are those for 1588-89 after which date Ferrabosco's name does not appear. The only occasion on which Ferrabosco, himself, received his pay was Lady Day, 1572. On all other occasions, his wages were given to assignees as follows:

Mich. 1569-1574 Joseph Lupo
1575-1577 John Palmer
1587-1582 Gomer van Awsterwyke

1580-1582 William Stubbs (on occasion)
after 1582 Ferrabosco's name is entered in the ordinary way, but there is no record of payment.

50. This raises the question whether the letter, dated 1567 but endorsed at Court as 1577, in which Ferrabosco protested his innocence in meeting the French Ambassador publicly, not privately, may really belong to the later year. The Ambassador's residence may have been a center for recusants; it certainly appears to have been kept under surveillance.

51. This resume of the letter appears in the *Calendar of State Papers, Rome, 1572-1578*, Volume II (London: 1926), pp. 458-59. It was quoted in a letter of W.H. Grattan Flood to the editor of *The Musical Times*, February 1, 1927, p. 158.

52. *Loc. cit.*

53. Arkwright, "'Master Alfonso,'" *ZIMG*, VIII (1907), p. 276.

54. Livi, *op. cit.*, p. 129.

55. Arkwright, "Notes," *MA*, III (1911/12), p. 225. Arkwright mistranscribed "figliolino" as "figlino Lino," a mistake corrected by Livi, *op. cit.*, p. 130. That this letter was written just before the English pay records for Alfonso cease can hardly be coincidence.

56. Kerman, "Master Alfonso and the English Madrigal," *The Musical Quarterly*, 38 (1952), p. 224. The original Spanish is found in Livi, *op. cit.*, p. 133.

57. Livi, *op. cit.*, pp. 129-30.

58. *Ibid.*, p. 132. Livi quotes the description of the manuscript volumes from B. Peyron, *Catalog of MSS. in the University Library of Turin*, 1899, p. 56.

59. *Primo libro de madrigali a cinque* (Venice: Gardane, 1587); *Secondo libro de madrigali a cinque* (Venice: Gardane, 1587). Kerman, in discussing the texts of these madrigals, points out that they lack the subtlety of many of Ferrabosco's manuscript madrigals such as appear in the Sambrooke MS. (NYPL, MS Drexel 4302) and Christ Church mss. 78-82. He speculates that the patron for the madrigals with more sophisticated texts might have been the Cardinal of Lorraine, but this is by no means certain, if even probable. (Kerman, "Master Alfonso and the English Madrigal," *MQ*, 38 (1952), p. 229).

60. Besides these madrigals, Ferrabosco had had other pieces published in anthologies, the first appearance being one chanson which appeared in the LeRoy-Ballard *Mellange de Chansons* of 1572 ("Aupres de vous"), the last being a five-part madrigal, "Ero cosi dicea," which appeared in the otherwise four-voice publication, *L'amorosa Ero rappresentata da' piu celebri musici d'Italia, con l'istesse parole & nel medesimo tono,* 1588. For complete bibliographical information concerning Ferrabosco's madrigals, see Kerman, *op. cit.*, and the same author's *The Elizabethan Madrigal.*

61. Book 1°: "Among the many favors which at various times Your Most Serene Highness has deigned to present to me, I consider the greatest and most notable that you have obliged me by your commands to bring to light my first [book of] madrigals." Book 2°: "My patron, the Lord Duke . . . commanded that I publish some of my madrigals."

62. Livi, *op. cit.*, p. 134, cites the Register of Deaths among the documents of the Convent of San Francesco where Ferrabosco was buried.

63. *Ibid.*, p. 138.

64. *Ibid.*, pp. 132, 135. In any case, there would have been no need to mention the "primogenito," for the inheritance passed to Carlo Emanuele at his father's death.

65. *Ibid.*, pp. 134-35, 138. Anfione, who seems to have shadowed Alfonso, remained in Turin until 1595 at the latest, when he listed among the musicians of the Magistrato degli Anziani in Bologna. He was released from service, apparently not at his request, when the Magistrates voted 6-2 against his nomination for continuance on May 19, 1598. He died ten years later (June 16, 1608) and, like his brother, was buried at the church of San Francesco.

66. Anthony Wood, *Athenae Oxoniensis*, Vol. I, in *Life of Wood*, edited, with additions by Philip Bliss (Oxford, 1848), pp. 67-68, note. (From Wood's MSS mus. Ashmolean 8568.106.)

67. Those records of Awsterwyke's pay which can be found in the Audit Office Declared Accounts are recorded in *MA*, Vols. I (1909/10) and II (1910/11), beginning Vol. I, p. 123, and ending Vol. II, p. 55.

68. Arkwright, "Alfonso Ferrabosco, the Younger," pp. 201-02. Quoted from the *Historical Manuscripts Commission, Hatfield House*, Part III, p. 869.

69. Thurston Dart, "Two new documents relating to the Royal Music, 1584-1605," *Music & Letters*, XLV (1964), p. 19.

70. *Ibid.*, p. 20. This annuity was paid up to 1601.

71. Arkwright, *op. cit.*, p. 202. Quoted from Anthony Wood, MS Notes on Musicians, Oxford, Bodleian MS Wood 19 D(4)f.49; Wood was apparently confused concerning Ferrabosco's output, for there are 4- and 6-part fancies and three 5-part innomines, but no 5-part fancies—unless Wood was referring to the 5-part dances or to untexted, instrumental performances of the motets, both unlikely confusions.

72. The allowance for mourning livery is cited from the Lord Chamberlain's accounts, Vol. 554, by Lafontaine, *The King's Musick*, p. 45.

73. Arkwright, "Ferrabosco, Alfonso," *Grove's Dictionary of Music and Musicians*, 2nd ed., 1904-1910, ed. by J.A. Fuller-Maitland.

74. Arkwright, "Alfonso Ferrabosco, the Younger," p. 201.

Notes for Pages 19-23

75. *Ibid.*, pp. 202-03.

76. Ben Jonson, *Complete Masques*, ed. by Stephen Orgel (New Haven: Yale University Press, 1969), p. 475. These songs were not published and have not been found.
    Frances Howard was only thirteen at the time of her marriage. She was the centerpiece of scandal a few years later in an affair with Robert Carr, a favorite of James I. That affair led to the annulment of their previous marriages and the murder, in the Tower, of Sir Thomas Overbury, a Seneca-like opponent to their match. James I created Carr Duke of Somerset, and the two lovers were married on December 26, 1613. This marriage was also celebrated with masques that night in the Whitehall Banqueting House by Campion's Masque dedicated to the Earl of Somerset with vocal music by Coperario and Lanier; on December 29 by Jonson's *Irish Masque* (a parody of Campion's masque); on January 4 by Middleton's *Masque of Cupid*; and on January 6 by *The Masque of Flowers* given at Gray's Inn.

77. *Ibid.*, p. 501.

78. John Aubrey, *The Natural History of Wiltshire*, written between 1656 and 1691, ed. John Britton (London: J.B. Nichols & Sons, 1847), pp. 80-81, quoted in Murray Lefkowitz, *William Lawes* (London: Routledge & Kegan Paul, 1960), pp. 4-5, note 2. Lefkowitz goes on to quote Thomas Fuller's *The History of the Worthies of England* (London, 1662) to the effect that the Earl of Hertford also supported the tutelage of William Lawes by Coperario. This is most likely where Lawes became acquainted with Ferrabosco whom, like his teacher, he memorialized by making use of one of Ferrabosco's bass lines in a composition, paying tribute to the older master in the title and referring to him familiarly as "Alphonso." Cf. Lefkowitz, op. cit., pp. 5-12, 140-42.

79. Aubrey, op. cit., p. 88, quoted in Lefkowitz, loc. cit. Wilton House, the estate of the Earls of Pembroke, was close by Amesbury and Wulfall.

80. The various manuscript collections which were copied out by Francis Tregian while imprisoned in Fleet Prison from 1609 until his death in 1619, particularly Egerton 3665 and the Sambrooke Book (NYPL Drexel 4302) which contain Ferrabosco's motets, almost all the four-part fancies, and much of the five-part dance music, were copied by 1619, and the organization of the manuscript indicates that the individual pieces were not copied "hot off the press."

81. Arkwright, "Alfonso Ferrabosco the Younger," p. 207, note 1. Burrell had bought the share before 1625, for on February 2, 1625, he petitioned Lord Buckingham to release him from his partnership with Innocent Lanier, "Who doesn't understand anything about the business." *Calendar of State Papers, Domestic*, 1623-1625, p. 466.

82. *Ibid.*, p. 207.

83. John S. Smart, *op. cit.*, pp. 189-91.

84. Arkwright, "Alfonso Ferrabosco the Younger," p. 208, note 1, puts it very well.

"The Ferrabosco family was evidently in high favour with the King. It looks very much as if these places were sinecures intended solely to provide salaries for favorite musicians."

85. *Calendar of State Papers, Domestic,* 1625-26, no. 569; and Rymer, *Foedera,* Vol. VIII, Part II, p. 162.

86. Lafontaine, *KM,* p. 61.

87. John S. Smart, in "Notes and Queries," *MA,* IV (1912/13), p. 191, gives several examples of these assignments, dating from 1619-1625, culled from the Exchequer Assignment Books.

88. This assignment, dated March 1618 from Greenwich, is in Ferrabosco's own hand. It was brought to my attention by Mr. Robert Ford who noticed it while cataloging a portion of the collection of the Friends of Music, Music Library, Yale University.

89. Arkwright, "Alfonso Ferrabosco the Younger," pp. 209-10.

90. Lafontaine, *KM,* p. 65. The letter of revocation was sent by Philip Herbert, Earl of Montgomery and then Lord Chamberlain, to Sir John Coke. The reason given was the prior promise of that position to Ferrabosco's son. See Denis Stevens, *Thomas Tomkins* (London: St. Martin's Press, 1957), p. 49. The original documents appear in the *Historical Manuscripts Commission, 12th Report,* i, 341 (Coke MSS, property of the Earl Cowper, K. 6., Melbourne Hall, Derbyshire).

91. Arkwright, *op. cit.,* pp. 212-13.

92. Lafontaine, *KM,* p. 63.

93. *Ibid.,* p. 59. He is also listed as a cornetist: *Ibid.,* p. 83.

94. Alfonso had sold his share of the patent by this time to William Burrell, for Burrell was involved in a dispute with Lanier on February 2, 1625: *Calendar of State Papers, Domestic,* 1623-1625, p. 466. (See above, note 81.)

95. Lafontaine, *KM,* p. 110. After the Restoration the positions were distributed as follows: Alfonso's place as composer of wind music—William Child (June 16, 1660) (*KM,* p. 114); Alfonso's place among the viols—John Hingston (*KM,* p. 115); Henry's place as composer—Matthew Locke (November 9, 1660) (*KM,* p. 118); and Henry's place as musician among the flutes—Thomas Bates.

96. *Ibid.,* p. 67.

97. A John Ferrabosco was born to Alphonso and Ellen Ferrabosco in 1626, and baptized on October 9 of that year (Arkwright, *op. cit.,* p. 213). John Ferrabosco appears in the records of the King's Musick in 1630 when a full fee for livery is paid to Nicolas Lanier in his name. (Lafontaine, *KM,* p. 75.) Another citation from earlier that year had authorized livery for John Ferrabosco "in the room of Henry Ferrabosco." [Wilibald Nagel, *Annalen der englischen Hofmusik von der Zeit*

Heinrichs VIII. bis zum Tode Karls I., Beilage zu den Monatsheften für Musikgeschichte, Bd. 26, (Leipzig: 1894), p. 42.] The boy was appointed to a full position, "for the windy instruments in place of Henry Farrabosco," on January 15, 1631. (Lafontaine, *KM*, p. 76) Since Henry remained in the service of the King as a musician, and there is no mention of John Ferrabosco's place after the Restoration, it seems most likely that this was an arrangement which provided for the training and upkeep of the child. His last appearance in the records of the King's Musick is in 1641 (*KM*, p. 110).

98. Peter Cunningham, *Handbook of London*, p. 313, cited in a correspondence by J.S. Smart appearing in *MA*, IV (1912/13), p. 263.

99. Arkwright, *op. cit.*, p. 214.

100. *Ibid.*, pp. 212-13. The records are a compendium of possible spellings of Ferrabosco.

101. Samuel Pepys, *The Diary of Samuel Pepys*, ed. Robert Latham and William Mathews (Berkeley: University of California Press, 1970-1976), 9v.: September 4, 1664 (vol. 5) and May 30, 1667 (vol. 8). Arkwright, in citing these (*op. cit.*, p. 213), speculated that Elizabeth Ferrabosco, daughter of Henry Ferrabosco and born in 1640, might have been meant.

102. Sir John Hawkins, *A general history of the science and practice of music* (1776; revised edition, 1853, reprinted New York: Dover, 1963, 2 vols.), vol. I, p. 480.

103. Marin Mersenne, *Harmonie Universelle* (Paris, 1636), Part 4, livre IV, proposition viii ("Expliquer la figure, la fabrique, l'accord & l'usage de la Viole"). Raymond Vaught identified this quotation and discussed the problems arising from Mersenne's truncation and transposition of the piece in "Mersenne's Unknown English Viol Player," *Galpin Society Journal*, 17 (1964), pp. 17-23.

104. Lafontaine, *KM*, p. 59.

105. André Maugars, "Response faite à un Curieux sur le sentiment de la musique d'Italie, escrite à Rome, le premier Octobre, 1639," printed in Ernest Thoinan, *Maugars Célèbre Joueur de Viole* (Paris, 1865), p. 32. [An English translation appears in J.S. Shedlock, "André Maugars," in Robin Grey (ed.), *Studies in Music* (New York, 1901), pp. 215-32].

106. *Ibid.*, p. 34.

Chapter II

1. Edward Doughtie, *Lyrics from English Ayres, 1596-1622* (Cambridge: Harvard University Press, 1970), p. 17. See also p. 16, from which the diagram on page 35 is derived.

2. The 10-syllable line, which is familiar from Continental poetry, is not represented among these ballad meters. In continental usage, the caesura occurs after the fourth syllable in this line. English usage increasingly varied from this norm as this line became the building block of blank verse or unrhymed iambic pentameter.

It was the very flexibility with which the English treated this line that made it so difficult to set to music in strophic fashion.

3. Sir Philip Sidney, *An Apology for Poetrie* [1595], In *Elizabethan Critical Essays*, 2 vols., edited by Gregory Smith (London, 1904), vol. I, pp. 204-205.

4. Catherine Ing, *Elizabethan Lyrics* (London: Chatto & Windus, 1951), p. 28. See also pp. 25-64.

5. Ibid., p. 155.

6. H.J.C. Grierson (ed.), *The Poems of John Donne* (Oxford, 1912), Vol. II, p. lv.

7. Brian Morris, "Not, Siren-like, to tempt," in *John Donne: Essays in Celebration*, edited by A. J. Smith (London: Methuen, 1972), p. 224.

8. Campion's work is easily accessible in Walter R. Davis (ed.), *The Works of Thomas Campion* (New York: Doubleday, 1967), pp. 287-317.

9. Ing, op. cit., p. 56.

10. The quality of music for a strophic song is ideally general, serving to represent a mood or manner which is shared by all strophes of the text. Each strophe of text, then, makes specific some aspect of the general mood which is presented by the music. Thus text and music work together on two different levels, the general and the specific. In the best examples of this kind, unexpected relations of mood and instance can be revealed. The requirements for such poetry are simple: consistency of diction, almost absolute repetitions of simple patterns of phrasing and rhyme, a reflection from one strophe to the next of the placement of important words, use of compatibly similar imagery, and the construction of a poem by addition rather than development. That is, the tone and thought of the poem, except in a narrative sense (cf. "Young and Simple Though I am," Ferrabosco *Ayres*, no. 8), can be extracted or extrapolated entirely from one strophe.

When the poetry does not meet these self-reflective criteria imposed by the nature of the experience of strophic song, song and text lose their fit. This is the main reason that it is a legitimate practice to sing only one strophe of, for example, Ferrabosco's setting of Donne's "The Expiration" ("So, so, leave off this last lamenting kiss," *Ayres*, no. 7), the prosody and syntax of which change considerably in the second strophe.

A refrain functions in much the same way: as a distillation of or commentary on the work. The refrain in a strophic song serves doubly as it becomes a reflective summing-up which is specifically informed by the individual strophes of text.

Refrains and strophic practices are not limited to the tuneful songs, although they are more prominent among those songs, the concern for speech-like declamation and individual words becoming more and more prominent in the serious lute songs and continuo songs. The play of wit (specific) and point (general) or of instance and mood can be made in both through-composed and strophic/refrain songs. The effect of musical repetition, even sequence, is, however, *sui generis*, and its associative capacity, in reflection, is here what is important.

11. Philip Brett, "Word-Setting in the Songs of William Byrd," *Publications of the Royal Music Association* 98(1971-72), p. 61.

12. Bruce Pattison, *Music and Poetry of the English Renaissance* (London: Methuen,[2]/ 1970), p. 86.

13. John Stevens, *Music and Poetry of the Early Tudor Court*, (London: Methuen, 1961), p. 107.

14. Brett, *op. cit.*, p. 63.

15. Morely, *Introduction*, p. 295, describes three important types of strophic Italian compositions: the *canzonetta* (which Einstein, *The Italian Madrigal*, II, p. 777, called "the counterfeit of the madrigal") with often AABCC form; the *vilanella*, a parody of the madrigal a3; and the balletto, AABB with "fa la" refrain – as being "by a general name called 'airs'."

16. For the influence of the French dance on Dowland, see James G. Smith, "John Dowland: A Reappraisal of his Ayres," unpublished D.M.A. dissertation, University of Illinois, 1973, pp. 224-232.

17. Alfred Einstein, *The Italian Madrigal*, vol. II, p. 611.

18. The development of later Caroline song, the problems of declamation, and the differences of Caroline and lutenist poetry are discussed most helpfully in an article by Eric Ford Hart: "Introduction to Henry Lawes," *Music & Letters* 32(1951), pp. 222-224. See also, Murray Lefkowitz, *William Lawes*, pp. 150-177; Ian Spink, *English Song, passim.*; Vincent Duckles, "English Song and the Challenge of Italian Monody," in *Words to Music* (Los Angeles: William Andrews Clark Memorial Library, 1967).

Chapter III

1. This formulation of the harmonic system with which Ferrabosco worked – both the concept and the expression – developed out of a series of discussions with Professor Murray Lefkowitz. I am grateful for his permission to present it here.

2. In effect, this results in a central tonal arena in which the minor is used as a chromatic inflection of the major, and vice versa, without weakening the tonal center. Thus, there are some of the ambiguities of tonal direction, such as are familiar from nineteenth-century chromaticism.

Chapter IV

1. Charles Burney, *A General History of Music from the Earliest Ages to the Present Period* (London, 1776; Dover reprint of Frank Mercer, ed., New York, 1935), Vol. II, p. 118.

2. *Ibid.*, p. 119. Burney did not transcribe the lute part in these examples, presenting instead the bass part only. The addition of figures for "Like Hermit Poore" emphasizes Burney's conclusion that the inner part-writing is rudimentary: "The Lute Accompt. is mere thorough base which the Chords implied by the figures placed over this bass wholly comprehend."

3. Five copies of the *Ayres* are known: British Museum (K.8.h.2); Royal College of Music, London (I.G.41), bearing the signature of the composer on the title page; Folger Shakespeare Library, Washington, D.C. (10827); Huntington Library, San Marino, California (59751); Newberry Library, Chicago (Case VM 1620 F36a). A facsimile edition, prepared from the British Museum copy and edited by David Greer, was published in 1971 by Scolar Press as vol. V in the series, *English Lute Songs, 1597-1632, A Collection of Facsimile Reprints* (general editor, F. W. Sternfeld). The *Ayres* have been transcribed and edited by E. H. Fellowes in *The English School of Lutenist Song Writers*, second series, XVI (London, 1927).

4. These works appear in Volume XIX (London, 1966) of *The English School of Lutenist Song Writers*, second series, edited by Ian Spink. Interestingly, these manuscript songs, like the manuscript concordances for various of the *Ayres*, are almost invariably for voice and continuo instrument, whereas the *Ayres* are printed in such a way that the singer and continuo player must look at the print from opposite positions at a table.

5. Ian Spink, "Sources of English Song, 1620-1660," *Miscellanea Musicologica*, I(1966), p. 133.

6. *Ibid.*, p. 136. Fellowes' description appears in *The Catalogue of Manuscripts in the Library of St. Michael's College, Tenbury*, (Paris, 1934), pp. 213-14.

7. *Ibid.;* See also J. P. Cutts, "Early Seventeenth-Century Lyrics at St. Michael's College," *Music & Letters* 37(1956), p. 221ff.

8. These monodies are important for their difference with published versions of the songs, eg., in *Le Nuove Musiche.* For more on this matter, see Nancy Maze, "Tenbury MS 1018: a key to Caccini's Art of Embellishment," *Journal of the American Musicological Society*, IX(1956), p. 61; and her unpublished M.Mus. thesis (University of Illinois, 1956), "The Printed and Manuscript Sources of the Solo Songs of Giulio Caccini."

9. Spink, *op. cit.*, p. 134.

10. Mary Joiner, "British Museum Add. MS 15117: A Commentary, Index and Bibliography," *Royal Music Association Research Chronicle* VII(1969), pp. 51-109. Joiner argues that the manuscript belonged to a musician employed in the London theatre, a conclusion with which David Fuller takes issue in "Ben Jonson's Plays and their Contemporary Music," *Music & Letters*, 58 (1977), pp. 66-67.

11. Peter Warlock, *The English Ayre* (Oxford, 1926), p. 96.

12. For information about the texts of these songs, see Edward Doughtie, *Lyrics from English Airs, 1596-1622*, (Cambridge: Harvard University Press, 1970), pp. 290-303;

560-71. This text is a translation of Desportes: "Je me veux rendre hermite," from *Amours de Diane*, II.8.

13. Vincent Duckles, "The Gamble Manuscript as a Source of Continuo Song in England," *JAMS* I(1948), p. 29.

14. Pepys, *Diary*, December 2, 1666.

15. These variants are presented synoptically by Ian Spink in *English Songs, 1625-1660, Musica Britannica*, Vol. 33 (London, 1971), p. 187.

16. The poem, in many sources, is a 14-line sonnet of which Ferrabosco's setting includes the first 4 and last 2 lines. Lanier's setting uses the last two lines as a refrain to each of three 4-line strophes.

17. Both settings appear in modern edition in *Poemes de Donne, Herbert et Crashaw, mise en musique par leurs contemporains*, transcribed and realized by A. Souris, introduced by Jean Jacquot (Paris: CNRS, 1961), pp. 8-11.

18. In this setting Ferrabosco has been consistent in breaking his lines after the fourth syllable, except in the middle section. It is hard to believe that the second strophe of this song was ever sung with any success.

19. Both of these appear in *John Donne: Essays in Celebration* (London: Methuen, 1972), edited by A. J. Smith: Brian Morris, "Not, Siren-like, to tempt," pp. 219-58; John Hollander, "Donne and the Limits of Lyric," pp. 259-72.

20. Hollander, *op. cit.*, pp. 262-63.

21. *Ibid.*, p. 263.

22. *Ibid.*, pp. 263-64.

23. *Ibid.*, p. 265.

24. *Ibid.*, p. 266.

Chapter V

1. The suavity of the second section of this song results from the flexibility of harmonic movement afforded by a sense of tonality which incorporates the resources (harmonic and melodic) of both the major and minor modes. In one sense this could be argued as the simultaneous availability of tonic (major/minor) and relative major (less often minor), in which the tonic clearly predominates. Thus, every degree of the scale, except the tonic, may be inflected; relations of fifths are available within each mode, relations by third move between modes (and modal expectations), and the 3rd, 6th, and 7th degrees of the scale lead active double lives. In addition, the subdominant of the tonic (major) becomes V/V of the relative major, serving therefore as a bridge between the major and minor areas of the tonic. The full use of these resources in Ferrabosco's music (and in that of other composers of the period) is accomplished without confusion of tonal area. In fact,

the question of tonic mode is almost always resolved (or rendered moot) by the raised third in the final cadence. Structurally and affectively the modal degrees have great importance within the piece, not as they affect the tonic, but in how they contribute to the perception of form and (textual) matters of expression. In this light, the appearance of the diminished fourth (e.g., e♭-b♮) occurs in the natural exploitation of these possibilities, as does its harmonic relative, the misspelled augmented triad (e.g.; g-b♮-e♭) which, in Ferrabosco, usually is developed out of melodic activity. Similarly, the use of ♭III and ♭VI in conjunction with V and V/V, with a characteristic "phrygian" or neapolitan effect, is another extension of this principle.

2. The scansion of the line follows Ferrabosco's setting; a variety of other possibilities exist depending on the emphasis placed on "thou" and whether "Heav'n" is treated as a monosyllable or disyllable, as it sounds. The point here, of course, is that the line begins with an accented syllable. The rising (iambic) stress pattern is not established until the latter half of the line. By emphasizing this first syllable in pitch, duration, and rythmic position Ferrabosco is responsive to the declamation of the text, although he is basically using a variant of a conventional formula (♩♩♩|♩) for setting the beginning of a line. But the fact that Ferrabosco varies the formula—much more, for example, than Lanier does in his setting of "Like Hermit Poore"—emphasizes the difficulty of discussing the effectiveness of setting English words to music. The problems are not simply those of duration and metric accent, but must include consideration of rhythm, harmonic movement, pitch, range, speed, and the quality of the musical gestures. Moreover, Ferrabosco's opening gestures are frequently musically arresting, sometimes at the expense of textual declamation.

3. That bass movement (mm. 7-13) provides its own sequences which are matched in Ian Spink's realization (Ferrabosco, *Manuscript Songs*, pp. 8-9) by "restless" sequences which both anticipate and reflect the vocal figure at "And restless man." This melodic figure acquires motivic importance when it returns in the second section of the song (m. 28), first in the bass as a prolepsis of the voice, then in sequence in the voice; the text is "to look for rest." Thus, "restless man" and his search for rest are musically unified and emphasized by the use of motive and sequence.

4. The prolepsis in the bass actually occurs deceptively at mm. 18-19 (where it attends the beginning of the triple-time in the voice), followed by the running descent to the lower occurrence of the G-F#-G figure. The prolepsis we hear as *vorimitation*, at measures 21-23 (G-d d-g), joins the two presentations, separated by an octave, of the G-F#-G figure.

5. The influence of the continental pattern of dividing 10-syllable lines with a caesura after the fourth syllable and the awkwardness it causes in this setting raise, along with the musical style of the song, the question of whether this song is a wholly English product or, perhaps, a translation from an originally intended (Italian?) text.

6. Regarding other instances of word-painting: 1) the triple-time of the melody ("*O world, betrayer* of the mind") is also appropriate for the first strophe only, not for the second ("Hail Death, the land I do descry"); 2) the diminished fourth of "being blind" is specific also to the first strophe and not to the words "them that die."

Chapter VI

1. This concordance was recognized by Edward Doughtie, "Ferrabosco and Jonson's 'The Houre-glasse,'" *Renaissance Quarterly* 22(1969), pp. 148-150.

2. *Ibid.*, p. 150.

3. This source poem was identified by Herford and Simpson: *Ben Jonson*, ed. C.H. Herford, Percy and Evelyn Simpson (Oxford: Clarendon Press), IX, p. 53.

4. Campion's setting appears in his *Fourth Booke of Ayres* (1617), ix. Lanier's setting, for three voices, was first printed in John Playford's *Select Musicall Ayres & Dialogues* (1652), sigs. Ee1^V-Ee2, and then, for four voices, in Playford's *The Musical Companion* (1673), sigs. Dd2^V-Dd3. Lanier's music also appears in British Museum MS Add. 11608 (c. 1650), f. 58 (first strophe only), and Edinburgh Library MS La. III.483, f. 194 (first line of text). The anonymous song appears in the National Library of Scotland, Advocates' MS 5.2.14 (c. 1640), f.8^V. For more information concerning the wide circulation of the text, see Doughtie, *Lyrics*, pp. 564-566.

5. Unlike the constant refrain of "Shall I seek" (#17), which distills the point of the song from the various strophes, the refrain function here is incorporated into the strophe. Sometimes, as in the example cited, the repeated lines serve as a pointed epigram which is particularly pertinent to the entire song. In every strophe, whether or not the epigrammatic style is so well achieved, this couplet provides a change of manner: the speaker's simplicity is abandoned and knowing irony (by contrast) is the effect. The change is from naive participation of knowing, observation, and the repeat emphasizes the detachment of the singer from the wide-eyed innocent, "young and simple." That that change occurs like a refrain provides the listener with the background and tone of the piece, against which the first four lines play their foreground drama unwitting of the less exalted real conditions of this particular game of love: "love he must – or flatter me."

6. Campion's setting appeared in Rosseter's *A Booke of Ayres* (1601) as the first song. It is a triple-time song, with active inner parts, which in no way matches the genuinely beautiful quality of the translation. Other poets and composers were attracted to this classic statement of *carpe diem*, the most direct imitators being Richard Crashaw, "Come and let us live, me Deare" *(The Delights of the Muses)*, and the poet of "My deerest mistresse, let us live and love" which was set by William Corkine in his *Second Booke of Ayres* (1612). There is also an anonymous setting of the anonymous poem "Come Laura come letts live and love" which appears in the Bodleian MS Don. c. 57, fols. 50-51. Herrick's related "Gather ye rosebuds while ye may" is another of the genre. Jonson's text appears in *Volpone*, III.vii, and was reprinted in *The Forrest*, no. V.

7. Hollander, "Donne and the Limits of Lyric," p. 264, n.1.

8. *Ibid.*, pp. 264-265.

Chapter VII

1. Stephen Orgel, *The Illusion of Power* (Berkeley: University of California Press, 1975), p. 39.

2. Jean Elizabeth Knowlton, "Some Dances of the Stuart Masque Identified and Analyzed" (Unpublished Ph.D. dissertation, University of Indiana, 1966), pp. 37-39.

3. See Knowlton, *op. cit.*, pp. 37-39, and Murray Lefkowitz, "Masque," [to be published in the sixth edition of *Grove's*] for succinct discussions of these matters.

4. Ian Spink, *English Song*, p. 40.

5. *Ibid.*, p. 41.

6. *Ibid.*, p. 43.

7. The attribution of recitative style to Lanier's contributions to Jonson's "Lovers Made Men" (1617) appeared only in the 1640 folio edition of various works, not in the 1618 quarto edition of the masque. Without the music, we cannot conclusively determine exactly what Jonson had in mind by his retrospective allusion to "stylo recitativo." It is more likely that Jonson had a simple declamatory style in mind, such as that Lanier used to set "Weep no more" (reset by Lanier as "Bring Away This Sacred Tree" in Campion's *Somerset Masque*)—a style closely kin with Ferrabosco's—rather than one derived from Italian recitative.

8. I am indebted to Dr. Murray Lefkowitz for this apt and succinct statement.

9. Peter G. Walls, "Music in the English Masque in the First Half of the Seventeenth Century" (Unpublished Ph.D. dissertation, Oxford University, 1978), p. 68.

10. Andrew Sabol, *Four Hundred Songs and Dances from the Stuart Masque* (Providence: Brown University Press, 1978), p. 25.

11. *Ibid*, pp. 25-26.

Chapter VIII

1. Jonson, *Complete Masques*, p. 58.

2. Walls, *op. cit.*, p. 54.

3. The exaggeration of "to" in the final line is awkward, but it is this "buoyancy" which allows it to move forward to the more important "doubt." I think that the performance of "stop-pe" must be monosyllabic, to follow the meter of the text which does not permit an extra syllable here. As presented in the *Ayres*, the second syllable makes sense only to indicate that the word was released on the second pitch.

4. The sophisticated prosody of these words makes the loss of the musical setting a

double-loss. Not only are the accents those of a speaking voice, but many variants of the basic iambic (rising) pattern, but the use of shorter and longer lines to articulate the structure. Particularly effective is the unrhymed fourth line "As now," which contrasts "brightened / So" with the dactylic feeling of "lightened / As now."

5. Walls, *op. cit.*, p. 62.

6. D.J. Gordon, "The Imagery of Ben Jonson's *Masques of Blacknesse and Beautie*," in *The Renaissance Imagination*, by D. J. Gordon, edited by Stephen Orgel (Berkeley: University of California Press, 1975), p. 145.

7. Jonson, *Complete Masques*, p. 514.

8. Ficino, *Commentary*, Or. 3, Cap. 2 (Basel, 1576) II, p. 1329, cited and translated in Gordon, *op. cit.*, p. 145.

9. Ficino, *op. cit.*, Or. 2, Cap. 2, p. 1324, cited and translated in Gordon, *op. cit.*, pp. 304-05, n. 46.

10. Gordon, *op. cit.*, p. 143.

11. Ferrabosco's setting has an ABB form with the final four lines repeated. This makes no textual sense, and an obvious improvement, textually, would be to repeat only the final couplet.

12. Doughtie, in his *Lyrics*, p. 570, gives more information on these points citing Donne's epistle "To the Countess of Huntingdon" as an explanation of the second line:

> Man to Gods image; Eve, to mans was made,
> Nor finde wee that God breath'd a soule in her.

Jonson refers to Macrobius to explain the argument of the entire song, and the particular passages from Macrobius's *In Somnium Scipionis* are cited by Doughtie from the translation of W. H. Stahl (New York: Columbia, 1952), p. 193:

> Thus the World-Soul, which stirred the body of the universe to the motion that we now witness, must have been interwoven with those numbers which produce musical harmony in order to make harmonious sounds which it instilled by its quickening impulse. It discovered those sounds in the fabric of its own composition.

And, from p. 195:

> Every soul in the world is allured by musical sounds . . . for the soul carries with it into the body a memory of the music which it knew in the sky.

13. Gordon, *op. cit.*, p. 152.

14. Jonson, *Complete Masques*, p. 73.

Chapter IX

1. Ferrabosco rarely presents a seventh chord so baldly as at "that," more often presenting sevenths in passing. Even more unusual, after the f♮ (as a seventh), is the overleap to g (instead of returning to c).

2. The fanfare quality of "courage where" (𝄽♪♪♩♩) does not wholly compensate for the awkwardness of trying to get through such a sluggish word so quickly.

3. One can see here all the devices of accent/stress being used: duration and anticipation ("Just-"; "his"), pitch ("his"), gesture ("his," "ha*t*ers"). The performer has the responsibility of avoiding stress and reversal on "(just)-ly," perhaps ironically by thinking in qualitative terms applied out-of-school: just-ly may his haters trem-ble.

4. The structure of the previous two songs, aab, is established by repeating the music which sets the first two lines of text for the third and fourth. That this pattern is broken at the words "Breaking all the bounds of place" can hardly be coincidental.

5. This is a particularly clear example of the difficulty in our anachronistic approach to, say, Ferrabosco's harmonic practice. Both major and minor harmonies built on every degree of the major scale are available to him, as are the harmonies built on the degrees of the parallel minor scale. In this scheme, the relative major (derived here from the awareness of the parallel minor) is a resource of any tonic—major or minor—and can be included as a relative to the plagal area because of its position in the circle of fifths. This is not bifocal tonality, but bimodal tonality.

6. Most of Fellowes's transcriptions of the *Ayres* are quite reliable. However, in the above example, Fellowes has simply misread the print and given quite a false impression of the entrance into the final flourish. His transcription at that point reads

This casts askew the metric frame of the song and completely confounds the grandeur of the gesture by advancing it both in time and in harmonic position.

Burney's transcriptions of these songs omit indications of the inflection of chords. His bass is unfigured (unlike the bass he gave for "Like Hermit Poore"). Fellowes's transcriptions are based only on the lute part. Burney seemed content, in these songs, to avoid the lute part entirely, relying on the bass viol part as sufficient to indicate the flavor of the accompaniment. This creates a tremendous problem in performance, for the flexibility of mode in these songs is lost, to a great extent, if chords above *a*, for example, can never be major, or those above *c* cannot be minor. Burney also notes that these songs were composed for the funeral of Sir Philip Sidney (d. 1591), information for which he gives no source.

7. Jonson, *Complete Masques*, p. 107.

8. *Ibid.*, pp. 117-18.

9. *Ibid.*, p. 120.

10. This gesture of address was also used in #7, "So, so, leave off," at the words "Turn thou ghost that way."

11. The transcription is a diplomatic rendering of the ornamented piece. There are numerous difficulties of textual clarity and underlay, some variant notes (the very first note of the accompaniment, for example, is A in the *Ayres*), and one change of word ("you" in place of "her" at the end of the first line of text). Accidentals, omitted here but known from the published version, are indicated here above the notes, editorially.

12. Jonson, *Complete Masques*, p. 122.

13. *Ibid.*, p. 140. The text of Ferrabosco's song differs slightly from this, notably in the substitution of "If" for the first word, "When." Whether Jonson's published text indicates a revision of his original or that Ferrabosco modified the text for his own purposes — or both — is unknown.

14. *Ibid.*, p. 140.

15. Spink, *English Song*, p. 41; see p. 117 above.

16. Disregarding the sequence, his setting of "Of worthy queens" is similar to Handel's in *Messiah* of "For unto us a child is born." In the latter case "For" must function as the beginning of a musical subject as well as a substitute for the sense of awe and joy better conveyed (gesturally) by a more energetic word meaning "behold!" In Ferrabosco's example (see Ex. 14) the figure emphasizes the "queens" by beginning off the beat and rushing toward the strong beat confirmed by the harmonic movement.

Chapter X

1. Ferrabosco, *Manuscript Songs*, p. 15.

2. Sabol, *Four Hundred Songs and Dances*, p. 552, however, argues that the original readings of these measures "make good musical sense." He leaves the measure intact.

3. Cutts mentioned the songs first in an article, "Original Music to Browne's Inner Temple Masque and other Jacobean Music," in *Notes and Queries*, n.s. I,5 (May, 1954), pp. 194-195. The quoted remark appears in his "La musique dans les masques de Ben Jonson," in *Les Fêtes de la Renaissance*, I, ed. J. Jacquot, (Paris: CNRS, 1956), p. 301.

Notes for Pages 165-184

4. The wide intervals at the beginning of phrases may have been filled in by division. Florid settings of songs in manuscript do not usually so embellish the very beginnings of phrases, but then those florid passages are more attentive to the cadential segment of the phrase. Only one of the three opportunities to fill in an octave leap is realized fully in "Why stays the bridegroom." One can hardly imagine, however, a singer not taking the liberty, well within accepted performance practice, of emphasizing the rhetoric by some ornament. This song lends itself to such decoration at the beginning of phrases more completely than most of Ferrabosco's others, although the long gestural triadic openings of many have been filled in by division. The *caveat*, of course, is that Ferrabosco often wrote out what, in effect, was rhetorical ornamentation, e.g. the "esclamazione" (approach from the lower third) which appears in "Oh! What a Fault" (#viii) and "Yes, were the Loves" (#20).

5. The final g of the tenor is reached only at the end of each section. That Ferrabosco avoided it at internal cadences makes its appearance more effective.

6. This is the same effect we had seen earlier in the sequence used to set "Of worthy Queens" in "If all the ages of the earth."

7. The answer to the textual question, "Could the world, with all her cost, Have redeem'd it?" is, of course, *no*. The answer which we, as observers of or fictive participants in the charmed world of the court (and this courtly entertainment), can give, however, is *yes* — that beauty is redeemed and not lost by the agency of the monarch whose presence has transforming and creative power.

8. The progression may better be served by first inversion chords for the second note of each member of the bass pattern. This emphasizes the final harmonies and doesn't muddy the waters where clarity is wanted. The use of root position chords throughout this sequence (1st inversion of m. 34, unless B is accepted as the proper note) contrasts minor chords in the first two measures with major chords in the latter two, upward root movement of a fifth with downward movement. This is certainly apt for "griev'd", although the larger contrast of subdominant and tonic is weakened.

Chapter XI

1. Ulrich Olshausen, *Das lautenbegleitete Sololied in England um 1600* (Frankfurt, 1963), p. 265.

2. Ian Spink, *English Song*, p. 44; Edward Doughtie, *Lyrics from English Ayres*, p. 571. See also J. P. Cutts, "Early Seventeenth-Century Lyrics at St. Michael's College," *Music & Letters* 37(1956), p. 232.

3. The bass line of mm. 23-24 has been torn from the manuscript, leaving only noteless stems, from which Spink's realization (followed above) is inferred. A more likely reading of those measures, based on these stems and Ferrabosco's harmonic pratice, which rarely in these songs has bass and voice moving in thirds and sixths except in sequential figures, is given here as a preferred alternative:

290   Notes for Pages 186-212

4. The word-painting (e.g., the extended notes and descending seventh of "perpetua morte" and the repetitions of "mille") and the text-setting with regard to longer and shorter notes and bar-line accents are two different aspects of a single response to the words. What is overwhelmingly apparent here, however, is the musical shape of the phrase: the subordination of textual immediacy and delivery to musical balance and coherence.

5. In Example 15, it would certainly be possible for the performer to intensify the presentation of the line, especially by means of forceful accents and rubato. Nevertheless, the setting does not stray far here from being quite metrical, and the harmonic and melodic shapeliness of the phrase makes it possible to be quite tender rather than forceful – a reading between the lines which the drama would certainly support, but which would be unusual in a setting like this.

6. The translation is by Ian Spink: Ferrabosco: *Manuscript Songs*, p. 42.

Chapter XII

1. Spink, *English Song*, p. 48.

2. In the later dialog, the distinction between a declamatory/recitative opening section and the concluding chorus would become clearer. Here, there is imitative duetting before the actual structural duet which begins only when the tonic is reasserted ("Then let us still together live and love"). Ferrabosco makes no attempt to change the meter for the chorus, and his dialogs follow the same pattern as the more declamatory songs which begin with forceful gestures over a continuo-style bass but retire into more tuneful lyricism with a more active accompaniment.

3. That the exaggerated length of "Say" and "Why" is similar to so many of Ferrabosco's opening gestures should come as no surprise. Their primary purpose is to attract attention to themselves, not to present the text.

4. This entrance should overlap the shepherd's question ("Sweet nymph, where art?"), so the contrast of the nymph's manner with that of the shepherd is made more directly. The bass is one measure too long in the passage immediately preceding the nymph's entrance, a problem Spink mentions without excising the extra notes: *Manuscript Songs*, p. 11.

5. The final cadence of this phrase is awkward, plummeting to G, when, by all rights, it should end on D. A possible revision is offered here, with apologies to stout English hearts.

Chapter XIII

1. Thomas Morley, *A Plain Easy Introduction to Practical Music*, R. Alec Harman, ed. (New York: W. W. North & Company, Inc., 1952), pp. 274-75. For a discussion of this problem with regard to Victoria, see Eugene Cramer, "The Significance of Clef Combinations in the Music of Tomas Luis de Victoria," in *The American Choral Review*, Volume XVIII, number 3 (July, 1976), pp. 3-11. The dispute concerning the relationship of clef combinations and transposition is reviewed in Arthur Mendel, "Pitch in the 16th and Early 17th Centuries," *Musical Quarterly*, Vol. XXXIV, No. 3 (1948), pp. 336-40. Additional significant work on this question, first introduced by Raphael Kiesewetter in his preface to *Galerie der alten Contrapunctisten* (1847), includes that by Siegfried Hermelink, "Zur Chiavettenfrage," *Bericht über den internationalen musikwissenschaftlichen Kongress, Wien: Mozartjahr 1956*, pp. 264-71; Caroline Miller, "Chiavette: A New Approach," unpublished Master's thesis, University of California, Berkeley, 1960; H. K. Andres, "Transposition of Byrd's Vocal Polyphony," *Music and Letters*, Vol. 43, No. 1 (Jan. 1962), pp. 25-37; and Carol MacClintock, *Giaches de Wert (1535-1596): Life and Works* (1966), pp. 205-11.

2. Morley, *loc. cit.*

3. *Ibid.*

4. *Ibid.*

5. In *Early English Church Music*, Vol. 15 (London: Stainer & Bell, 1974).

6. They are least smooth when Ferrabosco is trying to portray vivid activity: e.g., "quando caeli movendi sunt" in "Libera me." But in these motets, as in the songs, Ferrabosco often succumbs to the use of musical figures which serve themselves more than the text, as at the beginning of "Ego dixi domine." There is, however, much less of the typical off-beat gesture found in the songs.

7. Morley's comments (*op. cit.*, p. 249) support the argument that these motets *should* be considered together. Speaking about "Leaving the key," the Master says:

> A great fault, for every key hath a peculiar air proper unto itself, so that if you go into another than that wherein you begun you change the air of the song, which is as much as to wrest a thing out of his nature, making the ass leap upon his master and the spaniel bear the load. . . . . . and though the

air of every key be different one from the other yet some love (by a wonder of nature) to be joined to others, so that if you begin your song in Gam ut you may conclude it either in C fa ut or D sol re and from thence come again to Gam ut. . .

8. Arkwright, "Notes on the Ferrabosco Family," *MA* IV (1912/13), p. 49; the motet is given on pp. 50-54.

9. See Jack Pilgrim, "Tallis' *Lamentations* and the English Cadence," *The Music Review* XX (1959), pp. 1-6 He writes [p. 4] that this suspension form and the dissonances of cross-relation which resulted derived from "the dual conflict between the melodic urge of the suspension to attain its note of resolution and the harmonic desire of the composer to produce a complete chord at the same time." In its simpler forms, then, it is a vocal *acciaccatura*. Ferrabosco only presents the simpler forms, and this reasoning cannot stand up consistently with the many examples of cadences in the motets which are momentarily simply open fifths.

10. It is the $b^\flat$ inflection of d minor which colors the secondary dominant in an intervallic, "phrygian" manner: $d=i$, iv_6-V-i. At the same time the $f^\sharp$ points to g/G (and, with the $b^\flat$, keeps that g from moving toward C). This is a particularly good example of the use of parallel tonal pairs and the possibilities of moving between various intermediate tonal levels by third or fifth.

Chapter XIV

1. That this was more commemorative than liturgical is confirmed by the presence of a French text in the superius – in the manner of a medieval motet.

2. English *Lamentations* also appeared outside a sanctioned liturgical context: e.g., William Lawes's three-voice settings of George Sandys's paraphrases of 3 8-line portions of *The Lamentations of Jeremiah [Choice Psalms* (1648), nos. 5, 6, and 7]. As Dr. Lefkowitz points out (*William Lawes*, pp. 237-38), Lawes probably composed these during the period 1636-1639 for the King's Chapel. In addition, Lawes set portions of the second paragraph of the *Lamentations* as a 4-voice canon ("She Weepeth Sore in the Night;" see Lefkowitz, pp. 247-48). Considering Sandys's close relationship to court – he was a member of the King's Privy Council – and King Charles's approval of his metrical paraphrases of the psalms which appeared in 1636, dedicated to the King, these settings seem intended for the private devotions of a troubled King.

3. As a vocal movement, this piece is unusual in gesture. Dr. Lefkowitz informs me that the parts could quite easily be played by gambas. Whether this was the mode of performance, with, perhaps, one singer, is difficult to say.

Appendix I

Ayres, 1609

1. Known copies of the *Ayres*:
    British Museum K.8.h.2
    Folger Shakespeare Library 10827
        [lacks original after sig. H2; replaced in facsimile]
    Huntington Library 59751
    Newberry Library Case VM 1620 F36a
        [last leaf (K1) in facsimile; upper corners of I1, I2 repaired: pen facsimile]
    Royal College of Music I.G.41
        [Title page bears the signature of the composer; there is a correction slip pasted over some incorrectly aligned tablature rhythm-signs on sig. H2^v.]
2. Facsimile Edition:
    Alfonso Ferrabosco: *Ayres* (1609)
    Edited by David Greer.
        Volume 5 in *The English Lute Songs, 1597-1632; A Collection of Facsimile Reprints* (general editor, F.W. Sternfeld), (Menston, England: The Scolar Press, 1971). [The facsimile is of the British Museum copy of the *Ayres*]
3. Modern Edition:
    E.H. Fellowes, ed., *Alfonso Ferrabosco: Ayres,* in *The English School of Lutenist Song Writers,* second series, XVI (London, 1927).
4. Texts:
    Edward Doughtie, *Lyrics from English Ayres, 1596-1622* (Cambridge, Mass., 1971), pp. 290-303, 560-571.
    E.H. Fellowes, *Madrigal Verse, 1588-1632* (1920; 3d ed., rev. by F.W. Sternfeld with David Greer. New York, 1968), pp. 512-520, 745-746.
    [Both of these editions of texts use the British Museum copy of the *Ayres.*]

Title	Text Author/Source	Concordances[1]	Clef/Range[2]	Variants[3]
1. Like Hermit Poore Through-composed	[Raleigh?] Translation of Desportes, *Amours de Diane*, II.8, "Je me veux rendre hermite"		$S\flat$ d'-$e\flat''$	accomp. 10.2 e
2. Come Home my Troubled Thoughts ABB		Tenbury MS 1018, f.33 voice/bass This source presents a second strophe of text which was copied into the British Museum *Ayres*.	$S\flat$ d'-$e\flat''$	
3. Come Away, Come Away ABB	Ben Jonson *Masque of Blacknesse*, 1605	Christ Church MS 439, p. 31 voice/bass	$S\flat$ d'-d''	
4. Deere, When to Thee ABB		B.M. MS Add. 11586, f.38, #1 voice/bass	$S\flat$ d'-$e\flat''$	Voice 10.4 "a-fresh" $\underline{a}'$, not g'
5. Faine I would ABB		Christ Church MS 439, p. 21 voice/bass This source presents a second strophe of text.	Tr d'-f'	

Appendix I   295

6. Come, by Celia aaBCC	Ben Jonson *Volpone*, 1605 Adapted from Catullus, "Vivamus mea Lesbia"; See also Campion, "My sweetest Lesbia" in Rosseter's *First Booke of Ayres*, 1601, #1.	B.M. MS Add. 15117, f.20^v voice/lute	S^b c'-e$^{b''}$	accomp. 1.4 not In the *Ayres*, the lute time symbol is too far to the left at the beginning of the repeated first phrases ("spend not").

7. So, so, Leave off
ABB
	John Donne
	(first appearance of
	Donne's poetry in
	print)
		B.M. MS Add. 11586,
		f.38, #2
		voice/bass
			Tr d'-f''	accomp. 4.1 d'
				             b^b
				             g
				             G

8. Young and Simple
Though I Am
ABB
	Thomas Campion
	(See Campion's
	Fourth Book of Ayres
	1617), #9)
		B.M. MS Add. 24665
		f.53^v, #50
		voice/bass
		*Christ Church MS 439,
		p. 86
		voice/bass
			Tr g'-g''	accomp. 11.1 e'
				             c'
				             c

9. Drowne not with Teares aaBB		*Christ Church MS 439, pp. 88-89 voice/bass	Tr d'-f''	
10. I am a Lover aabb	Bartholomew Young, translator: Montemayor, *Diana*, from *Los Siete Libros de la Diana*, Valencia, 1559.	Christ Church MS 439, p. 29 voice/bass	Tr g'-g''	

296 Appendix I

Title	Text Author/Source	Concordances[1]	Clef/Range[2]	Variants[3]
11. Why stayes the Bridegroome A(aa')BB	Ben Jonson *Haddington masque*, 1608	Christ Church MS 439, pp. 60-61 voice/bass ornamented version	Tr e'-g"	accomp. 1.1 Christ Church: C *Ayres* (1609): A
12. Sing we then Heroic Grace aa'B			Tr f#'-e"	
13. Sing the Riches aa'b			Tr♭ g'-g"	voice 13.4 b'
14. Sing the Nobles Through-composed, in two sections		*Christ Church MS 439, p. 40 voice/bass	T c-g'	measure 20: Fellowes omitted two beats of rest before the vocal entrance at "Terror chased" and halved the harmony to fit under the words.
15. With what new Thoughts ABB		Christ Church MS 439, p. 25 voice/bass Tenbury MS 1018, f.34ᵛ voice/bass	Tr♭ f#'-a"	

16. Fly From the World Through-composed, in two sections	*Christ Church MS 439, p. 92 voice/bass Tenbury MS 1018, f.34ᵛ voice/bass	Tr b♭ g′-g″	voice 1.4 d″ 27.1 , not "o" lute/viol 29:
17. Shall I Seek ABB	*Christ Church MS 439, p. 91 voice/bass	Tr b♭ g′-g″	
18. If all these Cupids ABB	Ben Jonson *Masque of Beauty*, 1608 Christ Church MS 439, p. 93 voice/bass with ornamented final cadence	S♭ d′-e♭″	
19. It was no Pollicie ABB	Ben Jonson *Masque of Beauty*, 1608 *Christ Church Ms 439, p. 94 voice/bass	Tr d′-g″	voice 8.5: misprint in *Ayres* -- "earnest" as , instead of , which Fellowes gives without note.
20. Yes, Were the Loves ABB'	Ben Jonson *Masque of Beauty*, 1608 Christ Church MS 439, p. 96 (incomplete) voice/bass	T B♭-g′	voice 23.4: misprint in *Ayres*: b is misplace before f′, not ed′; corrected without note by Fellowes.

Appendix I

Title	Text Author/Source	Concordances[1]	Clef/Range[2]	Variants[3]
21. So Beautie on the Waters Stood aaBcc	Ben Jonson *Masque of Beauty*, 1608		A g'-g'	lute 1.1 e' c' g' c
22. Had Those that Dwell ABB	Ben Jonson *Masque of Beauty*, 1608		A f-a'	
23. If all the Ages ABB	Ben Jonson *Masque of Queens*, 1609	*Christ Church MS 439, p. 95 voice/bass	A g-a'	lute 10.1 g' e' c
24. Unconstant Love ABB		*Christ Church MS 439, p. 101 voice/bass	Tr♭ g'-g''	
25. O Eyes, O Mortal Stars	Guarini *Rime*, Venice 1598, Madrigal XII anonymous translation	Christ Church MS 439, p. 78 voice/bass Tenbury MS 1019, f.2 voice.lute The original Italian text is presented under the English words.	Tr♭ a'-g''	

[Dialogs]

26. Faire Cruell Nimph   Tr♭ a′-f′ ; A♭ f-g′

27. What Shall I Wish?   A♭ g-a′ ; A♭ a-a′   second voice 9,2,3 b
    ABB

28. Tell me, O Love   Tr f′-a″ ; T d-f′   lute 18,3 f
    first voice 40, not
    enough rests in
    Ayres
    viol 41-43, lacks a
    whole note c in
    Ayres

1. Concordances which are attributed are indicated by an asterisk. *
2. Fellowes, in his preface to the modern edition of the *Ayres*, confused the second-line Ms clef with the first-line S clef which is used for songs 1-4 and 6.
3. These are variants with Fellowes' edition, except for simple variants of chord-spacing which occur in the written out repeats of the 1609 *Ayres*. The first number is the measure (in Fellowes' edition); the second refers to the beat within the measure: e. g. , accomp. 10,2 e means that on the second beat of the tenth measure, in the accompaniment, there is an e (natural) in the *Ayres*, not an e♭, as in Fellowes.

Appendix II
Manuscript Songs: Concordances

Modern edition: *Alfonso Ferrabosco: Manuscript Songs*, transcribed and edited by Ian Spink, in *The English Lute-Songs*, second series, vol. 19 (London, 1966).

Title	Text Author/Source	Source/Concordances	Clef/Range
i. All you forsaken lovers AABB		*Cambridge: Fitzwilliam Museum MS 52.D.25 ("John Bull MS"), f.111^V voice/bass B.M. MS Add. 10337, f.47 voice/bass	Tr^b d$'$-g$''$
[Doe but consider this small dust]	Ben Jonson	*Carlisle Cathedral Library, Bishop Smith's part-books (altus/bassus, both texted)	
ii. Lo! In a Vale AABB		*Cambridge: John Bull MS, f. 108^V voice/bass	Tr^b e^b-g$''$
iii. Was I to Blame? ABB		*Cambridge: John Bull MS, f. 104^V voice/bass	Tr^b f$'$-a$''$
iv. Heav'n, Since Thou art ABB		*Cambridge: John Bull MS, f. 112 voice/bass	S^b f$'$-e$^{b''}$
v. Dialog: Say Shepherd Boy! ARR		*Cambridge: John Bull MS. ff. 100^V-101 voices/bass	Tr e$'$-g$''$; T B-e$'$ [# on 3d line]
vi. Nay, Nay You must not Stay Through-composed in two sections	Ben Jonson *Oberon*, 1611	*Tenbury MS 1018, f.36 voice/bass	T g-g$'$

Appendix II

Title	Text Author/Source	Source/Concordances	Clef/Range
vii. Gentle Knights ABB'	Ben Jonson *Oberon*, 1611	*Tenbury MS 1018, f. 37^V voice/bass	T^b B^b-g'
viii. Oh! What a Fault Through-composed in two sections	[Ben Jonson *Love Freed From Ignorance and Folly*, 1611]	*Tenbury MS 1018, f. 36^V voice/bass	Tr g'-g''
ix. Senses by unjust Force Banish'd Through-composed in two sections	Ben Jonson *Love Freed From Ignorance and Folly*, 1611	*Tenbury MS 1018, f.37 voice/bass	T c-g'
x. How Near to Good Through-composed in two sections	Ben Jonson *Love Freed From Ignorance and Folly*, 1611	*Tenbury MS 1018, f.37 voice/bass	T^b G-g'
xi. Udite Lagrimosi Spir'ti d'Averno Through-composed, in two sections	Guarini *Il Pastor Fido* III.6	*Tenbury MS 1018, f.35 voice/bass	Tr c'-f''
xii. Eterni Numi Through-composed, in two sections	Guarini *Il Pastor Fido* V.6	*Tenbury MS 1018, f.35^V	Tr f'-a''
xiii. O Crudel'Amarilli Through-composed, in two sections	Guarini *Il Pastor Fido* III.8	*Tenbury MS 1018, f.35^V voice/bass	Tr^b f'-g''
xiv. Lacrimar sempre il mio sommo diletto Through-composed, in two sections		*Tenbury MS 1018, f.36^V voice/bass	T c-d'

Appendix III

Concordances
Latin Motets and English Anthems

These tables provide information regarding the location of the motets and anthems in manuscript and published sources. In addition, the clef and signature of the source is indicated, as is the numbering of items within the source. The order of the motets a5 is taken from the Tregian anthology, or Sambrooke Book, NYPL MS Drexel 4302. Other pertinent information is given in notes.

The following abbreviations are used:

    c   cantus
    a   altus
    t   tenor
    b   bassus
    q   quintus
    Tr   treble clef
    S   soprano clef
    Ms   mezzo-soprano clef
    A   alto clef
    T   tenor clef
    Bar baritone clef
    B   bass clef

* attribution to Alfonso Ferrabosco (jun.) is made in the source.

♭ the parts in this source have a flat (♭) in the signature.

(1) numbers in parentheses refer to the number of the piece within the source. In several cases, for example Drexel 4302, Bodleian mus.sch c.45-50, and B.M. Add. 29366-8, these numbers are not consecutive throughout the manuscript, but refer only to the ordering of a particular group of pieces, usually by one composer, within the manuscript. For example, "Ego sum resurrectio" is the first of Ferrabosco's motets to appear in Drexel 4302 (on p. 89). Therefore, it is no. 1 in the manuscript section devoted to these pieces.

Appendix III

Concordances: Latin Motets a5

	NYPL MS DREXEL 4302	BODELIAN MSS mus sch c45 c46 c47 c49 c50					B.M. MSS Add. 29366 29367 29368 (=c45; =c50; =c46)			B.M. MSS Add. 29372-77 -72-73-74-75-76				
		c	a	t	q	b	c	b	q	c	a	t	b	q
a5 di Alfonso Ferabosco il figliuolo														
1. Ego sum resurrectio	1. p. 89 SMsATB♭ *	(1) S p48	A p22	T p22	Ms p24	B♭ p26	(2) S f37ᵛ	(1) B f36ᵛ	(1) A♭* f24ᵛ					
2. O nomen Jesu	2. p. 91 SMsATB *	(2) S p49	A p23	T p23	Ms p25	B p27	(3) S¹ f38	B¹ f37ᵛ	Ms²* f26 [=c49]	(14) S p178	A 178	T 178	B 178	Ms* 178 [=c46, c47]
3. Ego dixi Domine	3. p. 90 TrMsAABar *	(3) Tr p50	A p24	A p24	Ms p26	Bar p28	(4) Tr f38ᵛ	Bar f38	A[Ms]³* f26 [=c49]	(15) Tr p179	A 179	A 179	Bar 179	Ms 179 [=c46, c47]
4. Convertere Domine	4. p. 92 2ᵃParte TrMsAABar *	(4) Tr p50	A p25	A p25	Ms p27	Bar p29	(5) Tr f39	Bar f38ᵛ	A* f27					
5. Ubi duo vel tres	5. p. 93 TrTrMsABar *	(7) Tr p53	A p28	Tr p28	Ms p30	Bar p32	(8) Tr f40ᵛ	Bar f40	A* f28					

Appendix III

6. Libera me Domine	6. p. 94 2ªPars TrTrMsABar *				(8) Tr p54	A p29	Tr p29	Ms p31	Bar p32	(9) Tr f41	Bar f40ᵛ	A* f28ᵛ
7. Domine Deus	7. p. 96 TrMsAABar *				(5) Tr p51	A p26	A p26	Ms p28	Bar p30	(6) Tr f39ᵛ	Bar f39	*
8. Noli me	8. p. 97 2aPars TrMsAABar *				(6) Tr p52	A p27	A p27	Ms p29	Bar p31	(7) Tr f40	Bar f39ᵛ	A* f27ᵛ
9. Laboravi	9. p. 98 TrTrMsABar *									(Alfonso #4 untexted) Tr f34ᵛ	Bar f39ᵛ	A* f37
10. Lamentatio	10. p. 101 ATTBarB♭ *				(9) A p55				B♭ p49			
11. Tribulationem	11. p. 103 TrMsAABar * text:incipit only]											

1. MS Add. 29366 has a ♯ on B at the clef. MS Add. 29367 has, mistakenly, B♭ at the clef, but only there.

2. MS Add. 29368: The copyist first wrote out the text and was filling in the music for the alto clef part (cf. c.46), but stopped and scratched the whole thing out (f.25ᵛ). Then he copied the Ms clef part, apparently setting the numbering awry, for he used "prima pars" (intended for the uncopied Alto clef part of "Ego dixi") for the "secunda pars," "Convertere"

3. Still confused, the copyist here copied the music which should have Ms clef, but he used the Alto clef. (cf. c.49). The copyist had simply used the wrong book in copying the parts for "O nomen Jesu" and "Ego dixi."

Appendix III

NYPL MS DREXEL 4302	BODELIAN MSS mus sch c45 c46 c47 c49 c50					B.M. MSS Add. 29366 29367 29368 (=c45; =c50; =c46)					B.M. MSS Add. 29372-77 -72 -73 -74 -75 -76				
	c	a	t	q	b	c	b	q			c	a	t	b	q
12. O Domine	p. 104 2ªPars TrMsAABar * text:incipit only]														
13. Fortitudo mea	p. 106 SMsATB *														
14. Sustinuit anima mea	p. 106 SAATB♭ *														
15. [numbered, but blank]															

Concordances: Motets and Anthems (a4, a5)

Quare dereliquerunt (a4) London: British Museum   MS Egerton 3665, p. 51 AABar
    MSS Add. 29366, [lacking] Bar♭ *
                   29367, f. 37 Bar♭*
                   29368, f.25 A♭*
    MSS Add. 29372, p.18 A♭*
                   29373, p.18 A♭*
                   29374, p.18 Bar♭*
                   29375, p.18 Bar♭*

The following three anthems were published in Sir William Leighton's *Teares and Lamentaciones* of a Sorrowful Soule (1614).

In Thee, O Lord (a4)
    Leighton: *Teares and Lamentaciones*, #29 TrTrTrTr   *
    London: British Museum MS Royal App. 63, F.11 (#18)   * [see note 1]
                MS Add. 31418, f.20 (#28)   * [see note 2]

O Lord, Come Pitie my Distress (a5)
    Leighton: *Teares and Lamentaciones*, #32 SATTB   *
    London: British Museum MS Royal App. 63, f.19 (#31)   *
                MS Add. 31418, f.26ᵛ(#33)   *

In Depth No Man Remembreth (a5)
    Leighton: *Teares and Lamentaciones*, #55 SATTB   *
    London: British Museum MS Royal App. 63, f.31 (#55)   *
                MS Add. 31418, f.69v(#55)   *

[1] British Museum MS Royal App. 63 is a copy of Leighton's Teares for solo voice (cantus) with accompaniment of a treble viol and lute (written in tablature below).

[2] British Museum MS Add. 31418 is a late 18th-century transcript of the *Teares*.

Appendix IV

Motet Transcriptions

1. Ego sum resurrectio

New York, Public Library: MS Drexel 4302.
Oxford, Bodleian Library: MSS mus. sch. c.45-c50
London, British Museum: MSS add. 29366-29368 (S,B,A only)

        Ego sum resurrectio et vita
        Qui credit in me, etiam si mortuus fuerit, vivet.
        Et omnis qui vivit et credit in me
        Non morietur in eternum.

        John 11: 25-26

        I am the resurrection and the life:
        He that believeth in me, though
        he were dead, yet shall he live.
        And whosoever liveth and believeth
        in me shall never die.
        (King James Version)

Appendix IV

Appendix IV

Appendix IV

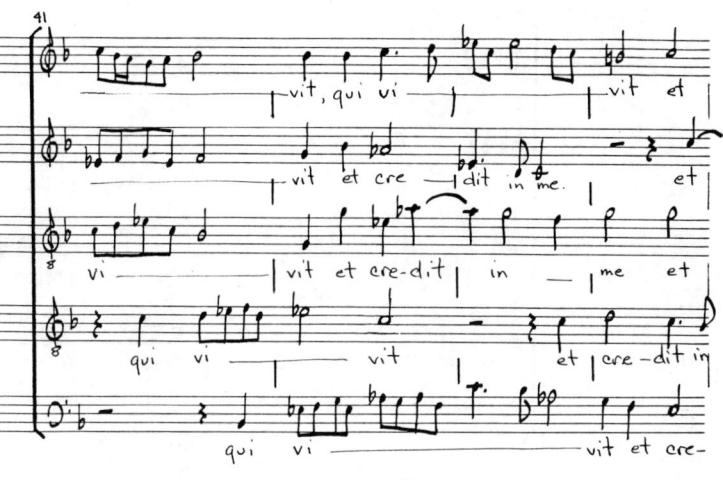

2. O nomen Jesu

New York, Public Library: MS Drexel 4302.
Oxford, Bodleian Library, MSS mus, sch. c45-c50.
London, British Museum: MSS add. 29366-29368 (S,B,Ms only)
          MSS add. 29372-29376

> O nomen Jesu, nomen dulce,
> nomen Jesu, nomen delectabile
> nomen Jesu, nomen confortans
> Quid est enim Jesus nisi salvator
> Ergo Jesu propter nomen sanctum tuum
> Esto michi Jesus et salva me.

> O name [of] Jesus, sweet name,
> delightful and comforting;
> For what is Jesus if not the saviour.
> Therefore, Jesus, by thy holy name
> be Jesus to me and restore me.

Appendix IV

3. Ego dixi, Domine miserere mei

New York, Public Library: MS Drexel 4302.
Oxford, Bodleian Library: MSS mus. sch. c.45-c.50.
London, British Museum: MSS add. 29366-29368 (Tr, Bar, Ms only).
          MSS add. 29372-29376.

> Ego dixi, domine miserere mei
> Sana animam meam
> Quia peccavi tibi.
>
> Psalm 41:4
>
> I said, "Lord, be merciful unto me;
> Heal my soul, for I have sinned
> against Thee."
> (King James Version)

Appendix IV

Appendix IV

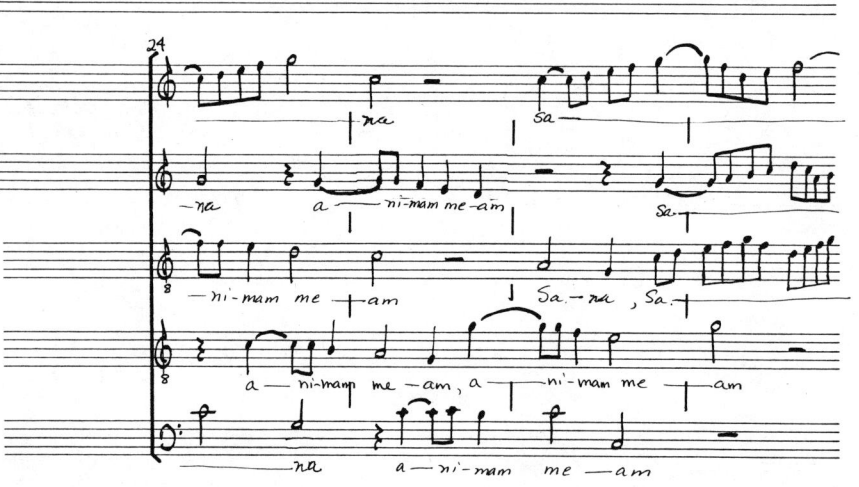

Appendix IV

Appendix IV

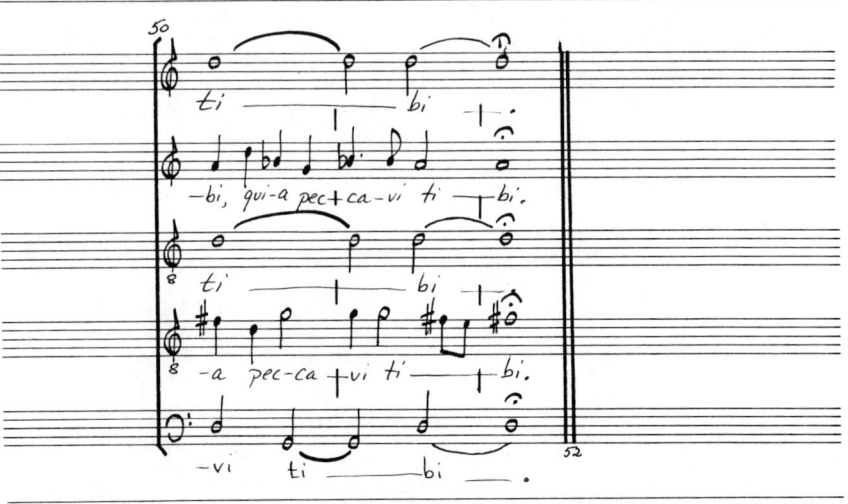

4. Convertere Domine usquequo

New York, Public Library: MS Drexel 4302.
Oxford, Bodleian Library: MSS mus. sch. c.45-c.50.
London, British Museum: MSS add. 29366-29368 (Tr, Bar,A only)

> Convertere Domine usquequo
> Et deprecabilis esto
> Super servos tuos.

Psalm 90:13

> Return, O Lord.
> How long before Thou show
> grace unto Thy servants?

Appendix IV

Appendix IV

Appendix IV

Appendix IV

5. Ubi duo vel tres

New York, Public Library: MS Drexel 4302.
Oxford, Bodleian Library: MSS mus. sch. c.45-c.50.
London, British Museum: MSS add. 29366-29368 (Tr,Bar,A only)

>Ubi duo vel tres congregati fuerunt
>In medio eorum sum
>In nomine meo.
>
>Dixi, Domine.
>
>Matthew 18:20
>
>Where two or three are gathered
>in my name, there am I in the
>midst of them.
>(King James Version)
>I said, "Lord"

Appendix IV

Appendix IV

Appendix IV

Appendix IV

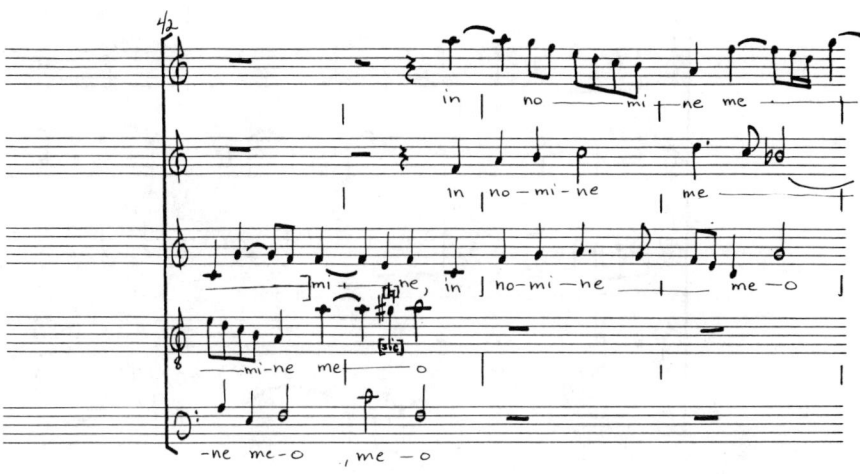

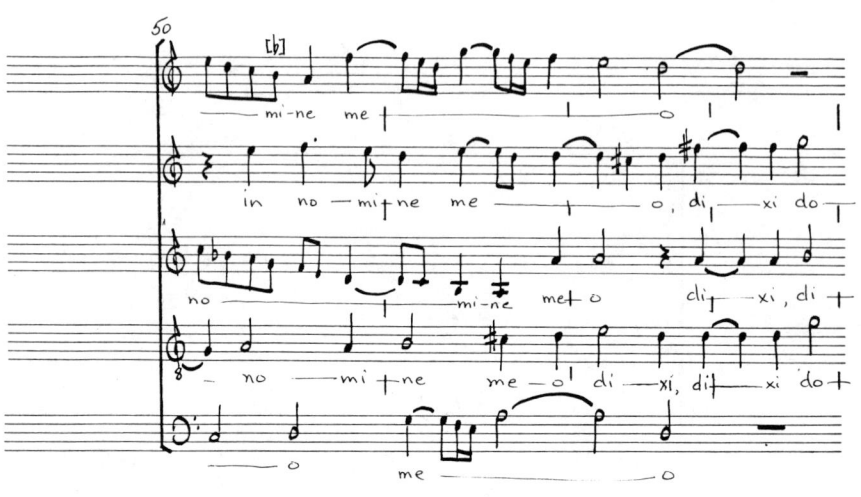

Appendix IV

6. Libera me, Domine

New York, Public Library: MS Drexel 4302.
Oxford, Bodleian Library: MSS mus. sch. c.45-c.50.
London, British Museum: MSS add. 29366-29368 (Tr,Bar,A only)

> Libera me, domine,
> de morte eterna,
> In die illa tremenda
> Quando caeli movendi sunt et terra,
> Dum veneris judicare seculum
> per ignem.

Responsory from the Office of the Dead

Deliver me, O Lord from eternal
death on that dread day when the
heavens and earth shall be moved,
when Thou shalt come to judge the world by fire.

Appendix IV

Appendix IV

Appendix IV

Appendix IV

Appendix IV

358 *Appendix IV*

7. Domine Deus meus

New York, Public Library: MS Drexel 4302.
Oxford, Bodleian Library: MSS mus. sch. c.45-c.50.
London, British Museum: MSS add. 29366-29368 (Tr, Bar only).

>Domine Deus meus
>Ne queso intres in iudicium
>Cum puero tuo
>delicta iuventutis meae
>et ignorantiae meae,
>Ne memineris unquam
>neve in finem iratum
>mea mala reserves.

>Lord, my God:
>Do not judge Thy child
>nor, in the wrathful end,
>remember the sins of my youth
>and ignorance
>or my evil deeds.

Appendix IV

Appendix IV

Appendix IV

Appendix IV

Appendix IV 365

8. Noli me proijcere

New York, Public Library: MS Drexel 4302.
Oxford, Bodleian Library: MSS mus. sch. c.45-c.50.
London, British Museum: MSS add. 29366-29368 (Tr,Bar,A only).

Noli me proijcere a facie tua
in tempore senectutis
Et cum defecerit virtus mea
ne derelinquas me
usque ad senectum in senium
ne declinas a servo tuo.
Sed in pace recipe animam meam
et misericordias tuas
in eternum cantabo:
Domine Deus meus.

Psalm 71:9, 18; Psalm 89:2

Cast me not off in the time of old age;
Forsake me not when my strength faileth.
Also when I am old and greyheaded,
O God, forsake me not.
But in peace receive my soul,
And I shall sing Thy mercies
In eternity: O Lord, my God.
(King James Version)

Appendix IV

Appendix IV

Appendix IV

Appendix IV

9. Laboravi in gemitu meo

New York, Public Library: MS Drexel 4302.
London, British Museum: MSS add. 29366-29368 (Tr,Bar,A only; untexted)

Laboravi in gemitu meo
Lavabo per singulas noctes
Stratum meum lachrimis meis rigabo.

I have labored in my moan.
Each night I shall weep and
moisten my bed with tears.

Appendix IV

Appendix IV

Appendix IV

Appendix IV

Appendix IV

Appendix IV

Appendix IV

10. Lamentations of Jeremiah

New York, Public Library: MS Drexel 4302.
Oxford, Bodleian Library: MSS c.45, c.50 (cantus, bassus only)

        Incipit lamentatio Jeremiae prophetae
Aleph.
        Quomodo sedet sola civitas plena populo!
        Facta est quasi vidua Domina gentium.
        Princeps provinciarum facta est sub tributo.
Beth.
        Plorans ploravit in nocte
        Et lacrimae eius in maxillis eius.
        Non est qui consoletur eam ex omnibus charis eius.
        Omnes amici eius spreverunt eam,
        Et facti sunt illi inimici.
Ghimel.
        Migravit Juda propter afflictionem et multitudinem servitutis;
        Habitavit inter gentes, nec inveniet requiem.
        Hierusalem, Hierusalem, convertere ad Dominum tuum.

The Lamentations of Jeremiah 1:1-3

Here begins the lamentation of the Prophet Jeremiah:

Aleph: How does the city sit solitary that was full of people! How is she become as a widow that was the queen of nations and chief among provinces; How is she become tributary.

Beth: She weeps sore in the night, and her tears are on her cheeks. Among all her lovers she hath none to comfort her: all her friends have dealt treacherously with her; they are become her enemies.

Ghimel: Judah is gone into captivity because of affliction and great servitude; She dwelleth among the heathen, she findeth no rest.

        Jerusalem, Jersusalem, Return to thy Lord.

Appendix IV

Appendix IV

Appendix IV

Appendix IV

3. Quomodo

Appendix IV

Appendix IV

1 PRINCEPS

Appendix IV

Appendix IV

397

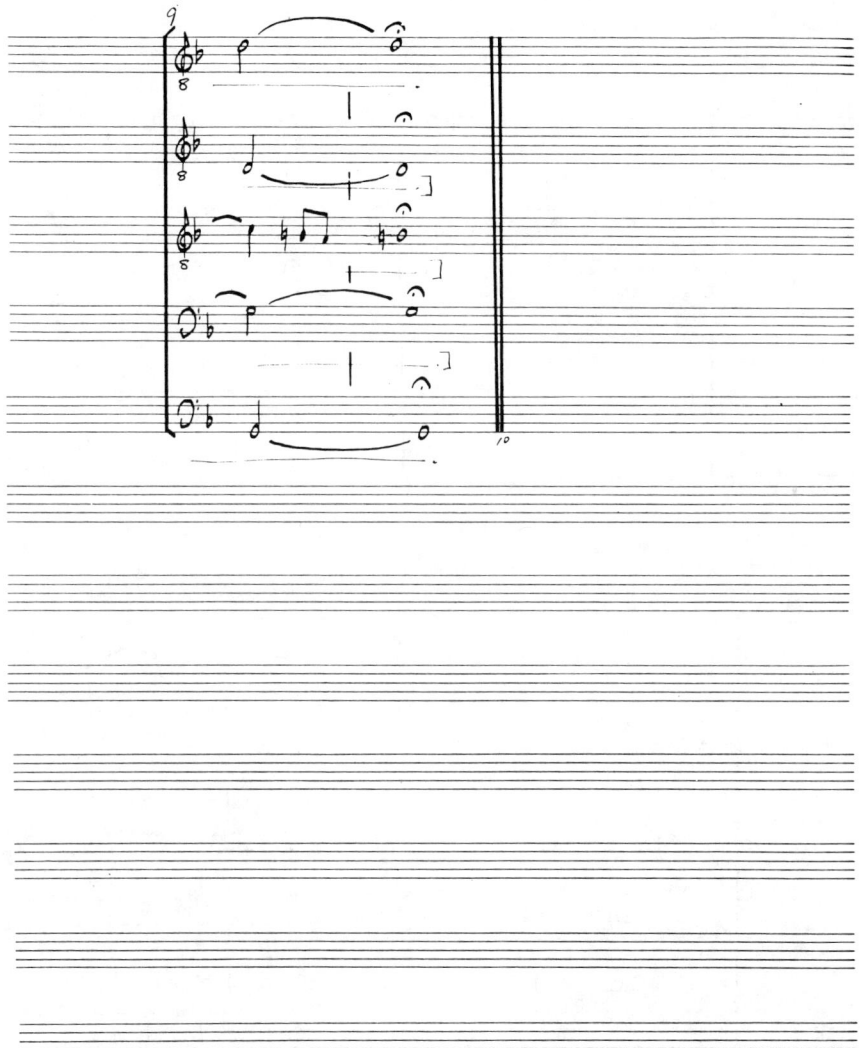

Appendix IV

6 Plorans Ploravit

Appendix IV

Appendix IV

7. Non est qui consolatur eam

Appendix IV

8.

Appendix IV

Appendix IV

9. Gimel

Appendix IV

Appendix IV

10. MIGRAVIT JUDA

Appendix IV

Appendix IV

11.
HIERUSALEM, CONVERTERE

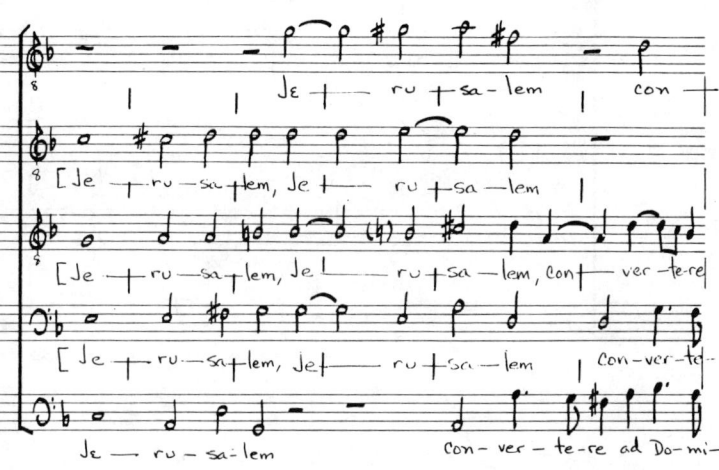

Appendix IV

11. Tribulationem et dolorem

New York, Public Library: MS Drexel 4302 (text: incipit only)

> Tribulationem et dolorem inveni,
> [et nomen Domini invocavi]
>
> Psalm 116:3,4
>
> I found trouble and sorrow.
> [Then I called upon the name
> of the Lord . . .]

Appendix IV

Appendix IV

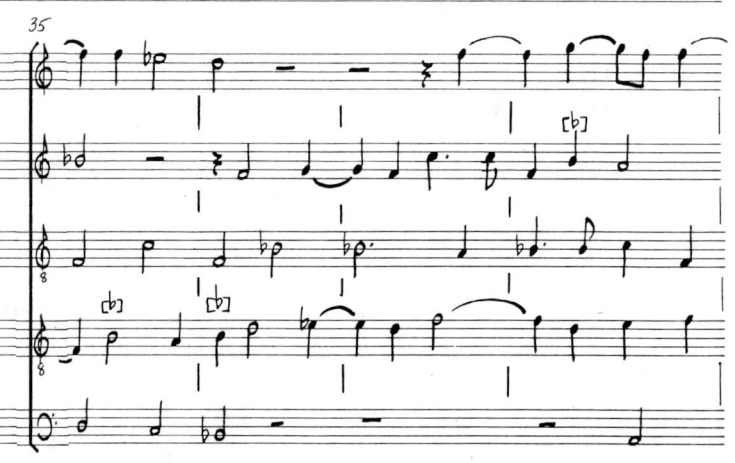

Appendix IV

Appendix IV

12. O Domine

New York, Public Library: MS Drexel 4302 (text lacking)

> O Domine ...
>
> O Lord, ...

Appendix IV

Appendix IV

Appendix IV

Appendix IV

13. Fortitudo mea

New York, Public Library: MS Drexel 4302.

> Fortitudo mea et laus mea Domine
> Et factus est mihi in salutem
> Vox exultationis et salutis
> In tabernaculis justorum.

Exodus 15:2

> The Lord is my strength and song,
> And he is become my salvation.
> The voice of rejoicing and salvation
> [is heard] in the tents of the
> righteous.
> (King James Version)

Appendix IV

Appendix IV

Appendix IV

14. Sustinuit anima mea

New York, Public Library: MS Drexel 4302.

> Sustinuit anima mea in verbo eius;
> Speravit anima mea in domino.
> A custodia matutina usque ad noctem
> Speret Israel in Domino.

Psalm 130: 5-7

> My soul is sustained in His word
> and hopes in the Lord.
> From the morning watch even till
> the night may Israel hope in the Lord.

Appendix IV

Appendix IV

Appendix IV

Appendix IV

Appendix IV

Appendix IV

Quare dereliquerunt me (a4)

London, British Museum: MSS add. 29367-29368 (Bar,A only).
                MSS add. 29372-29375.
                MS Egerton 3665.

Quare dereliquerunt me vires meae
Inundaverunt aquae super caput meum
Dixi Domine exaudi me
de lacu novissimo.

Wherefore does my strength fail and
the waters rise above my head?
I cried, "Lord, hear me," from this extreme sea of woes.

Appendix IV

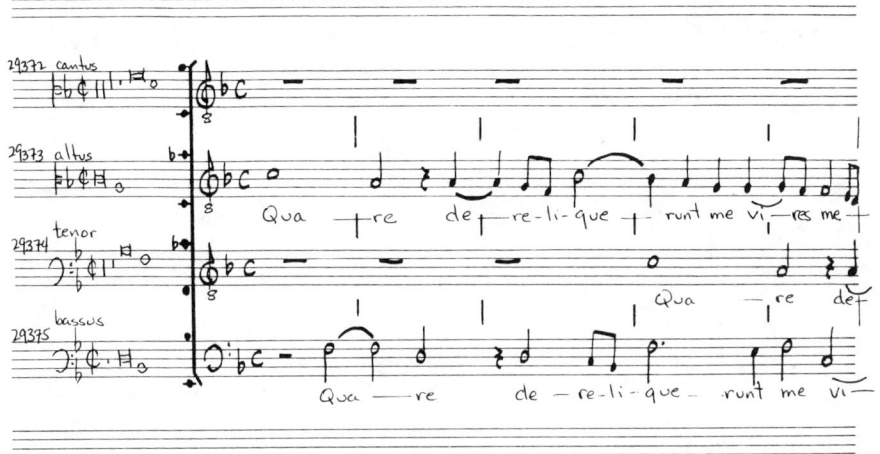

Appendix IV

Quare dereliquerunt me vires meae
Inundaverunt aquae super caput meum
Dixi Domine, Exaudi me de lacu novissimo

Appendix V

Motets: Table of Variants

The variants which appear in the manuscript sources, compared with the final transcriptions, are presented with the following information:

1. Part: 1-5, counting from the uppermost to lowest voice in transcription
2. Manuscript in which variant occurs
3. Measure number (transcription)
4. Order of note of measure, not counting rests
5. Variant (pitches are natural, unless an accidental is given)

For example:

O nomen Jesu

      2. c.49 : 3.3 f

The 3rd note of the 3rd measure of the 2nd highest voice part of "O nomen Jesu" is f#. In c. 49, it is given as f-natural.

The manuscript sources are abbreviated to their number:

NYPL Drexel 4302		4302
Oxford, Bodleian music school		
c.45-50		c.45,c.46,c.47,c.49c.50
London, British Museum		
Additional	29366-8	29366,29367,29368
	29372-6	29372,29373,29375,29376

Ego sum resurrectio

1.	29366:	13.3,4	e
	29366:	20.2	e
	29366:	33.3,5	b♭.
	c.45 :	33	no repetition of text indicated
	29366:	40.8	b♭
	c.45 :	41.6; 42.1	texting: "-vit, qui"
	29366:	51.1, rest	no rest; instead g′ ♩ with the syllable "-tur"

Ego sum resurrectio

2. c.49 :   24-25
   c.49 :   36.6   e
   4302 :   36.6   e
   4302 :   41.1,4 e

3. 29368:   5.1,2
   29368:   33.1   e
   4302 :   33.5   e
   29368:   33.2   e
   29368:   47.2   b
   c.46 :   47.2   b
   c.46 :   52.2   b♭
   c.46 :   65   texting: ♩ ♩̂ (-ter)-num.

4. c.47 :   20.2   "ad"
   c.47 :   35.3   f
   c.47 :   37.5   e
   4302 :   37.5   e
   c.47 :   64   omits "in"
   c.47 :   65   text underlay: ♫♩♫ ◯ [e]-ter-num.

5. 29367:   19.1   f
   c.50 :   30.4   f
   29367:   33.3   e
   4302 :   33.3   e
   29367:   42.4   e
   4302 :   42.4   e
   29367:   42.7   a
   29367:   47.1   b [see 3rd voice, 47.2]
   c.50 :   47.1   b [see 3rd voice, 47.2]
   c.50 :   51.1   f ♩

O nomen Jesu

1. c.45 :   30   texting: no repeat of "salvator"

2. c.49 :   3.3   f
   c.49 :   4.2   f
   c.49 :   8.3   f
   c.49 :   13.2   f
   29368:   36.3/37 ♫ ♩ omitted
   29376:   36-38   texting: ³⁶♩ ♩ ♫♩ ♩ ♩. ♪|♩ ♩ ³⁷ ³⁸ no-men sanc-tum, prop-ter no-men
   c.49 :   46.1   # placed after the c
   29376:   47-48   texting: ♫♩ ♩|♩ ♩ [mi-]-----chi Je-sus ♩ ♩

3. 29373:   28.3,4 c b (the stem on the b is crossed out)
   c.46 :   49.3   e
   4302 :   49.3   e

Appendix V 453

O nomen Jesu

	29373 :	49.3	e
	4302 :	53-54	implied texting: ♩ ♩ 𝅝 𝅗𝅥͡ (sal)-va me.
4.	4302 :	54.2	d♯ (followed by c; a mistake for the following variant)
	c.47 :	54.3	c♯ (preceded by d)
5.	29375 :	8-9	texting: ⁸♩♩ ♩ |⁹♩ ♩ [no]-men dul-ce
	c.50 :	21-22	texting: ²¹♩ ♩ ♩ 𝅝 con-for-tan-se [sic]
	29367 :	48.2	f

Ego dixi Domine

1. c.45 :   17.3   c   ♩ ♩
   29372 : 31.rest   In place of the rest, this manuscript has "sa-na,"
                      followed by a measure rest, and then the next phrase
                      (i.e., as in the transcription), followed by a two-beat
                      rest: ♩ ♩   ᴵ ♩. ♩♩♩ ♩. ♩♩♩ 𝅝 𝅝 ⊤[1]
                            sa-na
                               *   *

                      *: are not in other sources
   4302 :   43.4   ♩. ♪ instead of ♩
   c.45 alone of all the part-books used "salva" instead of "sana," beginning at measure
                      22. That salvation can be achieved only by the rsetoration and
                      healing of the soul makes this confusion of words meaningful
                      beyond accident.

2. c.49 :   191.   b♭
   c.49 :   35.4/36 ⎫
   29376 : 35.4/36 ⎬   ♫ \| ♩ ♩ ♩
                     ⎭   a g   a a g♯
                     texting:
                                 [-n i]-mam, me - [am]
   c.49 :   40.1   b
   29376 : 47.3,4   a ♩
   29376 : 51.1   b

3. c.46 :   30.4   f

4. c.47 :   21   texting as transcribed, despite repeated note
   c.47 :   52   f

5. 4302:   20-21   texting: ²⁰♩ ♩♩\|♩
                               me---i
   29375 : 39.3   b

Convertere Domine

1. c.45 :   11-13   texting: ♩ ♩. ♪ ♩ 𝄐 ♩ ♩ ♩
                     con--ver--te--re ad do--mi--ne [sic]
   4302 :   21.5   c
   4302 :   22.2   f
   c.45 :   22.3   g♯ (♯ intended for previous f)
   c.45 :   22.5   e♯ (♯ intended for previous f)
   c.45 :   23.3   c
   c.45 :   26.2   e
   29366:   30.3   b
   29366:   30.7   b
   c.45 :   30.7   b
   29366:   37-39   texting: ♪♪♪♩ ♩♪
                     [-lis] es--------to
   4302 :   44.3   f

2. 4302 :   19.3   f
   4302 :   22.3   c
   4302 :   22.8   f
   4302 :   26.6   b
   c.49 :   27.1   b
   c.49 :   27.4   e♭
   4302 :   34.8   f
   c.49 :   34   texting: ♪♪♩♩. ♪ | ♩
                     [-ca]-------bi-lis

3. 4302 :   11.2   b
   4302 :   24.1   f
   4302 :   25.3   b
   29368:   31.1   f
   4302 :   31.3   f
   29368:   31.3   f
   c.46 :   31.3   f (but see c.46:31,4)
   c.46 :   31.4   g♯ (♯ intended for previous f)
   c.46 :   37.5,6 ⎫ ♪♪
   29368:   37.5,6 ⎭ g b

4. 4302 :   18.4,6 f
   c.47 :   22.1   c
   c.47 :   24.5   f
   c.47 :   25.2   b
   c.47 :   34.7   f
   4302 :   34.7   f
                     ♩♪♪♪ ♩
   c.47 :   36.5   d c♭, not d
   c.47 :   44.1   f

5. 29367:   12.3,4 b
   c.50 :   16   texting: ¹⁶|♩. ♩|♩
                     us-que-quo
   4302 :   25.1   f

Convertere Domine

29367:	43.2,4	c
29367:	45	The copyist became lost, beginning the figure which appears in m. 45 but ending it with the conclusion of the figure in measures 53-55 of the transcription. He continues correctly from that point, but already lost are seven measures (as transcribed).

Ubi duo vel tres

1.
   c.45 : 32.3,4   g
   c.45 : 57   texting: [musical notation]
                       [do]----mi-[nus]
   c.45 :   Text concludes: "dixi dominus."

2.
   c.47 : 57.1   c b a, instead of c
   4302 : 58.4   c
   c.47 :   Text concludes: "dici dominus."

3.
   c.49 : 36-41   underlay unclear
   c.49 :   Text concludes: "dixi domine."

4.
   4302 : 26.1,2   e f
   c.46 : 31.2   g
   c.46 : 43.2   g (text: "mei," not "meo")
   29368: 43.2   g
   c.46 :   Text concludes: "dici domine."

5.
   29367: 13   texting: [musical notation]
                       fu----e---runt
   4302 : 23   texting: c d d
                       u---bi
   c.50 :   Text concludes: "dici domine."

Libera me

c.45, c.46, and c.49 reduce "Li-be-ra" to "Li-bra."

1.
   29366: 6.3   f
   c.45 : 6.6   e
   c.45 : 10   texting: [musical notation]
                       Li---be-ra me Do-[mine]
   c.45 : 12.1   c; A later hand has added a # underneath.
   4302 : 25.3   b

2.
   c.47 : 16.3   c
   c.47 : 34.4   c

3.
   c.49 : 4.2   a g, not a
   4302 : 13.2   f

Appendix V

Libera me

	c.49 :	14	texting:"(Libera) me-i [sic] domine" with not enough notes
	c.49 :	.3	b
	c.49 :	24.3/25	♩│♩ ♪ In di--e [sic]
	c.49 :	27.1	c b, not c
	c.49 :	45.3	e
4.	29368:	9	e e d
	c.46 :	11-13	texting: -ne, do--mi-ne li--bra me
	c.46 :	24.1	The eighth-note run in the manuscript begins on g and adds an extra eighth note, a, at the end.
	c.46 :	25.5	a is missing ( )
	c.46 :	31.3	b
	c.46 :	48.4/49	texting: ju---di-ca----re
5.	4302 :	39-42	texting: ter-ra

Domine, Deus Meus

1.	29366:	14.1	f
2.	c.49 :	37.4	d#
	4302 :	57-58	texting: [re]-ser--vis
3.	4302 :	18.3	d
	4302 :	20	
	c.46 :	29.1	f
	c.46 :	40.4	d
	4302 :	45.1	♩♩
4.	4302 :	18.4	
	c.47 :	28.3	a b, not a
5.	4302 :	11.3/-13	texting: me------us
	29367:	47.4	♩, not ♩

Noli me proijcere

1.	4302 :	3.2	c
	4302 :	.2,3	g,f
	c.45 :	17-18	texting: "deferit," instead of "defecerit"
	c.45 :	41-42	texting: [-as] a ser-vo tu---- o
2.	c.49 :	31.2	g
	c.49 :	34.2	f
	c.49 :	38.4	a

Noli me proijcere

3.   c.46 :   17.4   ♯ is placed after the f
    c.46 :   25   texting: "me-i" [sic]
    c.46 :   37-38   texting: "ne derelinquas," instead of "declinas"
    29368:   37-38   texting: "ne derelinquas," instead of "declinas"
    29368:   81-82   texting: omits "domine"

4.   c.47 :   15.4   f
    c.47 :   32   texting: "us-que-quo," instead of "usque"
    c.47 :   64ff.   texting unclear

5.   29367:   4.1   f
    c.50 :   19.2,3   b♯,a♯
    c.50 :   19.4   g
    29367:   19.4   g

Laboravi in gemitu meo

This motet appears untexted in Add. MSS 29366-8, slightly separated from the other motets by Alfonso Ferrabosco, jun., which appear in these part-books. The cantus and bassus parts are only partially texted in Drexel MS 4302. There is no signature indicating b♭ in Drexel 4302, nonetheless b♮ is often indicated by the use of the ♯.

1.   29368:   27.3   f ♩
    29368:   28.1   ♩ ♩   ♩
                               g g, not g
    29368:   34.2/35
                40   At measure 40, a portion of 4302 has been destroyed, and 29366-8 is the only source for this brief passage of from two to five beats (depending on the part) in transcription. Strangely, however, it is at this point where 29368 and 29366 "exchange" parts, relative to 4302, until the end of the motet.

    29366:   42.rest   ♪ 𝄾 , i.e., ♩ 𝄾 , continuing like 4302 on the fourth beat.

    29366:   47.2-4   ♩ ♩ (these notes appear in the third voice)

2.   4302 :   16.6   a g
                               ♩ ♩♩, instead of ♩♩
                               e e   e
               40.3   switch of 29368 to this part

    4302 :   45.4/46   e   ♩♩

    4302 :   50.3/51   e   ♩♩
    29368:   53-end   ♩. ♩ 𝅗𝅥 , not simply 𝅗𝅥

5.   17   At measure 17, portions of the lower two voices in 4302 have been destroyed. 29367 is the only source for the bass at this point (see also m. 41).

    4302 :   22.3   e ♩

Lamentations of Jeremiah

This set of *Lamentations* by the younger Ferrabosco appears in Drexel MS 4302 complete, but basically untexted except for the cantus and incipits in the bassus. The Bodleian Music School MSS c.45 and c.50 present the cantus and bassus fully texted.

Incipit Lamentatio

5. c.50 :   11-end texting: [musical notation]
   pro---phe-----tae

Aleph

1. c.45 :   7.6   b♭
   c.45 :   8.4   f

4. 4302 :   8   [musical notation] [sic]

5. c.45 :   texting: "Aleph" not repeated

Quo modo sedet

1. c.45 :   2.4   b♭
   c.45 :   6.2   b♭

4. 4302 :   8.3   f

A portion of measures 9-10 is lost from the lower two parts in 4302.

5. 4302 :   1-3   texting: [musical notation]
                               quo mo-do se-----det
   c.50 :   1-3   texting:
                    quo mo-----do se--det

c.50 :   9-11   This is the point where 4302 is lacking. c.50 presents its own problems and variants at m. 11 (when 4302 picks up again):   [musical notation]
-tas ple-a-na po--pu-lo.

The extra beat in "ple-a-na" [sic] is accommodated by shortening the last syllable of "populo." One can only wonder how this part was performed without a correction being made—if, indeed, performance from these part-books did take place.

Princeps Provinciarum

1. c.45 :   rest   Both these part-books grant only a 𝄾 rest,
5. c.50 :   rest   instead of the 𝄼 𝄾 appearing in 4302. The structure of the piece and the nature of the text ague that this rest, whatever the value, be treated as a pause—i.e., without definite duration.

Beth

1.	c.45 :	7.3	b
	c.45 :	text	In both part-books the text is given as "Bethalem." This variant is apparently deliberate and might argue to the point that these Catholic *Lamentations* were not only private and secret, but subversive as well: the fallen Jerusalem being the Anglican "Jerusalem" (founded by Joseph of Arimethea in legend), "Bethlehem," then, would refer to the true source of the Christian spring.
5.	c.50 :	text	

Plorans Ploravit

1.	c.45 :	17.1	b
5.	c.50 :	1.4	texting: Plo---rans plo-ra-vit in noc--te .
		[4302]	Plo-rans plo-ravit in noc-----te .

Non est qui consoletur

1.	c.45 :	8.2	g
3.	4302 :	7-end	The texting, implied by a ligature in the manuscript, is as follows: cha--ris, e-ius, cha-ris e----ius.
1.	c.45 :	5	texting: "*et* omnibus charis,"
5.	c.50 :	5	not "ex."

Omnes amici

The texting of this is not clear in c.45 and c.50, or it is simply faulty in Latin usage. The text of the passage, "Omnes amici eius spreverunt eam et facti sunt illi inimici," makes plural ("illi") what should be singular ("ei"), and confuses the "inimici" by appearing to be "inamice" or "nemici" or, even, "amici" (c.45: measure 15).

1.	c.45 :	7.1	b
5.	4302 :	18	The clef changes to the tenor clef after the rest, returning to the bass clef for the next section ("Ghimel"), although without indication. This is the only time the bass sings above c', i.e., above what would be one leger line in bass clef.
	c.50 :	20.4	b♭
	c.50 :	21-end	texting: [in]-- i-mi-ce

Ghimel

1.	c.45 :		The texting indicates that the first statement of "Ghimel" ends at the conclusion of measure 6, with the word repeated in measures 7-8.

Ghimel

	4302 :	4.4	b♭
3.	4302 :	2.4	f

Migravit

1.	c.45 :	8.2	c
	c.45 :	11.2	b
	c.45 :	12.2	b
5.	4302 :	11-13	texting:

♩ ♩. ♪ ♩. ♩ ♩ ♩
nem ser---------vi-tu-tis

Hierusalem

1.	c.45 :	8.3	b
	c.45 :	12.3	b

Appendix VI

Latin Motets and Lamentations: Texts and Translations

Latin Motets

1. Ego sum resurrectio et vita
Qui credit in me, etiam si mortuus fuerit, vivet.
Et omnis qui vivit et credit in me
Non morietur in eternum.

I am the resurrection and the life:
He that believeth in me, though
he were dead, yet shall he live.
And whosoever liveth and believeth
in me shall never die.

John 11: 25-26 (King James Version)

2. O nomen Jesu, nomen dulce,
nomen Jesu, nomen delectabile
nomen Jesu, nomen confortans
Quid est enim Jesus nisi salvator
Ergo Jesu propter nomen sanctum tuum
Esto michi Jesus et salva me.

O name [of] Jesus, sweet name, delightful and comforting;
For what is Jesus if not the saviour.
Therefore, Jesus, by thy holy name
be Jesus to me and restore me.

3. Ego dixi, domine miserere mei
Sana animam meam
Quia peccavi tibi.

I said, "Lord, be merciful unto
me: Heal my soul, for I have
sinned against Thee."

Psalm 41: 4 (KJV)

4. Convertere domine usquequo
Et deprecabilis esto
Super servos tuos.

Return, O Lord.
And how long before you show
favor concerning your servants?

Psalm 90: 13

5. Ubi duo vel tres congregati fuerunt
In medio eorum sum
In nomine meo.
Dixi, domine.

Where two or three are gathered
in my name, there am I in the
midst of them.
I said, "Lord"

Matthew 18: 20 (KJV)

6. Libera me, domine,
de morte eterna,
In die illa tremenda
Quando caeli movendi sunt et terra,
Dum veneris judicare seculum
per ignem.

Deliver me, O Lord, from eternal
death on that dread day when the
heavens and earth shall be moved,
when Thou shalt come to judge the
world by fire.

Responsory from the Office of the Dead

7. Domine Deus meus
Ne queso intres in iudicium
Cum puero tuo
delicta iuventutis meae

et ignorantiae meae
Ne memineris unquam
neve in finem iratum
mea mala reserves.

Lord, my God:
Do not judge Thy child
nor, in the wrathful end,
remember the sins of my youth
and ignorance or my evil deeds.

8. Noli me proijcere a facie tua
in tempore senectutis
Et cum defecerit virtus mea
ne derelinquas me
usque ad senectum in senium
ne declinas a servo tuo.
Sed in pace recipe animam meam
et misericordias tuas
in eternum cantabo:
Domine Deus meus.

Cast me not off in the time of old age;
Forsake me not when my strength faileth.
Also when I am old and greyheaded,
O God, forsake me not.
But in peace receive my soul,
And I shall sing Thy mercies
In eternity, O Lord, my God.

Psalm 71: 9,18; Psalm 89:2 (KJV)

9. Laboravi in gemitu meo
Lavabo per singulas noctes
Stratum meum lachrimis meis rigabo.

I have labored in my moan.
Each night I shall weep and
moisten my bed with tears.

11. Tribulationem et dolorem inveni,
[et nomen Domini invocavi]

I found trouble and sorrow.
[then I called upon the name
of the Lord.]

Psalm 116: 3,4

12. O Domine
[text lacking]

O Lord, . . .

13. Fortitudo mea et laus mea Domine
Et factus est mihi in salutem
Vox exultationis et salutis
In tabernaculis justorum.

The Lord is my strength and song,
And he is become my salvation.
The voice of rejoicing and salvation
[is heard] in the tents of the
righteous.

Exodus 15: 2 (KJV)

14. Sustinuit anima mea in verbo eius;
Speravit anima mea in domino.
A custodia matutina usque ad noctem
Speret Israel in Domino.

My soul is sustained in His word
and hopes in the Lord.
From the morning watch even till
the night may Israel hope in the
Lord.

Psalm 130: 5-7

(a4)
Quare dereliquerunt me vires meae
Inundaverunt aquae super caput meum
Dixi Domine exaudi me
de lacu novissimo.

Wherefore does my strength fail and
the waters rise above my head?
I cried, "Lord, hear me," from this
extreme sea of woes.

Lamentations

1. Incipit lamentatio Jeremiae prophetae
2. Aleph

The Lamentations of Jeremiah 1:1

3. Quomodo sedet sola civitas plena populo!
   Facta est quasi vidua Domina gentium.
4. Princeps provinciarum facta est sub tributo.
5. Beth

The Lamentations of Jeremiah 1:2

6. Plorans ploravit in nocte
   Et lacrimae eius in maxillis eius.
7. Non est qui consoletur eam ex omnibus charis eius.
8. Omnes amici eius spreverunt eam,
   Et facti sunt illi inimici.
9. Ghimel

The Lamentations of Jeremiah 1:3

10. Migravit Juda propter afflictionem et multitudinem servitutis;
    Habitavit inter gentes, nec inveniet requiem.
11. Hierusalem, Hierusalem, convertere ad Dominum tuum.

The Lamentations of Jeremiah 1:1-3

Here begins the lamentation of the prophet Jeremiah:
Aleph: How does the city sit solitary that was full of people! How is she become as a widow that was the queen of nations and chief among provinces; how is she become tributary.
Beth: She weeps sore in the night, and her tears are on her cheeks. Among all her lovers she hath none to comfort her: all her friends have dealt treacherously with her; they are become her enemies.
Ghimel: Judah is gone into captivity because of affliction and great servitude; She dwelleth among the heathen, she findeth no rest.
Jerusalem, Jerusalem, Return to thy Lord.

Bibliography

Manuscripts

Cambridge: Fitzwilliam Museum MS 52.D.25 ["John Bull"]
Carlisle: Carlisle Cathedral Library, Bishop Smith's Partbooks
London: British Museum [Library] MSS
        Add. 10337
        Add. 11586
        Add. 15117
        Add. 24665
        Add. 29366-8
        Add. 29372-7
        Add. 31418
        Egerton 3665
        Royal App. 63
New York: Public Library, MS Drexel 4302
Oxford: Bodleian Library, MSS mus. sch. c.45-50
        Christ Church Library MS 439
Tenbury Wells: St. Michael's College, MSS 1018, 1019

Primary Sources and Editions

Burney, Charles. *A General History of Music from the Earliest Ages to the Present Period* [London, 1776]. Dover reprint; Frank Mercer, editor, 1935.

Coperario, Giovanni [John Cooper]. *Rules How to Compose* [c. 1610]. Facsimile edition, edited by Manfred Bukofzer. Los Angeles, 1952.

Ferrabosco, Alfonso. *Ayres*. London: Thomas Browne, 1609.

_____. *Ayres*. [1609]. Facsimile edition, edited by David Greer. Volume 5 in *The English Lute Songs, 1597-1632; A Collection of Facsimile Reprints*. Menstion, England, 1971.

_____. *Ayres* [1609]. Edited by E.H. Fellowes, in *The English School of Lutenist Song Writers*, second series, XVI. London, 1927.

_____. *Manuscript Songs*. Edited by Ian Spink, in *The English Lute-Songs*, second series, XIX. London, 1966.

Hawkins, Sir John. *A General History of the Science and Practice of Music* [London, 1776]. Reprint of the 1853 edition, newly edited by Charles Cudworth. 2 vols. New York, 1963.

Jonson, Ben. *The Complete Masques*. Edited by Stephen Orgel. New Haven, 1969.

Leighton, Sir William. *Teares and Lamentaciones of a Sorrowful Soule* [1614].
Morley, Thomas. *A Plain and Easy Introducation to Practical Music* (1597). Edited by Alec Harmon. London, 1952.

Books and Articles

Andrews, H.K. *The Technique of Byrd's Vocal Polyphony.* London, 1966.
———. "Transposition of Byrd's Vocal Polyphony." *Music & Letters* 43(1962): 25-37.
Anglo, Sidney. "The Evolution of the Early Tudor Disguising, Pageant, and Mask." *Renaissance Drama*, n.s. 1(1968): 3-44.
Arkwright, G.E.P. "Alphonso Ferrabosco the Younger." In *Studies in Music*, edited by Robin Grey, pp. 199-214. London, 1901.
———. "'Master Alfonso' and Queen Elizabeth." *ZIMG* 8(1907): 271-277.
———. "Notes on the Ferrabosco Family." *The Musical Antiquary* 3(1911/1912): 220-228 and 4(1912/13): 42-54.
———. "Un compositore italiano alla corte di Elisabetta." *Rivista Musicale Italiana* 4(1897): 1-16.
Attridge, Derek. *Well-Weighed Syllables: Elizabethan Verse in Classical Metres.* Cambridge, 1974.
A Book of Masques, in Honour of Allardyce Nicoll, edited by T.J.B. Spencer and Stanley Wells. Cambridge, 1967.
Bontoux, Germaine. *La chanson en Angleterre au temps d'Elisabeth.* Oxford, 1936.
Bowden, William R. *The English Dramatic Lyric, 1603-1642.* New Haven, 1951.
Boyd, Morrison Comegys. *Elizabethan Music and Music Criticism.* 2d ed. Philadelphia, 1962.
Brett, Philip. "The English Consort Song, 1570-1625," *Proceedings of the Royal Musical Association* 88(1961): 73-88.
———. "The Songs of William Byrd." Unpublished Ph.D. dissertation, Cambridge University, 1965.
———. "Word-Setting in the Songs of Byrd." *Proceedings of the Royal Musical Association* 98(1971): 47-64.
Brotanek, Rudolf. *Die englischen Maskenspiele.* Vienna, 1902.
Chambers, Sir Edmund K. *The Elizabethan Stage.* 4 vols. Oxford, 1923.
Crum, Margaret. *First-Line Index of English Poetry 1500-1800 in Manuscripts of the Bodleian Library, Oxford.* 2 vols. Oxford, 1969.
Cutts, John P. "Ben Jonson's Masque *The Vision of Delight.*" *Notes & Queries*, n.s. 3(1956): 64-67.
———. "Early Seventeenth-Century Lyrics at St. Michael's College." *Music & Letters* 37(1956): 220-233.
———. "Jacobean Masque and Stage Music." *Music & Letters* 35(1954): 185-200.
———. *Musique de scène de la troupe de Shakespeare.* Paris, 1959.
———. "Robert Johnson: King's Musician in His Majesty's Public Entertainment." *Music & Letters* 35(1955): 110-125.
———. *Roger Smith, His Book: Bishop Smith's Part-Song Books in Carlisle Cathedral Library.* Publications of the American Institute of Musicology, Miscellanea, vol. 4. Rome, 1972.
———. "Le rôle de la musique dans les masques de Ben Jonson." In *Fêtes de la Renaisssance*, edited by Jean Jacquot. 2 vols. Paris, 1956.
———. "Seventeenth-Century Illustration of Three Masques by Jonson." *Comparative Drama* 6(1973/74): 125-134.
———. *Seventeenth-Century Songs and Lyrics.* Columbia, Mo., 1959.

Bibliography

Cyr, Mary. "A Seventeenth-Century Source of Ornamentation for Voice and Viol: British Museum MS Egerton 2971." *Royal Musical Association Research Chronicle* 9(1971): 53-72.
Dart, Thurston. "Rôle de la danse dans l' 'ayre' anglais." In *Musique et Poésie au XVIe Siècle*, edited by Jean Jacquot, pp. 203-209. Paris, 1954.
▬▬▬▬▬. "Two New Documents Relating to the Royal Music, 1584-1605." *Music & Letters* 45(1964): 16-19.
▬▬▬▬▬, and William Coates, eds. *Jacobean Consort Music. Musica Britannica*, vol. 9. London, 1955.
Day, Cyrus L., and E.B. Murrie. *English Song-Books, 1651-1702*. London, 1940.
Doughtie, Eward. "Ferrabosco and Jonson's 'The Houre-glasse'." *Renaissance Quarterly* 22(1969): 148-150.
▬▬▬▬▬. *Lyrics from English Ayres, 1596-1622*. Cambridge, Mass., 1970.
Duckles, Vincent. "The English Musical Elegy of the Late Renaissance." In *Aspects of Medieval and Renaissance Music: A Birthday Offering to Gustave Reese*, edited by Jan LaRue, pp. 134-153. New York, 1966.
▬▬▬▬▬. "English Song and the Challenge of Italian Monody." In *Words to Music, Papers on English Seventeenth-Century Song*. Los Angeles, 1967.
▬▬▬▬▬. "Florid Embellishment in English Song of the Late Sixteenth and Early Seventeenth Centuries." *Annales Musicologiques* 5(1957): 329-345.
▬▬▬▬▬. "John Gamble's Common-place Book: A Critical Edition of New York Public Library MS Drexel 4257." Unpublished Ph.D. dissertation, University of Calfornia at Berkeley, 1953.
▬▬▬▬▬. "The Gamble Manuscript as a Source of Continuo Song in England." *Journal of the American Musicological Society* 1(1948): 23-40.
▬▬▬▬▬. "Jacobean Theatre Songs." *Music & Letters* 34(1953): 88-89.
▬▬▬▬▬. "The Music for the Lyrics in Early Seventeenth-Century English Drama: A Bibliography of the Primary Sources." In *Music in English Renaissance Drama*, edited by J.H. Long, pp. 117-160. Lexington, Ky., 1968.
Einstein, Alfred. *The Italian Madrigal*. 3 vols. Translated by A.H. Krappe, Roger Sessions, and Oliver Strunk. Princeton, 1949.
Emslie, Macdonald. "Nicolas Lanier's Innovations in English Song." *Music & Letters* 41(1960): 13-27.
Evans, Willa McClung. *Ben Jonson and Elizabethan Music.* Lancaster, Pa.,
▬▬▬▬▬. *Henry Lawes, Musician and Friend to Poets.* New York, 1940.
Ewbank, Ingo-Stina. "The Eloquence of Masques: A Retrospective View of Masque Criticism." *Renaissance Drama*, n.s. 1(1968): 307-327.
Federhofer, Hellmut. "Matthia Ferrabosco." *Musica Disciplina* 7(1953): 205-233.
Fellowes, Edmund H. *Madrigal Verse, 1588-1632*. 1920. 3d ed., rev. by F.W. Sternfeld with David Greer. New York, 1968.
Fortune, Nigel. "Italian Secular Monody from 1600 to 1635: an Introductory Survey." *Musical Quarterly* 39(1953).
▬▬▬▬▬. "Italian Seventeenth-Century Singing." *Music & Letters* 35(1954).
▬▬▬▬▬. "Sigismondo d'India: An Introduction to his Life and Works." *Proceedings of the Royal Musical Association* 81(1954).
▬▬▬▬▬. "Solo Song and Cantata." In *New Oxford History of Music*, vol. IV, pp. 125-217. Oxford, 1968.
Fuller, David. "The Jonsonian Masque and its Music." *Music & Letters* 54(1973): 440-453.
Furniss, W. Todd. "Ben Jonson's Masques." In *Three Studies in the Renaissance.* New Haven, Conn., 1958.

Gombosi, Otto. "Some Musical Aspects of the English Court Mask." *Journal of the American Musicological Society* 1(1948): 3-19.
Gordon, D.J. *The Renaissance Imagination.* Essays collected and edited by Stephen Orgel. Berkeley, Calif., 1975.
Greer, David. "The Part-Songs of the English Lutenists." *Proceedings of the Royal Musical Association* 94(1968): 97-110.
Harding, D.W. *Words into Rhythm.* Cambridge, 1976.
Hart, Eric Ford. "Introduction to Henry Lawes." *Music & Letters* 32(1951): 217-225, 328-344.
Hollander, John. "Donne and the Limits of Lyric." In *John Donne: Essays in Celebration,* edited by A.J. Smith, pp. 259-272. London, 1972.
————. *The Untuning of the Sky: Ideas of Music in English Poetry, 1500-1700.* Princeton, N.J., 1961.
Ing, Catherine. *Elizabethan Lyrics.* London, 1951.
Joiner, Mary. "British Museum Add MS 15117: An Index, Commentary and Bibliography." *Royal Musical Association Research Chronicle* 7(1969): 51-109.
Jones, Edward Huws. "The Theorbo and Continuo Practice in the Early English Baroque." *Galpin Society Journal* 25(1972): 67-72.
Kerman, Joseph. "Byrd's Motets: Chronology and Canon." *Journal of the American Musicological Society* 14(1961).
————. *The Elizabethan Madrigal.* New York, 1962.
————. "The Elizabethan Motet: a Study of Texts for Music." In *Studies in the Renaissance* 9(1962): 273-305.
Knowlton, Jean. "Some Dances of the Stuart Masque Identified and Analyzed." 2 vols. Unpublished Ph.D. dissertation, Indiana University, 1966.
Lafontaine, H.C. de. *The King's Musick.* London, 1909.
Lefkowitz, Murray. *Trois Masques à la cour de Charles Ier d'Angleterre.* Paris, 1970.
————. *William Lawes.* London, 1960.
LeHuray, Peter. *Music and the Reformation in England, 1549-1660.* New York, 1967.
Livi, Giovanni. "The Ferrabosco Family." *The Musical Antiquary* 4(1912/13): 121-142.
Mazzaro, Jerome. *Transformations in the Renaissance English Lyric.* Ithaca, N.Y., 1970.
McGrady, Richard. "The English Solo Song from William Byrd to Henry Lawes." Unpublished Ph.D. dissertation, University of Manchester, 1963.
————. "Henry Lawes and the Concept of 'Just Note and Accent'." *Music & Letters* 50(1969): 86-102.
Meagher, John C. *Method and Meaning in Jonson's Masques.* Notre Dame, Ind., 1966.
Mendel, Alfred. "Pitch in the 16th and early 17th Centuries." *Musical Quarterly* 34(1948): 28-45, 199-221, 336-357, 575-593.
Meyer, Ernst Hermann. *English Chamber Music.* London, 1946.
————. *Die mehrstimmige Spielmusik des 17. Jahrhunderts in Nord- und Mitteleuropa.* Cassel, 1934.
Nagel, Wilibald. *Annalen der englischen Hofmusik von der Zeit Heinrichs VIII bis zum Tod Karls I. Beilage zu den Monatsheften für Musikgeschichte,* Bd. 26. Leipzig, 1894.
Nichols, John. *The Progresses of King James the First.* 4 vols. London, 1828.
Nicoll, Allardyce. *Stuart Masque and the Renaissance Stage.* New York, 1938.
Olshausen, Ulrich. *Das lautenbegleitete Sololied in England um 1600.* Frankfurt, 1963.
Orgel, Stephen. *The Illusion of Power: Political Theater in the English Renaissance.* Berkeley, Calif., 1975.
————. *The Jonsonian Masque.* Cambridge, Mass., 1966.
————. and Roy C. Strong. *Inigo Jones: The Theatre of the Stuart Court.* 2 vols. London, 1973.

Pattison, Bruce. *The Music and Poetry of the English Renaissance.* London, 1948.
Reyher, Paul. *Les masques anglais.* Paris, 1909.
Sabol, Andrew. *Four Hundred Songs and Dances From the Stuart Masque.* Providence, R.I., 1978.
Schofield, Bertram, and R.T. Dart. "Tregian's Anthology." *Music & Letters* 32(1951): 205-216.
Shedlock, J.S. "André Maugars." In *Studies in Music,* edited by Robin Grey, pp. 215-232. New York, 1901.
Smith, Hallett. *Elizabethan Poetry.* Cambridge, Mass., 1952.
Smith, James Gordon. "John Dowland: A Reappraisal of his Ayres." Unpublished D.M.A. dissertation, University of Illinois, 1973.
Spink, Ian. "Angelo Notari and his 'Prime Musiche Nuove'." *Monthly Musical Record* 87(1957): 168-177.
_____. "Campion's Entertainment at Brougham Castle, 1617." In *Music in English Renaissance Drama,* edited by John H. Long, pp. 57-74. Lexington, Ky., 1968.
_____. "English Cavalier Songs, 1620-1660." *Proceedings of the Royal Musical Association* 86(1960): 61-78.
_____. "English Seventeenth-Century Dialogues." *Music & Letters* 38(1957): 155-163.
_____. *English Song: Dowland to Purcell.* New York, 1974.
_____. *English Songs, 1625-1660.* Musica Britannica, vol. 33. London, 1971.
_____. "Lanier in Italy." *Music & Letters* 41(1960): 13-27.
_____. "The Musicians of Queen Henrietta-Maria: Some Notes and References in the English State Papers." *Acta Musicologica* 36(1964): 177-182.
_____. "Sources of English Song 1620-1660: A Survey." *Miscellanea Musicologie* 1 (1966): 117-136.
Stevens, John. *Music and Poetry in the Early Tudor Court.* London, 1961.
Strong, Roy C. *Splendor at Court: The Renaissance Spectacle and Illusion.* London, 1973.
Tovey, Sir Donald. "Words and Music." In *Seventeenth-Century Studies Presented to Sir Herbert Grierson.* London, 1938.
Ulrich, Ernest. "Die Musik in Ben Jonson's Maskenspielen und Entertainments." *Shakespeare Jahrbuch.* 73(1937): 53-84.
Vaught, Raymond. "The Fancies of Alfonso Ferrabosco II." 2 vols. Unpublished Ph.D. dissertation, Stanford University, 1959.
_____. "Mersenne's Unknown English Viol Player." *Galpin Society Journal* 17(1964): 17-23.
Walker, D.P. "Musical Humanism in the 16th and Early 17th Centuries." *Music Review* 2(1941): 1-13, 111-121, 220-227, 282-308; 3(1942): 55-71.
Walker, Ernest. "An Oxford Book of Fancies." *The Musical Antiquary* 3(1911/12): 65-73.
Walls, Peter. "Music in the English Masque in the First Half of the Seventeenth Century." Unpublished Ph.D. dissertation, Oxford University, 1978.
Warlock, Peter [Philip Heseltine]. *The English Ayre.* London, 1926.
Welsford, Enid. *The Court Masque.* Cambridge, 1927.
Westup, Sir Jack. "Domestic Music under the Stuarts." *Proceedings of the Royal Musical Association* 68(1942): 19-53.
_____. "Foreign Musicians in Stuart England." *Musical Quarterly* 27(1941): 70-89.
Willetts, Pamela. "Sir Nicholas LeStrange and John Jenkins." *Music & Letters* 42(1961): 30-43.
_____. "Sir Nicholas LeStrange's Collection of Masque Music." *British Museum Quarterly* 29(1964/65): 78-81.
Woodfill, Walter L. *Musicians in English Society from Elizabeth to Charles I.* Princeton, 1953.
Wulstan, David. "The Problem of Pitch in Sixteenth-century English Vocal Music." *Proceedings of the Royal Musical Association* 93(1966).

Index

An "(F)" following a title entry indicates that the music is by Alfonso Ferrabosco, the Younger.

Agricola, Alexander, 254
Agucchi, Giorgio, 8
"Aleph" (F), 256, 257, 258, 260, 262
"All you forsaken lovers" (F), 98-101
Allin, John, 157
Amaltei, Girolamo, 100
"Amarilli mia bella" (Caccini), 180, 190
Anne (queen of England), 156
Anthems. *See* Ferrabosco, Alfonso, the Younger, music, anthems
Ariosto, Ludovico, 36
Arkwright, G. E. P., 2-3, 229
Ascham, Roger, 40
Aubrey, John, 21
"Aupre de vous" (F), 274 n.60
Awsterwyke, Gomer van, 2, 17-18, 30, 273 n.49

Bacon, Francis, 40
Baif, Antoine de, 37
Baldwin, John, 11, 255
Ballard, Robert, 274 n.60
Balthasaris de Simonibus, Susanna, 10, 16
Banqueting House, Whitehall, 111-12, 117, 124
Barre, Leonardo, 7
Bassano family, 1
Bates, Thomas, 277 n.95
Bentivoglio, Anna, 270 n.10
Bentivoglio family, 1, 3, 7, 8, 269 n.4 and n.7
"Beth" (F), 256, 257, 258, 262
Boiardo family, 7
Bologna, 2-8, 270 n.10
Bravo, Giuseppe Torres Martinez, 14
"Bring away this sacred tree" (Lanier), 285 n.7
Browne, John, 21

Bull, John, MS, 55, 99-100, 200
Bunckley [i.e., Buncle], George, 28
Burney, Charles, 2, 51-52, 58, 59, 287 n.6
Burrell, William, 22
Busnois, Antoine, 253
Byrd, William: and Ferrabosco, 10-11; *Lamentations,* 254, 258; motets, 216, 218; musical style, 217, 223, 224, 238, 261; songs, 42-44, 58, 222

Caccini, Giulio: "Amarilli mia bella," 180, 190; madrigals, 36, 42; *Le Nuove Musiche,* 35-36, 42; songs, 55, 56, 57, 190
Cambrai, 253
Campeggi, Eleonora, 6, 8
Campion, Thomas: and Ferrabosco, 20, 52-54, 268; elegies, 22; masque songs, 117, 120; musical style, 36, 129, 180; "My sweetest Lesbia, let us live and love," 107; *Observations in the Art of English Poesie,* 37-39, 41, 101; *Somerset Masque,* 285 n.7; songs, 44, 57; "Young and simple though I am," 104-6
Carpentras [i.e., Genet, Elzéar], 254
Carr, Robert (Duke of Somerset), 276 n.76
Catullus, 107
Cecil, Sir William, 10
Chanson, 44, 94, 95
Charles I (king of England), 1, 20, 22, 30, 157
Charles of Guise (Cardinal of Lorraine), 8, 13, 274 n.59
"Chevy Chase," 61
Child, William, 277 n.95
Cimatoris, Michael, 7

Ciotti, G. B., 183
Cobham, Sir Henry, 14
Coke, Sir John, 277 n.90
Il Combattimento di Tancredi e Clorinda, 191, 199
"Come and let us live, me deare" (Crashaw), 284 n.6
"Come away, come away" (F), 72, 125-29
"Come home, my troubled thoughts" (F), 71-72, 126
"Come Laura come letts live and love," 284 n.6
"Come let us sound with melody," 38-39
"Come, my Celia" (F), 52, 95, 106-10, 284 n.6
Como (Cardinal of), 13-14
Contrari, Alfonso (Count of Ferrara), 6, 8
"Convertere Domine usquequo" (F), 229-34
Coperario, John: and Prince Charles, 20, 22, 23, 30, 276 n.78; musical style, 29, 44; songs, 55, 117, 276 n.76; *Songs of Mourning,* 22, 52
Corkine, William, 284 n.6
Cowper. See Coperario, John
Crashaw, Richard, 284 n.6
Crequillon, Thomas, 273 n.40
Crescenzi (Cardinal), 7
Cunningham, David, 27
Cutts, John P., 55, 164

Dandino, 13-14, 17-18
Daniel, John, 41, 117
Daniel, Samuel, 41
Dante, 36
"Dear, when to thee" (F), 92-94
Dering, Richard, 220, 229
d'Este, Lucrezia, 270 n.10
Dialogs, 199-201. See also Ferrabosco, Alfonso, the Younger, music, dialogs
"Doe but consider this small dust" (F), 100
"Domine, Deus meus" (F), 234-37, 241-43
Donne, John, 34, 39-40, 41, 52, 63-70, 94, 279 n.10, 286 n.12
Doughtie, Edward, 100, 180, 286 n.12
Dowland, John: and Burney, 51; and Ferrabosco, 268; *First Book of Songs or Ayres,* 42, 43-44, 101; "In darkness let me dwell," 57, 58, 209; "Lachrymae," 73, 91; songs, 42-44, 52, 55, 57, 58, 60, 94, 95, 121, 180
Dowland family, 1
"Drown not with tears" (F), 74-76
DuBellay, Joachim, 8, 36-37
Duckles, Vincent, 58
Dufay, Guillaume, 253

Earle, Giles, MS, 56

East, Michael, 216; *Medulla Musicke,* 273 n.43
"Ego dixi, Domine" (F), 215, 229-34, 248
"Ego sum resurrectio" (F), 221-29
Einstein, Alfred, 44
Elizabeth I (queen of England), 1-2, 3, 8-10, 12-14, 15, 17-18, 30, 58, 216, 254
Elizabeth Rogers Virginal Book, 56, 99
Emanuele, Carlo (Duke of Savoy), 2, 14-15
"Ero cosi dicea" (F), 274 n.60
Essex (Earl of), 19, 115, 276 n.76
"Eterni numi" (F), 186-89, 192
"The expectation" (Donne), 63-70, 279 n.10

"Fain I would, but O I dare not" (F), 95-97, 98
"Fair cruel nymph" (F), 203-6
Fancies, 2, 18, 30, 215, 275 n.71, 276 n.80
Farnese (Cardinal), 9
Fava family, 7
Fellowes, Edmund H., 55, 75, 202, 287 n.6
Ferrabosco, Alfonso, the Elder: biography, 1-2, 3, 7-18, 20, 29; music, 55, 183, 229, 248-49, 254, 255
Ferrabosco, Alfonso, the Younger
  biography, 1, 2, 15, 17-31, 267-68
  music
    anthems, 2, 249-51
    Ayres of 1609, 2, 19, 20, 30, 51-52, 54, 57-58, 64, 72, 95, 123, 132, 145-51, 157, 180, 200, 202, 203, 207, 209, 279 n.10, 281 n.3
    chanson, 274 n.60
    dialogs, 52, 56, 199-214
    fancies, 2, 18, 30, 215, 275 n.71, 276 n.80
    in nomines, 2, 30, 275 n.71
    Italian songs, 56, 57, 118, 120, 124, 179-98, 267
    Lamentations, 215-16, 217, 218, 219, 222, 225, 226, 253-66
    lessons, 2, 21
    madrigals, 2, 6, 15, 274 n.59 and n.60
    masque songs, 56, 57, 87, 114-78, 179, 267, 276 n.76
    motets, 2, 30, 215-51, 257, 267, 275 n.71, 276 n.80
    songs and ayres, 2, 30, 44, 51-58, 82, 94-95, 124, 215, 267-68
    viol music, 2, 30
Ferrabosco family, 1-31, 269 n.4, 270 n.83; Alessandro, 3; Alfonso (III), 22, 24, 28, 277 n.97; Anfione, 12, 16, 275 n.65; Annibale, 3-4; Carlo Emanuele, 15; Caterina, 15;

Index

Cecchino, 3; Domenico, 3; Domenico Maria, 1, 3, 6-8, 9, 10, 269 n.7; Elizabeth, 28, 278 n.98; Ellen, 23, 28-29, 277 n.97; Guidobaldo, 8, 16; Henry, 22, 24, 28, 277 n.97; Innocenzo, 7; John, 28, 277 n.97; Katherine, 28; Lodovico, 7; Mary, 28; Mostyn, 29; Susanna, 28
Ferrara, 6, 8, 270 n.10, 271 n.20
Ficino, Marsilio, 133-34, 141
Filmer, Sir Robert, 54
"Fly from the world" (F), 87-92
Fornari, Matteo, 271 n.20
"Fortitudo mea" (F), 244, 246-47
"Fuerent mihi" (Ferrabosco, the Elder), 248-49

Gabrieli, Giovanni, 240
Gagliardello family, 1
Gallus, Jacobus, 254
Gambara (Cardinal), 7
Gamble, John, 61
Gardane, Antonio, 6
Gascoigne, George, 40
Gaspari, Gaetano, 3
"Gather ye rosebuds while ye may" (Herrick), 284 n.6
Genet, Elzéar, 254
"Gentle knights" (F), 121, 161-66
Gesualdo, Carlo: madrigals, 192; "Moro lasso," 260
Gherus, Ramitius, 100
"Ghimel" (F), 256, 257, 258, 260, 264-65
Gibbons, Orlando, 43, 216, 218, 261
Giles, Thomas, 151, 157
Giles Earle, MS, 56
Giulio III (Pope), 7
Gombert, Nicolas, 10-11
Gordon, D. J., 133-34, 141
Grierson, H. J. C., 40
Gual: Quin, 21
Guarini, Giovanni Battista, 190-91; *Il Pastor Fido,* 55, 183; *Rime,* 180
Guidobaldo della Rovere (Duke of Urbino), 6, 270 n.10

"Had those that dwell in error foul" (F), 141-44
Haddington Masque (F), 19, 55, 115, 121, 123-24, 151-56, 160, 165, 180
Handel, George Friedrich, "For unto us a child is born," 288 n.16
Handl (Gallus), Jacob, 254
Harmonic practice, 47-49, 94
Harmony, 141-43

Harvey, Gabriel, 37, 40
Hawkins, Sir John, 29
"Heav'n, since thou art" (F), 52, 76-79, 87
Henry (Earl of Southampton), 21
Henry (prince of England), 2, 18-20, 22, 28, 29-30, 52, 115, 145, 149, 161, 216
Henry VIII (king of England), 22, 254
Herne, Hierome, 151
Hero and Leander, 44, 63, 118, 124, 198
Herbert, Philip (Earl of Montgomery), 277 n.90
Herbert, Philip (fourth Earl of Pembroke), 22, 30
Herrick, Robert, 284 n.6
Hertford (Earl of), 22, 30, 31, 276 n.78
Heseltine, Philip [i.e., Warlock, Peter], 2, 56-57, 58, 60
Heybourne, Sir Ferdinando [i.e., Richardsonus, Ferdinandus], 10, 273 n.39
"Hierusalem." See "Jerusalem"
Hilton, John, 199
Hingston, John, 277 n.95
Hollander, John, 66-70, 109-10, 212
"The houre-glasse" (Jonson), 99-101
"How near to good" (F), 125, 172-78
Howard, Lady Frances, 19, 115, 276 n.76
Hymenaie (F), 19, 20, 114, 115

"I am a lover" (F), 97-98
"If all the ages of the Earth" (F), 117, 120, 121, 157-60, 161, 177, 289 n.6
"If all these cupids" (F), 120, 132-33, 134-36, 138-41
"In darkness let me dwell" (Dowland), 57, 58, 209
"In death, no man remembreth thee" (F), 250-51
In nomines, 2, 30, 275 n.71
"In thee, O Lord, I put my trust" (F), 249
"Incipit Lamentatio" (F), 256, 257, 258, 260
India, Sigismondo d', 57, 190
Ing, Catherine, 36, 41
Innocenzo del Monte (Cardinal), 7
Inquisition, 9-10
"Io mi son giovinetta" (F), 6; Palestrina mass, 6
Irish Masque, 276 n.76
"It was no policy" (F), 132-33, 135-36, 138-41

James I (king of England), 2, 22, 29, 113, 114, 115, 118, 130, 134, 145, 149, 276 n.76
Jenkins, John, 17, 28, 51

"Jerusalem, Jerusalem" (F), 218, 245, 256, 257, 258, 266
John Bull MS, 55, 99-100, 200
Johnson, Robert, 55, 117, 180, 199
Jones, Inigo, 19-20, 29-30, 31, 111, 116, 151
Jones, Robert, 54, 55
Jonson, Ben: and Ferrabosco, 1, 2, 19-20, 21, 29, 51-53, 216; and poetry, 41; "Come away, come away," 125; "Come, my Celia," 106-10, 284 n.6; "Doe but consider," 100; *Haddington's Masque,* 19, 151-52; "The houre-glasse," 99-101; "How near to good," 174-75; *Irish Masque,* 276 n.76; *Love Freed from Ignorance and Folly,* 19, 161, 166, 174-75; *Lovers Made Men,* 124, 285 n.7; *Masque of Augurs,* 19; *Masque of Beautie,* 19, 132, 133, 141; *Masque of Blacknesse,* 19; *Masque of Queens,* 19, 156-57; *Oberon,* 19, 161, 164; *The Under-Wood,* 100; *Volpone,* 106-10, 284 n.6; "Weep no more," 285 n.7
Josquin des Prez, 271 n.20

Kerman, Joseph, 3, 274 n.59
Killegrew, Tom, 61
King's Musicians and Musick, 1, 18, 22, 23, 28, 277 n.97

La Hele, Georges de, 14
La Rue, Pierre de, 254
"Laboravi in gemitu meo" (F), 244-45
"Lachrymae" (Dowland), 73, 91
"Lacrimar sempre il sommo diletto" (F), 194-98
"Lagrime d'amante al sepolcro dell'amante" (Monteverdi), 199
Lamentations of Jeremiah the Prophet, 253-55; (F), 215-16, 217, 218, 219, 222, 225, 226, 255-66
Lanier, Andrea, 23
Lanier, Innocent, 22, 28
Lanier, Nocholas, 1, 24, 277 n.97; "Bring away this sacred tree," 285 n.7; *Hero and Leander,* 44, 63, 118, 124, 198; "Like hermit poore," 61-63, 94; *Lovers Made Men,* 124, 285 n.7; *Masque of Augurs,* 19; masque songs, 117-19, 124, 276 n.76; other songs, 55, 120, 199; "Young and simple though I am," 104
Lanier family, 1
Lassus, Orlando, 10-11, 216, 254, 273 n.40

Lawes, Henry: and Burney, 51; dialogs, 199-200, 201; songs, 118, 198, 268
Lawes, William: and Burney, 51; and Coperario, 22, 276 n.78; music, 29, 118, 198, 199, 268
Lawes family, 1
Leighton, Sir William, 2, 22, 249
LeRoy, Adrian, 274 n.60
Lessons, 2, 21
"Libera me" (F), 234-41, 248
"Like hermit poore" (F), 51, 52, 58-61, 65, 66, 87, 94; Lanier, 61-63, 94
Livi, Giovanni, 2-3, 269 n.4 and n.7
"Lo! In a vale" (F), 82-87, 94, 191
Locke, Matthew, 277 n.95
Lord Dudley's Master of the Horse, 9
Lorenzo (Cardinal), 6
Love Freed from Ignorance and Folly (F), 19, 55, 116, 122-23, 125, 161, 166-78, 183, 289 n.4
Lovers Made Men, 124, 285 n.7
Lowe, Edward, 61
Lupo, John, 273 n.49
Lupo family, 1
Lydiard, Hugh, 22

Macrobius, 141, 286 n.12
Madrigals. *See* Ferrabosco, Alfonso, the Younger, music, madrigals
Magnani, Vicenzo, 270 n.16
Malvasia family, 7
Manuscripts
    Cambridge, Fitzwilliam Museum, MS 52.D: 55, 99-100, 200
    Carlisle, Cathedral Library: 55, 99-101
    Cassino, Abbey of Montecassino, Codex 871: 253
    Chicago, Newberry Library, MS Case VM 1620 F36a: 281 n.3
    Dublin, Trinity College, MS f.5.13: 55
    Edinburgh, Library, MS La.III.483: 284 n.4
    Florence, Biblioteca Riccardiana, Codex 2794: 253
    London, British Museum, MSS Additional 10337: 56, 99; 11586: 56; 15117: 56; 11608: 284 n.4; 24665: 56; 29366-8: 215-16, 244; 29372-5: 248; 29372-7: 215; 29396: 61
    London, British Museum, Egerton 3665: 248, 276 n.80
    London, British Museum, MS K.8.h.2: 281 n.3
    London, British Museum, Royal Music Library, MS 24.D.2: 273 n.40

London, Royal College of Music, MS
 I.G.41: 281 n.3
New York, New York Public Library,
 MS Drexel 4302 (Tregian's Sambrooke Book): 215-16, 221, 226,
 244, 246, 255, 274 n.59, 276 n.80;
 4257 n.15: 61
Oxford, Bodleian, MS Don.c.57: 284
 n.6
Oxford, Bodleian, MSS Music School
 c.45-50: 215, 255; f.575: 64
Oxford, Christ Church, MSS 78-82: 274
 n.59; 439: 54, 123, 154, 180;
 979-983: 255
San Marino, California, Huntington
 Library, MS 59751: 281 n.3
Tenbury Wells, St. Michael's College,
 MSS 1018 and 1019: 55, 161, 166,
 169, 179, 180, 183
Washington, D.C., Folger Shakespeare
 Library, MS 10827: 281 n.3
Marenzio, Luca, 190, 273 n.40
Masque of Augurs (F), 19, 115, 116
Masque of Beautie (F), 19, 115, 120, 129-44, 145, 146, 149, 167
Masque of Blacknesse (F), 19, 72, 115, 125, 129, 133-35
Masque of Cupid, 276 n.76
Masque of Flowers, 276 n.76
Masque of Queens (F), 19, 116, 117, 120, 121, 156-60, 161, 177, 289 n.6
Masques, 111-16, 124. *See also Haddington Masque; Hero and Leander; Hymenaie; Irish Masque; Love Freed from Ignorance and Folly; Lovers Made Men; Masque of Augurs; Masque of Beautie; Masque of Blacknesse; Masque of Cupid; Masque of Flowers; Masque of Queens; Oberon; Somerset Masque*
Maugars, André, 29
Medulla Musicke, 273 n.43
Mersenne, Marin, 29
Middleton, Thomas, 276 n.76
"Migravit" (F), 256, 257, 258, 264-65
Monte, Philippe de, 273 n.40
Montemayor, Jorge de, 97
Monteverdi, Claudio: *Il Combattimento di Tancredi e Clorinda,* 191, 199;
 "Lagrime d'amante al sepolcro dell'amante," 199; musical style, 57, 180, 190, 206, 216-17; *L'Orfeo,* 192, 199; "Sfogava con le stelle," 183; "Si ch'io vorrei morire," 183
Montgomery (Earl of), 277 n.90
Morandi, Camillo, 270 n.8

Morley, Thomas: and Ferrabosco, 11, 15, 229, 280 n.15; musical ideas, 44, 219, 224, 234, 273 n.44; *Plaine and Easie Introduction,* 54
"Moro lasso" (Gesualdo), 260
Morris, Brian, 40, 66
Motets, 254. *See also* Ferrabosco, Alfonso, the Younger, music, motets
Mundy, John, 254
Musicians, King's, 1, 18, 22, 23, 28, 277 n.97
"My deerest mistresse, let us live and love" (Corkine), 284 n.6
"My sweetest Lesbia, let us live and love" (Campion), 107
Myriell, Thomas, 54, 215

"Nay, nay you must not stay" (F), 161-64, 167
Newcastle (Duchess of), 29
"Noli me" (F), 234-35, 241-43
"Non est" (F), 256, 258, 263-64
Notaries public, 8, 16, 270 n.8
Novelli, Giulia, 6, 8
Novelli, Guido ("dall'Arpa"), 6
Le Nuove Musiche, 35-36, 42

"O crudel'Amarilli" (F), 190-94
"O Domine" (F), 215-16, 244-46
"O eyes, O mortal stars" (F), 55, 180-83, 184
"O Lord, come pity my distress" (F), 249-50
"O nomen Jesu" (F), 216, 217, 221-29, 245
Oberon (F), 19, 55, 116, 161-67, 183
"Occhi, stelle mortali" (F), 180-83, 184
Ockeghem, Johannes, 253
"Oh! What a fault" (F), 166-70, 177, 289 n.4
Olshausen, Ulrich, 180
"Omnes amici" (F), 219, 256-57, 258, 263-64
"Or l'odiato nome" (F), 194
L'Orfeo, 192, 199
Orgel, Stephen, 111-12
Orlandini, Vincenzo, 16
Orpheus, 118

Paleotti (Cardinal), 13
Paleotti family, 7
Palestrina, Giovanni Pierluigi da, and Catholic Church, 7; "Io mi son giovinetta," 6; *Lamentations,* 254; *Missa Aeterna Christi munera,* 220; musical style, 216, 218, 223

Palmer, John, 273 n.49
Parsley, Osbert, 254
Pattison, Bruce, 43
Paul IV (Pope), 7
Peachum, Henry, 11, 229
Pembroke (fourth Earl of), 22, 30
Pepoli family, 7
Pepys, Samuel, 28, 61
Petrarch, 36, 41
Petrucci, Ottaviano, 253
Philips, Peter, 229
Pico della Mirandola, Giovanni, 36, 141
"Piu d'alto pin che in mezzo a un orto sia" (F), 6
Pius V (Pope), 254
Platt, Peter, 220
Playford, John, 61
Pléiade, 36
"Plorans ploravit" (F), 258, 262-63
Poetry, 33-46, 94, 95
Pope, Giulio III, 7; Paul IV, 7; Pius V, 254
"Princeps provinciarum" (F), 256, 258, 259, 261-62
Printers
  Ciotti, 183
  Gardane, 6
  LeRoy/Ballard, 274 n.60
  Petrucci, 253
  Playford, 61
Purcell, Henry, 118
Purcell family, 1
Puttenham, George, 37, 41

"Quare dereliquerunt me" (F), 248-49
"Quo modo" (F), 256, 258, 261

Radcliffe, Lady Elizabeth, 115
Raleigh, Sir Walter, 58
Ramsey, Robert, 199
Ramus, Petrus, 37
Rangoni family, 7
Rego, Pietro Vaz, 14
Richardsonus, Ferdinandus, 10, 273 n.39
Ripa, Cesare, 156
Rogers, Elizabeth, virginal book of, 56, 99
Ronsard, Pierre de, 37
Rore, Cipriano de, 6, 273 n.40
"Rose-cheekt Laura" (Campion), 37-38
Rosseter, Philip, 38, 101, 117, 284 n.6

Sabol, Andrew, 120, 121
Sambrooke Book (Tregian's, NYPL MS Drexel 4302), 215-16, 221, 226, 244, 246, 255, 274 n.59, 276 n.80
San Lorenzo e Damasco, Rome, 7

San Petronio, Bologna, 1, 6, 7
Sannazaro, Jacopo, 36
Saracini, Claudio, 57
Savoy (Duke of), 2, 14-15
"Say, shepherd boy!" (F), 200, 210-13
Schütz, Heinrich, 240
"Senses by unjust force banished" (F), 122-23, 169-72
Sermisy, Claudin de, 254
Seymour, Edward (Earl of Hertford), 22, 30, 31, 276 n.78
"Sfogava con le stelle" (Monteverdi), 183
Shakespeare, William, 21, 34, 39, 41
"Shall I seek to ease my grief?" (F), 101-3, 104, 284 n.5
"Si ch'io vorrei morire" (Monteverdi), 183
Sidney, Sir Philip, 9, 34, 36, 40
"Sing the nobles" (F), 145-51, 165
"Sing the riches" (F), 145-51, 165
"Sing we then heroic grace" (F), 51, 145-51, 165
Smith, Thomas (Bishop of Carlisle): part-books of, 55, 99-101
Snodham, T., 21
"So beauty on the waters stood" (F), 130-34
"So, so, leave off this last lamenting kiss" (F), 63-70, 279 n.10
Somerset (Duke of), 276 n.76
Somerset Masque, 285 n.7
Song, 42-46, 101, 116-19, 121, 179-80, 198. See also Ferrabosco, Alfonso, the Younger, music, Italian songs, and songs and ayres
Songs of Mourning, 22, 52
Southampton (Earl of), 21
Spain, 14
Spenser, Edmund, 33-34, 36, 37, 40
Spink, Ian, 54, 55, 61, 99, 116-18, 157, 164, 180, 198, 200-201
Stevens, John, 43
Stubbs, William, 273-74 n.49
Surrey, 33
"Sustinuit anima mea" (F), 244, 246-48

Tallis, Thomas, 10, 24, 273 n.39; *Lamentations*, 233, 254-55, 258; musical style, 217, 223, 233
"Tell me, O love" (F), 200, 206-10, 213
Text-setting, 94, 95, 117-19, 121-22, 126, 140, 146, 201, 216-17, 220, 234
Tinctoris, 254
Tite, George, 24
"To the Countess of Huntington" (Donne), 286 n.12
Tomkins, Nicholas, 20, 52, 54

Tomkins, Thomas, 22, 24, 28, 54
Tomson, William, 27
Tottel, Richard, 33, 39
Tregian, Francis, 30, 54; Sambrooke Book, 215-16, 221, 226, 244, 246, 255, 274 n.59, 276 n.80
"Tribulationem et dolorem" (F), 244-46
Turin, 14

"Ubi duo" (F), 234-41
"Udite lagrimosi spir'ti d'Averno" (F), 183-86
"Unconstant love" (F), 72-74, 91
Urbino, 6, 270 n.10
"Usquequo, Domine, oblivisceris me" (F), 6

Vaselli, Alessandro, 3
Victoria, Tomás Luis de, 254
Viol music, 2, 30
"Vivamus, mea Lesbia atque amemus" (Catullus), 107

Walls, Peter, 119, 126, 131
Walsingham, Sir Francis, 14
Ward, B. M., 273 n.49

Warlock, Peter, 2, 56-57, 58, 60
"Was I to blame?" (F), 79-82, 87
Weelkes, Thomas, 218
"Weep no more" (Jonson), 285 n.7
"What shall I wish" (F), 200, 202, 205
"When all the ages of the Earth" (F), 157
White, Robert, 254
"Why stays the bridegroom" (F), 55, 121, 123-24, 151-56, 160, 165, 180
Willaert, Adrian, 273 n.40
Wilson, John, 17, 55
Wilson, Thomas, 40
Wood, Anthony, 17, 18
Wyatt, Sir Thomas, 33

"Yes, were the loves" (F), 132-33, 136-41, 289 n.4
Yonge, Bartholomew, 97
Yonge, Nicholas, 11, 15
"Young and simple though I am" (F), 104-6, 110, 279 n.10; Campion, 104-6; Lanier, 104

Zarlino, 234

Cover illustrations: watermark examples selected from the *French Harpsichord Music of the 17th Century* by Bruce Gustafson, published by UMI Research Press.